# LOST HIGHWAYS

CREATION

# CREDITS

**Lost Highways**
*An Illustrated Guide To The Road Movie*
Jack Sargeant & Stephanie Watson (Editors)
ISBN 1 871592 68 2
CREATION CINEMA COLLECTION, VOLUME 15
© Jack Sargeant & Stephanie Watson & individual contributors 1999
*First published 1999 by:*
CREATION BOOKS
*Design/layout/typesetting:*
PCP International
*Design technician:*
Bradley Davis
*Photographs:*
From the Jack Hunter Collection,
by courtesy of the original film distributors.

**Editors' Acknowledgements:**
Thanks to: Kay Dickinson, Alan Gregory, Julian Weaver, Andru Clare, Jim Morton, Alistair Daniel, Adam Webb, Omayra Cruz and Ray Guins, Jonathan Rayner, Stuart Mitchell, Mikita Brottman & Christopher Sharrett, Peter Rojas, Karl Phillips, Ian Garwood, Estella Tincknell, Geraint Bryan, David Sorfa, Stephen Barber, Susan Picken, Ian Conrich, Jack Hunter, and everybody at Creation Books.

# CONTENTS

# CONTENTS

# Introduction

# LOOKING FOR MAPS: NOTES ON THE ROAD MOVIE AS GENRE

## Jack Sargeant & Stephanie Watson

*"We have found God in cars, or if not the true God, one so satisfying, so powerful and awe-inspiring that the distinction is too fine to matter"*
—Harry Crews, *The Car*

This book seeks to explore the expansive terrain of the road movie. Film genre may be viewed as being constructed in two ways; in the first the classic cinematic genres (most obviously the gangster film and Western) were defined by the early film industry as a way in which to regulate production and marketing. The second form of genre emerges from theoretical and fan writings retrospectively projecting a genre on a group of apparently disparate films – for example, *film noir*. The road movie paradoxically may be said to exist in neither – and both – zones simultaneously. Whilst the road movie is familiar to audiences as a distinctive genre emerging in the late sixties with the release of films such as **Easy Rider** (Dennis Hopper, 1969)[1] [see Chapter 4] and **Two Lane Blacktop** (Monte Hellman, 1971) [see Chapter 5], both of which appear to define many of the genre's key elements, the genre can also be retrospectively projected onto other films, which may not initially be thought of as road movies, but contain similar thematics. This is most apparent in films such as **The Wizard Of Oz** (Victor Fleming, 1939) [see Chapter 13] or **Gun Crazy** (Joseph H Lewis, 1949) [see Chapter 2], released as a cinematic adaptation of a classic children's story, and a crime film respectively.

Genre may be defined by a combination of recognizable elements of both narrative and *mise-en-scène*, and the road movie may be said to pertain to a particular iconographic and narrative trajectory, yet part of the nature of the road movie is its intertextuality and ability to combine with other genres. The road movie's status as an intertextual and generic hybrid allows it to be read through a variety of theoretical approaches which highlight different areas of film production. Such approaches are often complementary but not exhaustive.

The following, then, is a brief overview of the general themes of the genre. By necessity this introductory contextualization is broad and incomplete, allowing for new spaces of exploration to emerge from the essays that follow.

## CINEMATIC MYTHOLOGIES

On the surface, and as an American film genre, the road movie finds its roots largely in the classic Western film [see Chapter 1], and the youthsploitation films which emerged in the post-war boom of the fifties. However, as interpretations of these genres have changed, primarily via re-evaluations of American cultural and social history, so the road movie has emerged as a genre that exists as broadly critical of society and hypothesizes geographical movement as allied to cultural shifts both in America and beyond.

America is the mythical "land of dreams", a nation to which people fled from persecution, poverty and hardship in search of a better life. Modern America was founded by immigrants whose journeys from Europe did not end at the ports of the East Coast but spread across the country, firstly in wagon trains as settlers sought to find a "promised land", but later in cars as people pursued their dreams further west. There have been numerous mass migrations in the history of America, from the south to the north following the dissolution of slavery, the boom in the manufacturing industry and the growth in rural unemployment, from east to west during the gold rush, and again from east to west during the depression. As John Jerome writes: "America is a road epic; we have even developed a body of road art, Huck Finn to *The Grapes Of Wrath* to **Easy Rider**, cutting loose a path to the dream"[2]. Fordism led to the ready availability of mass-produced cars that enabled people to transverse the vast distances across the continent. Ultimately, in America, the freedom espoused in the constitution found its realisation within car culture.

While many who colonized the continent were farmers, establishing small rural communities (beginning with the Puritans and Quakers), it was the pioneering frontiersman who has emerged as the mythic, archetypal American hero. The frontiersman had an intricate relationship with the wilderness, he represented the first movement of European civilization, yet also understood the topographical nature of the landscape, having a relationship to it that was akin to, and informed by, that of the indigenous Native Americans. The mythology of the frontiersman as rugged individualist can be traced to the Old West, with historical figures such as Daniel Boone[3] emerging as the personification of the pioneer spirit. This figure, the lone individual, is not a criminal, but recognizes no legislation other than a combination of the natural laws demanded by survival in the wild and a quasi-Christian sense of moral certainty.

Such mythic figures also exist as separate to the heroes associated with Europe, having evolved to show the new sense of identity that was different from that of the "Old World", which was identified as a zone of constriction, as against the apparent freedom of the continent before them. This notion of a new or "born again" American hero pitted against the moral corruption of Europe, is very potent in American mythology. One of the major characteristics of the American hero is his[4] ability to transform his identity, to become someone else. As the nation aged, this attribute took on a darker side as dream turned into nightmare[5]. The ultimate American paranoiac expression of transformation, as a danger intrinsic to the nation's psyche, appears in the figure of the serial killer whose search for identity through killing others remains undetected within society.

This duality of good/bad power to transform identity was initially reflected in the American hero/anti-hero being pitted against the world around him. The dangers of transformation were seen to come from outside of the American psyche. Writers and filmmakers still generally favoured the "new democratic" American hero against that of the "Old World" aristocratic gentleman hero, whose fixed and hierarchical social status was based on his mythological Greek and Roman predecessors. Failure of the "new democratic" hero was invariably displaced onto some hidden "Old World" corrupt intervention. In later works, the hero often appeared as an anti-hero pitted against a corrupt and repressive American government, and ultimately society. The figure of the anti-hero is often a version of an earlier hero whose society has abandoned or disillusioned him with its corruptness. The American hero often overlaps with that of the anti-hero because of America's founding status of being a place of non-European beginning yet also trying to define itself against its European roots. This explains the road movie's dual trajectory of offering both escape and/or freedom.

One of the most enduring mythic figures to emerge is that of the outlaw, and especially the lone gunfighter, surviving by a combination of wits and skill; historical figures such as Billy the Kid and Pat Garrett became immortalized within Western films.

Convoy

Such figures are clearly echoed within the protagonists of road movies such as **Easy Rider, Vanishing Point** (Richard Sarafian, 1971) [see Chapter 6], or **Drugstore Cowboy** (Gus Van Sant, 1989), all of which feature characters who exist on the fringes of society[6]. The more ruthless – but nevertheless morally certain – gunfighters played by Clint Eastwood in films such as **The Good The Bad And The Ugly** (Sergio Leone, 1966) [see Chapter 1] find their counterparts within characters such as Max in the **Mad Max** trilogy (George Miller, 1979, 1982, 1985) [see Chapters 7 and 19], whilst the traveling vampires in **Near Dark** (Kathryn Bigelow, 1987) [see Chapter 9] recall numerous bandits and outlaws from countless Westerns.

The figure of the outlaw/anti-hero – especially in the road movies located within the American south – also emerges as an individualistic hero against a stupid, often comically absurd authority; see for example, the "good outlaws" of **Convoy** (Sam Peckinpah, 1978), or **Smokey And The Bandit** (Hal Needham, 1977) and its numerous sequels. In these films the very titles evoke the colloquialisms of CB Radio, the mode of communication of those in perpetual motion. In these films the character of the Bandit must also be seen as a representation of the mythical untamed Rebel Spirit of the south, unwilling to succumb to the economic dominance of the Union, akin to popular historical folk figures such as Jesse James[7]. An emphasis that was made even stronger in the television series *The Dukes Of Hazard* (Rodney Amateau, William Asher, 1979–1985), whose protagonists drove a car named the General Lee.

The heroines of **Thelma And Louise** (Ridley Scott, 1991) [see Chapter 11] are also "good outlaws", forced by necessity into a cycle of transgressions for which they eventually pay with their lives. The protagonists of road movies are often linked to crime (either they are fallen or about to fall, recalling the Western theme of law/lawlessness), whether as naive criminals on the run such as in **They Live By Night** (Nicholas Ray, 1949), or robbers in **The Getaway** (Sam Peckinpah, 1972) [see Chapter

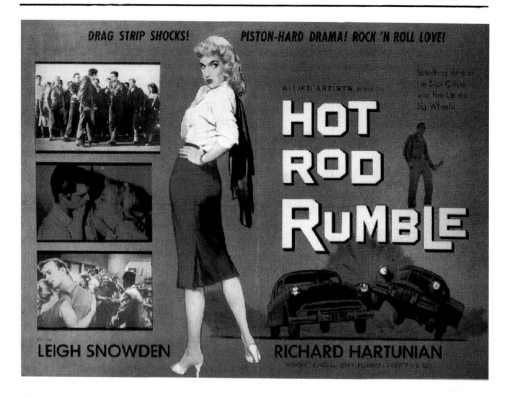

2]. This emphasis recalls the myth that it is possible to escape from the past and start again elsewhere, that roads eventually lead to freedom.

If it is the Western genre that provides the epic landscapes, the belief in freedom, the search for a better tomorrow, and the outlaw mythology, then the other influence on the road movie is the youth culture and the juvenile delinquency exploitation film. In America owning a car – or even having access to the family car – is a mark of independence, individuality and maturity. With the emergence of youth cultures in the aftermath of the Second World War, the car played a key role, representing an extension of the driver's identity. Cars frequently enable youth to draw a distinction with the conservative adult world of their parents, for whom cars are simply a mode of transportation. In cinema this relationship can be seen in films such as **Rebel Without A Cause** (Nicholas Ray, 1955) and **Hot Rod Rumble** (Leslie Martinson, 1957); (this emphasis on car culture also occurs in the irritating fifties nostalgia movies such as **American Graffiti** [George Lucas, 1973], and **Grease** [Randal Kleiser, 1978]). Many road movies recall this cultural construction of the car as a point of rupture with the recognizably adult world; thus even when protagonists are no longer young, the freedom of transportation enables them to rekindle a youthful spirit. Notably, both **Thelma And Louise** and **Kings Of The Road** (Wim Wenders, 1975) [see Chapter 16] include sequences in which the protagonists find themselves re-living a liberating rebellion, "free" from responsibilities that recalls youth. It is notable that, in the few road movies – frequently comedies – that neither depict youth, nor emphasize a move to a youthful state of mind, the protagonists often experience the road trip with a mixture of confusion, befuddlement, and even fear. In **National Lampoon's Vacation** (Harold Ramis, 1983), **Planes, Trains And Automobiles** (John Hughes, 1987), and **Lost In America** (Albert Brooks, 1985) the middle-aged protagonists are too old, too conservative, and ultimately too scared to undertake the psychic journey that is part of the geographical voyage. It is also notable that in these films the cars are all devoid

Faster, Pussycat! Kill! Kill!

of the mark of the driver's personality, instead they are stoically practical family vehicles or homogenized, sterile rental cars.

The juvenile delinquency genre can be traced back to the biker movie **The Wild One** (Laszlo Benedek, 1953) [see Chapter 3], and includes such films as **Dragstrip Girl** (Edward L. Cahn, 1957), **Hot Car Girl** (Bernard Kowalski, 1958), and **High School Confidential** (Jack Arnold, 1958), amongst countless others. These films frequently focus on car or motorbike culture, and often locate the protagonists' rebellion, sexual experiences[8], and dabblings in drink (and sometimes drugs) around cars. Cars also represent the chosen method of confrontation in many juvenile delinquency films; no juvenile delinquency movie is complete without either a race or chicken run sequence, scenes that occur in films ranging from **Rebel Without A Cause** to **Faster, Pussycat! Kill! Kill!** (Russ Meyer, 1966)[9].

However, the youth rebellion against the adult world emerged not just in largely imaginary cinematic representations of flick knives, greasers and chicken runs but also within a wider social context. In Jack Kerouac's beat novel *On The Road* (1957), the hipsters journey across both the country and through their own psyches. The two journeys combine, suggesting that only through experience can one know oneself. In Kerouac's novel, from which – as writer William Burroughs noted – "a whole migrant generation arose"[10], the road trip is as much an internal voyage as an external geographical movement, the inner voyage providing a "new frontier". Kerouac's life was evoked, with questionable success, in John Byrum's **Heart Beat** (1979). Following the beats' journeys youth culture, travel, and expanded consciousness became inexplicably linked within the popular imagination. This link was best illustrated by Ken Kesey and his Merry Pranksters who, in 1964, climbed onto a

Heart Beat

psychedelic-painted school bus to travel back from the West Coast with the "good" news – and copious quantities of LSD. Whilst Kesey may have been the first, his bus of stoned travellers was not the last; in 1968 the Manson family climbed upon their (ultimately) infamous black bus in order to expand minds and meet similarly disaffected individuals.

The drug culture of the sixties fed into the transgression of boundaries, both physical, social, and personal, which road movies highlight. Drugs offer a collapse of the interior/exterior duality that defines classic constructions of being, allowing and facilitating the expansion of the previously prescribed limits of the psyche, enabling the stoned mind to stretch across the landscape, free from the perceived constraints of the body, just as the body in motion is free from the constraints imposed upon it by the claustrophobia of the city. See, for example, the hallucinatory state of the biker protagonists of **Easy Rider**, actualized in a New Orleans graveyard, but suggested repeatedly by the *mise-en-scène* and stoned rock soundtrack. **Easy Rider** brings together the topographical scale of the Western, the energy of youth rebellion, the post-beat expanded consciousness, with the existential socio-political angst of the times with its now legendary marquee slogan "A man went looking for America and couldn't find it anywhere".

But the drugs in road movies are not just the beat and hippie drugs marijuana and LSD, for as times change so do prescriptions and by 1971 amphetamines also play their part; speed is the drug of choice in **Vanishing Point** and for the quasi-punk heroes in the similarly car-fixated **Repo Man** (Alex Cox, 1984). Heroin and opiates are less common in road movies (nodding out being less than practical when travelling across country) although **Drugstore Cowboy** manages to weave a junkie crime-wave road trip into its narrative, and the behaviour of the narcoleptic hustler Mike in **My Own Private Idaho** (Gus Van Sant, 1991) also echoes heroin lethargy.

Repo Man

## MAPS AND GAPS

Roads act as spaces in-between – they transverse apparently empty zones – and the boundaries both geographical and cultural that define social existence in the city or town no longer exist. There are no certainties on the road, only potentialities. Whilst journeys focus toward a final destination, detours are always possible. Other journeys never seek or reach a final destination, becoming extended wanderings with no clear teleological goal. In America's vast landscape, with its frequent seemingly endless straight roads, it is still possible to stray from the path.

The highway represents the circulatory system of the wider zone of the nation state, its routes criss-cross the barren landscape. The highway exists as a line that traces the borders and boundaries of established order, threatening to collapse into anarchy at any moment yet never fully disavowing the presence of civilization. The continual imminence of chaos on the highway becomes the object of terror in texts such as the horror film **Race With The Devil** (Jack Starrett, 1975) [see also Chapter 8], the science fiction films **Death Race 2000** (Paul Bartel, 1975) [see chapter 19] and **Mad Max**, and even the comedy **Planes, Trains And Automobiles**, in which Steve Martin is cast as a bewildered and lost traveller who is forced by the cancellation of his flight to transverse an ultimately alien mid-west by other means. This potential for disaster even on the supposed safety demarcated by the freeway belongs in part to the notion of the wagon trains, which crossed the supposedly uncivilized landscape at continual risk from attacks by native tribes, a myth that informs Westerns such as **The Covered Wagon** (James Cruze, 1923) and **Stagecoach** (John Ford, 1939) [see also Chapter 1]. This notion of an uncivilized wilderness just beyond the boundaries and safety of the city also occurs in films such as **The Hills Have Eyes** (Wes Craven, 1977) and **Deliverance** (John Boorman, 1972) [see Chapter 15], in which the traditional racial "other" of the

The Warriors

Western is replaced by the mythical notion of the psychopathic interbred rural community which survives by preying on luckless, lost travellers.

The vision of the open road eternally vanishing into the horizon always promises greater possibilities and journeys to come. Road movies offer audiences a glimpse at an ecstatic freedom. Following the classic Westerns the *mise-en-scène* emphasises the vastness of the terrain, not only locating the individual protagonist's journey within the greater zone of the wilderness, but also allowing the audience the visual pleasure of the spectacle of the landscape, itself a mythical and poetic aspect of the construction of the American identity.

Yet in the genre's emphasis on the spaces between there is a simultaneous acknowledgement the power of the city. In road movies the city can be both the place from which protagonists flee and/or the final destination. It can represent both the past which must be escaped, as in **Thelma And Louise, Wild At Heart** (David Lynch, 1990) [see Chapter 17], and **True Romance** (Tony Scott, 1993) [see Chapter 10], and the holy grail which offers future possibilities as in **Easy Rider, Mad Max: Beyond Thunderdome**, and **Kalifornia** (Dominic Sena, 1993) [see Chapter 10]. The city itself can represent a microcosm of the larger country, and journeys within the city can become mimetic representations of the larger cross country road trips, with protagonists facing the same dilemmas, questions, and search that happen in the narratives of classic road movies. Such parallels occur in Wim Wenders' film **Summer In The City** (1970) and Walter Hill's urban warfare, juvenile delinquency classic **The Warriors** (1979).

Like the city, the status of the home maintains an ambivalence in the genre. It can be a place of constraint, hardship and danger from which protagonists must flee as a result of circumstantial necessity (as in **The Grapes Of Wrath** [John Ford, 1940], **Badlands** [Terrence Malick, 1973] [see Chapter 10], **Paris, Texas** [Wim Wenders, 1984] [see also Chapter 16], and **Natural Born Killers** [Oliver Stone, 1994] [see Chapter 10]), yet the search for home can also be the reason for the quest in certain road movies

The Passenger

**(Alice In The Cities** [Wim Wenders, 1973] and **The Wizard Of Oz).**

Other road movies see the protagonists searching for a new place that they can call home **(They Live By Night, Mad Max 2)**, but these destinations may be illusions and dreams, and protagonists frequently suffer and often die before reaching their promised land. For the protagonists of many road movies the actual road becomes a home-from-home, a haven on radials; in **Two Lane Blacktop, Vanishing Point, Kings Of The Road, Mad Max**, and **Near Dark** the continually transforming terrain has become the true home, the films' characters lose themselves in their journeys. This sense of losing a static home or sense of identity is particularly evident in later films where disillusionment and cynicism preclude the ability to either motivate the search for, or find a social and/or spiritual home. The search for, and rejection of a static home, can be likened to the desire for, and escape from, fixed social roles and identities.

The desert, more than any other space within the genre, acts as a symbolic zone in which recognizable signifying practices collapse and identity loses its previous boundaries (for example, Michelangelo Antonioni's **The Passenger**, 1975). It exists as a void in which long-established meanings vanish, the insane heat drives images to haze and nothing is as it once seemed; the sun burns into the retina, human life and the individual subject are always at risk from greater forces and/or the continual threat of pure chaos. Historically the desert is a space in which protagonists are tested and emerge as transformed, in narratives that go back to the Bible, and Jesus' forty days and nights spent in the wilderness. The desert is a zone that exists outside of quantifiable time, its temporality is more geological than anthropological, as Jean Baudrillard observed: the desert "is a kind of suspended eternity"[11] with each day

Something Wild

forming a microcosm of a year's seasons.

The desert is a zone that is suspended as both an originary place that has yet to form a recognizable shape, yet simultaneously offers a zone that connotes the imaginary post-apocalyptical terrain. The journeys made in road movies frequently bisect the desert; it offers freedom and possibility in **Easy Rider** and **Thelma And Louise**, a confrontation with insanity in **Natural Born Killers** and **Kalifornia**, transformation in **The Adventures Of Priscilla, Queen Of The Desert** (Stephan Elliott, 1994) [see Chapter 12], eventual growth and development in **Walkabout** (Nicholas Roeg, 1971) [see Chapter 13], personal armageddon in **Duel** (Stephen Spielberg, 1971) [see Chapter 8], **Race With The Devil**, and **The Hitcher** (Robert Harmon, 1986) [see Chapter 8], and the spectre of global apocalypse in **Damnation Alley** (Jack Smight, 1977) [see Chapter 19] and the **Mad Max** trilogy.

## NARRATIVE POTENTIALS

On the road anything appears possible because nothing seems fixed, the journey itself represents a degree of seduction as the protagonists leave the confines of their world and see the geographical expanse of their future before them (a seduction mirrored within the *mise-en-scène* of the genre which depicts the geographical panoramas as one of its key visual pleasures, for example Monument Valley which emerged as a location in the Western and then found its resonant echo within the road movie). As the past vanishes in the rear view mirror new liaisons are formed and new potentialities emerge.

The journey offers the protagonists multiple possibilities, as they either search for a better future or escape the constraints of the past. In recent years the genre has emphasized romance on the road, as in **Near Dark**, **Something Wild** (Jonathan Demme, 1986), **True Romance**, and **Love And A .45** (C. M. Talkington, 1994); or as a result of

My Own Private Idaho

juvenile delinquent-inspired couple-on-the-run movies such as **Badlands, Wild At Heart, Kalifornia** (which twists the conventions by focusing on two couples searching – for very different reasons – for new lives) and **Natural Born Killers**; however, many classic films in the genre frequently imagine same sex friendships. These male/male friendships are formed from a kinship that is fused on the road via a (frequently temporary) shared mutual status of "being-in-transit"; see, for example **Easy Rider, Kings Of The Road, Butch Cassidy And The Sundance Kid** (George Roy Hill, 1969), and **Rain Man** (Barry Levinson, 1988).

Same sex friendships also served as the central motif of the seven Bob Hope and Bing Crosby comedies: **Road To Singapore** (Victor Schertzinger, 1940), **Road To Zanzibar** (Schertzinger, 1941), **Road To Morroco** (David Butler, 1942), **Road To Utopia** (Hal Walker, 1946), **Road To Rio** (Norman Z. McLeod, 1948), **Road To Bali** (Hal Walker, 1953), and **The Road To Hong Kong** (Norman Panama, 1962). These comedies frequently contain jokes based on the nature of the friendship between the two men, and similar jokes *vis-à-vis* male friendships occur in other road comedies such as **Planes, Trains And Automobiles**. If these films acknowledge the homosocial nature of such friendships, they attempt to circumnavigate any interpretation of the friendship as homosexual by introducing either love-interests or featuring scenes in which protagonists declare their heterosexuality by discussing their families. It is primarily in films that are identified as queer, such as **My Own Private Idaho** and **The Living End** (Gregg Araki, 1992), that the homosexual potentiality of male/male friendships is articulated. The male/male friendship is effectively parodied in **Thelma And Louise**, in which the key friendship is female/female, but notably in this film too the heroines are defined as heterosexual via their love interests.

The quest drives many protagonists of the road movie, as they travel in search of a better future, a new life, or greater potentialities. The quest theme recalls the original mythic journeys such as that detailed in Homer's *Odyssey*, but its modern form

Charlie Is My Darling

places emphasis on in the voyage taken westwards, intrinsic to American history and the western mythology. The notion of the quest also hints at the wider aspects of the genre, in films not immediately associated with the road, yet bearing many of its narrative accoutrements, ranging from Jim Jarmusch's postmodern Western **Dead Man** (1995) and the *Star Trek* television series (1966–1969).

## REMIX

As America developed as a nation, blues, folk, and country music inevitably formed an oral historical tradition, with numerous songs detailing the hardships of life, and often dealing with the theme of travelling across the country. With the development of rock and roll, which borrowed heavily from these earlier traditions, such themes became a recognizable part of the cultural image reservoir, and early American rock and pop songs celebrated a teenage life which almost invariably revolved around surfing, romance, and cars[12]. These themes of the relationship between American musical traditions and the road are explored in Rudy Wurlitzer and Robert Frank's 1987 cult feature **Candy Mountain.**

Music is also linked to the road by virtue of the travelling musicians from the early blues men through to rock musicians in air conditioned coaches. These journeys form the basis of films such as the Rolling Stones documentaries **Charlie Is My Darling** (Peter Whitehead, 1965) and **Cocksucker Blues** (Robert Frank, 1972), D.A Pennebaker's Dylan tour movie **Don't Look Back** (1966), and, more recently, films such as Uli M. Schuppel's tour documentary of Nick Cave And The Bad Seeds, **The Road To God Knows Where** (1990). These tour films exist in an aesthetic zone that is separate from the rock concert film; there is less emphasis on the spectacle of the performance or the finality of the show, than on the seemingly endlessness of the journey, and the music is almost incidental to the repetition of the black top. This sub-genre also informs the intertextual nature of the "rockumentry" satire **This Is Spinal Tap** (Rob Reiner, 1983) [see also Chapter 16, which explores the use of popular music in Wim Wenders' road movies].

More than anything else it was through **Easy Rider** that the road movie has been linked to rock music. Throughout **Easy Rider** music acts as a signifier for travel, for the voyage itself, as well as a reflection on the protagonists' state of mind during the journey; thus in **Easy Rider** the ideals of the bikers are captured and described by the lyrics of the songs, and the visual *mise-en-scène* similarly accompanies the music. Such was the success of **Easy Rider**, and the popularity of its soundtrack, that the use of rock music in road movies occurs repeatedly.

Musical sub-cultural styles offer much of the iconography for the road movie – from the crumpled jazz suits worn by the protagonists of **Strangers In Paradise** (Jim Jarmusch, 1984), through the denim-leather-and-attitude of youth-on-the-run movies such as **Badlands** and **Natural Born Killers**. This emphasis on style is best articulated by Sailor Ripley in **Wild At Heart** when he states: "This snakeskin jacket symbolizes my individuality and belief in personal freedom". Ripley's statement offers a knowing pastiche on the understated iconographic bad boy leather jacket worn by the social outcast, most notably in classic film role models such as Marlon Brando in **The Wild One** and, more specifically, in **The Fugitive Kind** (Sidney Lumet, 1960).

## BEYOND AMERICA

Road movies emerged from America, where notions of the open road and travel form part of a potent cultural myth far more powerful than in Europe where all possible routes were mapped before long before their nation states consolidated, thus many of the preceding observations apply primarily to the American manifestation of the genre. The subsequent interest in, and production of, road movies in other cultures normally exists as a critique of American (and, often, by extension, capitalist culture) or as homage to the classics of the genre.

The essays included within this volume focus on all aspects of the road movie, tracing its roots from the Western, *film noir*, and biker/juvenile delinquency films through to the emergence of the genre in its classic form as articulated in **Easy Rider**, **Two Lane Blacktop**, **Vanishing Point** and the more recent **Thelma And Louise**. *Lost Highways* also explores the less travelled roots of the road movie; examining its links to children, to horror, to science fiction and to other travel and quest oriented movies. *Lost Highways* opens the road movie genre to Europe and beyond, and into other less-examined areas demarcated by the auteurs Lynch, Cronenberg, and Jodorowsky. *Lost Highways* is an attempt, finally, to map the intricate routes, both familiar and less known, of this vast genre.

# NOTES

1. **Easy Rider** is often cited as the first modern road movie, see for example Mikita Brottman, "Tombstones In Their Eyes: Easy Rider And The Death Of The American Dream" in Jack Hunter, ed, *Dennis Hopper: Movie Top Ten*; Creation Books, 1999.

2. John Jerome, *The Death Of The Automobile: The Fatal Effect Of The Golden Era, 1955–1970*; Norton: New York, 1972, p.103.

3. The frontiersman Daniel Boone (1734–1820) played a central role in the colonising of Kentucky before moving onwards to Missouri.

4. Women and non-whites were excluded from a "realistic" portrayal of the parts they played in American history, partly because they were excluded from the role of adventurer but mainly because their histories involved other agendas which did not serve the dominant ideology. Hence many stories have been ignored until recently and remain problematized. The adventure genre, with its focus on physical action, is essentially a male genre. The female/male, passive/active divide is a cultural construction which is very difficult to convincingly override. This greatly problematizes adventure films with heroines such as **Thelma And Louise**. This is partly due to what on the surface appears to be factual, namely that women did not travel on their own, they stayed at home and so on. However the reasons for this were generally due to cultural and social constraints. This artificial conditioning of women is reflected in the fact that America as a new nation was unable to totally ignore the reality of its social heroines. However, film like any other cultural artifact reflects and furthers the priorization of the American hero as male, and the overt act of penetrating the American landscape, shooting guns, composing seminal written tracts and speeches and so on, retains a distinctly male bias.

5. For example in the gothic romances of Nathaniel Hawthorne, and the gothic/mystery tales of Edgar Allan Poe. Often these stories feature a fragmentation or doubling of identity, and play on a paranoia that this transformation is undetectable, that the villain appears normal. This tradition continued into the twentieth century, particularly in the work of Southern gothic writers where the concept of change has a slightly more problematic history – because of slavery – to that of the North.

6. In part this betrays the genre's relationship to the Western, but the borderline criminal/outsider is also a key element to much classic American travel/road literature from Mark Twain's *Huckleberry Finn* to Jack Kerouac's *On The Road*.

7. Brothers Jesse (1847–1882) and Franklin James (1843–1915), alongside Cole Younger (1844–1916), learned much from the Confederate bandit leader William Clarke Quantrill. Between 1866–82 the James-Younger gang became popular amongst the rural populace for their crimes, beginning with the robbery of the bank at Liberty, Missouri, in February 1866.

8. The sexual fetishization of the car is also represented in Kenneth Anger's short **Kustom Kar Kommandos** (1964), which depicts a muscleboy lovingly polishing his pink dune buggy.

9. **Faster, Pussycat! Kill! Kill!** is the culmination of Russ Meyer's b/w trash trilogy, which commenced with **Mudhoney** (1964) and **Motorpsycho!** (1965). Set in the desert – a crucial road movie zone – the film shows a gang of three pneumatic, dune buggy-riding girls who terrorize two shack-dwellers – an old man and his retarded son – and a young couple. The film thus offers an inversion of "pit-stop" films such as **The Hills Have Eyes**, where it is conventionally the travellers in the wilderness who are preyed upon by its denizens. Furthermore the couple – also traditional road movie predators – likewise fall victim to the trio of dominant, physically superior females in a typically perverse Meyer flourish. With plenty of sex and violence (the gang leader, Varla, is eventually crushed by a car) – not to mention a wild desert drag race – **Faster, Pussycat! Kill! Kill!** melds and twists several car/road movie tropes to maximum, impacted pulp effect.

10. William S. Burroughs, "Remembering Jack Kerouac", in *The Adding Machine: Collected Essays*; London: John Calder Publishers, 1985, p.176.

11.  Jean Baudrillard, *America*; Verso: London and New York, 1988 (1986), p.121.

12.  Numerous traditional songs detail the relationship of the working classes to the continent, from blues songs to folk songs such as "This Land Is Your Land". Many religious songs also detail movement and the search for religious freedom, even death and transcendence is detailed as a physical movement i.e. "Swing Low Sweet Chariot". The relationship between youth and motor transport is detailed in classic songs such as "Little Deuce Coupe", "Tell Laura I Love Her", "Leader Of The Pack", "Route 66", "Dead Man's Curve", and many, many others. The notion of travel and escape also informs sixties love songs such as "By The Time I Get To Phoenix" or "24 Hours To Tulsa", as well as nostalgic narrative songs such as "Phantom 309".

## Chapter 1

# The Western

# FROM RIDING TO DRIVING: ONCE UPON A TIME IN THE WEST

## Stephanie Watson

### THE ROAD AHEAD

The road has a central place in the American psyche which can be seen in relation to North America's formation as an international economic and political power. As a positive ideological metaphor of legislation, progress and emancipation, it does however also have negative connotations of ruination, exploitation and limitation. The road has countless associated metaphors which centre around the theme of travel and transgression from one position, ideological or otherwise, to another. The vehicle which enables that movement, both metaphysical and literal (human, horse, automobile, space rocket, military weapons, computer technology etc.), can be seen as the metaphor/catalyst which gives the road a contemporary representation. For example, the road movie in its most literal form is about a car journey, but it also incorporates, and sometimes disguises, other contemporary concerns. For example the destruction of the road (America in some aspect), by the same technology which enabled the car's literal and mythic status in the first place. In other words the promise of the road forwards is also accompanied by the fear of going too far, sliding off the map, or simply being trapped along the same piece of road with no hope of progression.

The Western genre embraces the concept of the road in both literal and figurative terms. In many ways the Western has acted as progenitor, guardian and checkpoint for the American road into history. If the road movie follows the route already laid down then in many ways the Western can be seen as the pioneer or progenitor of the route which other American genres would follow. The Western genre wraps American history beneath a myth of origin which forwards a historical fight for personal freedom and liberty set against the hardships of an expansive landscape of extremes. The myth inferred is that once this landscape was successfully traversed and conquered it would allow for the birth of a civilizing nation where all men were at equal liberty to fulfil their potential, at least that is what the American Dream and Thomas Jefferson's Declaration of Independence appear to promise. However beneath all dreams and declarations of intent there lies a hidden nightmare world of exclusion where other voices are distorted and silenced. The Western genre in all its media representations is concerned more with consolidating the dream than paying heed to the nightmare. As Richard Slotkin notes in *Gunfighter Nation* "Genre space is also *mythic space*... it is a setting which is not only rooted in a culture's myth/ideological tradition. It is also a setting in which the concrete work of contemporary myth making is done. This is particularly true of the Western, whose roots go deeper into the American cultural past than those of any other movie genre"[1].

America has been represented in European mediums of representation since its European "discovery" in 1492, initially described in exotic terms in travellers' tales which though factual entertained their European audiences with sights and events both inspiring and terrifying. Tales of a more specifically western character arose after the beginning of the nineteenth century when the vast area of land west of the Mississippi became more readily open to exploration and later settlement following Thomas Jefferson's Louisiana Purchase of 1803. At a cost of $15 million, double the federal budget, Jefferson bought the land from the French in order to secure North America; British claims to Oregon were abandoned in 1846. To secure the Western River and potential commercial passage to the Pacific, Jefferson commissioned the 1804–6 Lewis and William Clark expedition. The Spanish based in Mexico lost out on the east-west, Missouri–Pacific route although they sent out two unsuccessful expeditions to intercept and, if necessary, eradicate the American party. Jefferson believed that settlement of the west would take over one thousand generations, however the canoes of the 1804–6 Lewis and Clark expedition (which included an African-American slave called York, inherited by Clark from his father, and George Drouillard a half-French, half-Shawnee hunter and interpreter employed by the expedition), very quickly gave way to horses, prairie wagons, trains, cars and eventually planes as the western lands experienced one form of economic bonanza and migration after another. The Native Americans, perceived as a threat, were increasingly decimated by the incoming European populations, and they possessed little ability to defend themselves or their land. The history of the west has always incorporated the duel tension of opportunity, of exploiting the land to make a quick buck, or settling the land such as in the case of farmers to make a more long-term investment. The latter half of the nineteenth century saw an explosion in immigration to the west with ensuing social tensions. The discovery of gold and the ensuing Californian Gold Rush of 1849 highlighted the bonanza culture, other bonanzas included that of cotton (1830s and 1850s), silver and gold in the Mountain West (1849–1880's), cattle (1870–85), wheat (1880s), and dryland products (1900–20), plus the oil boom in the south-west in the early twentieth century. Contrary to popular mythology that the west has always been a space of rugged individualism where individuals can make their fortunes, the federal government was the biggest landholder in the western states, funding the expansion of such enterprises as the railroads, and still holds over 50% of the land. This bonanza culture attracted many immigrants and provided a strong cultural mixture of Native Americans, Spanish, Russians, French and British. Other first wave Europeans and Americans such as African Americans were lured by the rosy portraits of fertile land and opportunity disseminated by the growing newspaper market and also the rail roads. Many Westerns explore the tension between the mobile outsider who is able to instill a natural moral order but not obey federal authority and the embryonic community allied to eastern civilization. An attempt to delineate the boundaries of the Western genre can be attempted in relation to the technological advances and industrial growth of the nineteenth century. When the horse gave way to the train and then the car, the belief in freedom of movement as a way of life became less convincing.

The Western genre originated in the literature and theatre plays of the latter half of the nineteenth century in the form of dime novels or pulp magazines, which owed much of their mass popularity to advances in printing techniques and developments in marketing and distribution. Dime novels were generally short (30,000 to 50,000 words), and aimed at the youth and working class market, but were actually popular amongst a much larger cross-section of society. Dime novels were adventure stories, ranging in theme from pirates to urban detectives, but with a majority emphasis on western figures of pioneer and frontier exploration such as cowboys, Indians, outlaws, and backwoodsmen.

Slotkin notes that the influence for the dime novel came from the merger of two earlier genres which arose in New England. The first was the late seventeenth century "captivity narrative" based on the popular personal account of Mary Rowlandson. This quickly became the main narrative theme for the eighteenth century American novel often involving a woman or Christian minister being captured during savage Indian wars and entering a wilderness where Christianity and civilisation are non-existent, and thus offer a figurative descent into Hell which is akin to madness. This was essentially a passive victim narrative. These narratives were both based on fact and also fictional accounts. The second narrative which arose in the early eighteenth century offered celebration of Indian fighters and then wilderness hunters. The first was written by a contemporary of Mary Rowlandson, Benjamin Church and focused on his skills in Indian tactics which enabled him to defeat and kill King Philip. This conception of the American hero as Indian fighter reached full historical expression in the eighteenth century figure of Daniel Boone whose career and public celebrity had an impact on literature and mythology. These influences were combined in the nineteenth century when the captivity narrative of redemption through suffering was integrated with the triumphalism of the Indian war story, a triumph of civilization over savagery, where white hunters/warriors rescue white women held by savages. The notion of a savage wilderness versus civilization was a popular theme which informed western narratives.

James Fenimore Cooper's Frontier Romances (published between 1823–50) codified frontier representations seen in other genres such as the personal narrative, the history, the sermon, the newspaper item, the street ballad, and the "penny dreadful". Cooper projects causality for problems in contemporary Jacksonian America back into a fictionalized past. Cooper conceived that the white/Indian conflict was America's central historical trope, he felt that the central ideological justification for American history hinged on the Indian question. His Leatherstocking novels use the white/Indian conflict as a central opposition for illustrating and interpreting fundamental oppositions in terms of contemporary concerns such as the rise in immigrants to the west and problems of class and gender divisions.

Cooper offers compromises by offering a whole spectrum of segregated and inter-mixed society. This inquiry is particularly explored and continually re-worked in Western films concerning the position of ethnicity, particularly that of Native Americans. Cooper's fictional hero is Hawkeye, who knows the Indians so well that he can supposedly pass for one. Hawkeye was based on Daniel Boone who offered an ideological model for future versions of the frontier hero incorporated and manipulated by antebellum historians, journalists and politicians, with particular application to the question of Indian policy, emigration and westward expansion. The man who knows Indians is seen as a mediator/interpreter, or even one who could defeat his enemy by knowing his enemy, or using his own enemy's savagery.

The Indian metaphor had many uses within social policy, often used as a veiled form of scapegoating other elements of society, such as those seen in the social crises of the latter half of the nineteenth century. For example the long cycle of American economic expansion ended in 1873, the banks panicked resulting in twenty years of the worst economic depression that America has had. The land reserves that Jefferson had envisaged lasting a thousand generations with the same amount to spare again seemed to be running out in only three or four. During the 1876–77 period America was dealing with urban class unrest in the wake of the 1874 Tomkins Square "riot" culminating in the Great Strike of 1877; the collapse of Reconstruction in the South with race riots and Ku Klux Klan outbreaks (slavery being officially abolished in 1863, but mainly effected at the end of the Civil War in 1865); the failure of western development by securing the opening of land by the railroads and failure to solve the "Indian question", resulting in the Sioux War of 1876 and the disaster of Custer's Last Stand (Custer was himself another great western self-publicist whose exploits were mingled with fiction, as in 1874 when at the age of thirty-five he published his autobiography, *My Life On The Plains*). These crises and the increasing opportunity to travel the western lands attracted writers such as Mark Twain, who produced both documentary and utopian/dystopian works. Newspapers had by 1850 become an influential medium for distributing information and opinion, and backing the concept that corporate industry demanded a hierarchical structure in direct contradiction to the founding ideology of equal rights, white workers, Native Americans, and African Americans were represented as "red skin savages" who raised the "The Red Spectre of the Commune".

This racist underpinning of civil unrest with allusions to the divide between civilization and wilderness has coloured political rhetoric, both internal and international, to the present day. For example the concept of the original inhabitants, the Native American, as "savage" became an accepted and useful political tool both during pioneer settlement and then throughout the twentieth century as a metaphor for the dissident or social "outsider". The fact that there was no major threat of destroying/removing white settlements on a large scale basis after 1700 mattered little to the rhetoric of racism and America's need for an enemy against which it could define itself. This racist rhetoric is particularly highlighted in relationship to communism and warfare such as America's involvement in Vietnam in the 1960's[2]. Frontier rhetoric has also served America as a powerful tool of political renewal, for example John F. Kennedy, an eastern politician, used the concept of the "New Frontier" in his 1960 acceptance speech as the Democratic candidate for President.

In the first decade of the twentieth century, when film was becoming a popular and commercial medium the Western became the subject of many early American films. Film and other forms of visual and literary representation have played a very important role in formulating and naturalising the national identity of a country which is relatively young in terms of world history. The Western formulae is deeply embedded in the America's conceptualisation of its own history and presentation of what it means to be an American. Many influences led to this formulation of American identity. Western films offer a distorted and romanticized picture of events which had only just passed out of living memory in the early twentieth century. Western films therefore played an important role in disseminating the myth created by America's founding ideology which based itself in a factually acceptable and recent past. This was problematic in the beginning when many of the west's historical participants were still alive to tell the tale, the real tale(s), but the need for an American tradition to root its political and social formation won out against conflicting versions of the truth. Throughout the twentieth century the Western has surfaced to reformulate the contemporary ideology, particularly at crisis points where the nation has had a collective identity crisis or need to "find itself". Sometimes critical, these films always pay homage to the myth of America's formative history in one way or another. The Western is intricately tied to America's history and the passage from the Western to the road movie highlights America's struggle with its self-conscious recognition of its dependency upon a story of progress and moral righteousness (Manifest Destiny) which was only partially based in fact and was often violently and oppressively implemented.

Many of the west's key figures quickly exploited the American peoples' investment in a founding narrative by using the nineteenth and early twentieth century's rapidly expanding forms of media, technology and distribution such as newspapers and film to publicize their exploits both real and imagined. Figures such as Bill Cody (a.k.a. Buffalo Bill) formed part of the growing entertainment market, becoming legends in their own lifetime. Cody, scout and showman, was a self-publicist and published his autobiography in 1879, *The Life Of Hon. William F. Cody, Known As Buffalo Bill* which was fairly reliable, and 557 dime novels were published about him, including four by the dime novel author Ned Buntline, whose first novel about Cody, *Buffalo Bill, King Of The Border Men*, led Cody to national and then international fame with the aid of a stage play – The Scouts Of The Prairie (16 December 1872, Chicago) – in which Cody appeared as himself. There were originally around fifty touring "Wild West" shows, of which Cody's was the most popular. Cody performed in "Buffalo Bill's Wild West And Congress Of Rough Riders" show which presented a distorted picture of battles and feats of bravery, touring major political rallies and also internationally before heads of state such as Queen Victoria, fuelling the national myth. Cody also took part in contemporary political conflicts, employing Native Americans in his shows, such as Sitting Bull who toured with the show for one season. In 1890 during problems over the Ghost Dance, Cody tried to intervene between Sitting Bull and General Nelson Miles but Sitting Bull was killed before Cody could see him. Cody later made films of these political events.

This acknowledged crossover between fact and fiction is still potent in contemporary America where the Western connection lends a sense of authenticity and prestige to figures involved in other walks of life. This confusion of reality and fantasy is less discernable in older national traditions. In America, there has always been a close relationship between the creation of a mythical conception of its history and its continual reconstruction of that myth through representation. America's founding mythology is readily open to pastiche and postmodern interpretations because it was founded on the loss and subsequent discovery of a new ideal. The Western at its inception as a genre expressed a nostalgia of loss for something which had only just been barely found and formulated. The recent nature of the myth called for a rapid smoothing over of its rough edges, such as the decimation of an already existing culture. However as time progressed and the 1880's period which is primarily dealt with in Western films became the more overtly historical past, these fissures became less easy to deal with, and the black and white world of the Western found the divide between wilderness and civilization was not unproblematic. The Western is so highly open to intertextual positioning, the picture of a pioneer frontier west can be used in almost any context from political speech to aftershave advertisements to identify something as American, white, masculine and patriotic, tinged with the promise of individuality, freedom and physical strength or violence. The characters, situations and speech are stereotypical and understood to instill certain values on those who evoke them, and a particular response from those who receive them. The Western is a highly formulaic genre, with repetitive narrative structures and black and white value structures (particularly within B-movie and later television series as opposed to the main feature – but less popular – A-movie films which incorporated contemporary issues and fashions).

The Western is an effective mythology because unlike other genres which led on from it – such as the gangster movie – it exploits nostalgia for a lost past which is recognisably authentic and easily "naturalized" within a powerfully symbolic American natural landscape. The West's landscape of extremes, of vast and soaring canyons is essential to its central place in the national identity. It is the last frontier on the east to west road across America, it represents in socio-economic terms the first authentically American birth of culture, and perhaps crucially it represents a culture free of technological creation, including that of representation such as film. There are obviously fissures in this belief because the myth of the West was both formulated and disseminated via the mediums of literature and film, and the Native American population was decimated and enslaved not only by warfare, forced re-location, and European diseases such as small pox, but crucially by advances in gun technology during the latter half of the nineteenth century which allowed for multiple and more rapid firing. However the West and its associated myth is viewed as an authentic historical locale free of the machinations of reproductive technology.

The sense of nostalgia or loss and its contingent desire to find that which never existed, is an extremely powerful explanation and motivation for a country whose origin was self-consciously constructed in tension with older European origins and founding myths. America has had various western discourses both secular and religious imposed upon it since Europeans first arrived in 1492. This has created a self-conscious awareness that its founding history has been distorted through myth, applied interpretation. European histories and myths of origin have obtained much of their accepted/naturalized position by virtue of the fact that their creation was seen to be handed down in an oral rather than literary or visual tradition, thus allowing for the easier acceptance of hierarchical and stasis systems such as class systems and monarchy. There is a certain self-conscious awareness that America has both copied and reinterpreted older European myths to suit its particular experiences. This awareness is less detectable in Europe where changes in national myths generally occur over longer periods of time and without such an obvious dependence on representational modes such as newspapers and film.

Christianity was transplanted to America in the guise of a journeying Adam who had been given the opportunity to be literally born again, not so much to find a paradise or Eden from which he was expelled, but to have access to it in the first place. This new Eden necessitated battling through the Wilderness which was seen as both virgin yet savage, assumed to be there for the taking once its hostile forces had been conquered and tamed. From the beginning of European settlement religion was quickly organised for secular application, for example in the South during slavery Christian doctrines of original sin were incorporated by the white slave-owning population as justification for their inhumane treatment of African-Americans. Sin was interpreted as blackness, therefore the opposing structure of slavery interpreted the Bible's conflict between good and evil so that "whites" became sinless and "blacks" became sinful. Likewise the puritan settlers of New England sought to tie biblical interpretation down by giving it a materialistic application to the point where the word of God and letter of the law became elevated to the point of supreme adulation and truth, allowing little room for opposing interpretations which might undermine both their beliefs and their rigid social hierarchy based on religion.

However, the American translation of European mythology has created a society which is both aware of the self-conscious creation of its own mythology and yearns for authenticity yet is also antagonistic towards any imposition of tradition which it feels to be deceptive and limiting of the individual's right to freedom. The Western fits this psyche perfectly, essentially a secular adventure genre it plays out the conflict between the individual's right to freedom and transformation irrespective of religion, and the desire for possession and settlement, set against a hostile environment with obstacles which might bring about the downfall of the hero. The heroes the Western evokes are young, white, active men who have a healthy disregard for undemocratic laws yet essentially recognize, and fight for the rights of the democratic settlers.

North America has a duel history of dispossession and possession. Firstly the early European discovery of America and later exploitation of the land and settlement was dependent on consolidating dispossession of the native inhabitants (Native Americans, Mexicans). This was perhaps more overt in the case of Native Americans, many of whom had a transmigratory way of life and viewed possession of the land in very different terms to the European settlers. Secondly, the European explorers/settlers sought a life of freedom and opportunity in opposition to their dispossessed status in their native European homelands. This structure of loss and acquisition applied to a wide social cross-section of Europeans, ranging from monarchies to social outcasts. Some Europeans felt they were escaping to America to avoid the socio-economic and/or religious oppression they suffered in Europe, to begin their lives again. Others simply saw America as a "New World" to further their financial and political aspirations, recreating violent systems of exploitation and extending them, for example the "Peculiar Institution" of slavery in the Southern States, an appalling system of human rights abuse towards Africans and a further feudal oppression of poor European immigrants. From its inception as a nation after the American Revolution and in Thomas Jefferson's Declaration of Independence of July 1776, America has been idealized as a land of equal opportunity. Undoubtedly it did and still does offer different opportunities to those of the European homelands. However like all nations, many were excluded from equal opportunity, and America was divided between those who had, and those who had not.

In terms of a white Euro-centric history America is a relatively young nation, its central political cohesion and economic development as a nation state has occurred from the 1870's onwards. Its expansion in terms of population, settlement, governmental organisation and industrial infrastructure began prior to this but was interrupted and then accelerated when slavery was finally outlawed and the American Civil War had seen the Northern States defeat and decimate the Southern States slave-dependent economy. In simplified terms, America's development can be seen in terms of waves or frontier advances with a basic east to west history of exploration, exploitation and settlement alongside waves of economic depression and prosperity as its economy became less based on small-scale individual and agrarian gain or "bonanza" geological gains (Californian Gold Rush 1849 etc.) and more geared towards large-scale industry and business entrepreneurs.

America's founding myth of the frontier and the American Dream, the history of cinema, and the history of the Western film genre are interdependent. Both the myth and the Western genre began before cinema, but it was cinema (and other forms of media) which gave the myth and the Western genre their powerful imagery, with shared and internationally recognizable symbols. Westerns began in fiction, in both popular and more documentary forms, in spectacular Wild West Shows and reconstructions, theatre plays and radio serials, and then at the beginning of the twentieth century in short films – mainly in the form of simple generic adventure B-movies and often as serials, but also as longer and more complex A-movie features and epic films, after 1950's television also incorporated Western series. Images of the west had long been popular with landscape painters and photographers, but it was film, and in the 1930s film with sound, that brought the west into focus as a site of movement and growth for the nation as a whole. The advent of film ensured that Western motifs became more readily acceptable and narratives became less complex and more based on physical action than literary mediums.

## BUILDING THE YELLOW BRICK ROAD
The Western is the father of the road movie, they share many common elements; but in many ways the road movie is not just an updating of the Western into the technological age where motorized transport replaces horse, or simply a distillation of ideological motifs and generic characters (such as the heroic white male cowboy who, as the twentieth century progresses, is seen as an anachronistic desperado gunfighter in an increasingly ambiguous moral universe with nowhere left to go in the vast western landscape). The road movie may be the Western's son, but it is a wayward son, a prodigal son who contests his father's authority, and searching for a true parental hero finds either disillusionment or orphanage. The road movie is in many ways a reformulation of the Western, which by following its routes in search of promised gold finds only empty dreams. Of course, the division between myth and actuality always existed in the Western, by its use of a text or image which offered greater verisimilitude than the reality. For example, many films which specify an exact geographical locale were often filmed elsewhere, although this was not made apparent. For the Western, above all other considerations, offered a distorted view of

history which was less concerned with showing the real America(s) and more concerned with cathartic entertainment and sometimes political intent, basically offering adventure stories with a patriotic veneer. The history of the Western as cinematic product and ideological reference material illustrates this point.

The latter half of the nineteenth century and the beginning of the twentieth century saw many technological and industrial advances with a resulting impact on society and entertainment which allowed the national myth to become inseparable from its representation in the realms of both politics and media. This created an overlap between fact and fiction, both within the entertainment product and within its reception in the larger social arena. It is not surprising that D. W. Griffiths' **Birth Of A Nation** (1915), based on Thomas Dixon's best-selling and pro-Ku Klux Klan historical romance *The Clansman* (1904), should make use of Western imagery, neither is it a surprise that the film had political backing. By the beginning of the twentieth century, the public was eager for representations of an American way of life and history. As the west became a more authentically historical locale, its representations could depart more from the reality. Many of the first American films were short documentaries, for example Thomas Edison produced documentary footage from 1894 featuring scenes of western life such as cowboys at work, "Indian" scenes, landscape vistas, and Buffalo Bill's Wild West. In 1898 Edison's company made two films, **Poker At Dawson City** and **Cripple Creek Bar-Room**, which registered a shift from documentary to dramatic film – though the films had some basis in contemporary life, for example Cripple Creek was the site of the biggest gold strike and gold mining site in Colorado 1890–1901. Edison's 1903 film **The Great Train Robbery** by Edwin Porter is often cited as being the first Western, or first such film with narrative action and close-up; originally a stage play, it was based on an actual event that took place in 1900.

There are discrepancies around the film's status as first Western, for example other films had used similar techniques, and the film **Kit Carson** by the American Mutoscope and Biograph Company was copyrighted in September 1903, whereas **The Great Train Robbery** was copyrighted in December 1903. Also, the verisimilitude of the film was somewhat debatable since the ten-minute film contained outdoor shots but was filmed in New Jersey – film production at this time was located in the East. However, the film was the biggest commercial success yet seen and spawned countless imitations by both Edison and its competitors; **The Great Bank Robbery, The Bold Bank Robbery, The Little Train Robbery, The Hold-Up Of The Mountain Express**, and so on. The Western as a film genre was quickly listed in distributors' catalogues, but by 1911 reviewers were complaining that the genre was "a gold mine that had been worked to the limit"[3].

This closure on the Western was not new either in relation to the genre or to its companion, the frontier myth, and is intricately tied to the idea that America's frontier with its ensuing promise of individual opportunity, the ability to transform from one person/nationality to another is lost in the past. The fact that this warning was frequently repeated with any new advance in technology or society, and at a very early point in America's myth creation might indicate that those values were never concrete or available in the first place. For example the historian Frederick Jackson Turner, delivered a seminal essay at the World's Columbian Exposition in 1893, entitled "The Significance Of The Frontier In American History", where he makes the point that "the frontier has gone", fearing for the effect that this will have on the American character and American democracy which he sees as being dependent on the westward challenge against the wilderness. The Western is a genre which increasingly appears to mourn the loss of a golden land where a man could be a hero and this sense of loss is deeply embedded in the road movie. The division between civilization and wilderness and the ensuing sets of oppositions that this creates forms the foundation for the Western but is also reveals fissures in the national myth – particularly within an A-movie format, for example in many of John Ford's films a tension exists between the wilderness as desert and the wilderness as garden.

The success of **The Great Train Robbery** and its imitations led both to the formation of a Western genre and partly to the shift in film production from the East to the West coast, with the eventual formation of Hollywood. The Patents Company's attempt to monopolize film production in the East also forced this geographic shift, but it did allow film companies to have access to authentic western locales and characters such as unemployed cowboys and Native Americans living on reservations, who had previously found employment with the Wild West Shows, who could act or offer technical advice. During the 1911–20 period various western towns were bidding to become the centre of film production, including Los Angeles, a western town with cultural and commercial links (via railroad) to the cattle and mining frontiers of Arizona, New Mexico, and West Texas. The Selig-Polyscope Company of Chicago led the way in sending film troupes on location to the west, while others based themselves on location, such as the Bison company who contracted with the Miller Brothers 101 Ranch Wild West show and who had a huge area of ranches in Oklahoma complete with rodeo arena, cowboys, Native Americans, herds of buffalo, stagecoaches and so on. Bison 101 was relatively short-lived but popular action films were made under the directorship of Thomas Ince, who streamlined production establishing standard industry practices. The Universal film company followed Bison 101's lead and built a huge studio five miles to the north of Los Angeles; the studio's opening in 1915 was attended by William Cody (Buffalo Bill). Universal also bought another ranch in the San Fernando Valley ensuring that it became the biggest producer of Westerns during the 1920s.

By 1910 it could be said that the Western had become the first cinematic genre and the first American film contribution. Out of the 1001 films made in 1910, 213 (21%) were Westerns. This high percentage remained fairly continuous with a brief intermission in the 1930s partly due to the economic Depression but perhaps more crucially to the introduction of sound. Between 1926–1967 a quarter of all feature films made in Hollywood were Westerns, and as such can be seen as a foundation for Hollywood. 1923 saw the production of the first Western epic **The Covered Wagon**, a ten reel film by Paramount costing an unprecedented $782,000, shot in Utah and Nevada, which charts the Californian Gold Rush and the conflict within a large party of emigrants who are headed to Oregon to set up farms. When news of the Gold Rush reaches them half of the group choose to try and make a quick buck in California. The film quickly became one of the biggest grossing silent films, spawning many imitators. John Ford's 1924 epic, **The Iron Horse**, traces a similar theme and is perhaps the best known such epic.

The 1930s saw the development of sound and the need brought about by the Depression to entice cinema-goers with double features, hence the creation of the A-movie feature film and the B-movie, or bottom half of the bill movie. B-movies were produced by independents and quickly became prolific, many were filmed as series, and were produced on a production line basis and sold by regional distributors to cinemas on a block-booking basis of a whole season's films, often at a flat rate of $25–$30 per play off. A-movies were produced by the major studios who had to pay for their own nationwide network of distribution. Some B-movie producers consolidated their position under economic hardship by placing themselves under the Republic company umbrella. B-movies were temporarily hit in the 1930–31 period by the introduction of sound; most small independent film companies could not initially afford the technology, cameras had to be heavily insulated to cut out the noise of the movement, limiting mobility and therefore location shots, in addition the small rural movie theatres which were the mainstay audience for B-movie Westerns found wiring for sound to be a large financial burden. B-movie Western production dipped during this period while the film companies waited to see if sound would catch on; it did, and the companies eventually increased production.

The B-movie Western moved further away from realism during the 1930s with the increasingly formulaic cowboy hero who remained popular until the 1950s when he was transformed into the gunfighter. The figure of the cowboy had received increasing prominence throughout the 1920s, various actors often with skills in horsemanship and previously allied to the Wild West Shows had reached stardom. In the 1930s Gene Autry, "the singing cowboy", rose to stardom further codifying the moral clean-cut behaviour of the western man of adventure. Fans identified the role with the star and Autry was simply billed as himself in performances; likewise series were built around stars and actors were allowed little room to play other roles. In 1943 Autry was succeeded by Roy Rogers, who remained the top cowboy star until 1954 when production of Western series was ended. The major studios cut back on Westerns during the 1930s/'40s. The independents were much more dependent on the Western and during the second World War period, 1941–5, half of their feature films were Westerns (313 out of 645). In this same period the eight major studios produced between half and a third of all Westerns made, but it represented only 15% of their output.

Only John Wayne stands as an actor who was able to cross between the fields of A and B-movies, starring in John Ford's seminal Westerns such as **Stagecoach** (1939), an A-movie Western which revitalized the major studios' production of A Westerns and produced iconographic scenic views of Monument Valley; **The Searchers** (1956), often cited as a seminal influence on other American film genres and as a link in its theme of the quest narrative to many road movies; and **The Man Who Shot Liberty Valance** (1962), which reveals the complicity between media and myth-making. John Wayne was so closely identified with the Western hero that it comes as little surprise that the American public equated his film persona with his own identity, illustrating the much-quoted newspaper editor's statement in **The Man Who Shot Liberty Valence**, "When the legend becomes fact, print the legend". America looked to the Western genre for its real-life heroes and created them.

Wayne's final appearance in Don Siegel's **The Shootist**, three years before his death from cancer in 1979, as a dying gunfighter with opening clips from his many Westerns, created an aftermath of adulation for Wayne and the values his roles embedded. This included the tearful appearance by actress Maureen O'Hara before a congressional committee to plead that her dying co-star be awarded the U.S. Medal of Freedom – even though Wayne only ever played military heroes, never serving as one. It can be little surprise either that this media authentication of history was again seen in the election as President and the media trimmings and White House Western decor, surrounding the former actor and California Governor Ronald Reagan who likewise was an actor-soldier. This trend of fiction meets fact, film actor meets politics, includes James Stewart who was named as a Pennsylvania Ambassador in 1948, and also Clint Eastwood, former mayor of Carmel, California.

The films of John Ford, and the starring roles that John Wayne played in many of them, stand as seminal markers in the history of the Western film genre, and as markers for the western's link to the road movie. In particular, the films of director Sam Peckinpah, can be seen as re-working Ford's work in a modern, more cynical context. Peckinpah's films not only highlight the nostalgia felt in Ford's films for a less complex and morally certain past, but also debunk the myth that such a past really existed other than through the rose-tinted glasses of the media.

Ford's films focus on the central movements and themes that marked both the west's formation and its decline in terms of social colonization and technological innovation. For example, the building of the first transcontinental railroad contrasted against figures from the "Wild West" (**The Iron Horse**); the democratisation and "stock" figures of western society and mythology such as the drunken doctor, the

The Searchers

Southern gambler and so on, (**Stagecoach**); the loss of a clear-cut conception of the Native American "other" and the inability to obtain the American pioneer dream of rural homestead (**The Searchers**); the intervention of law in the West, the consolidation of community values and life with the introduction of the railroad, and media manipulation in creating the national myth (**The Man Who Shot Liberty Valance**). Ford's films often provide different ways of interpreting the same key themes of the estern myth.

Ford's films are notable for bringing a complexity of human motivation and character to the mythical figures of the west that the audience can identify with to some extent. His characters often face moral dilemmas, often mixing comic elements with more serious considerations. Ford's films mix this human dimension with both the mythology of the west contained in dime novels and historical events, and in addition to this Ford produced highly coherent narratives and spectacular visual imagery, all of which create memorable and distinguishable cinema. This mixture of fiction and fact, however revised, gave Ford's films a certain questioning ability, an inability to smooth over certain tensions and contradictions in the mythology of the west.

**The Searchers** in particular foreshadows the uneasy nostalgic vision of America turning to disillusion as seen in the Westerns of the sixties, and the road movie genre itself. The film is set in 1868. John Wayne plays the ex-confederate Ethan Edwards, who is seen as a homecomer to his brother's farmstead on the Texas frontier. Ethan's brother, sister-in-law and eldest daughter are killed by Comanches, whilst the youngest daughter, Debbie, is taken captive and becomes one of the wives of Chief Scar. Ethan, alongside Martin Pawley, a part-Cherokee orphan adopted by Ethan's brother, spends five years tracking Debbie, who has accepted her new life. Ethan, who it is implied loved his brother's wife, has a revenge motive to kill what to him is the "sexually" –

and therefore "racially" – soiled Debbie. Pawley prevents Ethan from doing so. Pawley kills Chief Scar and rescues Debbie. Ethan initially attempts to ride down the escaping Debbie, but then relents, lifts her up and returns her to the white settlement. Pawley returns to the settlement and marries his white sweetheart.

The closing scene is one of the most memorable of all Westerns, as the audience see Ethan refusing their invite to enter the homestead, he stands outside of the darkened interior framed by the doorway, silhouetted against the bright light outside. Wayne's character is ambiguous, he is a searcher although his goal is not defined, and an avenger for justice, but a morally distorted justice. The character of Martin muddies Ethan's fight as white avenger against the Indians. Martin, as part-Cherokee hero who marries into the white settlement, distorts the racial divide. Martin also doubles and critiques Ethan's role of hero. This is not to say that the Native American representation in the film is politically correct or historically accurate. However it does show that American hero no longer has a clearly defined identity, he has become an anti-hero with confused motivation who cannot find a home. With the character of Ethan, it appears that America has lost its heroes because they lack a place to belong in America, and their heroic status was always part media construct. The search will continue for Ethan because, without a goal, he does not know for what he is searching. This notion of nostalgia or loss for a sense of belonging or direction found in **The Searchers**, overlaps with America's founding mythology and feeds directly into the road movie genre. The search for a home, for an American identity in the road movie is seen as more desperate, hopeless, and urgent because the suspicion lurks, as seen in the character of Ethan, that it was perhaps always an impossible and non-existent dream.

**The Outlaw** (1943, but begun in 1940) starring Jane Russell and produced by Howard Hughes is credited with introducing sex into the genre and also marking its decline, alongside **The Ox-Bow Incident** (1942) starring Henry Fonda, which has a less heroic and more bleak view of frontier life. **The Outlaw** introduced a new tendency in A-movies to offer social commentary and more complex character motivation. B-movies remained pretty consistent during this period, which also saw the rise of MGM musicals and film noir. A more cynical worldview and psychological interests were filtered into the A-Westerns. Hollywood found itself facing further commercial setback and commercial wariness with the 1948 Supreme Court "Paramount decision" which forced the division of the studios from their chains of theatres. The late 1950s saw a further relaxation of other taboos in films such as the inclusion of homosexuality and incest, and a move away from more traditional Western themes, other taboos such as miscegenation remained conservative in their portrayal. The sympathetic Native American theme which had been popular in some of the very early Westerns received further prominence in **Broken Arrow** (1950), but its treatment is now seen as being much less liberal partly due to its total evasion, through the lead female character's death, of the possibility of a Native American/white American relationship. With the exception of Tonto, there are no Native American heroes in the B-Western and very few in the A-Western between 1920–50.

1954 saw Republic release its final series Western, **Phantom Stallion** and from then on it was the turn of the television Western series, some like *The Lone Ranger* had begun in radio and quickly spun off into other media. The television series were the training grounds of future Western actors and film directors such as Clint Eastwood (*Rawhide*, which began in 1959 and was listed among the top 25 television shows of the 1959/60 season), and Sam Peckinpah, the director of 1960s "nowhere-left-to-go" Westerns such as **The Wild Bunch** (1969). The television series were popular but were declining by the 1970s when the industry initiated demographic audience research and discovered that the audiences their Western series attracted were similar to that of the B-Movies and did not appeal to either women or a more urban population. This was similar to the findings of the major studios in the 1930s who turned away from the Western and created the more urban genre of the gangster movie, and then "Victorian Empire" adventure films which fed into Western films after their revival in 1939.

By the 1950s the major film studios had lost interest in the Western and the Independent companies had collapsed, major studio production of Westerns fell from 27% in 1953 to 9% of their output in 1963. However the 1960s saw a revival in the Western from non-American sources which became both consumers and then producers of Westerns, the almost unthinkable had occurred. The first hint of new revival came with the popularity of **The Magnificent Seven** (1960), produced and directed by John Sturges, a film which was more popular in Europe than America and set in Mexico. The emphasis moved away from the lone gunfighter whose morals and motivation had become increasingly cloudy to that of the gunfighter gang whose motivation is clearly monetary. In 1962 a German film company began production of Western stories based on Karl May novels and 1964 saw the emergence of the Italian director Sergio Leone with his trilogy of "dollars" spaghetti Westerns, **Per Un Pugno Di Dollari** (1964, *aka* **A Fistful Of Dollars**), **Per Qualche Dollaro In Piu** (1965, *aka* **For A Few Dollars More**), and **Il Buono, Il Brutto, Il Cattivo** (1966, *aka* **The Good, The Bad And The Ugly**). The films star Clint Eastwood as an enigmatic gunfighter who radiates silent mystique and also violence to the stirring soundtracks of Ennio Morricone. These later Westerns see an increase in violence and also in the amorality of the gunfighter where the previous choice between money and morals becomes more cynical; this trend had been seen earlier in Westerns such as **Santa Cruz** (1954), but it became more pronounced as the gunfighter shifted towards the mercenary open to the highest bidder. Leone's silent gunfighter does retain a set of personal ethics, but the "Man With No Name" has an almost haunting quality, a signifier for one for whom the west or America has a place for, but who must continually return to set the record straight because of the hypocrisy and fallibility of civilization. His motivation is self-orientated, but for revenge and money, not ethics which are seen to have no place here. If the American Dream stresses the ability and freedom to become whoever one wants to be then Eastwood's nameless, silent stranger expresses the alienation and emptiness of the national myth.

1969 saw the release of "nowhere-left-to-go" Westerns which hint at the end of the West and the beginning of a new era of technological civilization. For example, the gently critical **Butch Cassidy And The Sundance Kid** (dir. George Roy Hill), which features a motorized pushbike, and Peckinpah's more overtly cynical and violent **The Wild Bunch** which was the most popular and controversial of the 1969 Westerns. Noted for its graphic slow-motion violence, influenced by Italian film, and related by critics to civil unrest on the streets of America, Peckinpah's film portrays a more brutal West with unscrupulous killers and outmoded gunfighters who are visibly old and unable to fit in with their last option of being bank robbers or paid mercenaries. The film expresses a nostalgia for the Western myth of the cowboy, but seems to imply that it had once existed but became quickly outdated. To further this point Peckinpah introduces the presence of the car (invented in 1885 but not accessible to most of the American public until 1907 when Henry Ford set up a production line for his Model-T). The car (also seen previously in Peckinpah's **Ride The High Country**, 1962 as a symbol of the West's decline), is presented as a symbol of debauchery and destruction which sweeps over a pre-existing lifestyle, in much the same way as the railroad was seen to do in **Stagecoach**; however the overtones are more pessimistic in **The Wild Bunch**, where railroads are also corrupt and do not just bring in change.

The end-sequence of Peckinpah's film shows a framed still-shot which gradually burns away emphasizing the mythic, media construction of the West and its transparency as fiction. This highlighting of media complicity can be compared to many Westerns which use media forms to lesser degrees of consciousness, and also to later

The Wild Bunch

films such as Clint Eastwood's **Unforgiven** (1992) which draws similar conclusions to Peckinpah's film. The film is critical of Western mythology but is essentially more conservative. This is emphasized in the closing-sequence where a documentary text relating to the hero's future life is seen to pass over the desolate scene of his abandoned farmstead. In other words, the critical distance between film and its awareness of the complicity of media in the creation of myth is lessened by not showing it as the means of representation. The relationship between the means and portrayal of media such as newspapers in Western films highlights the relationship between myth and reality.

## A MAN WENT LOOKING FOR AMERICA...

1969 also saw the release of **Easy Rider**, often cited as the first road movie in terms of its quest narrative (particularly that of spiritual identity). The film makes full use of previous Western motifs such as the expansive landscape, but such symbols are imbued with a very overt cynicism and self-consciousness, whereby the patriotic symbols of the Western are shown as meaningless signifiers. For example the two main characters are called Wyatt (Peter Fonda), and Billy (Dennis Hopper); Wyatt wears a helmet with an American flag design, whilst Billy is clad in a pioneer suede fringed outfit – modern day pastiches of two legendary and much distorted Western figures, the lawman Wyatt Earp and the outlaw killer Billy the Kid. The message is clear, there are no heroes for late 1960s society to rely on, the great American heroes were not only dead, but mythical in the first place. The quest for identity, the escape of becoming someone else was not a viable option, as the film's advertising makes clear, America and its people needed a new forms of identity to express their discontents and fulfil their dreams. **Easy Rider** charts a motorcycle journey across the nation, whereas most road movies focus on the car, creating a more insulated/alienated version of the quest for identity without the same sense of rugged individualism.

Production of Westerns did not cease after 1969, but the Western myth was largely debunked as the search for new directions indicates and Hollywood no longer saw it as playing a central role in film production. Once again other genres such as the crime, horror, and science fiction film became more popular than the Western. If the Western remained popular it was in terms of adding significance (increasingly ironic or as pastiche) to other genres, or by being influenced by themes from its own descendent genres such as the spiritual/psychological quest of many road movies. This is evidenced by Don Siegel's casting of Clint Eastwood in **Coogan's Bluff** (1968) as an Arizona sheriff pursuing his quarry through the urban frontier, in this case New York, and then later as an unorthodox Western detective in a series of films starting with **Dirty Harry** (1971). Siegel also cast Eastwood in **The Beguiled** (1970), Southern Gothic in style and tension, but Western in its theme of the Civil War as it traces one Union soldier's psychological/escape route.

Eastwood himself as actor/director made some of the best Westerns during the 1970s, including **High Plains Drifter** (1972) which owes much as tribute to the work of Siegel and Leone, and **The Outlaw Josey Wales** (1976), a commercial flop but a critically successful revenge movie tinged with tenderness, which places a Western emphasis on the landscape. Eastwood continued to resurrect the Western in the 1980s with **Pale Rider** (1985), a more "socio-realistic" pro-community narrative with a shift away from gunfighter towards more traditional cowboy (Hollywood in general was less keen on the Western in the 1980s partly due to the huge financial flop of the extravagant **Heaven's Gate** in 1980). However, Eastwood was successful with **Unforgiven** (1992), in which he debunks the Western myth making full use of its genre symbols, for example the characters could be seen as the dysfunctional and unheroic versions of those stock Western roles found in the films of John Ford, particularly **Stagecoach** and **The Man Who Shot Liberty Valance**. The film is essentially conservative, showing that whilst the role of the gunfighter might have been less glamorous than painted it provided better gains than either the choice of farmer stricken with hardship and poverty, or that of urban bourgeois capitalist. **Unforgiven's** mixture of conservatism (return to order), and critique of national mythology might, as has been suggested[4], be due to the fact that its script was written in the 1970s but it was produced in the aftermath of the reactionary '80s.

Eastwood's latest film as actor/director/producer, **Space Cowboys** (2000) might on release, provide an interesting take on the space/astronaut theme with relationship to America's founding myth. The film sees Eastwood as retired astronaut, with former U.S. airforce buddies (including former Western actor James Garner), enter space on an emergency mission to repair a 1960s satellite which is due to crash into the earth with dire consequences for humanity. Eastwood's character is the only one who can save the world, with his knowledge of the outmoded satellite technology. He will only agree to lead the mission on the condition that his former friends, who never made the astronaut training program, come with him on his last and potentially fatal space flight. This show of male loyalty mixed with individualism and bravery has all the hallmarks of the classic Western and reviewers are already describing its pre-production in Western terms, accusing its backer Warner Brothers of "staking out a claim" on the late Summer film release slot. The Western may have shifted its representational grounds, the mythmakers of the West and the Western may be dead or grey, but neither their ideology or imagery is forgotten.

# NOTES

1. Slotkin, R. *Gunfighter Nation: The Myth Of The Frontier In Twentieth-Century America*, p.254.

2. See Slotkin, R., *Gunfighter Nation* for a fuller discussion of this phenomenon.

3. *The BFI Companion To The Western*, ed. Edward Buscombe, p.24.

4. Leighton Gist, "Unforgiven" in *The Movie Book Of The Western*, eds. I. Cameron & D. Pye, 294.

# 'EL TOPO':
# THE ROAD TO ATROCITY

## Stephen Barber

Alexandro Jodorowsky's life is the ultimate road movie narrative. Incessantly on the road or on the run between countries and continents, surrounded by a peripheral entourage of freaks and mentally damaged individuals, and moving with sudden transitions from obscurity to ephemeral celebrity and back again, Jodorowsky has been one of the great legendary, but subterranean, figures of experimental art and cinema from the 1960s to the present. His pre-eminent film, the "mystical Western" **El Topo** ("The Mole"), released in 1971, charts the road to atrocity and revelation with lacerating force. Jodorowsky was already forty-two when he made **El Topo**, and had a history of two decades of experimental theatre performance behind him, mostly staged in Mexico: his principal inspiration in this performance work was Antonin Artaud's Theatre of Cruelty, although Jodorowsky insists that, if asked to choose between Artaud and his own obsessions as his main creative source, he prizes his own compulsions above all cultures. Jodorowsky has been associated for over thirty years with the renowned Spanish theatre director and filmmaker, Fernando Arrabal[1], although Jodorowsky's South American origins provide him with an ability to dissect human illusions and the sheer worthlessness of human existence with a naked power barred to any European.

El Topo was immediately taken up and revered on its New York release, early in 1971, by figures such as Dennis Hopper (whose film **The Last Movie** of the same year has much of the intricate rawness of Jodorowsky's work) and John Lennon, and at various points until the beginning of the 1980s it appeared that Jodorowsky's vision might be co-opted by Hollywood. This never happened. Jodorowsky soon lost the rights to **El Topo**, a pattern that seems to have recurred with almost all of his subsequent films – in fact, Jodorowsky claims never to have made any money whatsoever from any of his films, until the Accatone cinema in Paris paid him 500 francs (around £50) for a screening of his film **Santa Sangre** (1986) in 1999. He believes that, with a virulent and stubborn vision such as he has pursued since his first film, **Fando And Lis**, he can expect to make no more than a film each decade. Although Jodorowsky has a number of film projects in development, over a decade has now passed since his last film, **Santa Sangre**, and he is still looking for a producer for his next project.

In Paris, where he now lives, Jodorowsky is celebrated primarily as a successful comic-strip book (*"bandes dessinées"*) author; he works in collaboration with a number of artists, providing extravagant narratives which the artists illustrate, and in 1999 he produced the narrative for the first ever comic-strip book entirely created by digital image technology.

El Topo has followed a twisted road. The film achieved a legendary status in Britain during its short period of visibility (and the screenplay, heavily annotated by Jodorowsky, was published in Britain in the early 1970s), but the film disappeared rapidly from view there, as it had done in the United States. Ownership disputes plagued the film for over twenty-five years, and the aura of **El Topo** as a lost masterpiece of supreme cruelty achieved overblown proportions. Jodorowsky made a rare (probably unique) appearance in Britain in 1996 for the festival "Incarcerated With

Artaud And Genet" at the Institute of Contemporary Arts, and El Topo was screened on British terrestrial television (its first ever showing on television anywhere in the world) in the following year, giving it a new, if tenuous, existence.

El Topo is the ultimate projection of individual obsession and self-mythification: it carries the relentless and endless interior journey which is the mark of the road movie, and the entire trajectory of El Topo is that of a multiplicitous searching into the interacting roles of the individual, of god and of violence. But El Topo also indelibly marks the moment when the ecstasy of the 1960s counterculture overturned into massacre, assassination, and terror, and here too it captures the definitive moment of the road movie, at the turn of the 1970s, as a visual sledgehammer blow aimed at the head of American fundamentalism, militarism and ignorance.

At times, El Topo moves with extraordinary slowness, at other times with a cardiac frenzy reminiscent of the momentum driving another great disillusioned Mexican road movie of the early 1970s, Sam Peckinpah's Bring Me The Head Of Alfredo Garcia, which also terminates in a ferocious bloodbath and with the suicide or self-sacrifice that is the only way to mark the end of the road with dignity. The narrative of El Topo is a journey from atrocity to atrocity, punctuated by bouts of revelation, and structured in two parts.

Although the more fatuous British critics of the film, such as Christopher Frayling, have argued that El Topo's narrative is incoherent, in fact it is a superbly plotted film, intricate and lucidly contradictory from its first to last moment. In the first shots of the film – using an iconography intentionally drawn from the Western film genre – a gunfighter in black leather, "El Topo" (played by Jodorowsky himself), shaded by a black umbrella, is travelling through a desert, carrying his naked seven-year-old son with him on his horse. They reach a town which is running with a river of blood and whose population has been decimated: El Topo ascertains that a bandit known as "The Colonel" has committed the outrage with his gang of cretins. He tracks them down at a Franciscan mission, slaughters the gang (Jodorowsky choreographed their bloody demise with advice from the technicians of Peckinpah's The Wild Bunch, castrates The Colonel (who dies in a sequence of abject humiliation exactly prefiguring the castration scene in Santa Sangre), and releases The Colonel's sex slave, a young

woman who accompanies El Topo and forces him to abandon his son.

They wander in a desert, and the woman incites El Topo into a new quest, to kill the four Gun-Masters who live in the desert. As El Topo picks off the four Masters, through treachery and cunning, he finally becomes convinced of the futility of his quest and shatters his gun; a female gunfighter who has been jealously following El Topo and seducing the woman then shoots down El Topo.

In the second part of the film, El Topo awakens twenty years on, from a coma induced by his shooting, to find himself in a cavern populated by dispossessed, inbred freaks; these freaks, who have saved El Topo and regard him as their deity and source of salvation, have been imprisoned in the cavern many years earlier by the population of a nearby town which views them as its detritus – "born from incest and deformed". El Topo now reverses his earlier self-directed quest and resolves to help the freaks, who want to return to the town, even though this is clearly a desperate and utterly futile aspiration. Now shaven-headed and dressed in sackcloth, El Topo decides to build a tunnel from the almost-inaccessible cavern to the outside world, and goes to visit the town with the young dwarf woman who has been caring for him.

The town is a hell of greed, murder and arcane power systems, with a bogus morality. Even though the town is evidently much worse than the cavern, El Topo goes ahead with his plan and, to earn money for the tunnel's construction, performs mime acts (Jodorowsky trained for many years in France with the mime artist Marcel Marceau) for the crass townspeople, and suffers execration and subjugation. He decides to marry the pregnant dwarf and they visit the town's priest, who turns out to be El Topo's abandoned son, now an adult who is furious to see his father and resolves to kill him once the tunnel is built. But, when El Topo finishes the job, the son changes his mind, wailing "I can't kill my Master".

The liberated torrent of freaks immediately pour down into the town where they are promptly massacred by the townspeople. El Topo, in turn, massacres the townspeople before immolating himself (in a sequence which must have evoked the burning monks protesting against the Vietnam war at the time of the film's release). El Topo's son, now wearing the gunfighter's black leathers, rides out of town with El Topo's dwarf wife, who has given birth to El Topo's new child at the very moment of his death.

Although El Topo has reductively been labelled a "metaphysical" or "allegorical" or "psychoanalytical" Western, its concerns are far more those behind the road movie: it is an exploration of the essential matters of sex and isolation and subjugation and death, all of which obsess and compel the protagonists of the road movie[2]. In fact, little in El Topo is oblique or symbolic, and Jodorowsky's scepticism (along with that of all authentic surrealists) towards the power structures of psychoanalysis means that he is interrogating new ways of creating human communities, and reversing ideas of health and illness, rather than confirming existing theories. All of Jodorowsky's films embody the search of peripheral individuals to group together as an oppositional, antisocial community: a preoccupation which is the core of the road movie's journey. Jodorowsky's special insistence on the stature of the freak as his preferred human being emphasizes his engagement with those who disturb or overturn society or who have special insights into its malignancy.

Indeed, Jodorowsky still prizes freaks above all other human beings: at the ICA in 1996, he met the eminent opera director Peter Sellars and declared that he was a freak of such distinction that it was worth the effort of having crossed the Channel just to have got a look at him. But Jodorowsky, unlike many of the filmmakers and artists whose work hit its peak of notoriety at the turn of the 1970s, is not against the idea of the family; Jodorowsky cast all of his own sons in Santa Sangre, and his son Brontis plays the young, abandoned son in El Topo. Instead, Jodorowsky refutes hypocritical human societies based on greed, expulsion and subjugation.

Like many road movies, El Topo has a hallucinatory quality, in which the identity of the characters can fluctuate and reverse from moment to moment (El Topo himself declares: "I am God" as he castrates the Colonel; later, in the cavern of freaks, he asserts: "I am not God"). The film's journey itself is precipitated by these abrupt reversals of identity, in which resuscitations and obliterations occur with contradictory tenacity. The aberrant merit of El Topo is to make these transmutations the central element of film narrative itself (as they are in David Lynch's Lost Highway, 1997), and to inflict the gruelling challenge of such a journey of cuts onto the film spectator.

At the same time, El Topo is a film of laughter: the film directs disabused laughter at the ludicrous pretensions and ambitions of the film and of Jodorowsky himself, but also at the idiocy of the society he derides. Jodorowsky believes that laughter is the last surviving sign of humanity. Jodorowsky's films have the reputation of being too harsh in their caustic depiction of the human species, but he is still especially attacked for the cruelty towards animals in his work (although only a number of rabbits and sheep died during the making of El Topo, Jodorowsky's subsequent film, The Holy Mountain (1973), in many ways a much more extreme film than El Topo, contains images of whole processions of crucified animals). Jodorowsky now presents the animal massacres and eviscerations of his early 1970s films as being "of their time" – certainly, in Japanese experimental cinema of the same period, no film ends without the strangulation or beheading of at least one chicken (see, for example, Shuji Terayama's Emperor Tomato Ketchup [1970]) – and claims that he was ignorant of animal rights.

While the film may evoke the historical atrocities of the time of its making, El Topo remains a contemporary film precisely because of its exploration of the visceral: its incision into the matter of the body, and its salutary blurring of the borders between animal and human life. Like all unique films, El Topo shows what is deemed unshowable. It is a scream of laughter at futility, at the intricate endgames and absolute cruelty of human existence: a journey into the matter of the end.

# NOTES

1. Arrabal is the director of such films as **Viva La Muerte** (1970) and **J'Irai Comme Un Cheval Fou** (1975).

2. Jodorowsky has commented in defence of his own film: "With every new picture, I must change myself, I must kill myself, and I must be born. I must kill the actors and they must be born. And the audiences, the audiences who go to the movies, must be assassinated, killed, destroyed, and they must leave the theatre as new people. This is a good picture."

Chapter 2

# Pulp Noir
# On The Road

# NOWHERE TO RUN: PULP NOIR ON THE ROAD

## Geraint Bryan

When we think of *film noir* we usually imagine a dark, rainy urban setting but there is another American *noir*. An American *noir* that explores the bleak heartland of America and one where rootlessness and desperation dominate. In films like **Detour** (Edgar G. Ulmer, 1945) and **Gun Crazy** (Joseph H. Lewis, 1949) the fatalism of *film noir* is transplanted to the open road to create a pulp aesthetic of frantic getaways, doomed love and feverish violence.

It is now quite difficult to imagine how mainstream Hollywood produced a genre that had such a pessimistic view of human nature as *film noir*, especially in view of the restrictive conventions of the time. Yet America's own violent history demanded such genres as the western or the gangster movie. The gangster movie acted as a contemporaneous commentary on real events happening in American society (rather like gangster rap now). The *film noir* took the tough thrills of the gangster movie but dispensed with the sociological moralisation of such films as **Angels With Dirty Faces** (Michael Curtiz, 1938) or **Little Caesar** (Mervyn LeRoy, 1930). In its place came a psychological realism that highlighted the existential anguish of the individual. The real genesis of *film noir* was the pulp novel, which provided an easy supply of new material for the studios. Existing outside of the traditional conventions of literature and originating in the first mass produced magazines, the pulp novel introduced a fast-paced narrative that titillated audiences with its concentration on sex, violence and the dark side. The pulp novel emerged from a context of an America still suffering from the economic hardships of the depression and the impact of organised crime during prohibition. Writers like Dashiell Hammett drew upon their own experiences (in his case as a Pinkerton detective) to create a raw, "hard-boiled" fiction that explored a deadly, amoral world whereby each action determined survival.

These themes were married to increasingly adventurous film techniques. It was the boom in film production in the thirties and forties which allowed directors and cameramen the freedom to explore new stylistic ways of seeing. Their job was to bring in films quickly and on a small budget; innovations were often born as solutions to practical difficulties rather than intended artistic advances. B-movies in particular would provide fertile grounds for experimentation as they were not governed by the same degree of commercial consideration and studio control given to main features. Technical and thematic innovation were brought too by the wave of European *émigrés* fleeing the onslaught of Fascism and alerted to the new opportunities in Hollywood. Bringing with them a world view psychologically shaped by the trauma of events in Europe and a technological expertise (particularly in lighting), they had much to do with the look and mood of what would be retrospectively named *film noir*. In particular, Hollywood would borrow heavily from German Expressionism with its visual style of oblique camera angles, light and dark contrasts and ominous shadows. This new stark vocabulary perfectly matched the moral ambiguities of the brutal pulp fictions and the two together would come to define *film noir*.

It was one of the most notable *émigrés*, Fritz Lang, who initiated the most durable theme of road movies through the years by coupling *amour fou* -mad love – with the crime movie to produce the lovers on the run film. In Europe Lang had made, amongst many others, **M** (1931) and **The Testament Of Dr. Mabuse** (1933), two

They Live By Night

masterful studies of evil and a corrupted world. **You Only Live Once** (1937) is one of his earliest American films. Henry Fonda plays Eddie Taylor, an ex-criminal seeking to escape his past. Tried and committed for a murder he is innocent of, Taylor escapes and goes on the run with his wife (Joan Graham). Rejected by the small town America they travel through, they are forced to live on their wits and outside the law. When they finally reach the border and it seems that freedom is within their grasp, they are cold-bloodedly killed in a police ambush. The brutality of this ending would be reprised in a number of lovers on the run movies, notably **Bonnie And Clyde** (Arthur Penn, 1967). There is a bitter irony that Taylor can only attain freedom through death, which is presented as a release from the repressions of American society. Lang's vision is remarkable for its disdain for authority and for its jaundiced view of notions of justice. The film is imbued with a grey, grainy realism that suggests an environment that is permanently threatening to suffocate the lovers.

Another film from this period which took the lovers in flight theme and gave it a *noir* overlay was Nicholas Ray's **They Live By Night** (1948). Later lionised by French film critics as one of the great Hollywood *auteurs*, i.e. a director whose stylistic imprints and concerns could be traced throughout his work, Ray's debut contains many of his later themes, noticeably a sympathy for society's outsiders. **They Live By Night** concerns young convict Bowie (Farley Granger) who breaks out of prison with two hardened, experienced criminals. Bowie is persuaded by them to join in a series of violent robberies. While hiding out he meets and falls in love with Keechie (Cathy O'Donnell). Yet his failure to extricate himself from his violent surroundings means that their love affair is ultimately doomed. Whilst in some respects a standard pot-boiler, Ray does succeed in giving the film a kinetic energy which is epitomised by the shot of the getaway car disappearing behind a cloud of dust; a shot taken by helicopter (which at

the time was highly unorthodox). As in **You Only Live Once**, the protagonists are seen as the helpless victims of a harsh, brutal world.

If these films sit comfortably within genre conventions, **Gun Crazy** is something else altogether. For *film noir* staples such as the femme fatale, impending violence and psychological complexity substitute a sexually rapacious female lead, a fetishistic obsession with guns and a motivational explanation that goes no further than the film's title: Gun Crazy! The nature of the film can be gleaned from its lurid poster, a tight, split-skirted wearing Peggy Cummins posing with two guns, and its attendant tag line: "Thrill Crazy... Kill Crazy". Director Joseph H. Lewis was a veteran of numerous B-movies and employed an economical approach which heightened the sheer visceral energy of the film. Asked many years later on the advice he gave his two young leads, John Dall and Peggy Cummins, Lewis commented: "I told John, 'Your cock's never been so hard', and I told Peggy, 'You're a female dog on heat, and you want him. But don't let him have it in a hurry. Keep him waiting'"[1].

After the relaxation of strict censorship codes, forties films were able to explore sexuality, and in particular female sexuality, in a way that had been impossible a decade earlier. *Film noir* became noted for its depiction of the *femme fatale*, granting female characters a hitherto unknown autonomy as they controlled the destinies of those around them. Yet if *film noir* used euphemism, innuendo and an implicit symbolism to convey female sexuality, Lewis went much further. Audiences did not need a working knowledge of Freudian symbolism to understand the eroticism of Cummins' handling of the guns. It is Cummins' sexuality that dominates and drives the film as Dall's own sexual drives are sublimated into the couple's obsessive gun fixation.

**Gun Crazy** begins surprisingly conventionally, as a series of witnesses testify on the behalf of the young Bart Tare who is in court for stealing a gun. This was a standard plot device of the time which served to give reassuringly sociological explanations for deviancy. One senses Lewis is barely interested in this and the rest of the film dispenses with explanation to instead present the couple as a force of nature (erotically) impelled to shoot and rob. Released, after a spell in the army, Bart (John Dall) returns to his small town and is taken to a carnival by his childhood friends. Here he engages in a competitive display of sharpshooting with Laurie Starr (Peggy Cummins). Bart regards Laurie with a lustfulness that endures for the entire movie. After joining the carnival, a jealous Bart fires a gun at Laurie's seedy boss and lover. Understandably he calls the pair "a couple of wild animals" and fires them both. They then hit the road and from here the film becomes increasingly frantic. After a quick montage of their honeymoon which ends bathetically with a shot of a pawnshop, the couple embark on a series of robberies that become increasingly ambitious as they in turn become more obsessed with each other. Bart is portrayed throughout as a passive victim driven by a lust he cannot control. Laurie is the dominant partner, yet she too is equally powerless to control events. "I've never been much good," she confesses early in the film and later we learn of a mysterious incident where she shot a man in St. Louis. Divorced from both family and society they inhabit their own existential world where the only tangibles are their desires. That their identities are so malleable is graphically illustrated in the film, as they each appear at various moments dressed as cowboys, prim office workers, soldiers and sinisterly stylish in macs, shades and berets.

Unusually for a film of this period, location shots are used throughout. The film feverishly traverses New Mexico, Arizona and California as the film contrasts the banal tranquility of smalltown America with the desperation of the couple. At one point Bart states: "Everything's going so fast... it's all in such high gear," which could equally serve as a commentary on the film's visual style. The first major robbery, on the Hampton Building and Loan Company, is filmed in a fluid one-take, three-minute shot which highlights them at the height of their powers. This contrasts with the snappy

Gun Crazy

editing and frenetic camerawork used to depict the latter tense and complex robbery of a payroll office as they become increasingly desperate. The film memorably climaxes with them hunted down and trapped in a swamp. The swathes of mist used were apparently to prevent the expense of using extras. However their dramatic impact lies in the way they symbolically represent the distance Bart has come from the unseen childhood friends who implore him to surrender. Despite the exciting amorality of the film, neither of the two are unsympathetic characters. Bart continually and futilely attempts to get them to give up the fugitive life, yet normality is never an option for them. When they are dressed "respectably" it is to rob a bank, when they go to a dance with other young couples they end up fleeing through a back exit. It is their fate to have a love for each other that goes together like "guns and ammunition". **Gun Crazy** is the ultimate pulp B-movie, but it is also so much more than this. Arguably the fastest and toughest film of its era, its themes and visual style would be plundered by many thrillers in the years to come.

At this point, it is worth considering the mythological potency of the road in the American cultural psyche. Directly fed by the history of the early pioneers, travel has often been seen as a symbol of American utopianism. The theme of self-discovery through immersion in the American landscape has been expressed throughout much American film and literature. In this context the road takes on the heroic qualities of a quest as the participants undertake a journey that is both geographical and metaphorical (Kerouac's novel *On The Road* is the best example of this). Even in a film as graphically downbeat as **My Own Private Idaho** (Gus Van Sant, 1991), the road is seen as a hallucinatory idyll which offers the promise of reinvention and escape from the predatory harshness of the city. In this analysis the road becomes a symbol of hope and transformation. The remarkable aspect of the road *noir* films is how obstinately and defiantly they stand outside this tradition. Working as a direct inversion of the many road movies, the road in the *noir* movie offers not hope but negation. The fugitives move because they've got no choice and so in a dark twist the road represents not freedom but imprisonment. In searching for the visual motifs of this road *noir*, the psychic landscape that these themes inhabit, it is interesting to consider the paintings of Edward Hopper. In the thirties and forties he painted a series of pictures featuring empty roads, desolate hotel lobbies, railway tracks disappearing into infinity, gas stations and diners. If the psychic geography of the road *noir* is to be found anywhere it is in paintings like "Four Lane Road", "Western Motel", and "Route 6 Eastham". These are desolate, anonymous landscapes quite different from the epic grandeur of much American landscape painting. When people do appear they look lost in the transitory environments of hotel lobbies and station waiting rooms. Their influence on cinema can be seen in **Psycho** (Alfred Hitchcock, 1960). The Bates Motel was based on Hopper's painting "House By The Railroad". Indeed the first half hour of **Psycho** exists as a road *noir* movie, as Marion Crane drives with the stolen money through a nightscape of driving rain and neon road signs, before the film veers off into something stranger altogether.

It is precisely this landscape that Edgar Ulmer's **Detour** inhabits. **Detour** is the ultimate road *noir*, with the kind of fatalistic belief in destiny usually encountered in Greek Tragedy. We first encounter Al Roberts (Tom Neal) in a half empty diner. He looks beat up, wired and when a friendly truck driver attempts to engage him in conversation, he snaps back "my mother taught me to never speak to strangers". When the truck driver plays a seemingly innocuous record on the jukebox, he loses it completely screaming for it to be switched off. Clearly he is a man at the end of his tether, he has reached the end of the road. How he came to this state of affairs is revealed in flashback, a common *film noir* narrative device of the time.

The flashback takes us back to Roberts playing piano in a New York nightclub. We are introduced to his girlfriend Sue, a singer at the club. Although his voice-over narration claims that at this point "I was a pretty lucky guy", the evidence suggests otherwise. His girlfriend wants to leave him to seek fame in Hollywood, to which he responds "That's the most stupid thing I ever heard of", and his talents as a musician go unappreciated. This section represents a normality in Roberts' life before things go seriously wrong. Yet wearing the lugubrious, down-mouthed expression he will keep for the entire movie, it is evident that his future is not to be filled with optimism. The one optimistic gesture he makes is to spend a tip on a long distance phone call to his girlfriend in LA; impetuously he promises to join her. It is on such whims that fate hangs and he is soon hitching a ride with wealthy businessman Haskell. Haskell's affluent affability vividly contrasts with the broke, taciturn Roberts. However it is entirely in keeping with the bleak worldview of **Detour** that Haskell is not what he appears to be. His money has been made in a shady betting operation and he is making the trip to con some money out of his wealthy father; more sinister still are the scratches on his arm from a "dame with claws" whom he threw out of his car. While Haskell rests, Roberts takes the wheel. It is a typically rainy *noir* night and Roberts tries to rouse Haskell only to discover he has died in his sleep. As he opens the car door Haskell falls, hitting his head. Deciding he will be framed for the murder of Haskell, Roberts concludes that his only option is to assume the man's identity and drive to LA where he can sell the car.

That we absolutely accept such preposterous logic is due to the power of **Detour**'s strange, enclosed, fate-driven world. **Detour** has the unreal quality of a nightmare in which choice and action are powerless. Later Roberts becomes even more helpless as he picks up a hitcher only to discover that she was the woman thrown out of Haskell's car. Vera (Ann Savage) identifies him as an impostor and blackmails him into giving her the money for the sold car and tries to involve him in a far-fetched scheme to impersonate Haskell to claim his dying father's inheritance. Imprisoned with

Detour

her in dreary hotel rooms, the film climaxes with the bizarre accidental murder of Vera by Roberts. Left to roam the country in a dead man's identity, Roberts as Haskell is also being sought for the murder of Vera; he bemoans that: "Fate – or some mysterious force – can put the finger on you or me, for no good reason at all".

Whilst intended as a straightforward *film noir* B-movie, the sheer weirdness of **Detour** pushes it beyond such genre conventions and it emerges as something of an oddball classic. **Detour** has none of *film noir*'s poetic realism, instead opting for an escalating hysteria – driven by the constant paranoiac voice-over – that takes the road inwards into the private realms of psychic disturbance. Loaded with dream sequences, the film invites us to question whether any of these events are "real" at all (a point emphasised by the ambiguous ending). The sneering, snarling Ann Savage is less a femme fatale than an avenging witch dredged from the subconscious. Tom Neal's gloomy pessimism is a world away from the tough hero of *noir*. His cynicism has not been earned like that of a world-weary Bogart, but comes from a defeatism so acute as to be pathological. In a strange case of life imitating art, ex-boxer Neal was later sentenced to ten years for the involuntary manslaughter of his wife.

**Detour** was a classic product of the "poverty row" studios, shot in an incredible six days. Director Ulmer (who also made the Universal horror classic **The Black Cat** in 1934) would spend his career grinding out cheap B-movies. In **Detour** the technical limitations complement the atmosphere of the film so that the artificiality of the back projections used for the driving scenes, perfectly mirror the unreality that pervades the film. Had Kafka been forced to churn out scripts for B-movie studios then you feel **Detour** would be the result.

These films would refuse to sink into obscurity and their pulp-derived energy and amorality would become a source of inspiration for the New Hollywood of the sixties and seventies. Robert Altman would remake **They Live By Night** as **Thieves Like Us** (1974), and Terrence Malick's **Badlands** (1973) would also revisit a pulp *noir* world of murderous young lovers adrift in a bleak Nebraska. Perhaps the film most influenced by the forties road *noir* films was the film that would kick-start the New Hollywood,

**Bonnie And Clyde**. Here, the charged violence of the earlier films is married to a more politicised reading that saw Bonnie and Clyde as, in the words of scriptwriter Robert Benton, "aesthetic revolutionaries"[2]. The influence of, in particular, **Gun Crazy** is everywhere to be seen. The sexual dominance of Laurie over Bart is given a sixties psychological twist in the impotence of Clyde. Faye Dunaway's vampish look of mac and beret, then very much epitomising sixties chic, was taken directly from Peggy Cummins' look in **Gun Crazy**. Finally, the manic energy and amorality of **Gun Crazy** is made explicit in **Bonnie And Clyde**, which introduced new levels of screen violence to mainstream cinema.

If the films of the forties were imbued with the unease and uncertainties of the times, American filmmaking of the seventies was informed by a cynicism and brutality that came, in part, from a post-Vietnam disenchantment. After **Bonnie And Clyde** the films became harder and tougher. At the forefront of this new lean, mean cinema was Sam Peckinpah, whose **The Wild Bunch** (1969) was Peckinpah's revisionist take on the Western; a film which gloried in its replacement of the Fordian romantic notion of the west with a vision that reduced the genre to its most brutal elements [see Chapter 1]. Peckinpah's raw, no-frills approach was perfect for the *noir* road movie. If there had always been an existential subtext to the *noir* road movie, one where identity was forged in a world of total instinct, then Peckinpah, with his dark meditations on the violence inherent in the American dream, was the perfect director to update this for the seventies. Peckinpah's **The Getaway** (1972) was adapted from a Jim Thompson pulp novel. Even amongst pulp novelists Thompson's works stand out for their bleakness and vivid depiction of neon-tinged lowlife[3]. Walter Hill, who would later direct the classic urban car thriller **The Driver** (1978), provided the minimal hard-boiled screenplay which allowed Peckinpah's cynicism full rein. Both Peckinpah and star Steve McQueen were in need of a hit, which lead Peckinpah to reduce **The Getaway** to a recipe of high-octane visceral thrills. Although Peckinpah was reputably displeased with the final cut, for which he blamed McQueen, **The Getaway** stands as one of the great post-*noir* films of the seventies.

The film opens with one of Peckinpah's greatest sequences; a montage of accelerating images showing the dehumanising effect of prison on McQueen. This sets up a mood of taut desperation which will endure for the rest of the film. McQueen stars as Doc McCoy, who is released from prison at the start of the film. His release has been secured by Benyon, a corrupt local politician, so that McQueen can pull off a bank job. Unknown to Mcqueen, his wife (Ali McGraw) has slept with Benyon as part of the deal. This corrupt and duplicious world informs the whole of **The Getaway**, whose plot is propelled by a series of double crossings. No one is what they appear in this film, from the corrupt southern establishment to the polite man, who helps McGraw with her baggage, who turns out to be a conman. Even Slim Pickens as the good ole boy at the film's end (an ending whose sentimentality somewhat jars with the rest of the film) is bought off. As McQueen states: "You want to know what I trust? In God I trust – it's the words written on the back of every bill".

After the killing of Benyon, Mcqueen and Mcgraw make a desperate escape with the money from the bank job down to El Paso where Benyon's henchman are waiting. Also in pursuit is Rudy (Al Letteira) a brutal bankrobber who tried unsuccessfully to double-cross McQueen and who has kidnapped a trashy Sally Strothers and her beleaguered husband. If the portrayal of the relationship between McQueen and McGraw is often cynical, then that between Letteira and Strothers is positively sado-masochistic. This is Peckinpah painting humanity at its basest, and Letteira brings a real thuggish menace to his role.

**The Getaway** takes place across the American southwest, a terrain Peckinpah would revisit again and again. These are seen as lawless lands with the border promising an elusive freedom. Throughout the naturalistic camerawork captures a

trashy Americana of hot-dog stands, gun shops and dilapidated hotel lobbies. The small towns McQueen travels through are full of potential danger meaning he may have to make a "getaway" at any time. The "getaway" is what counts – the means are irrelevant. At different points in the film they will make this getaway in a trashed car, a greyhound bus, train, an old pick-up truck and most memorably of all in a garbage truck. This is one of the key shots in all of Peckinpah, a testament to his own dark humour, as McQueen and McGraw are thrown onto a garbage heap. We momentarily see the plate on the truck and its judgement on the couple – "TRASH". McQueen is the immovable rock the film revolves around, the one point of certainty in a tumultuous, chaotic landscape. **The Getaway** moves with an energy which is almost psychotic and inhabits a world of crazed desperadoes. The violence of the film is both balletic and visceral, complete with Peckinpah's trademark slow motions and fast edits.

If the road in the earlier pulp *noirs* was sinister and had the ominous threat of the unexpected, in Peckinpah's hands it has become a singular force of violence. This is the end of the road, an end which is sure to be marked by the sound of a twelve-gauge shotgun[4].

# NOTES

1. D. Peary, *Cult Movies*; Delacorte Press, New York, 1981.

2. Peter Biskind, *Easy Riders, Raging Bulls*; Bloomsbury, 1998, p.23.

3. Jim Thompson is probably the greatest of all the classic hard-boiled crime novelists, churning out lurid pulps to order in the 1950s. His books, such as *Savage Night* and *King Blood*, easily transcend the confines of the dimestore novel with their depiction of a godless world populated by losers, boozers, criminals and corrupt lawmen. Other films made from Thompson's novels include: **The Killer Inside Me** (1976), **After Dark, My Sweet** (1990), and **The Grifters** (1990).

4. Yet Peckinpah managed to up the ante one more time with **Bring Me The Head Of Alfredo Garcia**, in 1974. This dark classic, starring Warren Oates, really is the road movie that leads to hell and damnation [see Chapter 8].

# Chapter 3

# Biker Movies

# REBELS OF THE ROAD:
# THE BIKER FILM

## Jim Morton

Much of the tension in any road movie comes from the potential for chaos that lies around the bend or at the next truck stop. The most perfect personification of this is the biker. This pot-smoking, grime-coated, speed-addled, Harley-riding stereotype started back in the early fifties, after a group of motorcycle enthusiasts got a little too rowdy in Hollister, California. The incident was turned into an article for *Harper's Magazine*, and then eventually into the sensational movie, **The Wild One** (1953, starring Marlon Brando)[1]. The truth of the group in Hollister was far more prosaic than the motley characters in Laszlo Benedek's film, but, as is often the case, life started imitating art, and the image of the rampaging, socio-pathic biker gang was born.

By the early sixties, Marlon Brando's Johnny had been reduced to the caricature of Eric Von Zipper in the Beach Party movies[2], but the bikers were mutating. In California, a group called the Hell's Angels was growing in numbers, getting more rebellious and – most importantly – learning the joys of heretofore unknown recreational drugs. In 1965, Thomas Lynch, Attorney General of the State of California, filed a report on motorcycle gangs, painting them as unwashed thugs, wreaking havoc on the highways of that State. In the report, the Hell's Angels were named as the worst of the lot. Shortly afterward, a motorcycle rally in Laconia, New Hampshire turned violent and the Angels were blamed, even though there were no Angels in attendance. Now all eyes were focused on California's favourite outlaws. The timing could not have been better. In January, 1966, "Mother" Miles, the leader of the Sacramento branch of the Hell's Angels, died. The funeral procession was huge. Bikers from all over the country showed up (including some members of rival gangs). The sight of thousands of Harley-Davidsons in procession was enough to warrant plenty of press including a picture in *Life* magazine.

Director Roger Corman, always on the lookout for new movie ideas, was thumbing through a copy of the magazine when he came to the Angels' funeral procession. Struck by the graphic power of the photo, Corman thought that the a movie about these rebels might do well at the box office. He called Charles B. Griffith, the man who wrote some of Corman's best features, including **Little Shop Of Horrors** and **Bucket Of Blood,** and the two of them arranged to meet with some local Hell's Angels. After an evening of story-telling and beer-drinking, Griffith and Corman left with plenty of material for a movie.

The movie was to be called "All The Fallen Angels". Corman wasn't completely happy with Griffith's script so he had his young production assistant doctor the script. Corman required that all of the actors who played bikers in the film know how to ride their Harleys. The lead was to be played by George Chakiris, but when he asked that a stunt double do his riding for him, Corman had him replaced with the man who was to play the second lead, Peter Fonda. For added realism, biker extras were culled from the ranks of the Venice Chapter of the Hell's Angels.

Before its release later in 1966, the movie had a change of title. What had been "All The Fallen Angels" became **The Wild Angels**. The film is a little light on plot. After an Angel, fittingly named "Loser", gets shot by the police, his fellow gang members try to break him out of the hospital. Lacking the requisite medical attention,

Loser promptly dies. During the funeral the gang flips out, rapes Loser's wife and trashes the church. At the end, "Heavenly Blues" (Peter Fonda) is left wondering what he is going to do with his life.

The Hell's Angels were helpful to Corman's production because they thought that he was making a film that would vindicate them. Instead, **The Wild Angels** features the biggest gang of nitwits to hit the screen. The Hell's Angels sued Corman for slander and defamation of character for five million dollars. Eventually, they settled out of court for $300,000.[3]

Whatever the Angels thought of the film, the general public loved it. The song, "Blue's Theme" by Davy Allan and the Arrows was an AM radio hit as well. **The Wild Angels** was chosen to play at the Cannes Film Festival, much to the horror of some American officials. The film's success was a call to cameras in Hollywood. The race was on to produce more biker films. The first one out of the starting gate was **Devil's Angels**. Like **The Wild Angels**, this was also an AIP feature and also featured a script by Charles B. Griffith. Corman had been slated to direct it, but he was busy working on a script by Jack Nicholson called **The Trip**, so ex-Art Director Daniel Haller took over the helm. **Devil's Angels** starred John Cassavetes as the aging leader of a pack of bikers. Cassavetes took the part to finance his own low budget features. This was an inspired bit of casting. In 1956, Cassavetes had made a splash playing Frankie Dane, a young gang leader in the television drama, *Crime In The Streets* (which was later made into a movie by Allied Artists). Casting him here as an aging gang leader, brought the idea to its logical end: the aging gangster now a pathetic loser with nowhere left to go.

**Devil's Angels** was released in 1967, and did not do as well at the box office as **The Wild Angels**. The big hit biker film of that year was **Hell's Angels On Wheels**. **Hell's Angels On Wheels** was produced by Joe Solomon, a man who had practically grown up in the exploitation film industry.

Joe Solomon got his start as a boy when he helped his father print posters for theatres. Later he became the advance publicist for **Mom And Dad** (William Beaudine, 1944), one of the original "Birth Of A Baby" films. After several ups and downs in the movie world, Solomon invested everything he had in the making of **Hell's Angels On Wheels**. The film cost $200,000 to make and pulled in a several million at the box office. Joe took the money and invested in another biker film (**Angels From Hell** [Kurt Neumann, 1968]), and then another (**Run, Angel, Run** [Jack Starrett, 1969]). Soon, he had enough money to start his own production company, Fanfare Productions.

**Hell's Angels On Wheels** is arguably the best biker film of them all. It starred Jack Nicholson as a loner who meets up with, joins, then later splits from a group of Hell's Angels. Like **The Wild Angels**, this film has a mere skeleton of a plot, and also features real Hell's Angels, including Sonny Barger, the gang's leader at the time. Unlike **The Wild Angels**, the Hell's Angels actually endorsed this film. It was directed by Richard Rush, a talented, but often self-indulgent director, best known for **Psych-Out** and **The Stunt Man**. The real star of the film was cinematographer Laszlo Kovacs. Kovacs got his start with Ray Dennis Steckler, shooting the infamous **Incredibly Strange Creatures Who Stopped Living And Became Mixed-up Zombies**. Kovacs was still a newcomer, but Rush let him do what he wanted, so Kovacs experimented with odd lenses and funny angles. With **Hell's Angels On Wheels**, Kovacs became the preferred photographer for the biker genre, he lensed more than any other cinematographer. The films he shot include **The Savage Seven** (1968, Richard Rush's follow-up to **Hell's Angels On Wheels**), **Easy Rider** (Dennis Hopper, 1969), **The Rebel Rousers** (Martin B Cohen, 1967), and **Hell's Bloody Devils** (Al Adamson[4], 1967). As with Jack Nicholson, **Easy Rider** led to **Five Easy Pieces** (Bob Rafelson, 1970); Kovacs then progressed to more mainstream features including **New York, New York** (Martin Scorsese, 1977), and **Ghostbusters** (Ivan Reitman, 1984).

Hell's Angels On Wheels

The Rebel Rousers

# HE'S A Cycle PSYCHO

When he wanted a gang...
HE STOLE ONE!
When he wanted a girl...
HE GRABBED ONE!
When he wanted a cop...
HE BOUGHT ONE!

The Company that brought you
"HELL'S ANGELS ON WHEELS"
now brings you...

# ANGELS FROM HELL

THE STORY THAT TELLS IT LIKE IT IS!

COLOR BY PERFECT

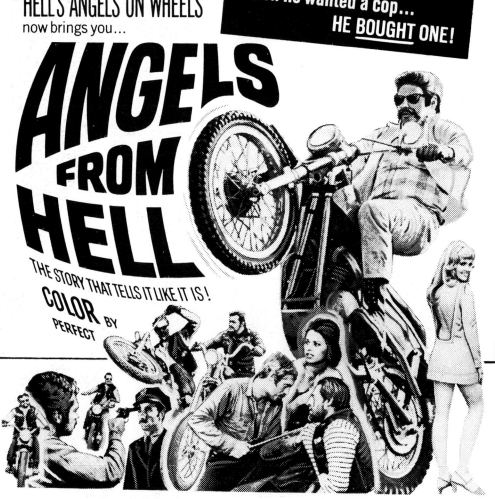

A BIG CHROME BABY and a BLACK LEATHER DOLL ...both Hotter, Faster, Tougher than most men can handle.

BURWALT PRODUCTIONS Presents

# THE HARD RIDE

Another film that did well that summer of 1967 was **Born Losers,** starring a young, unknown actor named Tom Laughlin. Laughlin also directed the film under the pseudonym, "T.C. Frank." In **Born Losers,** Laughlin played a Vietnam vet, who was also half-Indian. The name of this character was "Billy Jack", and **Born Losers** was followed with a sequel by that name. **Billy Jack** (Laughlin, 1971) was an even bigger hit than **Born Losers,** or, for that matter, **Born Losers, Hell's Angels On Wheels** and **The Wild Angels** combined. The film was a phenomenon and led to a remarkably bad sequel, **The Trial Of Billy Jack** (Laughlin, 1974). Years later, this character would be resurrected in a thin disguise by Steven Seagal in **On Deadly Ground,** a film so bad it makes **The Trial Of Billy Jack** look majestic.

From 1967 to 1970, no fewer than fifteen biker films were released[5]. Many well-known actors appeared in these films, including Harry Dean Stanton, Bruce Dern, Jack Nicholson, Diane Ladd, and William Smith. The market for these films was teenagers, so it was just a matter of time before the biker film was cross-bred with that other teenage favourite, the horror movie. The first attempt at this was **Werewolves On Wheels** (Michael Levesque, 1971), a film about a gang that crosses paths with a witch and ends up being turned into lycanthropes. Barf bags were handed out at the door.

Another attempt was also one of the few biker films to come out of Britain[6]. It was called **Psychomania** (aka **The Death Wheelers,** Don Sharp, 1972), and was the story of a motorcycle gang led by an occult fanatic who worships a bullfrog, and promises the gang members immortality if they kill themselves. The name of the gang is, quite logically, "The Living Dead".

A late entry to the field of Harley horror (and not a bad one either) was **Northville Cemetery Massacre,** made in 1977 by William Dear. The film tells the story of a corrupt town sheriff, who brutally rapes a leading citizen's daughter and blames a local biker gang. The grisly final shootout occurs in the town cemetery. Dan Hoskins' **Chopper Chicks In Zombie Town** (1989) is the only recent addition to this sub-genre of any note.

Herschell Gordon Lewis, the man who gave us **Blood Feast** and **Two Thousand Maniacs,** put his own grisly stamp on the biker genre with **She Devils On Wheels.** Although fairly tame by Gordon standards, it is gorier than most other biker flicks. This time the bikers are females, as they are in **The Mini-Skirt Mob** (Maury Dexter, 1968), and **Sisters In Leather** (Zoltan G Spencer, 1969)[7]. The problem with all of these is the problem of women and Harleys. Few women (or men, for that matter) had the upper body strength needed to manoeuvre these metal monsters (a constant problem for actors and non-biker extras in these films). The usual fix was to give them slightly smaller bikes – Triumphs and Nortons. The best exception to this is Dixie Peabody, who really does ride her own Harley in **Bury Me An Angel,** the story of a woman on a mission of vengeance for the death of her brother ("A Howling Hellcat, Humping A Hot Hog On A Roaring Rampage Of Revenge", the ads proclaimed). Dixie Peabody looks good on a Harley and looks like she knows how to handle it. Unfortunately, she can't act to save her soul. **Bury Me An Angel** was written and directed by Barbara Peeters, who later went on the direct **Humanoids From The Deep.**

Since the biker films were invading the theatres at the same time as the blaxploitation flicks, it wasn't long before those two genres were also combined. The first was **The Black Angels** (Lawrence Merrick, 1970), followed by the likes of Matt Cimber's **The Black Six** (1974), but the best was **Darktown Strutters** (William Witney, 1975), a film so bizarre it defies any meaningful description.

Every angle on Angels was exploited and explored, with the possible exception of space monsters (Johnny Legend reportedly tried to sell this idea to a studio back in the early seventies, but no one was interested). One of the most inane premises was **The Losers** (Jack Starrett, 1970), in which a gang of bikers is hired by the president to

She Devils On Wheels

rescue soldiers in Cambodia. Years later, Sylvester Stallone would borrow this basic concept (as idiotic as it is) for **Rambo II**. **The Losers** was also remade (as **Nam Angels**) by Cirio H Santiago in 1989. **The Losers** might have done okay at the box office in spite its stupidity, but the film broke the cardinal rule: the bikers were riding dirt bikes which, while more practical, destroys the image. A good biker always rides Harleys – nothing else will do. Even **The Wild One** loses points in the biker community for its use of Triumphs, a bike that Angels sneered on vehemently until the Japanese bikes came along to take over the bottom rung of uncoolness.

In 1970, Avco-Embassy released **C.C. And Company**, starring American football hero, Joe Namath as a lone biker, Ann-Margaret as his love interest and biker film regular William Smith as the bad guy. Directed by Seymour Robbie, the film did okay at the box office thanks to the drawing power of its stars, but one thing became abundantly clear: Joe Namath was no actor. He made two more films that year and then moved on to other enterprises, appearing only occasionally in films after that.

By some accounts the best biker film is also the best road movie, and that film is **Easy Rider** [see Chapter 4]. Co-written by Peter Fonda and Dennis Hopper and ostensibly directed by Hopper, **Easy Rider** is the famous tale of two bikers who sell a huge amount of cocaine to Phil Spector and decide to retire to Florida. During their trip across the country, they meet hippies, rednecks and New Orleans prostitutes. The get busted, beat-up and stoned, and wind up dead on the side of the road. Critics and the public alike gave the film high marks. Like any good movie, it came along at just the right time, and seemed to sum up the feelings of many people about life in the United States. Some people thought that the film was anti-Southern, but Fonda and Hopper were actually trying to say something about the intolerance and stupidity of the entire country.

Although there were a few biker films made in the seventies[8], the real climax of the genre occurred on December 6th, 1969, at the Rolling Stones concert at the Altamont Speedway near San Francisco. Claiming they had been hired as security, the Angels stomped on spectators and performers alike, cold cocking Jefferson Airplane's Marty Balin. Black spectator Meredith Hunter was stabbed to death in the chaos that reigned under the Angels' "supervision", and the whole thing was captured in the sometimes harrowing Maysles' documentary **Gimme Shelter**[9]. Suddenly, the Angels were no longer funny symbols of rebellion. They were really as dangerous as everyone said they were. This same conclusion is reflected in Hunter S. Thompson's book *Hell's Angels*, which starts as an inside and defensive observation of the gang, but ends with Thompson leaving a gathering under threat of his life.

There were other factors at work as well. The sudden hike in gas prices in the early seventies turned the highways from places of exploration into a method of getting from point A to point B. Speed and Safety laws were passed that took all the fun out of the open road. In many States, helmet laws were passed, and there is just no way to look cool in a helmet. Bikers tried by using helmets shaped like those of Nazi stormtroopers. Other laws on fork and handlebar extensions removed the more outrageous-looking bikes from the road.

In the end, however, the biggest factor in the demise of the biker film was the public's lack of interest. The well had run dry – and it was a pretty shallow well to begin with. We wouldn't see interesting bikers on the road again until George Miller's Australian road classic **Mad Max** in 1979 [see Chapters 7 and 19].

# NOTES

1. Before **The Wild One**, motorcycle groups had seldom been portrayed at all, and then only as very tame (as in **Teenage Devil Dolls** [1952]). Later '50s entries such as Edward L Cahn's **Motorcycle Gang** (1957) did little or nothing to improve on the Brando template.

2. The one notable exception being Kenneth Anger's dazzling underground classic **Scorpio Rising** (1964), which vividly depicted the fetishistic, homo-erotic and scatological rites of a (real) neo-Nazi New Jersey bike gang, using montage techniques and utilizing a pop music soundtrack to revolutionary effect.

3. **The Wild Angels** may have been the first Hell's Angels picture, but exploitation king Russ Meyer scored a year earlier with his own tale of psychotic bikers, **Motorpsycho!** (1965). In this typical "roughie", starring Meyer regular Haji, three cycle thugs go on a cross-country rape and murder spree. Their leader (played by Stephen Oliver), is one of the earliest screen examples of the deranged Vietnam Vet. Meyer's next film was his masterpiece **Faster, Pussycat! Kill! Kill!** (1966), a film which obliquely intersects the road movie genre [see Introduction].

4. Al Adamson, the notorious exploitation movie director, also made the violent biker films **Satan's Sadists** (1969, with Russ Tamblyn) and **Angels' Wild Women** (1972, "Hot, Hard And Mean...Too Tough For Any Man!! They'll Beat 'Em, Treat 'Em And Eat 'Em Alive!").

5. Others include: **The Glory Stompers** (Anthony M Lanza, 1967, starring Dennis Hopper); **Savages From Hell** (Joseph Prieto, 1968); **Hell's Chosen Few** (David L Hewitt, 1968); **The Cycle Savages** (Bill Brame, 1969); **Naked Angels** (Bruce D Clark, 1969); **Hell's Angels '69** (Lee Madden, 1969); **Wild Wheels** (Kent Osborne, 1969); **Free Grass** (Bill Brame, 1969); **Angel Unchained** (Lee Madden, 1970); and **Angels Die Hard** (Richard Compton, 1970). A pair of homicidal bikers also figure in David C Graham's gore entry **The Undertaker And His Pals** (1967).

6. The first British biker film is generally considered to be **The Leather Boys** (Sidney J Furie, 1963), a story, with homosexual undertones, of England's biker/rocker café sub-culture. Sex also predominates Jack Cardiff's **Girl On A Motorcycle** (1968), starring Marianne Faithfull as the girl who rides naked under leather to be united with her lover (Alain Delon). Psycho bikers figure briefly in Anthony Balch's **Horror Hospital** (1973), and real Hell's Angels were employed by Ken Russell in **Tommy** (1975).

7. **Sisters In Leather** is also notable as a sexploitation entry featuring plenty of female nudity and lesbianism. Bikers would also figure in such hardcore, abusive porno productions as **The Cheaters** (1971), **Revenge Of The Motorcycle Mama** (1972), **Sleazy Rider** (1976) and **Little Orphan Dusty** (1976). And female bikers still crop up in modern hardcore productions; **Biker Chicks In Love** (1991), **Motorcycle Mistress Mamas** (1991) and **Butt-Banged Cycle Sluts** (1995) being three typical examples.

8. Notably: **Angels Hard As They Come** (Joe Viola, 1971); **The Hard Ride** (Burt Topper, 1971); **The Jesus Trip** (Russ Mayberry, 1971); **Chrome And Hot Leather** (Lee Frost, 1971); **The Peace Killers** (Douglas Schwartz, 1971); **The Dirt Gang** (Jerry Jameson, 1972); and **Hellriders** (James Bryant, 1974). A deranged Vietnam Vet biker is the protagonist of Brad Grinter's extraordinary trash horror **Blood Freak** (1971), while Leo Garen's **Hex** (1973) is a bizarre story of bikers in 1919, who arrive at a Nebraska farm inhabited by two sisters with supernatural powers. One sister uses Native American magic to destroy most of the gang. Equally odd is George Romero's anomalous **Knightriders** (1981), featuring bikers who stage mediaeval jousts with hogs instead of chargers. Romero had previously included a marauding biker gang in his zombie classic **Dawn Of The Dead** (1978). Bikers became increasingly reduced to an adjunct in various road/action/psycho movies from the '70s onward, such as **Savage Abduction** (John Lawrence, 1973), **Death Weekend** (William Fruet, 1976), Clint Eastwood's **The Gauntlet** (1977), and the bizarre SF epic **Deathsport** (Henry Suso/Allan Arkush, 1978). The last "pure" biker film must be genre queen Kathryn Bigelow's debut, **The Loveless** (1981). Co-directed by Monty Montgomery, and starring Willem Dafoe and Robert Gordon, **The Loveless** recalls Kenneth Anger's **Scorpio Rising** in its attention to every

eroticized, fetishistic detail of the ('50s) biker's zippered leather and polished chrome universe.

9.  A more postive view of the Angels can be found in Kevin Keating's authorised documentary **Hell's Angels Forever** (1981).

# Chapter 4

# 'Easy Rider'

# GET YOUR KICKS: 'EASY RIDER' AND THE COUNTER-CULTURE

## Alistair Daniel

*"A man went looking for America and couldn't find it anywhere"*
—Billboard ad for **Easy Rider**

**Easy Rider** (1969) is one of the legendary success stories of cinema history. From a budget of $375,000 it grossed over $50 million worldwide on first release, picking up a prize for "Best Film By A New Director" at the 1969 Cannes Film Festival on the way. But if the film's phenomenal return on its modest investment is remarkable, for anyone familiar with the notorious history of its making, it is still more amazing that it was completed and released at all. The arguments over who really wrote the script (credited to Peter Fonda, Dennis Hopper and Terry Southern) have raged unresolved for 30 years, while the apparently spontaneous innovation which characterises the film was as much the result of a chaotic production process as a deliberate artistic approach. The climactic Mardi Gras footage, shot first on 16mm stock by a hastily-assembled crew, was largely unusable. While location scouting in the south, Hopper was arrested for smoking dope. Drugs played havoc with the professionalism on set, and by the end of the shoot, according to Peter Biskind, the crew "were so out of it that they had the wrap party, and then realized they had forgotten to shoot the second campfire scene... so they had to shoot it later"[1]. Towards the end of the principal shoot all the motorbikes were stolen. In post-production Hopper – once described as "the worst editor that's ever been"[2] – tinkered with the final cut for months, his preferred version lasting over four hours. At one point he "wanted to run the credit sequence upside down"[3]. It was only when the film was rigorously cut in Hopper's absence in the winter of 1968 that the final 94 minute version emerged.

Of course such stories only contribute to the cult of **Easy Rider**: its haphazard birth seems to embody the spirit of spontaneous creativity in defiance of rigid studio control, validating its romantic counter-cultural appeal. Certainly this spirit, once ordered by the final cut, offers a clue to **Easy Rider**'s extraordinary resonance with audiences, but this is not quite enough in itself to account for both the film's commercial success and its enduring popularity.

**Easy Rider**, like its stars, did not quite come out of nowhere. Raybert, its small but forward-looking production company, was situated on the lot of the major studio which financed it, Columbia. Hence Hopper (as director) and Fonda (as producer) had all the benefits of the backing of a major studio, and little of the interference. Furthermore, all three stars, Fonda, Hopper and Nicholson, plus photographer Laszlo Kovacs, already had a certain caché with a cult audience, having worked for Roger Corman at AIP. Fonda, aside from having a famous actor father and sister had starred in Corman's 1967 film **The Trip**, while Dennis Hopper had been on the fringes of Hollywood for years, understudying James Dean as a teenager for the part of Goon in **Rebel Without A Cause** (Nicholas Ray, 1955). Persuading Terry Southern, a celebrated novelist and screenwriter, to work for scale on the script, and securing a cameo appearance by Phil Spector were both major coups which further enhanced the film's of-the-moment credibility.

If the cast was not unknown, nor is the film's scenario entirely unfamiliar. Drawing on a sublime landscape familiar from countless westerns, **Easy Rider** deliberately situates itself both in relation to America's mythologised past and its film history. The vast beauty of the landscape is remade here for a new era, shot through with the intrusive power and noise of modern machinery, and coupled to a rock soundtrack which injects a jarring, fierce contemporaneity into the timeless backdrop. **Easy Rider** was one of the first films to use a soundtrack of assorted contemporary rock, and its unrestrained energy was irresistible to a youth audience hitherto obliged to look to pop rather than film for sympathetic representations of its desires and values.[4] Though Wyatt and Billy spend near half the running time of the film on the road, the music and the fast editing, far from diluting the impact of the off-road scenes, intensify the effect, hurtling us at greater and greater speed towards the film's conclusion.

## THE ODD COUPLE
At the heart of the film is the odd, barely-articulated relationship between the contemplative Wyatt/Captain America (Fonda) and the manic Billy (Hopper). Theirs is a classic personality clash typical of buddy movies and comedy double acts, with Fonda playing the straight man to Hopper's frenetic buffoon. Every opportunity is used to contrast their personalities. While Wyatt is quiet, contemplative, slightly melancholy, Billy is an inarticulate snickering adolescent, whose main conversational tactic is to repeat anything he hears in a jeering tone. In the airfield scene, where Wyatt and Billy sell the coke on to their "connection" (Phil Spector), Fonda is first seen gazing up at the aircraft passing low overhead. While Billy crouches, wincing and covering his ears as each plane passes with a deafening roar, Fonda remains upright, standing on an upturned crate. The effect is to make Fonda appear almost twice Hopper's height, adding a physical dimension to the absurdity of their unlikely pairing. Even their bikes are designed to differentiate them: Fonda's has much higher, almost ridiculously high, handlebars, making his posture appear improbably stately even at high speeds, while Billy's bike is much lower, causing him to crouch aggressively. These early visual contrasts establish the tensions in Wyatt and Billy's relationship, tensions which are never resolved, but which open up a space for the film to explore the motivation and potential of the counter-cultural life they represent.

## A NEW AMERICAN CINEMA
**Easy Rider** is rightly celebrated both for its representation of counter-cultural life and its introduction of radicalism in filmmaking and politics to something approaching mainstream Hollywood. After a decade of increasingly obsolete musicals, costume dramas and (conventional) Westerns, churned out by a weary studio system undermined by television, the late sixties saw an overdue flood of filmmaking responsive to contemporary life. In 1967 Arthur Penn's **Bonnie And Clyde** caused shockwaves with its unblinking violence [see also Chapter 10], and that same year Mike Nichols' **The Graduate** delivered a satirical slap in the face of complacent middle America. In the last year of the decade John Schlesinger's **Midnight Cowboy** – which complements **Easy Rider** with its central character's progression from country to city, and its equally energetic editing – was a comparable meditation on the gulf between urban and rural life, and between ideals and reality. But, in some ways, **Easy Rider** surpasses all these films for the raw energy of its affect. Encompassing "all the tropes of the counter-culture, from libidinous pleasure, spontaneity and rebellion to aesthetic hipness"[5], it aspires to be the definitive portrait of its era.

Experimenting wildly throughout filming, many of Fonda and Hopper's innovations endure. Admirers of underground American film and the French New Wave, they incorporated elements of both (hand-held cameras, fast non-sequential editing) into **Easy Rider's** visual style. They also claimed to have improvised dialogue, and picked up untrained extras along the way. Accidental chemical stains on the film were happily incorporated into the final cut. Panning across the landscape, cinematographer Haskell Wexler deliberately incorporated "lens flair" – allowing sunlight to reflect off the lens of the camera – a technique traditionally shunned for interrupting the onscreen illusion, but deliberately adopted by the New American Cinema to afford a documentary-style feel of immediacy. The innovative, perhaps modish editing style which cuts rapidly back and forth between the current scene and the next still startles and disorientates at first, while the hallucinatory scene at the Mardi Gras, edited from footage shot in infamously chaotic fashion, is still a remarkable evocation of a trip – in both senses – gone badly wrong. The mixture of surrealist images (fisheye lenses, a man in a suit dancing with an umbrella among the gravestones) with a complex overlapping of soundtracks embodies the dark underside of psychedelia, and remains unsettling and portentous.

## KINGS OF THE ROAD
Wyatt and Billy's journey across the South both invokes the pioneering spirit of the early settlers (and the innumerable westerns which mythologised them) and self-consciously reverses it in a contrary movement from west to east. The duo are on a modern pilgrimage, a journey at once literal, geographical and spiritual. They leave Los Angeles in search of New Orleans, specifically the Mardi Gras, a utopian multicultural carnival space of celebration, display and parade (which contrasts markedly with the

stilted, permit-only parade they encounter and mockingly disrupt on the way), but they are also looking for more than this[6]. Their quest is marked with moral overtones. Reversing the established social structures which mark them out as criminals and delinquents, the film initially positions the duo as true representatives of American values. Alternately named as superheroes ("This is Captain America and I'm Billy!") and legendary Western figures Wyatt (Earp) and Billy (the Kid), the pair take on a (half serious, half ironic) nobility in their journey across the deep South.

With its (albeit obscure) quest delineated by the road and embracing the people of country, town and city along the way, **Easy Rider** places the road movie firmly in the tradition of the picaresque, a genre perfectly suited to politicised, state-of-the nation social commentary. Using this framework, the film pits counter-cultural values against rural insularity to produce an inflammatory call for change, launching an uncompromising attack on the perceived bigotry of the white population of the American South. Character after character is a hastily-sketched study in monstrosity, in corruption, racism, violence, patriarchy, no doubt influenced by Hopper's location scouting in the South[7]. Fonda was in no doubt about the political nature of his project. At Cannes in 1969 he "wore the uniform of a Union cavalry general and a bushy fake beard to the première. The symbolism was evident to him, if nobody else; it was meant to suggest that he and his generation were engaged in the second Civil War."[8]

## GOD DAMN THE PUSHER
Though the characters make few overtly political statements, only on the most superficial level is **Easy Rider** not a political film. In fact it engages with major social

issues of racism, drugs, the North-South divide, systematically unpicking the absurdities and hypocrisies of conservative America. In a move calculated to provoke, the opening scene sees "Captain America" snort coke from a wing mirror. Thereafter the issue of drugs, still one of enduring controversy, is made central, with the duo lighting joints at every campfire scene. When George first joins them Wyatt offers him some grass with the words "Do this instead", a phrase which directly links Wyatt and Billy's illegal dope-smoking with George's drink problem, which merits no more than the occasional sleep-over in jail. Having recognised that what he is being offered is not an "ordinary" cigarette (tobacco being another of his socially acceptable habits), George is instantly uncomfortable, expounding in one breath a string of commonplace objections to marijuana: "I've got enough problems with the booze and all... I can't afford to get hooked... it leads to harder stuff". Wyatt simply regards him with a serene patience. Once George has accepted the joint, Billy has a sudden vision of a "satellite", moving impossibly across the sky. This prompts George to launch with total sincerity into a comically preposterous tale about UFO sightings in Mexico:

*"We seen forty of 'em flying in formation. They have got bases all over the world; ever since 1946 when the scientists first started bouncing radar beams off of the moon and they have been living and working among us in vast quantities ever since. The government knows all about 'em."*

George's visions under the influence of drink are even more vivid than Billy's stoned imaginings, and prompt the amusing sight of an incredulous Billy criticising someone else for talking nonsense: "I think it's a crackpot idea man!" Through this ironic strategy the film demonstrates the arbitrariness of social mores which sanction some addictive hallucinogenic substances and demonise others. Wyatt's quiet pensiveness while consuming the same quantity of grass as Billy demonstrates the complex interaction of personality and substance. Wyatt is the equivalent of a man who can hold his drink, Billy is not.

## WEIRDOS

**Easy Rider** seeks to further enhance its subversive credentials by attempting to align its central characters, its drop-out white liberals, with other marginalised and dispossessed groups. In this respect, their route is significant. As Barbara Klinger points out, "The terrain most idealised in the film – the Southwest – is at once the land of displaced peoples championed by the counter-culture (eg., Native Americans and the Hispanics) and the site of iconography for the hippie movement, since hippie clothing and lifestyles mimicked the buckskin naturalism of the early settlers."[9] As Wyatt and Billy move east, passing though poor black settlements on the edge of town where children peer out at them timidly from doorways, they become associated with the civil rights movement through George. George is a lawyer for the ACLU, the American Civil Liberties Union, and his hard drinking points to the stress of a career spent struggling to represent minorities through the worst years of civil unrest in the South. With a weary cynicism he professes to be able to help them "if you haven't killed anybody – least not anybody white". The encounter with George seems to further politicise Wyatt; during the acid trip sequence in New Orleans after George's death, Wyatt clenches his raised fist in a black power salute[10].

But there is defiance in Wyatt from the start. Adorning his crash helmet and bike with the stars and stripes is an attempt to reclaim the American flag, to resist the establishment's efforts to position the counter-culture as "un-American". Language is employed in the same way. The label "weird" is the site of a continual struggle between Wyatt and Billy and the hicks they encounter. Billy's first intelligible line in

the film is a comment on the Mardi Gras to which they're heading: "Mardi Gras man, that's gonna be the weirdest man". When arrested for "parading without a permit" he protests: "A bunch of weirdo hicks – parading without a permit man!". Not surprisingly, Billy does not consider himself "weird": "I never thought of myself as a freak," he comments honestly. In Madame Tinkertoy's, the New Orleans brothel recommended to them by George, Billy cavorts with a girl, mimicking the Southern drawl of the rural society they have temporarily escaped. He then immediately undercuts this parody: "I'm really from New York man, I just have a weird accent". For Billy it's the Southern hicks who are "weird", who do not fit into the West Coast society with which he is familiar. Out here though, as he is acutely aware, it is clearly Billy himself who is considered "weird". His deployment of the word to describe others is an attempt to reverse the prejudices directed against him, and assert the validity of his own identity. When the girl tugs his hair asking "Is this your real hair?" and fondles the bone necklace he wears, he tugs *her* hair and touches her breasts, throwing her questions back at her. For once, Billy's mocking repetition works, successfully exposing and undermining the arbitrary nature of social conventions which dictate, for instance, that men's hair should be short and women's long. The girl has already conceded the point: "I'm kinda a freak myself," she confesses. What Billy, and the film as a whole, makes plain, is the relative, subjective nature of "weirdness", or its opposite, "normality". In so doing it champions youth culture's right to self-expression. The right to be weird, different, individual, is a direct challenge to the existing social structures which demand that individuals conform to a recognisable group. And it is the assertion of this right that makes Wyatt and Billy a threat. Their mere presence in the South is interpreted everywhere they go as an incitement, a provocation. As George, a Southerner, explains to Billy, "they're scared of what you represent to them... freedom... talking about it and being it, that's two different things". Billy and Wyatt represent a threat by refusing to accept their allotted position in a rigorously demarcated society. Their carefree crossing of state and parish borders on the noisy and ostentatious symbols of their freedom is a direct challenge to those who pretend not to acknowledge the social constraints to which they submit.

In **Easy Rider** it is the Southern hicks and their police officers who are forced to confront this challenge. "You name it, I'll throw rocks at it, sheriff" says one as Billy, Wyatt and George, a motley trio of incongruously dressed outsiders, enter the café where he sits. But naming "it" is precisely what they find most difficult. While the trio wait in vain to be served they are subjected to a string of what George calls "country witticisms", each of which successively attempts to place the group in a different category: "put her in a women's cell", "put her in a cage", "looks like a bunch of refugees from a gorilla family", "that's some Yankee queers, check out the flag on that bike". In the course of two minutes the hicks succeed in identifying Wyatt, Billy and George as members of a whole string of social groups who do not fit their conception of normality, including men with long hair, Yankees, gays, black people and women. In so doing, they successfully brand as "weird" an overwhelming majority of the population of the United States.

## ALL CITIES ARE ALIKE

An unblinking portrait of a corrupt and bigoted society enraged by the image of its own ugliness, it could be argued nonetheless that **Easy Rider** undermines its own impact by caricaturing what it attacks. George is the only white Southerner not demonised, but he is the exception that proves the rule. But if the film makes of the rural South a scapegoat, responsible for or representative of all the maladies in contemporary society, the city is implicitly no better. Though LA makes space, we can assume, for Wyatt and Billy to adopt their hippie identities without fear of attack, it is inadequate in other ways, as their flight into the desert makes plain. The Stranger, also from "a city", summarises the discontent with urban life in a single dismissive phrase: "all cities are alike". The only urban scenes in the film are at the Mardi Gras in New Orleans, but what should have been the ecstatic culmination of their search becomes a nightmare. By this point George is dead and Wyatt and Billy wander through the non-stop hour carnival jaded and bewildered. The industrial technology of modernity is also imbued with strongly negative tones: the noise of their bikes frightens the rancher's horses, the scream of passing aircraft makes Billy double-up, and the nightmarish acid trip is accompanied by the soundtrack of an oppressively monotonous piston from the oil refinery which overlooks the graveyard. In this way **Easy Rider** maintains an ambivalence about the contrasting forms of community. The city is ugly and oppressive, the country beautiful but dangerous.

## BORN TO BE WILD

This ambivalence extends to the counter-culture itself. Certainly hippie culture is not the only way of life the film endorses, and its endorsement is not unconditional. The opening track, Steppenwolf's "Born To Be Wild", which accompanies the first carefree shots of Billy and Wyatt enjoying what appears to be the freedom of the road, introduces the dual theme of the "wild", which is both an anti-establishment individual expression of free will, and an affinity with nature, with "the wild". Billy and Wyatt are thus initially positioned as romantic figures reacting against the ordered space of the city, with its overdeveloped institutions and police force, and embracing the land with its scattered settlements and environmental self sufficiency. This links them to the romantic myths of a traditional, rural agrarian society. Perhaps the most positive figure in the film is the rancher who welcomes Wyatt and Billy when they have a puncture. Wary but not judgmental, he allows them to change their tire in his barn while he shoes a horse. A much commented-on deep focus shot of the horse in the foreground being shod, with its twentieth century equivalent receiving similar treatment in the barn behind, draws host and guests together. In the next scene they join the farmer's family for dinner, where they are introduced to his Mexican wife and the camera pans over the faces of their Anglo-Hispanic children. Fonda has nothing but praise and admiration for their way of life: "No, I mean it. You've got a nice place. It's not every man who can live off the land, you know. You do your own thing in your own time. You should be proud." It's a utopian scene of rural self-sufficiency, peace, and racial integration. And it has nothing to do with the counter-culture.

In fact, the idea of a single "counter-culture" is carefully deconstructed throughout the film. As Klinger puts it, "Wyatt and Billy are California hippies, incarnating, respectively, the 'cool' existential and wild paranoid hippie types drawn from the state most recognised as a counter-cultural Mecca."[11] These are not the student radicals of Antonioni's **Zabriskie Point** (1971)[12]. Nor are they the Christian zealots of the commune. The commune scenes, which bring them into contact with another form of hippie life, serve to emphasise their difference from it. Though, as the Stranger explains, these people are also city kids, escaping into the desert with unprepared optimism, and though Wyatt again expresses admiration for their project ("They're gonna make it" he comments, surveying a group scattering seeds on unpromisingly barren land), their religious fervour sits oddly with Wyatt's existential doubt. Billy, his paranoia exacerbated by an odd encounter with the Stranger, is desperate to leave. Wyatt is more intrigued, but he too, ultimately moves on. Shortly before leaving, the Stranger gives them LSD, commenting "When you get to the right place with the right people; a quart of this." "You know, this could be the right place," he adds, to Wyatt. "Yeah I know," he replies "...But I just gotta go." Something tells Wyatt it isn't. The Stranger himself does not quite fit with the other commune-dwellers. His almost relentless flippancy at the campfire scene which precedes their arrival contrasts with "Jesus" (the leader)'s passionate sincerity, while his dress is more in the urban psychedelic style than the others. In fact he resembles no one more than John Lennon circa *Sgt. Pepper*, with pink flares, a purple Victorian-style military jacket, small round shades, and an unkempt moptop framed by a drooping moustache. Like George, he is an equally incongruous passenger on the leather-clad Wyatt's bike.

## I JUST GOTTA GO

Of course, the commune scene also highlights the contrasts between Wyatt and Billy. Though clearly invested with a certain amount of symbolism, they are not simply Everymen for the counter-culture. In fact, they are so clearly differentiated it is hard to see just why they are together. Billy has conveniently appropriated only the most hedonistic elements of the counter-culture, the desire to get high and get laid. He does not have anything which could be called a philosophy. Wyatt seems more principled, but his ultimate motivation is enigmatic. From the first scene Wyatt, as Billy notes, is "pulling inside, getting a little distance". "Yeah well," says Wyatt, "I'm just getting my thing together." But we can never be quite sure what Wyatt's "thing" is exactly. At the very beginning he throws his watch away in the desert, and at the commune claims to be "hip about time", yet he refers repeatedly to their distance from New Orleans in terms of days rather than miles. His admiration for elements of the ranch and the commune life point obliquely towards a desire for a settled self-sufficiency, but he is impelled from within to keep moving: "I just gotta go".[13]

For all his apparent serenity, his behaviour is almost as unstable as Billy's. In the New Orleans churchyard, away from the Mardi Gras, surrounded by tombs and the drone of machinery, accompanied by Billy and the two prostitutes they've hired for the occasion in a bizarre tribute to George's memory, Wyatt finally breaks open the LSD given him by the Stranger, dragging them all into despairing hallucinations. Can he really believe this is "the right place and the right people"?

At least Billy's aims, by contrast, seem clear enough. Wild-eyed with fear at the gas station where the Stranger refuels their bikes, he protests: "Everything we ever dreamed of is in that teardrop gas tank". For Billy "everything" is the money, for Wyatt, perhaps, it is the petrol that the money buys. In the last campfire scene Billy still adheres to the money/freedom equation, exclaiming triumphantly: "We've done it. We're rich, Wyatt. Yeah, man. We did it... We're retired in Florida now mister... You go for the big money, man, and then you're free, you dig?" After all their experiences, his words protest too much. "You know Billy. We blew it," replies Wyatt, enigmatically refusing to elaborate on the most discussed line of the film. The scene is immediately followed by another road scene, more apparent urgency, more insistent pop soundtrack, but they are beyond New Orleans now, beyond their only stated aim, they are not going anywhere, they are just going. Wyatt and Billy might never run out of road but they run out of direction. Although their directionless urgency recalls the Beat ethos of the previous decade, Wyatt and Billy are more like jaded, exhausted ghosts, their vitality ebbing away in the wake of George's death. Past New Orleans they are locked into a Beckett-style cycle of despair. Unlike Beckett's characters, who are unable to move, they are unable to stop, but the end result is the same.

## WE BLEW IT

For all their rebellious posturing, their West Coast cool, Wyatt and Billy are not quite the new American heroes they would like to be, and they know it. Their behaviour often has little to do with the utopian principles of hippie culture and more to do with its flip-side of self-serving irresponsibility. The drug-deal which facilitates their journey makes a mockery of their identification with the marginalised, since they buy the coke from a group of Mexicans and sell it at a sizeable profit. Aside from the criminality of the act, this is a simple capitalist transaction, with Wyatt and Billy happily positioning themselves as the bourgeois middle men whose labour is no more than a little mediation between the producer and consumer.[14] In this context, the use of Steppenwolf's "God Damn The Pusher" immediately after the opening deal begins to seem rather less ironic that it at first appears. Furthermore, in their continual search for an alternative way of life, their interest in other people and communities is cursory at best. Not for nothing was the film originally titled "The Loners". Billy's initial interest in George is only prompted by the realisation that he can help them get out of jail. Even in the Mardi Gras, the foursome wanders through the crowds observant but non-committal, the one moment of interaction outside the group is Billy's brief inaudible exchange with an old black man. They regard each other with mutual suspicion, and move warily away. Wyatt's raised fist comes in the middle of the LSD sequence: a gesture unconnected with any dialogue, it seems less a political statement than a random motif from his hallucinating consciousness, a sign without a referent, emptied of context and meaning.[15]

Despite their companionship, their own relationship is not that of equals. In the drug-deal scene at Los Angeles airport there is a shot through the car window which establishes the power relations between Wyatt and Billy. The shot shows their buyer (Spector) in the driver's seat, with Wyatt leaning on the window at the far end. On the left of the screen the wing mirror shows Billy and the buyer's bodyguard watching the deal take place. This split screen effect, which displaces the small, distant figures of Billy and the bodyguard to the far left of the screen, delineates two clear master/servant relationships. A neatly choreographed, almost farcical scene ensues in which everyone gets in and out of the car performing various minor tasks. First the bodyguard helps Wyatt get into the car to count the money, then Billy holds the door for the buyer while he gets in the back. By the end of the wordless scene we are left in no doubt who is the architect of the deal, and who follows noisily behind.

## ACROSS THE LINES

This scene encapsulates the film's use of framing and mirroring effects; both literally in the use of mirrors and metaphorically in the symmetry of the two pairs of figures, establishing a pattern of pairing which is repeated throughout. The self-consciously schematic structure serves to heighten our awareness at every turn of the omnipresence of the borders, frames and limitations that structure the world of the characters. These borders are not empty symbols, they have real, oppressive powers of containment which work their influence over everyone. The rancher, in awe that Wyatt and Billy have come all the way from LA, comments "when I was a young man I was headed for California but, well, you know how it is", indicating his wife. In the farmer's case, marriage waylaid his youthful plans of exploration. Something more sinister is at work with George, who confesses to having tried to get to the Mardi Gras "six or seven times... never got further than the state line". What exactly stops him at the state line is not explained, but it seems to be the symbolic power of the border itself.

While everyone else has trouble crossing lines, Wyatt and Billy, on the other hand, blissfully blast through them. Or so it seems to the hicks. Aside from knowing the right buyers in LA, what enables them to complete the drug deal, we infer, is their ability to cross and recross the Mexican border to make the initial purchase and sell the cocaine on. But Wyatt and Billy live in the same world as the hicks, and their (literal) transgressions come at a price. The greatest irony of **Easy Rider** is that neither Billy nor Wyatt possess the freedom they appear to embody. Their wilful independence, their Bacchanalian freeloading, freewheeling self-expression is a conscious act of hubris; an offence not against classical gods but those mortals who nonetheless control life and death in their local realm. One of the hicks who insults them in the café predicts they will not "make the parish line". His prediction is a statement of intent, as it is he and the others who club George to death in his sleep in the next scene. That it is George, the one who understands and articulates the nature of their aggression and fear, who dies, only serves to endorse his analysis. If freedom cannot be enjoyed without retribution, it is not freedom at all.

In the wake of his death, George comes to seem a more serious figure than at first we are encouraged to take him for.[16] The genius of his UFO speech is that it is at once a comic diversion and a telling parable. The story is a Kurt Vonnegut-esque sci-fi fantasy at once endearing, spaced-out, and overtly allegorical. The "Venutians" are a civilisation "more highly evolved" than our own, the proof of their superiority being that they have "no wars, no monetary system, no leaders". Sounding like a Marxist utopia in which the state has long since withered away, it is not surprising that the "government" refuses to publicly acknowledge the Venutians' existence, regarding their promotion of "equality for all" as "too shocking" for general consumption. The humour of the scene allows some critical distance from George's naive Cold War allegory, but the power of the central idea – that the absence of war, of money, of hierarchy and control, is "too shocking"; that we all invest in it, find comfort and order in subordination and conflict – lingers. And it reminds us of Wyatt and Billy's own tacit participation in the world of leadership and monetary systems. Small wonder Billy reacts with scorn, while Wyatt's more measured response is equally evasive; he quietly changes the subject. Though George's energetic fluctuation between comic intoxication and measured seriousness is sometimes hard to swallow, Lee Hill rightly regards George as "the film's moral centre"[17]. It is almost certainly George who makes Wyatt realise that "we blew it".

Perhaps Wyatt, in accepting total responsibility for their failure to break the mould, is a little hard on himself. What **Easy Rider** argues, is that "freedom", whether in a modern democracy or not, is always qualified, localised, organised into pockets of behaviour and appearance which are acceptable only in specific places and contexts. Wyatt and Billy are not innately outsiders, they are positioned as such as much as they actively differentiate themselves. They try to stop at a motel, but are refused a bed. They try to have lunch at a café, but are driven out by threats. After George's murder, the earlier scene in which the trio perform stunts and do bird impressions to a soundtrack of The Holy Modal Rounders' "If You Wanna Be A Bird" takes on a pathetic quality. The camera follows and overtakes them as they flap their arms absurdly, zooms in and pulls back. It looks dynamic, but it is a hopelessly inadequate simulation of the real freedom of flight. The jump cuts which move us back and forth in time may disrupt traditional Hollywood representations of time, but their most potent effect is to prime us for tragedy. There is a heavy sense of determinism in the flashforward/back structure, a suggestion that the story has already been written which undermines the character's perception of the road as a source of unlimited freedom, a mode of being without end. The confirmation of this comes in the brothel, where Wyatt notices an inscription on the wall: "death only closes a man's reputation". Immediately he sees a flashforward of his own death, of his bike in flames on the roadside, seen from a spectral position above. Countless shots frame Wyatt and Billy through windows, or from behind the burnt out frame of a derelict building. It seems to illustrate the entrapment of the poor figures who watch them as they pass, but it's a far more ambivalent technique. In the jail Billy has a run-in with George, who has accidentally banged the door while Wyatt sleeps. The two regard each other from either side of the door, which is constructed entirely from metal bars. First Billy is seen, behind bars, from George's angle, and then the shot is reversed. The scene is the most overt to problematise the idea of inside/outside, to question our assumptions about who is more free than who. The fact that the viewer is constantly obliged to observe the onscreen characters through bars and frames represents an implicit challenge to our comfortable position as spectators. Moved to pity by the experiences of the characters on the other side of the frame, we cannot quite be sure of our own safety.

The final sequence, when it comes, is almost a relief from the despair to which Wyatt has succumbed. For an instant, speeding along the highway for help after Billy has been shot, Wyatt seems to recover some of the energy and purpose of the earlier scenes. His own death, shot in a flurry of cuts which make the slow-motion bullet ballets of films such as **Bonnie And Clyde** seem mannered and childish[18], emphasises the brutality of the murders, and suggests the characters are less important than the story itself. The hicks, charging back down the road in their pick-up, blow Wyatt off the road with a single gunshot. Here the final close up is an image not of Wyatt's body but of his bike; the human is replaced by the symbol. The shot is a final demonstration of **Easy Rider**'s ambivalence about its protagonists and the counter-culture, for it is Wyatt's oil tank which explodes at the hicks' gunshot; the tank which contains the drug money, but also the tank with the painted flag, the tank on which Wyatt, in one of his finer moments, tried to reclaim America for his generation. **Easy Rider** is too astute a film to offer pat solutions, instead it presents us simultaneously with a critique of its generation and a challenge to do better, the relevance of which has outlasted the period it encapsulates.

# NOTES

1. Peter Biskind, *Easy Riders, Raging Bulls*; London: Bloomsbury, 1998, p.70.

2. Quote attributed to Bill Hayward in Peter Biskind, *Easy Riders, Raging Bulls*, p.70.

3. Peter Biskind, *Easy Riders, Raging Bulls*, p.70.

4. This too, was partly an accident. According to Biskind, the newly-formed supergroup Crosby, Stills and Nash were originally hired to provide a tailor-made score, but when this fell through the editors had to fall back by and large on the soundtrack already in place.

5. Barbara Klinger, "The Road To Dystopia: Landscaping The Nation In **Easy Rider**", in Steven Cohan and Ina Rae Hark (eds.), *The Road Movie Book*; London: Routledge, London, 1997, p.180.

6. They, or rather, *he*. The singularity of the promotional billboard's "a man" suggests that this is Wyatt's quest rather than Billy's.

7. The dialogue in jail where Hanson describes what the police did to "the last two longhairs" who arrived, shaving their scalps with rusty razor blades, may, as Peter Biskind relates, have been inspired by a similar narrow escape experienced by Hopper.

8. Peter Biskind, *Easy Riders, Raging Bulls*, p.73.

9. Barbara Klinger, "The Road To Dystopia: Landscaping The Nation In **Easy Rider**", pp.182–3.

10. The original screenplay made the characters' identification with the civil rights movement more overt. According to Lee Hill, Southern's shooting script had a scene in which Wayne & Billy "exchange pleasantries and briefly ride with a group of black bikers". (Lee Hill, *Easy Rider*; BFI Publishing, London, 1996, p.42.

11. Barbara Klinger, "The Road To Dystopia: Landscaping The Nation In **Easy Rider**", pp.182–3.

12. For one thing they are too old. Fonda was 28 when shooting started, Hopper was 32.

13. See Klinger for a discussion of the allusions to Kerouac's *On The Road* in **Easy Rider**.

14. Lee Hill notes that the title, **Easy Rider**, is slang for someone who lives off another's earnings, implying a critique of the "easy money" strategy which is the foundation of the whole trip.

15. Some of the protagonists' failings could be levelled at the film itself. The earnest but ultimately flimsy parallels drawn between Wyatt and Billy and Afro-American experiences in the South only highlight the fact that non-white characters remain entirely marginal figures in the final cut (the only sign of a native American is a mask and headdress glimpsed in the midst of the crowd at the Mardi Gras), while even the female characters are given little to do save fawn on the male leads.

16. By turns serious and absurd, with ideas alternately loopy and astute, Hanson is a complex, perhaps unlikely character, obliged to carry a large share of both the film's energy and meaning. Rip Torn was originally hired to play the part, but it's hard to imagine anyone better equipped than Nicholson. In the role that finally launched him it is possible to see something of both sides of his subsequent career, the restrained intensity of his celebrated seventies roles in **Chinatown** and **Five Easy Pieces**, and the later self-parodying grotesques of **The Shining, The Witches Of Eastwick** and **Batman**.

17. Lee Hill, *Easy Rider*, p.35.

18. A more direct contrast might be drawn with the spectacular ending of **Zabriskie Point**, in which a bourgeois mansion on a desert outcrop is detonated by student militia. The final slow-motion sequence of abstractly-falling debris, which lasts several minutes, is the opposite both in style and content of **Easy Rider**'s denouement, since, contrary to **Easy Rider**'s angry cynicism about the prospects for real social reform at the end of the sixties, it indulges radical left fantasies in a way which seems particularly naive by 1971.

# 'Two Lane Blacktop'

# NO BEGINNING. NO END. NO SPEED LIMIT: 'TWO-LANE BLACKTOP'

## Adam Webb

On release in September 1971, Monte Hellman's **Two-Lane Blacktop** had the ingredients of a sure-fire hit. Trailing the wake of **Easy Rider**, the factors necessary for a successful road movie were all present. Classic cars duelling across the States. *Check*. A cult director from the Roger Corman stable. *Check*. On-the-road nihilism and existentialist plot twists. *Check*. A journey towards the meaning of America today. *Check*. And on top of this, two spunky rock musicians in James Taylor and Dennis Wilson as its stars. Taylor, following the release of *Sweet Baby James*, was riding the peak of commercial success and enjoying a high-profile relationship with Joni Mitchell, the Queen of the Folk Singers. Wilson, as drummer for the Beach Boys, had been an icon of Californian sexuality for over a decade. A hyperbolic *Rolling Stone* article written on location and a full year before release date had journalist Michael Goodwin hailing an "instant classic" – "a film about road racers and their women, cross-country adventure, the Great God Speed". Though recognised predominantly in Europe for his Westerns **The Shooting** and **Ride The Whirlwind** (both starring, and the latter scripted by, Jack Nicholson), Hellman was granted $900,000 to break into the lucrative youth market. This was his first fully financed movie. Universal Pictures had expectations here.

But the film bombed. The end result was a major disappointment to the distributors. Far from being an action-packed bonanza **Two-Lane** was cold-centred and slow moving; a drifting arthouse irony about road racers almost too disinterested to race. Wilson and Taylor looked cool but said little beyond one syllable. There was no human connection with the two leading players, and they remained strangers to the audience. A resulting lack of promotion ensured it played for little more than a few months before being struck off like a failed experiment. To this day it remains unreleased on video – an infrequent occupant of the graveyard shift on cable TV. Hellman went on to direct **Cockfighter** (1974) and **China 9, Liberty 37** (1978) before obscurity beckoned, Dennis and James returned to music, while co-stars Warren Oates and Harry Dean Stanton (both Hellman regulars) progressed onwards and upwards with their careers.

Which begs the question: what went wrong? Why was **Two-Lane Blacktop** so ignored on release and why has it remained such a cinematic rarity? It was released in 1971 after all, when the road movie genre was at its peak – a by-product of the endemic introspection sweeping the remnants of the US counterculture as it limped wearily into the new decade. Collectively Woodstock, Monterey, Free Love and LSD had achieved little of what they promised. Altamont and Manson had exposed the fraudulent Hippy Dream, LBJ's "War On Poverty" had failed, conflict in Vietnam had escalated, and arch conservative Richard Nixon was secure (for a while) in the White House. The optimism and hopes so intrinsic to our images of the previous decade had seemingly evaporated, replaced by the traditional values of the Silent Majority. Governmental power flexed its muscles and ruled supreme at Kent State University and Attica Prison. During that pre-Watergate era the achievements of the 1960s appeared illusionary. The voices that called for change in 1967 were now questioning their very

identity. This was apparent musically with the revival of country and folk music (mellow AOR songs by the Laurel Canyon dwellers who had survived LA burnout) and cinematically with the anti-hero loners portrayed in **Easy Rider** and **Vanishing Point** (released the same year) – individuals who journeyed through the American heartland on missions of self-discovery. Lost souls for lost times.

And within these strict parameters **Two-Lane** existed for the same reasons. Rudy Wurlitzer and Will Cory's screenplay was at first glance simplicity itself: two nameless drifters known to us only as The Driver (Taylor) and The Mechanic (Wilson) roam Nowheresville USA, hustling dollars by racing their powerful but plain grey '55 Chevy. Along the way they pick up The Girl (played by Laurie Bird) and unintentionally start a race against the yellow Pontiac driven by GTO (Warren Oates), a middle-aged wannabe hipster. Straight out of Tom Wolfe's essay *The Kandy-Coloured Tangerine-Flake Streamline Baby*, the race is for "pink slips" – the first car to Washington wins the opposition's automobile – the ultimate racing grudge match. All three male characters compete for the attention of The Girl while GTO provides entertainment along the way by spinning his self-deluding life story to an assortment of hitchhikers. The race itself finally becomes meaningless and the actors drift away as easily as they came together. The film closes when the actual celluloid we are watching catches fire and burns out. The construction and setting appear plotless and bleak; the performances realistic to the point of amateurism – as if we have actually invaded the living space of two non-descript humans for the course of a few hours.

It was this pure realism and the failure to conform to Hollywood's cinematic standards that set the film apart. "I like surface polish like in Hitchcock's **North By Northwest**," admitted Hellman during the film's making. "But I'm not talking about perfection exactly – who would want a perfect movie?" Our archetypal expectations of the genre are let down at every turn and at every possibility. Where were those wide-open spaces captured by wide-angled lenses? Where was the glorious American scenery, the mountains, the deserts and lakes? Where was the Byrds and Steppenwolf soundtrack or the blaxploitation narration of DJ Soul Power? Why did every scene start with potential but never reach fruition? It was as if the machinery was in place but tension, reason and excitement were being wilfully denied.

Our view of the road is terminally confined to the front seat of the '55. For long periods shots linger on the expressionless faces of the drivers. Despite opening to the sound of police sirens the action is scarce and the actual races devoid of tension. There are few of **Easy Rider**'s beautiful rolling vistas, and the pace is lethargic; the camera work remains resolutely static as characters move in and out of focus. The landscape becomes increasingly peripheral to the journey and is in the main unremarkable – all faceless fields and small towns inhabited by unremarkable people. The atmosphere is predominantly dank and close and it seems to rain permanently. This is an America that is nowhere and could be anywhere; a rural backwater dotted intermittently with diners, garages and motels.

For a film headlining with two rock stars there was little in the way of music and nothing but screaming engines over the opening credits. The Doors playing *Moonlight Drive* is featured in one small segment, but that aside the music is limited to the radio in the Chevy (which The Driver soon turns off for added concentration) and GTO's tape collection. There was no *Born To Be Wild* – only The Girl breaking into a spontaneous and off-key version of *Satisfaction*. In 1971, the Rock industry was celebrating its own self-importance as the affluent survivors of the '60s mythologised the past and sang contentedly, as if their struggles in that era had actually borne achievement. Hellman simply presents the music as a disposable soundtrack: a distraction to which most of the characters are ambivalent. Only The Girl is enamoured with the GTO collection of "Rock, Soul, Hillbilly and Western". Everyone else exists in the backwater world outside of LA, San Francisco or New York, where the most popular station plays country, and the rock revolution passed by unnoticed. The hillbilly who spits out, "You ain't Hippies are ya?" as if they are something from another world is typical of the faces they encounter on the road. The majority of the country remained untouched by the boasts of the '60s and, as later decades would testify, remained true to the conservative spirit of the American Dream.

The characters themselves appear one-dimensional. The Driver and Mechanic share no bonds except the car. Conversation revolves around engine performance and the relationship is realised only while hustling at the race meets and dragster derbies. Wilson reels off the vital statistics of opposition motors and selects a likely victim for Taylor to goad into racing. The quest for spare parts is given equal importance to the competition. Even when Laurie Bird appears, climbing without reason or explanation into the back of the Chevy, there is no tension and she is accepted as a passenger without question. As meaningless as the rest of the characters, The Girl sleeps with The Mechanic (though he does nothing to pursue her) only to brush off the vague advances of The Driver. ("You bore me," she retorts coldly to his small talk about "the freaky bugs"). This is a bleak worldview where communication is non-existent – and even portrayed as weakness. When GTO finally resists his boasting to attempt a confession on how his life fell apart The Driver's response is chillingly numb. "I don't wanna hear about it. It's not my problem." In many respects **Two-Lane Blacktop** was the first modern slacker movie. Welcome to the '70s.

Indeed, it was left to Warren Oates to provide all traces of humanity. An experienced actor compared to the other main players (at this point in his career he had starred in **The Wild Bunch** and **Return Of The Magnificent Seven**, as well as Hellman's existential Western **The Shooting** (1966), his depiction of the gregarious GTO saves the movie from a total emotional void. He is a tragi-comic figure who exists only

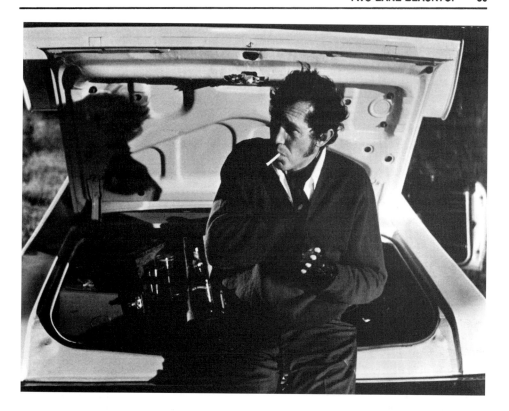

through the differing fairy tales of his life story with which he regales each unfortunate hitchhiker. We have no idea who he really is or what he is doing on the road, only of his constant desire to impress or befriend his passengers. A middle-aged loner in a changing array of colourful V-neck sweaters and cravats, he is desperate to prove himself and his virility, though no-one is interested by his spiel. He offers out pills ("I've got other items dependin' on which way you wanna go: up, down or sideways"), flaunts his tape collection and makes cringing attempts to speak hip. The only reaction he garners is the unwanted hand of Harry Dean Stanton's gay cowboy – "I'm not into that. This is competition, man. I ain't got no time." To his other passengers he is looking for a new thrill after testing jets, or on a mission to make millions for The Organisation, or on his way to New York after winning the car in Vegas shootin' craps or finally, to the old lady and child on their way to the cemetery, he is going to fix his mother's house in St Petersburg Florida. Spinning people what he believes they want to hear, his whole identity is bound to the tales of his imagination.

GTO is a lonely cipher, but there are more than enough hints that he is harbouring a secret, or that he at least has a soul. His engaging smiles, sense of humour ("Champagne. Caviar. Chicken sandwiches under glass," he drawls on entering another forsaken diner) and concern for his fellow racers win our sympathy. Of the three male characters he at least actively pursues The Girl, promising her fantasies of a life in Chicago or building a house in Florida or Arizona while she sleeps. A potential situation with some good ol' local boys is diffused when he claims the occupants of the '55 are related and he is their manager – "We're a big family but we know how to keep it together, you know what I mean." He alone drives towards a purpose – even if, irony of ironies, the world he inhabits is pure fantasy and that purpose is never revealed. GTO also gets the best lines in the film and Oates delivers with relish: "All that speed is gonna run over you one of these days. You can't be a nomad forever

unless you flow with it like me"; "I'll have a hamburger and an alka seltzer"; and best of all, "If I'm not grounded pretty soon I'm gonna go into orbit".

And yet all that Hellman actually achieved with **Two-Lane Blacktop** was intentional. The film that looked haphazard and meandering was in fact intricately formed, designed to provoke feelings of unsettlement. Surmised perfectly by the promotional slogan that appeared on the poster (No Beginning. No End. No Speed Limit!) the whole essence of the movie was its own meaninglessness. It was the perfect brutal reflection of a smug self-satisfied year when the shit of the peace and love era was really hitting the fan. (After the fanfares of the '60s came this horrifically deathly silence). A whole film constructed like the never-ending layers to an unsolvable puzzle, where everyone is lost and nothing has purpose. The race, the centre point of the whole exercise, became unimportant after ten minutes when the two sides start helping one another. Eventually the audience themselves become unwilling participants in this spectacle – watching a non-story without end is a meaningless experience in itself! In an act of total subversion Hellman had presented Universal, not with the film about nihilism that they so desired, but a film that actually *was* nihilism.

Hellman took the road movie genre far beyond the failed dreams of **Easy Rider**. Intelligent and thought provoking, **Two-Lane** in all its glorious open-ended detail was a perfect allegory of the early 1970s. The one flaw was the alienation of its potential audience. The American public and Universal Pictures preferred a comforting image of the present and found Hellman's vision unpalatable. The disappointments of the '60s had left most people wanting stability in their art as opposed to challenge and radicalism. The complexities of the real world demanded soothing bubblegum simplicity. And this was not a phenomenon intrinsic to film, as Neil Young was to discover. The average punter demanded the unthreatening country rock sound of

*Harvest* or *After The Goldrush* rather than the black existential melodrama of *Tonight's The Night* or *On The Beach*. Much like the Reaganite '80s, when bland corporate rock ruled the airwaves, the unthinkable truth in the shape of Watergate or the secret bombing of Cambodia demanded an AOR soundtrack. Maybe only now with hindsight can we make sense of and appreciate this.

America the Superpower, that could put men on the moon and inflict democracy wherever it pleased, was not at peace with itself. Beyond the huge and powerful city centres and the glory of the Stars and Stripes was the timeless vacuum where nothing ever changed. Between the government propaganda of the greatest nation on earth and the liberal ideals of the counter culture was this god-fearing land where it was forever 1954. **Two-Lane** was the road to this meaningless place with its car races, small-mindedness, and sheer mindnumbing ordinariness that, according to Hellman, was the real "America today". The only escape from the cities and the remnants of the previous decade was to this wasteland: bleached-out, numb, lonely and emotionless.

A bleak film then, but not without an absorbing beauty. A strange existentialist journey to nowhere, but given the outstanding performance of Warren Oates, and Dennis Wilson's iconographic presence, compelling and watchable. For Hellman it had been an abstract departure from the Cormanesque B-movies and Westerns for which he had been renowned – and his bravery was rewarded by a marked downturn in his career. Left behind by the likes of Coppola and Scorsese, it was in 1987 as Assistant Director of Filmography on **Robocop** before he next worked on a project of significant proportions.

However, for aficionados his reputation as an original and inspired filmmaker remained intact, and in 1991 he approached the unknown Quentin Tarantino who was hawking a script entitled **Reservoir Dogs**. After helping secure the funding Hellman ended up as Executive Producer, but the young director has paid homage to the importance of his work on several occasions. In different hands his ideas and techniques – updated and reissued – have found success elsewhere, but unlike other pioneers the original films remain obscure and rarely seen. In Tarantino's own words, "It's a real shame there are no new Monte Hellman pictures showing in our movie houses". And though it is unlikely that Quentin's patronage will lead to a revival of Travolta-like proportions, the sentiment is a worthy one. **Two-Lane Blacktop** was simply too dark for success, but its flawed glory and defiant intent stand testament to a unique and maverick talent that peaked out of time. Considering the sterility of present-day Hollywood, we film fans can only hope it might return.

# Chapter 6
# 'Vanishing Point'

# 'VANISHING POINT': SPEED KILLS

## Jack Sargeant

Based on a screenplay by Guillero Cain, Richard Sarafian's **Vanishing Point** (1971) was produced by the British company Cupid, who had previously been responsible for Jean-Luc Godard's sixties urban guerrilla/Black Panther fixated Rolling Stones documentary **One Plus One** (aka **Sympathy For The Devil**, 1968). Inspired, in part, by the death of a youthful Californian driver who refused to stop at a police roadblock and subsequently crashed and died, the original **Vanishing Point** script was reported to have contained a more overt existential narrative. In the final edit the film emerged as a chase movie, a genre under which it would eventually be marketed. On its American release in January 1971, the film played for only two weeks[1], however after attaining a degree of cult success in Europe the film was re-issued in America on a double bill with William Friedkin's **The French Connection** (1971). The film's cult status grew when it was re-issued in 1975, once again as half of a double bill, with John Hough's **Dirty Mary Crazy Larry** (1974) under the advertising banner: "3½ hours of high performance action as two great chase films return... together!"

The narrative of **Vanishing Point** opens in the desert, the noise of massive bulldozers dominating the soundtrack, as the machines are driven across the highway, forming an impassable steel wall. A helicopter, flying reconnaissance, locates the suspect in the desert – it is a 1970 white Dodge Challenger bearing Colorado plates. At the road block groups of civilians and police stand watching the road, there is an air of anticipation. The white car comes face to face with the road block and does a U-turn, but comes face to face with three police cars. The car swerves off of the road and into the desert. The desert is littered with the shells of burnt out cars and old tires. Pulling up amongst them the car stops and – to a gospel style organ – the driver climbs out. He walks around his car, climbs back in, and drives back towards the barricade, ignoring a "stop" sign and numerous glowing flares scattered across the road. A black car races past in the opposite direction. The image freezes, credit: "California – Sunday – 10.02AM".

Cut to night, the sound of a train running over a crossing, a second credit: "Two days earlier". The driver – Kowalski (Barry Newman) – is delivering a car to Denver, Colorado. Rather than stay in the city he insists on immediately taking another car back to San Francisco, and his employer reluctantly agrees. On his way out of town, Kowalski stops by a street corner, to see Jake (Lee Weaver II) and score some amphetamines. The drug dealer, who doubles as a pimp, offers him the choice of a woman to spend the night with, but Kowalski rejects his offer, stating he has to be in San Francisco on Sunday, at 3.00PM (although he does not actually have to be there until Monday): "I gotta get moving". Jake doubts him, "You can not make it", they bet double or nothing on the bennies Kowalski has just gulped down. Ignoring all street signs Kowalski leaves town.

Dawn the following day, and Super Soul (Cleavon Little), a blind black DJ is walking through the dusty western town of Goldfield towards the radio station where he works. His steps are slow, but the second he enters the studio and begins his broadcast he becomes energised. Notably, the view from Super Soul's window, dusty brown desert, and blue sky, is punctuated with a vivid red "stop" sign.

On a desert road two motorcycle cops try to pull over Kowalski's car,

presumably to complete a routine stop. Kowalski speeds off, forcing one bike from the road, and escaping the other. As the police motorbike spins from the road in a shower of dust, Kowalski has a flashback to his own days as a motorbike racer. Super Soul is playing a hard driving soul music, and listening to the police radio with his engineer when he hears about Kowalski's initial encounter with the police. Kowalski is being pursued by two police cars, but once again eludes capture. The film cuts to another of Kowalski's memories, this time to a demolition derby. Back in the present the road across the desert stretches before him. A Jaguar pulls up next to him and its driver demands to know "got any balls in that mother?" The two cars begin to race across the desert, Kowalski tight-lipped, eyes ahead, foot on the gas, the other driver laughing and cheering. The sports car spins out of control and crashes. Kowalski – in a sudden display of concern – stops his car and runs to check on the crashed car; the driver is dazed but fine, hearing police sirens Kowalski climbs back into his car and the pursuit continues until the highway patrol are forced off his tail at the Nevada border.

At a gas station in Nevada, Kowalski is served by a woman. This triggers a flashback to his time spent as a cop, watching in the rearview mirror as his partner attempts to rape a youthful suspect in the back seat of their car, and eventually stepping in to intervene. As he drives away we hear Super Soul broadcasting: "and there goes the Challenger being chased by the blue, blue meanies on wheels, the vicious strapping squad cars after our known driver, the electric sitar, the demi-god, the super driver of the golden west ...our soul hero, in his soul mobile... the last beautiful free soul on this planet. It is written, if the evil spirit arms the tiger with claws, Brahmin provided wings for the dove".

As the Nevada police begin to pursue Kowalski more details emerge from their files; the "speed maniac" they are pursuing is a legitimate car delivery driver. Throughout the film the police radio and news journalists reports gradually reveal more information: Kowalski is a great driver, but never made the grade during his racing days. He served in Vietnam and was honourably discharged in 1964 – having been awarded a medal of honour, he served in the San Diego police force and was promoted to Detective First Class before being dishonourably discharged having been busted outside a courtroom for smoking marijuana. Since 1966 Kowalski has had a succession of driving jobs.

Kowalski evades capture by driving into the desert. Super Soul starts talking to Kowalski directly in his broadcasts – "you can beat the police, you can beat the road, you can even beat the clock, but you can't beat the desert" – telling him of the popular support for his trip. Kowalski turns the radio off.

In the desert Kowalski remembers his relationship with his lover Vera (Victoria Medlin), who fantasies that he may arrest her for "trying to turn him on" to drugs. "Only if you make war on war will you overcome it," she tells him, whilst talking about the scar that he bares from his experience in Vietnam (a scar that is not seen in the narrative). She leaves the beach hut and enters the sea to surf. A shot of her board bobbing in the foam from the waves suggests to the audience that she has drowned (a fact later verified by the media in the film). The flashback is disturbed by a blow-out.

Whilst changing tires Kowalski disturbs a rattlesnake – before he can move a wondering prospector in the desert appears, and captures the snake. The prospector (Dean Jagger) promises to show him the way out of the desert in exchange for a ride. The prospector trades snakes with evangelical Christians who have set up a prayer meeting in the desert. Kowalski takes him to the meeting, but the Christians no longer want his snakes, and free them. Kowalski leaves the desert and heads for the Nevada/California border.

On the highway Kowalski meets two travellers, stranded next to their broken car. He gives them a lift. Both of them are coded as gay, with lispy tones – "You think we're queers". They attack him, he beats them both ("Oh no please, it hurts," whines one) and kicks them from the car. Super Soul broadcasts barely coded messages to Kowalski – telling him of police traps set at the major roads into California. The radio station is attacked as a gang of thugs try to silence him. In the desert Kowalski meets a biker (Timothy Scott) who invites Kowalski to his ranch, "You need any help?" Kowalski declines, then, after a moment's thought, asks the biker for some speed. The two head to the biker's shack in the desert. Here, amongst the wreckage of various cars and bikes, Kowalski meets the biker's girlfriend (Gilda Texter), who drives aimlessly in circles around the tin buildings, naked on her motorbike. Whilst at the biker's ranch he hears another Super Soul broadcast, but this time telling Kowalski to drive into California via the freeway he is already on. Kowalski is suspicious – something is different in Super Soul's voice. The biker agrees to go and check the route, to see if there is a trap. Whilst Kowalski waits with the woman, the biker disappears. She offers to fuck Kowalski, but he declines. "You don't fancy me?". He admits he does, but does not want sex, asking instead for a cigarette. She drives off. The biker returns, and warns Kowalski of the trap – "More cops than I ever seen". The biker climbs into a pile of auto parts next to his shack and pulls out a siren, then, using the light from his motorbike, disguises Kowalski's car as a police car. The two drive toward the police barricade and – with lights on and siren wailing – force the police, who believe the car to be one of their own, from the road. By the time they realize what is happening it is too late. Kowalski is almost home.

In the ruined studio Super Soul begins to broadcast, "This radio station was named Kowalski in honour of the last great American hero to whom speed means freedom of the soul, the question is not when is he going to stop, but who is going to stop him?"

California: the highway patrol office is a hive of activity, Kowalski – pursued by a helicopter – races towards his destiny. At the town of Cisco bulldozers are driven

into place across the highway. Locals, hippies and cops gather on the road side, united in their desire to witness Kowalski's possible capture. Kowalski drives towards the steel barricade – he smiles – and plows his car into the blades of the bulldozers. The car explodes in a ball of flame. Credit: California: Sunday – 10.04AM. As the fire is extinguished the assembled crowds slowly drift away.

**Easy Rider** was shot at the tail end of the optimistic sixties; even the drug smuggling activities of its central protagonists are legitimized by the usage of the Steppenwolf song "Pusher Man" in the soundtrack. The bikers are – as the film's publicity stated – existential heroes who are possessed by an urge to find freedom, searching for an authentic America, although in the final eventuality they are unable to find it. This search for a pure, essential America – even if it no longer could be said to exist – informed the film's protagonists' hope and dreams. The film is, ultimately, close to the road movie's western roots with its utopian belief that with the expanse of the continent lies the inherent freedom at the heart of the American Dream. Eventually the bikers' inability to find the visionary America that they are searching for is characterized by an overriding sense of melancholia, and the film is infused with a nostalgia for the original quests to explore the massive continent with its vast cinematic spectacles across the wonder of the landscape.

In **Easy Rider** the optimism of the sixties ultimately comes face-to-face with the conservative "straight culture"'s oppression somewhere on a back road outside of New Orleans, but this ending is one which frustrates and angers the audience, who read the bikers' killers as the "other" and representative of a culture that will ultimately undergo social change. Further, even if the heroes met their sticky end on the highway, the audience was nevertheless offered numerous images of the "potential" of a "new", "ideal" America with its cultural identity still embedded in the mythology of the Dream; represented by optimistic scenes of communal living and so forth (as one of the bikers states, whilst looking at a shrub of land set aside at the commune for growing food, "They're going to make it").

In the two years between the Summer 1969 cinema release of **Easy Rider** (following a successful première at the Cannes Film Festival earlier in the year) and the Spring 1971 release of **Vanishing Point**, any remaining fantasy of sixties optimism had been ruthlessly dissipated. 1969 saw the supposedly love oriented counter culture vanish in pools of blood and gun smoke; in August, Sharon Tate *et al* were killed by members of the Manson Family, and in December the Rolling Stones concert at Altamont turned into a nightmare for many. As the counter culture paper the *Berkeley Tribe* described the rock festival in their headline: "Stones Concert Ends It – America Now Up for Grabs"[2].

As a result of the massive increase in aerial bombardments of Vietnam and the inevitable spread of the conflict into Cambodia, as well as the large scale police brutality at the Democratic Convention in Chicago in the summer of 1968, the student protest movement – which had been largely non-violent – became increasingly confrontational. In the June of 1969 the Weathermen emerged from the growing ranks of student dissent. No longer pledged to democracy, the Weathermen believed in immediate and violent revolution. By August 1969 the first Weathermen bombings occurred in a wave of random violence that would continue into the early seventies. The Weathermen's politics were extreme and brutal; following the Tate/LaBianca killings and the revelation that one of those slain had a fork stuck into his fleshy stomach, Bernadine Dohrn, leader of the guerrilla group, announced 1969 as "The Year Of The Fork". As the conflict in Vietnam worsened, and with the election of Richard Nixon, the anti-Vietnam protests grew in popularity, but by the end of the summer of 1970, following numerous college riots and confrontations between students and the national guard, the remaining student protest movement was all but forgotten. Any optimism about socio-political change or pretence at a love oriented counter culture had vanished.

**Vanishing Point** – for all of its iconographic and narrative references to the American hero[3] – is a film based neither in a melancholia or nostalgia for a mythical America, but in the ultimate nihilistic recognition that the only remaining option is a wilful annihilation. Characterized by this nihilism **Vanishing Point** denies the liberal humanism inherent within the narrative of **Easy Rider**, instead it strips communication between individuals and social exchange to their most perfunctory forms. The remnants of the hippies in **Vanishing Point** are presented as grubby and dirty, as borderline street-people in Denver – they are no longer the "innocent" and "beautiful" people that they once were. Most appear fascinated by Kowalski purely as a media-generated myth which alleviates their stoned boredom.

The belief in any mystical/religious interpretation of the world has also disintegrated, the sixties search for spiritual enlightenment has ended in the desert, where all that is left is a rudimentary form of quasi-fundamentalism manifested by the preacher and his congregation who appear to be interested only in pure spectacle and mindless celebration, engaging in rituals of snake handling and handclapping. Notably, when the leader of the Christians, the suitably named J. Hova, throws the rattlesnakes onto the ground he cries "Free the vipers" – the viper, of course, is the Biblical symbol of Satan; such a gesture, alongside the Christians' anger at the prospector for bringing Kowalski to their meeting, and the remote location of their secret desert prayer meeting, suggests that these worshippers are concerned more with notions of the apocalypse – the main preoccupation of the Manson Family, coded as "Helter Skelter" – than any of the shared enlightened lifestyle presented in the commune scenes in **Easy Rider**.

In contrast to the popular mythology that constructed the hippies as sexually liberated, **Vanishing Point** presents any sense of sexual contact as pointless or

unpleasant, with Kowalski refusing to have sex with either the prostitutes in Denver, or with the naked woman on the motorbike (a character who, similarly bored, seems to offer Kowalski sex more from a sunburned/drug-fried sense of *ennui* than either romantic passion or animal lust). Similarly the two hitchhikers that Kowalski picks up are immediately identified as homosexual, and positively ooze sleaze and degeneracy, serving to emphasize that, despite Kowalski's refusal of sex with the naked woman, he nevertheless is not homosexual. If sex is seen to represent a union of others – a momentary sharing or merging of identity – as well as, in its most biological form, reproduction – by negating the act of sex within the diegesis Kowalski re-enforces his status as an absolute outsider. Further, by negating sexual contact Kowalski is negating the possibility of the emergence of his own identity, suggesting once more that he has entered an abyss of nihilism. Even in his memories sex is constructed as negative, either as the grasping cop molesting the runaway in the back of the police car, or linked to the death of Vera and hence marked by unhappiness.

Unlike the protagonists of many road movies Kowalski is travelling alone. There is no one with whom he can share the experience of the journey, no one with whom to talk, instead he is plagued by recurring memories of the repeated failures and tragedies that have punctuated his life. The nearest figure to a companion in the film is Super Soul, yet the two men share little in common. Despite Super Soul's perceived closeness and link with Kowalski (he refers to Kowalski's "soul" and "soul mobile" linking the concept of Kowalski's auto-*geist* with his own name), the driver turns the radio off when he is lost in the desert – silencing the DJ's voice[4]. Silence itself becomes a major thematic of Kowalski's persona, he barely talks, and avoids linguistic communication where possible, even in the flashback scenes he hardly speaks. Communication itself has been rendered as an almost hopeless task.

Kowalski is not interested in an existential search for either himself or for any authentic manifestation of the American Dream, what little the audience know about him emerges from the flashbacks which punctuate his journey and a few briefly glimpsed newspaper headlines. What these mnemonic glimpses reveal more than anything is that, subsequent to his military experience, he has failed or lost everything that has mattered to him; thus the urge to get to San Francisco by 3.00PM on Sunday represents his one – perhaps final – opportunity at achieving a degree of success, as well as guaranteeing him free amphetamines should he make it in time. Whilst Super Soul constructs Kowalski as the "last great American hero" the evidence presented to the audience suggests that rather than manifesting "freedom of the soul" Kowalski is haunted by his memories, trapped in a psychic cage of his own making, however fast he moves he is inevitably unable to outrun himself. Notably the *mise-en-scène* of the film allows repeated glances into the rearview mirror, further emphasizing Kowalski's inability to forget. His memories – rather than receding into the distance -- emerge through his repeated backwards gaze (his flashback to his experiences as a cop are structured literally on this look into the mirror).

The film's star, Barry Newman, has suggested that Kowalski "smiles as he rushes to his death at the end of **Vanishing Point** because he believes he will make it through the roadblock. Deep down, Kowalski may have believed he wasn't going to make it, but that's the basis of an existentialist film"[5]. However, it is clear that he cannot cross the steel wall of the bulldozers' blades, indeed Kowalski's death is assured, his brief pause and moment of reflection prior to deciding to take the final death trip suggests that, rather than believing he will complete. his journey, he recognizes the only freedom he can ultimately find is the silence of death[6].

In scenes that were edited from the version of the film that was eventually released, Kowalski picks up a female hitchhiker (played by Charlotte Rampling) who is also heading for San Francisco. Kowalski and the women talk, and she asks him his astrological sign. According to Barry Newman, the couple "end up spending the night together in the desert. Suddenly she says 'Don't go to San Francisco', and vanishes. She was the symbol of death"[7]. The scene was cut because it was believed that audiences would not understand its symbolism, and the film was ultimately marketed as a B-movie[8]. Nevertheless, this scene, had it remained in the film would further suggest that Kowalski knew of his imminent death, and that by pursuing his journey he would die[9]. Furthermore this scene would also have suggested Kowalski engaged in sex, thus by cutting the sex scene from the film, sex is literally under erasure. If the scene remained in the film it would have suggested not only an inevitable link between sex and death – with the hitchhiker representing death – but also that Kowalski was fucking death.

The inherent nihilism of the film further emerges within its cyclic structure, it opens immediately prior to Kowalski's death, and closes with the spectacle of his car in flames. There is a grim atmosphere of inevitability to the film from its first scene. As Kowalski races towards death at the film's opening he passes a black car driving the opposite direction. The camera swings to follow this black car, it is the same car that Kowalski drives to Denver. The dramatic device serves to link the opening scenes with the subsequent action set two days previously, however it also suggests a broader cyclic structure, as if Kowalski is endlessly trapped within the twin loops of the journey (back and forth, from San Francisco to Denver to San Francisco, and, presumably, back yet again) and his speed-wracked nervous system. Similarly when Kowalski drives into the Nevada high-desert and loses his way an aerial shot reveals the circular route he has taken, his tracks crossing over themselves in a massive loop.

This notion of a temporal collapse is repeated throughout the film; during Kowalski's first pursuit by police cars on Saturday morning the sun is low in the sky and the long shadows suggest dusk, yet the film cuts to show crisp mid-morning light. As the chase ends and Kowalski flees the State successfully a subtitle reads "Nevada Saturday 11.43AM". When Kowalski reaches California with the assistance of the biker a subtitle reads "California Saturday 7.12PM", the film then cuts to Sunday morning.

Saturday night has been erased from **Vanishing Point**, causing some confusion to audiences and writers on the film who often mistakenly describe Kowalski's planned trip as taking sixteen hours. Moreover, the loss of scenes depicting Saturday night, as well as the frequently dusty desert lighting, mean that a large section of the film appears to transpire in a temporal zone characterized by an endless dusk/twilight haze. This adds a dream-like spectral quality to the film that also hints at the imminence of Kowalski's apocalyptic destiny. At the film's climax Kowalski can see a burst of light from between the steel blades of the bulldozers, in a blaze that represents the rising sun as a symbol for his own self-sacrifice as he breaks through the ultimately endless, meandering, pointless loops that have demarcated his life and annihilates himself.

Vanishing Point, unlike other road movies, makes little use of the landscape through which Kowalski travels; there are few panoramic shots, in the main part the visual emphasis is on the car/road/rearview mirror. What long shots occur in the film do so in order to locate the protagonists within a terrain but these, frequently short, shots – unlike those in **Easy Rider** – do not celebrate the pure visual pleasure of the landscape.

In **Vanishing Point**, amphetamines are the drug of choice. Speed – as a drug – represents the antithesis of the sixties obsessions with expanding consciousness. Whilst the psychedelic drugs and marijuana consumed in **Easy Rider** open the protagonists' minds to the greater beauty of the world, speed narrows experience and perception to a pin-prick on the horizon. Speed is a functional drug devised and consumed for practical purposes, it does not allow for the bourgeois luxury of contemplating stoned realities[10]. As a drug it serves to further separate Kowalski from any notional sixties sub-cultural hero. Instead the amphetamines act to link Kowalski directly with the Dodge Challenger he is driving to San Francisco, fusing man and car in a celebration of pure (terminal) velocity.

The film's distributors also acknowledged this velocity, and – at the time of its release – **Vanishing Point** was marketed in part as a large-scale chase movie. Further, **Vanishing Point**'s publicity celebrated the audiences' viewing experience as a form of speed psychosis, with the advertising slogans stating: "Watch carefully because everything happens fast. The chase. The desert. The shack. The girl. The roadblock. The end." and "Tighten your seat belt. You never had a trip like this before". The driving scenes in **Vanishing Point** were frequently shot with the cameras under cranked, thus creating the illusion that the cars were driving faster than they actually were. For example during the race scene between Kowalski and the Jaguar the cars actually drove at about 50mph, but in the finished film the race appears to be much faster. This emphasis on driving and pursuit further emphasizes the film's engagement with the chase genre. As a pursuit-oriented road movie, **Vanishing Point**, in part, leads the way for lightweight films such as **Slither** (Howard Zieff, 1972), Sam Peckinpah's country song inspired **Convoy** (1978), and the broadly comic chase movies of the late seventies, such as the **Smokey And The Bandit** (Hal Needham, 1977) and its numerous sequels.

Yet the film's unshaking nihilism, the certainty of Kowalski's demise, the temporal distortion, and the abandonment of a recognizable linear narrative in favour of the gyre-like structure punctuated by flashbacks, all serve to place **Vanishing Point** within a cycle of films that announce an increasingly harsh, hopeless, post-sixties/early seventies world view. As such **Vanishing Point** may be seen to be a part of the nihilistic, sometimes brutal body of early seventies films that includes Monte Hellman's **Two-Lane Blacktop** and Peckinpah's 1974 road-to-hell classic **Bring Me The Head Of Alfred Garcia** [see also Chapter 8]. Road movies were now less concerned with notions of beatitude and more fascinated by the potential for the degeneration of the human condition and the ultimate loneliness of existence on the road.

# NOTES

1. In an article in *Musclecar Review*, the actor Barry Newman states that the film was "dumped... in neighbourhood theatres as a multiple release, and it was out of the theatres in less than two weeks" – Barry Newman, quoted in, Paul Zazarine, "Behind The Scenes Of The Movie Vanishing Point" in *Musclecar Review*, March, 1986. Note also that the film has a cult following amongst American car fans; as Paul Zazarine's article on the film testifies, it was motivated by "a tidal wave of **Vanishing Point** mania".

2. Cited in David Caute, *'68 The Year Of The Barricades*, Paladin: London, 1988, p.396.

3. These references to the American hero are apparent not only within the diegesis (via Super Soul's radio monologues) but also in the publicity material surrounding the film which described Kowalski as a "latter-day 'cowboy' whose mounts are souped-up cars", and "like the legendary cowboy, the hero... is a loner, a man with his own peculiar sense of freedom" (*Vanishing Point Pressbook*, p.6).

4. It should be noted however, that Kowalski's listening to Super Soul's show, and Super Soul's closeness to Kowalski does announce the possibility for friendships based on equality across the perceived racial divisions. Notably the police and representatives of straight culture who beat Super Soul and his technician and refer to Super Soul as "nigger", and are seen referring to him as inferior or an upstart, while Kowalski and the Biker both appreciate Super Soul. Kowalski is also clearly close to the drug dealer, once again suggesting his friendships with blacks. Of course despite the film's nods to multi-culturalism it is the music-oriented disc jockey Super Soul and the drug dealer who are black, not the main protagonist, and as such the black characters should be read in part as stereotypes that would occur repeatedly in both action and exploitation films of the seventies.

5. Barry Newman, quoted in, Paul Zazarine, "Behind The Scenes Of The Movie Vanishing Point".

6. This is in contrast to most road movies (ie **Easy Rider** or **Thelma And Louise**) in which protagonists are killed as a result of their freedom (real or perceived) and their unwillingness to be constrained.

7. Barry Newman, quoted in, Paul Zazarine, "Behind The Scenes Of The Movie Vanishing Point".

8. It is telling that the film was marketed as a B-movie, suggesting that the distributors perceived a change in public tastes that would negate too much narrative complexity.

9. Note also that Charlotte Rampling's name appeared on the video box artwork for **Vanishing Point**'s initial video release, despite her absence from the film.

10. Speed, as Jim Hogshire has observed, is linked to "truck drivers, and other examples of stand-up citizens just getting the job done" (Jim Hogshire, *Pills-A-Go-Go: A Fiendish Investigation Into Pill Marketing, Art, History And Consumption*, Feral House: Los Angeles, 1999, p.106). It should also be observed that in the psychedelic heyday of Haight-Ashbury many hippies espoused the belief that, whilst LSD et al were beneficial, "Speed Kills".

## Chapter 7
# The Antipodes

# LOOP THE LOOP
# AND CRASH HEAD-ON:
# AUSTRALIAN
# ROAD MOVIES

## Jonathan Rayner

The recurrence of examples of the road movie genre within Australian cinema since its revival at the end of the 1960s has been linked to a variety of cultural, commercial and social imperatives. These conditions have pertained to all types of popular and art cinema productions coming out of Australia over the last thirty years. However, not only have there been different emphases and initiatives affecting the production of specific types of Australian film at certain periods, but different film genres (including indigenous film categories as well as generic types imported and adapted from Hollywood) have been advantaged or disadvantaged as a result. As a commercially-oriented and youth-targeted genre, the road movie in its Australian incarnation has been subject to both local and overseas competition. More costly American popular films have maintained a high profile with Australian audiences during the renaissance of the national film industry. At the same time, other home-grown film genres (such as the period film and the male ensemble drama in the 1970s and '80s) have been granted governmental financial support and received a favourable reception from Australian cinema-goers.

The road movie can be seen to encapsulate the same debates and embody the same difficulties as other forms of recent film production within the Australian cinema. At its inception, the new Australian cinema, its practitioners and critics were divided between an aspiration for a national film industry to rival Hollywood on popular, commercial terms and a desire for a cultural cinema which would explore, define and broadcast a recognisable national identity. These two objectives were successfully, but embarrassingly combined in the popular, vulgar "Ocker" comedies of the early 1970s (such as **The Adventures Of Barry McKenzie** [Bruce Beresford, 1972]). Subsequently, a more decorous union of the principles was accomplished in **Picnic At Hanging Rock** (Peter Weir, 1975). which was styled in emulation of the 1960s art cinema and was successful in Australia and Europe. The Australian road movies made during and since the resurgence in local production have also needed to align themselves with the cultural or commercial poles which have dominated production: "polarisation between 'international' product and indigenous film began to displace the earlier one, film as industry and commerce vs. film as art, in the late seventies."[1]

At a superficial level, it may appear that the aesthetically refined and literary-based period film would emphasise national heritage, articulate national culture and appeal directly to the local audience, while the youth-oriented road movie must gravitate towards the commercial and generically based cinema which seeks an international audience. In fact, the exploration of contemporary Australian culture became an integral part of the travel through the natural and social landscape which the locally-made road movies enacted. In some cases such commentary is pertinent and direct, as rural and urban circumstances and relevant social issues are encountered en route (e.g. **Backroads** [Philip Noyce, 1977]). In others, the relationship with the land affects the portrayal of the environment and human activity and mobility within it (The **Mad Max** trilogy [Dr George Miller, 1979/82/85]): "...the road and the journey... have a central function, either in the form of a moral discourse, a tale of personal development, or as a reflection of society itself."[2]

## AUSTRALIAN ROAD MOVIES AND CONTEMPORARY SOCIETY

The use of the road movie genre as a site for the definition of Australian-ness and the exploration of specific Australian concerns is evident from the first decade of the film revival. The identification of a particular national perspective upon the car as an icon and its status within popular culture grows out of the Australian Gothic films, but is also discernible in **The FJ Holden** (Michael Thornhill, 1977). The title of Thornhill's film refers to a much-prized model, the FJ, the first all-Australian car built by a home-grown car manufacturing company in the 1950s. The car functions as a teenage symbol, connected to a particular era and the sexual maturation and rites of passage with which it has become associated. This relationship is important in the development of road movies within Australia, even though **The FJ Holden** is not located fully within the itinerant, picaresque traditions of the genre and concentrates instead on the circumscription of everyday suburban existence in Sydney. Instead, the car and the sexual liaisons which it inspires and which take place in it provide an opportunity to explore a national and idiomatic perspective on teenage culture: "the issue of adolescent sexuality is a key element in the search for identity... [in **The FJ Holden**] Anne submits to the unwelcome attentions of Bob as a preliminary to a more protracted session with his mate Kevin... There is both resignation and pleasure in Anne's submitting to Kevin – and submitting is what it usually amounts to for the girls in these films. Whatever their social class, their sexual conditioning negates the possibility of their being the instigator. Insofar as sexual experience is a key element in their adult identities, it will be as passive receiver."[3]

This portrait of an Australian victimhood, suffering the constraint of social circumstances and expectations, is also present in Thornhill's other film work, and in similar conflations of road movie, teen pic and social commentary in Australian film. In **Queensland** (John Ruane, 1976), the desire of the central characters is to break out of the unimaginative drudgery of routine through escape from Melbourne by road. Although they depict varying generations and their respective stresses and aspirations, Ruane's and Thornhill's films share a common treatment of suburban entrapment and the illusory or unattainable freedom of the road:

*"Queensland is the other place, not easily reached from Melbourne, mid-winter, when you get your car back from being in hock over gambling debts and find it will barely make it to the corner, let alone out of the suburb... The final, epic crane shot up from street level watches Doug's broken-down Holden start, stop, and crawl uncertainly through the maze of streets, a thousand miles to go. Doug's quest is deeply futile, locked in the city. FJ Holden uses a few similar epic crane shots; the final one pulls up and back from Kevin's entrapment at last by parents, police and a stunted future."[4]*

A more hard-edged critical commentary of Australian social structures, connecting racial relations with the natural landscape and human geography is seen in **Backroads** (Philip Noyce, 1977). An archetypal white Australian (played by Bill Hunter, the ubiquitous face of Australian patriarchy in films of the 1990s) maintains a tense friendship with an Aboriginal companion while they travel through the sparsely-populated rural environment. The threat of entrapment, implied from their usage of a stolen car, persists through the film's frame compositions, with images of the blank landscape bounded by the limited frames of the car windows. Within this context, the liberation of the road is squandered in flight. The desired evasion of authority is replaced by a duplication, within the car's confined space, of the tensions present in contemporary society:

*"Places like the black shanty town and roadside café are given documentary realism, and John Emery's script is finely attuned to naturalistic speech and the lazy violence that can lie beneath its laconicism. But the world inside the car is emblematic, not documentary. Black and white, male and female, enclosed within a detached alienation, speeding nowhere."[5]*

Less confrontational but no less pertinent considerations of Australian-ness, including the representation of youth culture and race relations, can be found in contemporary generic hybrids which combine road movies and rock musicals. **Oz** (Chris Lofven, 1976) updates and transplants to Australia the narrative of **The Wizard Of Oz** (1925/1939) [see Chapter 13], and **Wrong Side Of The Road** (Ned Lander, 1981) follows the journey and experiences of an Aboriginal reggae band on tour in South Australia.

The amalgamation of road movie features with other generic bases underlines the international recognition of the itinerant, picaresque film narrative, which works counter to the national and cultural specificity of some of the previous examples. The goal of "internationalisation" of Australian film products suggests a reliance on foreign (Hollywood) generic models, narrative constructions and even stars in order to exploit overseas as well as local markets. **Road Games** (Richard Franklin, 1980) [see also Chapter 8] epitomises this trend, being a commercially-oriented Australian production which employed American actors in principal roles. The casting of Stacey Keach and Jamie Lee Curtis (prompted also, in the latter's case, by her fame from recent films such as **Halloween** [John Carpenter, 1978]) provoked opposition from Australian Equity which called for the substitution of indigenous acting talent.[6] The film's plot is equally derivative and lacking in Australian specificity, though its location of menace within the empty and featureless natural environment connects it with the cycle of Australian Gothic films made during the 1970s and 1980s. The Gothic treatment of human existence within, travel through and reaction to the oppressive landscape is culturally specific, and uses the iconography of the road movie in exploring the national psyche.

## ROAD MOVIES AND THE AUSTRALIAN GOTHIC
The rootlessness and disaffection suggested by the suburban Australian road movie can be compared to generalised Western depersonalisation within the urban environment and the desire to return or travel to the perceived rural idyll. Within Australian culture, the perception of the interior country as a romantic retreat is countered by the immensity and intractability of the desert continent:

*"The Romantic desire to find oneself spiritually in Nature has in Australia to deal with a material version of nature that is antithetical to Romanticism: inverted in season, in mood and meaning, the Australian landscape as mirror to the soul reflects the grotesque and the desolate rather than the beautiful and the tranquil."[7]*

The portrayal of rural communities within Australian Gothic films is based on their otherness in comparison with urban environments and their inhabitants. These differences are exposed by the arrival of outsiders, travellers journeying from the civilised fringe of the country to the secluded interior. Travel by car, the subsequent discovery of aspects of individual and communal identity, and the hybridisation of B-picture genres found in the Gothic connect these films closely with the original road movie model.

In **The Cars That Ate Paris** (Peter Weir, 1974) discussion of the centrality and lethality of the car within Australian culture is initiated. This subject is more fully developed in the **Mad Max** films, but the predilection for and reliance upon automobiles that Weir's film uncovers underlines this close cultural association, which is presupposed in the Australian film industry's production of indigenous road movies. In the American road movie, the car and highway can be interpreted as liberating or restorative, objects of aspiration or agents of transformation for travellers. By contrast, in Australian road movies the car is acknowledged as a prerequisite to survival in rural areas, just as it is a symbol of status in suburbia. The road itself is often unremittingly straight, existing as the shortest distance between locations of importance across a barren territory. Emphasis rests on arrival rather than on the journey, in contradiction to the developmental principle attached to travel in the road movie genre. The heroes of Australian Gothic film are propelled into zones of conflict by the car or motorbike, and likewise resolution of conflict is dependent on the vehicle's mobility and lethalness.

In **The Cars That Ate Paris**, the hero Arthur Waldo enters the bush town of Paris when the car his brother is driving crashes on a country road. His brother is killed and Arthur is hospitalised, and is left unable to drive because of his traumatic experience. While he is marooned in Paris, Arthur gradually realises that the town subsists on a twilight economy of car parts and valuables looted from crashes vehicles, and that the "accidents" themselves are engineered by the town's inhabitants. The town's barter system uses a car-currency, of tyres, oil, petrol and spares. The survivors of the crashes are also absorbed and recycled, ending up either as "veggies" in the town infirmary or being adopted by local families. Arthur is welcomed into the mayor's family, which is already augmented by "second-hand" orphaned children. Although his automotive disability prevents his departure, Arthur's knowledge of the town's secret means that he must be silenced, and so he is offered the job of traffic warden. He is tasked with reining in the increasingly disruptive behaviour of Paris' youth, who threaten the town with beweaponed cars built out of the many wrecks. Eventually a car-based civil war erupts and the town is destroyed. Out of fear and for his own protection Arthur takes the wheel again and kills one of the attacking "cars" and, liberated once more, drives off into the night restored in his self-esteem and mobility.

Arthur's arrival in Paris compares with the righteous intervention of the hero of a Hollywood Western, who saves the endangered homesteaders before riding out into the wilderness. However, his inability to drive, scorned by the youths like the cowardice of a cowboy too yellow to draw, undermines expectation and parodies the quoted genre. This bathetic approach is furthered by Arthur's collusion with immoral authority. Instead of exposing corruption he colludes with it, and this unheroic portrayal is completed by his destructive rather than redemptive, moral violence at the film's climax. Rather than saving the town, he assists in its destruction, and the exodus of Paris' inhabitants, now let loose on the country's roads, suggests the radiation rather than containment of anarchy. Arthur's immobility, enunciated through the stasis of non-driving and exaggerated by his appointment as an inefficient "parking officer" unable to control even stationary vehicles, is replaced with uncontrolled and dangerous movement. His return to the road, and the spread of Paris' population, are indicative of the specific social criticism (applicable to Western society in general but Australia in particular) contained within Weir's film:

*"While it reverts to the oblique and grotesque in its approach to the question of how to be an Australian film, Cars doesn't strain for an answer. It is, of course, commenting on something deeply embedded in the Australian ethos: that we would die without our cars and to prove the point we daily risk dying in them. The spike-encrusted cars coming out of the darkness to prey on civilisation form the crowning image... It works*

*as a suggestive, dark, comic fantasy, uneven in its success, but rich in some of the perversity it unearths from the underside of the Australian psyche.*[8]

**Cars'** influential use of vehicles as weapons and its propensity for wider social commentary were highlighted by its circulation in America under the title **The Cars That Ate People**, and it providing the inspiration behind Roger Corman's black comedic science fiction film **Death Race 2000** [see Chapter 19].[9] The generic hybridity, dark humour and equivocation on the nature of heroism found in Weir's film carry over into the best known and internationally successful examples of Australian Gothic, the **Mad Max** trilogy.

## MAD MAX: JOINING THE RAT CIRCUS

Dr George Miller's post-apocalyptic trilogy derives its popularity, impact and commercial success from the strong generic basis of its narrative characterisation and iconography. Elements derived from the Western (the lone avenger, the beleaguered homestead, the desert landscape), science fiction (societal collapse in the near future), the biker movie[10] and the police thriller are alloyed in self-conscious parody and pastiche. As a youthful amalgam of Ethan Edwards (**The Searchers**) and Harry Callahan (**Dirty Harry**), Max assumes heroic tasks which increase in scale and destructiveness as the cycle progresses. However, uniting and defining the trilogy are its fetishisation of the vehicles and dehumanisation of the hero, and its recognition of the car's elevated status as key to plot, character and action. The specific Australian landscape in which the action takes place is central to the film's examination of the national car culture.

Max's similarity to the Western hero extends beyond his revenge motivation to acknowledge his inseparability from the outlaws he combats. In **Mad Max** the policemen of the Main Force Patrol (defined in its title by mobility and violence) inhabit the same blank desert, dress in the same fetishised costumes and employ their vehicles and weapons (and, in an echo of **Cars**, their vehicles *as* weapons) in the same ways as the opposition, the nomad biker gang. In theory, the hero's actions are devoted to the preservation of society and upholding of justice, but in practice the Patrol are losing the battle against the encroaching forces of darkness. The highways they protect exact an ever-increasing death toll. After the titles, the trilogy's defining image (a straight road stretching to infinity across a featureless landscape) is accompanied by signs bearing the skull and crossbones and the name "Anarchie Road". Additionally, the validity of the Patrol's fatal pursuits is also undermined. The majority take place away from urban areas, and so are worthless as law enforcement. Furthermore, when the first chase "heads for population", the police vehicles are seen to represent a greater danger to civilian bystanders than the Nightrider's stolen V8 interceptor.

The desperate and vain attempts by his colleagues to stop the Nightrider are succeeded by Max's mechanical but clinically efficient actions. Our introduction to the character is tantalising and fragmented: close-ups of his hands tending his engine, his expressionless face hidden behind dark glasses and details of the controls and dashboard connect him conclusively with his vehicle. Choosing a stretch of straight road for the automotive duel, Max drives at the Nightrider head-on. Max's refusal to flinch causes an instantaneous emasculation and emotional breakdown in his foe, who crashes fatally immediately afterwards. Only when he dismounts to view the resulting explosion does Max remove his dark glasses (which have rendered him robotically impassive until this point) and express emotion. Several key themes and aspects of characterisation originate from this exposition. Masculinity and the revelation of emotion are connected with driving, since self-image is based on skill and courage behind the wheel. The interconnection of heroism and machinery, and the blank

Mad Max

landscape upon which one is articulated by the other, emerge as one of the trilogy's primary concerns.

In his car Max is all-powerful, but is demoralised by the pointlessness of the Patrol's efforts to safeguard society. Since the vicissitudes of the legal system release those criminals they do catch, the Patrol's duties degenerate into the pursuit of personal vendettas. It is this increasing inseparability between the gangs and the Patrol which prompts Max to quit, before he is submerged in the thrill of the "rat circus" on the highway. Max is only tempted to stay with the offer of using the last V8 interceptor, and leaves on an indefinite holiday. The hero's weakness, and the target of the biker's revenge is Max's family. While in uniform, Max's wife Jessie and their child represent a source of strength and a haven for retreat, since their home is divorced from both the town and the highway. However, when on leave from the Patrol, Max makes the mistake of taking his family on holiday on the road, presenting them as targets when they become one with the vulnerable society he has previously striven to protect. Despite being pursued across the countryside, it is on the road that Jessie and Sprog are attacked, and it is through the road that Max seeks redress. Significantly, the loss of his family reduces Max, in the words of the hospital staff tending Jessie, to a "zombie": the integration of the character with his vehicle and his role, and the convergence of the machine and dehumanised, mechanical behaviour is completed with Max's campaign of vengeance. Vehicles are instrumental in the destruction of Max's enemies, as he chases the Toecutter into a head-on collision with a truck and handcuffs Johnny to a burning car. While it extends the debt to science fiction implied in **Cars'** narrative of societal breakdown, like Weir's film **Mad Max** also connects unerringly with contemporary Australian culture:

*"Miller's film... has a message embedded in its dark action: this country's insane and deadly road culture. Many Australians like to use their cars as lethal weapons, and there is an aggression on the roads unlike that found elsewhere (as well as a bloodthirsty approach to, and obsession with, motor accidents on the television news). Out of that, Miller fashioned an ethos of the future."[11]*

## WHITE LINE NIGHTMARE: MAD MAX 2

The offer of the last V8 interceptor, the car driven to death by the Nightrider, equates Max with the gangs when he enacts his revenge at the end of the first film, and when he is found alone in the desert at the beginning of the second. His similarity to his adversaries (the "dogs of war" led by the Humungus) is extended by the embellishment of his black leather costume (the remnants of his uniform) just as his association with machinery is exaggerated by the mechanical joint which supports his injured knee. His kinship with the enemies of civilisation is made explicit by Pappagallo, the leader of the "white tribe", who likens them all to "maggots living off the corpse of the old world". The annihilating blankness of the desert environment renders progress futile, just as the Max and the gangs burn petrol in their vain searches along the roads for more. The roads are no longer even an attenuated socio-economic infrastructure, but an infinite arena for running battles. However, this "blighted place" is where Max is re-humanised, as he finds a society to protect and a role to fulfil. Again, in parallel with the classical Western hero, the community Max fights for is one he is excluded from joining, but the resumption of heroic status and the gradual reconnection with other people point to the use of the featureless desert stage as a setting for purposeful activity. While the white tribe travel out of the desert with their hoard of fuel to start a new settlement, Max's undertakes a metaphorical journey out of a human, emotional wilderness even though the desert remains the archetypal milieu.

Max's union with the road and his car is broken when the V8 is destroyed. Prior to this he had refused to help the white tribe break out from the Humungus' siege by driving their tanker, but on his return to their camp he insists on assuming this role. Where earlier he had professed that he had everything he needed in his car ("everything but a future", Pappagallo observes), he now accepts gladiatorial battle with his nemesis, Wez. His motives for doing so are unclear, since again he defends a society he cannot join, and notably the members of the white tribe who join him on the suicide mission are those mimicking his skills (the Warrior Woman) and connections to machinery (the crippled mechanic). The final battle takes place on the same straight road through the unbroken, flat landscape which formed the first film's abiding image. In resuming violent, heroic activity Max justifies the mythic appellation (used as the film's title in America) of "the Road Warrior", applied to him by the narrator. The *tabula rasa* of the desert forms the backcloth to the performance of skilful, lethal road combat, but it is not a neutral setting since its vacuity echoes the nihilism of the destruction and Max's solipsistic existence. The final revelation that the tanker was filled with sand, not petrol, underlines the ambiguity of Max's commitment. Perhaps he has been abused by the society he saves, or perhaps he acknowledges that this is the only way he could save it. Arguably he would have acted as he did irrespective of the potential benefits or glory, since he has been defined by driving, combat and the road since his first appearance. The truck's reversal of its course, to travel in the opposite direction down the same straight road serves two purposes. It re-emphasises the repetition and inescapability of Max's role, inextricably linked to the road, and precipitates another climactic head-on crash, with the vehicle driven by the Humungus. Identical collisions feature in the climactic car combat of the third film in the series, when the mutated truck-locomotive smashes an opponent to pieces, and Max engages

Mad Max 2

in a final game of chicken with Ironbar. The hyperbole and repetition of these death-blows is again interpretable in a specific national context:

*"In **Mad Max**'s climax Max kills the leader of the motorcycle gang who has been responsible for the death of his wife, child and friends. The generic convention leads us to infer that Max will extract ultimate retribution by his own hands. But he does so not by his own hands, gun or car. Instead he forces the bikie into a head-on collision with a truck... The truck appears out of nowhere. There is hardly a truck in the rest of the film. Is it too outlandish to suggest that this disruption of the film's carefully contrived diegetic world works for its Australian audiences because it captures all too well the motorists' routine nightmare of their own death? It is a death which comes from not paying enough attention to the road and is delivered by that most impersonal of agencies, a semi-trailer."*[12]

The re-appearance of the truck as final arbiter of conflict in the trilogy and the annihilating conclusion enacted in the head-on collision hold great symbolic significance. The ubiquitous hazard of the enlarged semi-trailer in rural areas, coupled with its inconceivable invisibility on straight roads, transforms the truck into a potent, culturally specific *deus-ex-machina*. Judgement is handed to the anonymous machine in the first film, then subsequently appropriated by the hero who drives into head-on collisions wearing the invulnerable armour of his driving skill and nerve. The ambiguity of Max's heroic status is traced across his moral descent, associated with the outlaw V8, to his redemption, enacted through the scourging righteousness of the truck.

## THE CRIMINAL PICARESQUE
In the 1990s the Australian road movie has diversified. Films have appeared with an

apparently closer allegiance to the forms and themes of more conventional American road movies, in concentrating on youth and romance with criminality as the impetus behind the cross-country journey. **Kiss Or Kill** (Bill Bennett, 1997) and **Heaven's Burning** (Craig Lahiff, 1997) share certain features (the pursuit of couples across the rural landscape, the multiplication of pursuit by police and other groups seeking retribution), but combine the commercial stress on youthful couples with Gothic and contemporary elements.

In **Kiss Or Kill** a young couple, Alan and Nicole, head across the desert from Adelaide to Perth to evade the police. They are pursued by detectives because of a series of robberies they have committed in the city, but also have in their possession a video tape incriminating an ageing football star. The couple's route is revealed by a trail of unexplained murders, which may have been committed by Nicole (as she is prone to sleep-walking) or by Alan (as they need more money to complete their escape). Both the police and the football star pursue them. The journey seems to incriminate the couple further, and the deaths of all they meet *en route* heightens their suspicion of each other. Rather than being a flight from justice, their trip becomes an attempt to overcome their personal traumas and paranoia.

The film uses jump-cuts continually to exaggerate the speed of travel and events. The constant excision of detail and interruption of the diegetic flow disadvantages the viewer, and articulates the partial knowledge the characters have of each other. This conspicuous editing technique fuels the couple's suspicions and dynamises their fateful progress. Subjective narration, which offers Nicole's thoughts at the film's beginning and end but relays Alan's uncertainty as to her actions in between, is served by this departure from seamless narrative practice. The characters' departure from the familiar urban environment also adds to the sense of dislocation. Reaching an outback town, one of the following cops reflects "It's not the end of the world, but you can see it from here". As in **Mad Max** and other Gothic representations of rural Australia, the uncanny landscape appears inscrutable or threatening. Stan the motel owner tells the couple that though the land is "flat as a pizza" on top, beneath it is riddled with unfathomable caves. This unknown quality reflects the characters' limited knowledge of each other, and in contrast to expectation neither the trip nor its conclusion offer any enlightenment. While the detectives manage to solve the riddle of the bodies, Alan and Nicole remain ignorant of the truth. In a parody of personal revelation on the road, the junior cop tells his superior of his private life. The account of his adoption as a child, his family's Jewish roots, and his child's illness is florid, melodramatic, and entirely untrue. Even when they are delivered to their remote destination and a future guiltless existence, Nicole's final voice-over assures us that she will never reveal the defining trauma of her childhood to Alan.

In **Heaven's Burning**, a doomed romance between victims of circumstance develops as a Japanese woman and an Australian man go on the run. She fakes her own kidnapping to escape from her husband, but is taken hostage during a bungled bank robbery. The getaway driver intervenes and shoots the other gang members when they threaten to kill her. Subsequently the couple's romantic attachment grows as they are pursued by the police, the surviving gang members and the humiliated husband. While neither the driver, Colin, nor the errant wife, Midori, intend harm, their engagement in and disengagement from marriage, criminal activity and passion are always attended by violence – in shootings, deaths, car chases and crashes. The use of violent scenes as punctuation to the travel and romance serves to meet popular expectations for a road movie audience, and to underline the fated nature of their relationship. The line of the road carrying them to their destiny is echoed by the lifeline on Midori's hand, which a palmist informs her foretells the death of a loved one. The bandage she ties over her palm in an attempt to avert this fate precedes the bandages applied to Colin. His hands are nailed to a table by the vengeful gang members but he frees himself when Midori is threatened.

Colin's crucifixion and Midori's nationality foreground the film's contradictory attitudes to race within modern, multicultural Australia. The father of the Afghan bank robbers is characterised as brutal and sadistic, yet he declares that his sons are softened by life in Australia. When leaving an interview with the gang family, Inspector Bishop remarks that with the mosque and the "yodelling" of the muessin down the street "we may as well be in fucking Arabia". Midori's husband Yukio, bent on killing her for dishonouring him, also conforms to an unpalatable racial stereotype. A truck driver accuses Colin of the "mongrelisation" of Australia when he learns of his relationship with Midori. Before he is killed, Colin's father curses Yukio with the "bad karma" resulting from Japan's record in the Pacific War. By contrast, the love between Colin and Midori, and her belief in the freedom and opportunity that life in Australia could offer her suggest a positive outlook upon trans-Pacific relations and an endorsement of multi-cultural society. The wounding of Colin and his defence of Midori suggest an updating and modification of **A Town Like Alice**[13]. Such a rewriting of a national text might be completed if the couple were allowed to reach freedom, but their massed pursuers and the fate inscribed on Midori's hand are inescapable. The unattainability of paradise, irrespective of the distance travelled, which is suggested by the film's title, is confirmed by its ending in a car crash at the coast. Ironically in a country of such scale, the hunted couple run out of road, and time.

## TRAVEL TO THE HEARTLAND

The protagonists of **Kiss Or Kill** and **Heaven's Burning** share a rootlessness engendered by their lack of stable family backgrounds. Alan is disowned by his rich father, and Nicole is orphaned at an early age. The members of Colin's family exist for years without contact, and Midori leaves her husband only to be abandoned by her lover in Japan. The prerequisites of isolation and difference defining road movie protagonists also apply to "Spider" (Brad), a young ambulance driver and Rose Doherty, a sick widow in **Spider And Rose** (Bill Bennett, 1994). A year after her husband's death in a car crash, Rose leaves hospital to travel to her son's farm in rural New South Wales to celebrate her seventieth birthday. On his last day before quitting, Spider is given the unenviable job of delivering Rose to her new home. The antagonism between them arises from generational difference, exacerbated by his disengagement from his job and responsibility and her bitter loneliness. Predictably the journey softens both characters and produces reversals of fortune. They discover an unexpected similarity between their experiences of squats during contemporary unemployment and the "lean-tos" used as houses during the Depression. When a crash leaves Spider with a broken leg, she lends him her walking stick while she drives a "borrowed" tractor. *En route* Rose compares notes on bereavement with a man of her own age, who offers her a different journey and life with him. She turns him down, but on arrival at the farm she discovers that this is not to be her final destination. Avoiding her family's plan to put her in an old people's home, she heads out onto the road again, leaving Spider to find his own way back to Sydney.

Although the characters represent an unusual pairing, the narrative of **Spider And Rose** marks it as a quite conventional road movie. Both characters undergo significant change. Before he leaves, Spider's boss tells him to "take a drive and think about what you're pissing away". Spider's decision to resign is not attributable to his hedonism or lack of commitment, but on the price dedication to the ambulance service has cost him in the past. Rose's determination and her handling of her own family throw Spider's upbringing and present problems into perspective. Despite the age gap the film does not sentimentalise either character or demonise the unsympathetic family, and instead provides a final image of fleeting, vulnerable but worthwhile liberation on the road. Reaching the family precipitates the recognition of personal identity and aspiration, even if it does not represent the attainment of a home.

A road film which foregrounds the experience of the older generation is **Over The Hill** (George T. Miller, 1992). Despite being a commercially-oriented production aimed at overseas markets (with the casting of the American Olympia Dukakis and British Derek Fowldes), Miller's film explores the lifestyle of the "grey nomads" – retirement-age travellers who live on and off the roads of Australia as "middle-class gypsies". Alma Harris, a widowed American woman refuses to move in with her son's family and leaves to visit her daughter in Sydney. She arrives unannounced in the middle of her son-in-law's election campaign. Rebuffed, she buys a reconditioned American car from her granddaughter's boyfriend and heads out into the country. There she meets travellers on both sides of the law, and begins a hesitant relationship with Dutchly, a divorced, retired dentist. Her subsequent experiences circling the desert ("looping the loop" rather than taking the shortest route across the centre), meeting Aboriginal women and testing her own and the car's full potential enlighten her as to the problems in her relationship with her family. The desert again exists as an important landscape, but not threatening as in previous examples. Rather the setting is constructed as a viable alternative: like **Mad Max** the human actions within it, rather than the location itself, are given intrinsic meaning through their relationship to communities and individuals inside and outside it. Like Rose, Alma eventually insists on her freedom, refusing to be restricted within her offspring's homes and returning to the road with her new partner. The last images of their two vehicles heading into the distance emphasises the positive and transcendent treatment given to the road and the landscape in Miller's film.

Stephan Elliott's **The Adventures Of Priscilla, Queen Of The Desert** (1994) [see also Chapter 12] represents one of the most positive adaptations of the road movie format to Australia. The story of two drag queens and a transsexual travelling from Sydney to Alice Springs to put on a cabaret show encompasses elements of the musical, the Western and the Australian Gothic alongside its road movie basis. Along the way the unconventional trio encounter bigotry and prejudice in outback towns. The trip is developmental for all three principal characters: Bernadette comes to terms with her bereavement, Adam is encouraged to examine his confrontational nature and Tick is forced to admit his marriage and parenthood. While Bernadette begins a relationship with Bob (played by Bill Hunter), Tick evaluates his relationship with his son. The film's characters, their trek across the desert landscape and their goal at the centre of Australia reflect its capacity to debate issues of nationality, sexuality and masculinity. Aspects of the Hollywood Western, in the theme of individual endeavour symbolising nation-building during travel to the western frontier, are also quoted and parodied. Their destination, the geographical and metaphorical heart of Australia, suggests that the film's problematic but positive reconciliation of male and female, gay and straight, transsexual and bisexual characteristics is emblematic of a necessary journey to be undertaken in contemporary society. In depicting characters which contradict national stereotypes of masculinity (in the artists themselves but also particularly in Bob's attraction to them), the film challenges pervasive images of landscape and manhood which the Australian cinema has previously helped to propagate. In moving from the popular urban environment to the mythologised interior, the drag troupe's odyssey implies the possibility, even necessity of personal and communal travel towards an objective of tolerance:

*"The 'suburban surreal' of **Priscilla** screams that things are happening, that the 'tyranny of distance' is easily obliterated by three drag queens on a bus, and that people of every imaginable ethnic and sexual mix can look equally silly to one another."*[14]

## CONCLUSION

The road movie in Australia has performed several roles, in line with the varying emphases that have been placed on production since the revival of the film industry. The potential commercialism of the road movie genre has been down-played because of the appropriation of some of its tropes by the Gothic films, the tendency towards social commentary and the generic hybridity which have marked Australian film since 1970. The twin goals of cultural representation and commercial viability have been served by Australian adaptations and revisions of the road movie: social criticism in the realist mode of **The FJ Holden** or **Backroads** is continued in a lighter vein by **Priscilla**, while the Gothic or melodramatic intensities of **Mad Max** or **Heaven's Burning** retain a pertinent national and cultural specificity despite an obvious popular intent. Racial, sexual and generational conflict within contemporary society are all addressed through the road movie format, as they are to varying degrees within other indigenous and imported genres in recent Australian film. The road and the journey in Australian films are not uniformly positive, restorative or transformative, and recognition of this aids appreciation of a down-beat, inconclusive tone to the majority of Australian film narratives, irrespective of their genre. The difficulty or even impossibility of humanity making a lasting impression on the indomitable and near-limitless landscape is an abiding theme of revival films. The futility of action or movement finds its partner in the victimisation of protagonists in the Australian cinema, for whom control over events or circumstances is lost or never gained. In such examples the road symbolises a postponement of the task of addressing problematic issues, but offers no chance of evading them conclusively. Conversely, the blank landscape and the straight road can represent an unmarked page on which human activity can be impressed. This individualistic and humanistic stance, perhaps reflective of the vestiges of pioneer settlement, is well attuned to the character-defining action of **Max**, the enlightenment of **Over The Hill**, and the transformative journey of **Priscilla**.

# NOTES

1. Susan Dermody and Elizabeth Jacka, *The Screening Of Australia Vol.I: Anatomy Of A Film Industry*; Sydney, Currency, 1987, p.35.

2. Ron Eyerman and Orvar Lofgren, "Romancing The Road: Road Movies And Images Of Mobility" in *Theory, Culture And Society vol.12 #1* (1995), 53–79, (p.60).

3. Brian McFarlane, *Australian Cinema 1970–1985*; London: Secker and Warburg, 1987), pp.152–3.

4. Susan Dermody and Elizabeth Jacka, *The Screening Of Australia Vol.II: Anatomy Of A National Cinema*; Sydney, Currency, 1988, p.122.

5. Op.cit., pp.115–6.

6. Dermody and Jacka (1987), pp.144–5.

7. Graeme Turner, *National Fictions: Literature, Film And The Construction Of Australian Narrative*; London: Allen and Unwin, 1986, p.30.

8. Dermody and Jacka (1988), pp.95–6.

9. David Stratton, *The Last New Wave: The Australian Film Revival*; London, Angus and Robertson, 1980, p.64.

10. Most notably **Stone** (Sandy Harbutt, 1974), Australia's best-known biker movie prior to **Mad Max**, although Miller's desert vistas and Gibson's loner also vividly evoke **Electra Glide In Blue** (1973), James William Guercio's expansive motorcycle cop movie.

11. Scott Murray, "Australian Cinema in the 1970s and 1980s", in Scott Murray (ed.), *Australian Cinema*; St Leonards: Allen and Unwin, 1994, p.95.

12. Tom O'Regan, *Australian National Cinema*; London: Routledge, 1996, p.105.

13. Jack Lee's 1956 film **A Town Like Alice** is the saga of women prisoners of the Japanese in Malaysia.

14. Adrian Martin, "More Than Muriel", *Sight And Sound* vol.5 #6 (1995), 30–32, (p.32).

# IN GOD'S OWN COUNTRY: OPEN SPACES AND THE NEW ZEALAND ROAD MOVIE

## Ian Conrich

A New Wave of New Zealand cinema commenced in 1977 and the production of more than eighty per cent of this national film industry has been concentrated into the last quarter of cinema's first century. One genre that has been associated with recent New Zealand film is the road movie, and this can be approached though questions of cultural characterisation. The New Zealand road movie foregrounds geographical representations of the country while presenting an examination of male endurance, lawlessness, and the importance of the motor vehicle. Within the scope of this article initial thoughts on these characteristics will be established in relation to films such as **Goodbye Pork Pie** (1980), **Race For The Yankee Zephyr** (1981), **Battletruck** (1982), **Carry Me Back** (1982), and **Shaker Run** (1986).

### LANDSCAPE

A prevalent view of New Zealand is that it is a country of abundant nature, capable of providing both tranquillity and shelter; a land on the edge of the world that appears to serve as a distant and ideal refuge. Offering isolated, untouched and uninhabited spaces of natural beauty New Zealand has been referred to as "God's Own Country" or "Godzone" – a reference to the pastoral values with which it has been associated. The glorious landscape has dominated many of New Zealand's films and location shooting has become standard filmmaking practice; in fact it was not until 1993, with **Desperate Remedies**, that a New Zealand film was produced entirely within a studio. The French filmmaker Gaston Méliès, who produced shorts for the American market as early as 1912, was the first director to exploit the lush New Zealand landscape for dramatic purposes, establishing the setting for a common narrative of this early cinema – the love story. Foreign filmmakers have continued to exploit the local geography, and Ringo Lam's **Aces Go Places IV** (1986) is a good example of the "chase movie" employing a variety of locations for action sequences.

New Zealand offers vast open spaces, seemingly endless roads, rich sunlight, different climates and a diversity of landscapes – wet Wellington; warm resorts such as Napier; the glacial Southern Alps and the snow covered mountains of Queenstown; and the agricultural steppes of the Canterbury Plains. The importance of the New Zealand landscape for presenting a variety of location possibilities was demonstrated by the 1988 American film **The Rescue** where New Zealand functioned as a substitute for North Korea; more recently New Zealand has served as the location for Peter Jackson's fantasy of Middle-Earth in his **Lord Of The Rings** trilogy.

### EXPLOITATION

It was in the early 1980s that foreign-supported productions were most dominant in New Zealand. Overseas film companies exploited a tax loophole but, furthermore, New Zealand's natural resources were mined and used as inexpensive movie backdrops. One example is the off-road movie **Race For The Yankee Zephyr** (1981), an Australian-New Zealand co-production which stars, amongst others, Donald Pleasance and George Peppard. Chased by a group of international criminals intent on locating a recently unearthed cargo of Second World War treasure, a trio of "locals" (which includes an old buffoon called Barney, played by Pleasance) traverse the rugged and often inaccessible New Zealand terrain. The three "locals" are thrown together and, despite their differences, manage to bond through adversity. Filmed around Queenstown, the locations are largely mountainous, or set upon or on the edge of vast lakes. The opening shot of the film establishes the difficulties of journeying over the land as a helicopter flies closely along the contours of a hilly range, whilst attempting to track at speed an escaping deer. When the three locals are, themselves, hunted and their helicopter crashes, they retreat to an isolated cabin where, overnight, a land-buggy is constructed utilising available parts, in a style that would have impressed television's The A-Team. From the surrounding country, men arrive to work throughout the night and build a vehicle with caterpillar tracks that is best described as a cross between a helicopter and a tractor – "she goes like a flippin' Ferrari", chuckles Pleasance. Displaying typical Kiwi ingenuity, an off-road vehicle is created that allows the chase to continue over a part of the New Zealand landscape that is, often, devoid of roads.

Post-**Mad Max**, many independent film companies produced their own low-budget, but inferior, imitations of a particular neo-apocalyptic road warrior vision [see Chapter 19, note 2]. New Zealand's own contribution was the Harley Cokliss-directed **Battletruck** (1982) – "It was the most evil machine the world had seen... but somehow it had to be stopped!", declared the advertising for the British video release of the film. Made the year after **Mad Max 2** (1981), the similarities between the two films are all too apparent. **Battletruck** is set in 1994, after the oil wars, and presents a lone motorbike-riding "cowboy" who aims to defeat a dictator and a community of future barbarians, who are in control of an armour-plated juggernaut that thunders along a barren landscape. Filmed on location around Central Otago on New Zealand's South Island, the producers of **Battletruck** attempted to fashion a Kiwi **Mad Max** by exploiting the local "wasteland". In *Mapping The Godzone*, William J. Schafer wrote of his experiences of driving through country just south of where **Battletruck** was filmed – "for twenty minutes... [you] do not see a car in any direction. You experience a sudden solipsistic foreboding, a Twilight Zone premonitory twinge: Where are all the people? Where is everybody? No wonder **On The Beach** was set in the Antipodes – a ready-made postapocalyptic vacuum".[1]

## IDENTITY

Both **Race For The Yankee Zephyr** and **Battletruck** are New Zealand films, yet they offer little for a discussion of national cinema or cultural identity. The first New Zealand road movie was the John O'Shea-directed **Runaway** (1964), an art-house styled film inspired by the modernism of filmmakers such as Michelangelo Antonioni; unfortunately, it lacked popular success. **Goodbye Pork Pie**, made seventeen years later, had a greater impact and is regarded as the prototype New Zealand road movie. This Kiwi car-caper stole the interest of a local population that had, generally, found it a curious experience hearing and seeing themselves reflected on screen. On its release, in 1981, **Goodbye Pork Pie** was watched by an estimated one sixth of the New Zealand population and media coverage included a shot of then Prime Minister Robert Muldoon wearing a promotional tie-in baseball cap. National press quoted Robert Muldoon as saying that the film "used the country well for a back-drop", whilst Mrs Muldoon said that she "was also caught up in the action and the scenery"[2]. **Goodbye Pork Pie** was the first New Zealand film to receive a nationwide release in the United Kingdom and its promotion included a competition in the monthly magazine *Film*

*Review*, which offered the prize of a British Leyland Mini, a replica of the bright yellow car driven in the film. Competition questions included "How do cars travel from the North Island to the South Island in New Zealand?" and "When the Mini gets to Wellington it experiences that city's usual weather feature. What is it?".[3]

The film is essentially concerned with the journey of two men – John and Gerry, who call themselves the Blondini Gang – driving from Northland, at the top of the North Island, to Invercargill at the bottom of the South Island, to reunite John with his girlfriend. Their journey is anything but a direct route and despite their journey's urgency they are drawn to visit a number of different destinations. The complete tourists, as they travel they collect souvenirs, little flags from the places that they have visited, which are attached to the car aerial. Later, it is these, their symbols of freedom and movement that they are most reluctant to sell when offering parts of their car – the grill, bonnet, bumper – to finance further stages of their journey.

Romantic notions of freedom are encouraged by a land that almost seems to demand exploration. But there are other issues to consider for the fascination of the Pakeha (non-Maori) population with perpetual journeying. It could be argued that the Pakeha have experienced difficulties in establishing a sense of place and identity in New Zealand and that they have become "tourists" overawed by a vast primordial New Zealand landscape. There is also the idea that the perpetual journeying is a movement away rather than a movement towards. As a character in **Goodbye Pork Pie** declares, it is "perhaps better to travel when you've nowhere to be".

## HEGEMONY AND RESISTANCE

New Zealand's straight roads provide, for the individual, an easy escape from the restrictions and confines of repressive authority and the many tightly structured communities. The country has been very much bound by committees, local boards and, at times, rigid moral values. As Lyndsey Head writes, New Zealand "silenced freedom with law and we became (in H.G. Wells's definition) a Community of Obedience, rather than a Community of Will".[4] New Zealand has been described as a series of "village" communities where everyone knows everyone else's business and good neighbours still exist. These communities enforce conformity, suffocating expressions of individualism.

In contrast, the car provides mobility, the potential for adventure and the chance to break for the open spaces, where regulation is absent. It also facilitates the defiance of authority and the police are the hegemonic force that is most often resisted. As Monte Holcroft writes "[i]t was easier and safer to jeer at authority from a moving vehicle".[5] One popular image of the New Zealand police is that they are incompetent and ineffectual, and they have been continually ridiculed in New Zealand films to the point, in the late 1980s, when the police force felt the need to withdraw their technical and official support from all commercial movie productions.

The New Zealand road movie contains many instances of anti-authoritarian behaviour and a repeated mocking of the police. In **Goodbye Pork Pie** they are shown to be incapable of thwarting the Blondini Gang's car journey. Eluding the authorities on the North Island the Blondinis arrive, by ferry, on the South Island, where the local police have been alerted to the need to stop a yellow Mini. One of the first South Island policeman that we are shown is presented as sexually impotent, and he can only be aroused by his wife whilst pretending to apprehend her for a traffic offence. But as they are fumbling in his police car the yellow Mini speeds past. The policeman frantically starts his car and gives chase, only to quickly lose control and drive into a lake when his seatbelt becomes caught in the steering wheel and his undone trousers become trapped around his ankles.

A similar mocking of the New Zealand police occurs in **Carry Me Back**, a comedy concerning two brothers attempting to secretly transport their dead father's body from the North to the South Island, so they can claim that he actually died on his farm, thereby allowing them to receive their inheritance. At one point the brothers are close to catching the ferry that will take them between the North and South Islands but they are stopped by a policeman for committing an illegal U-turn. Whilst one brother distracts the policeman, another jumps from their truck and steals the police car keys; the brothers then drive off leaving the policeman stranded. In their sociological study of the New Zealand male, Jane and James Ritchie comment that the "image of the outsider battling authority and, at least for a time, winning, connects powerfully with New Zealand attitudes to authority and the fragile controls that curb male aggression".[6]

## CARS AND MASCULINITY

The road movie is a strong example of the male popular cinema in New Zealand which is the product of an industry traditionally dominated by men. Concerned most with reflecting the aspects of a male Kiwi culture the road movie has presented a series of road exploits – car chases, crashes and out-driving the police – which are viewed in New Zealand as tests of masculinity and acts of "heroism". As Tom Brooking wrote in his article "Wheels", his autobiographical view of New Zealand masculinity: "Paul and I were the only guys in our class not to have a serious road accident in our first year of driving. Among the others, rolling a car was a badge of courage, a kind of initiation into male puerility".[7]

The monotony of the open and endless roads in New Zealand encourages tests of endurance and speed. The lack of activities and distractions offered by many small towns, and the level of boredom experienced, in particular, by young males has led to the emergence of the New Zealand *hoon*. A Kiwi version of what British people would loosely call "boy racers", one interpretation of hooning is that it is aimless and crazy driving, and often occurs whilst under the influence of alcohol.[8] Tom Brooking distinctly remembers similar experiences on a Saturday night when he and his friends would pile into the ancient car, anticipating a long and exciting "spin". "We headed north out of town and on to a long straight, where I wound the vehicle up to its maximum speed of 60 m.p.h. As the needle touched 60 the ancient steed began to shake, rattle and veer about. The 'speed wobbles' signalled the end of the speed test and was greeted with shrieks of delight. Then we dropped back to the comfort of 55 m.p.h. Next we killed time by trying to run down possums."[9]

An unfortunate consequence of this, in New Zealand, is the many accidents and road deaths. New Zealanders Jane and James Ritchie write that "[o]ur driving standards and annual road toll are a national disgrace. The death rate here (3.56 per 10,000 registered vehicles) is higher than in any similar country".[10]

Road movies such as **Goodbye Pork Pie** and the political thriller **Shaker Run** glorify such dangers and give prominence to the performance of many wild stunts. One of the more startling images in the New Zealand road movie occurs at the end of **Shaker Run**. For much of the film an ex-racing driver, turned stunt car showman, is chased by government agents keen to retrieve a container carrying a lethal virus. The roads in New Zealand may appear endless, but as an island the country does, ultimately, present an enclosed road space. With all possible roads having disappeared, the protagonists seem cornered; the only route is straight over the coastal cliffs. This is the ultimate drive to freedom but, unlike **Thelma And Louise** [see Chapter 11], this journey is not terminated and the car is hooked, at the last moment, to a helicopter and flown away from the mainland to safety, leaving the chasing villains, without the aid of flight, to crash to the rocks below. **Shaker Run**, like other New Zealand road films, is both a celebration and an extension of folk heroism and depicts a culture for which car driving appears central.

# NOTES

1. William J. Schafer, *Mapping The Godzone: A Primer On New Zealand Literature And Culture*; University of Hawaii Press, 1998, p.5.

2. *The Dominion*, 17 March 1981.

3. *Film Review*, November 1981, vol.31 #11.

4. Lyndsey Head, "Culture On The Fault Line", in (ed.) Michael King, *Pakeha: The Quest For Identity In New Zealand*; Auckland: Penguin, 1991, p.31.

5. M.H. Holcroft, *The Village Transformed: Aspects Of Change In New Zealand 1900–1990*; Wellington: Victoria University Press, 1990, p.39.

6. Jane and James Ritchie, *Violence In New Zealand*; Wellington: Huia Publishers, 1993, p.94.

7. Tom Brooking, "Wheels", in (ed.) Michael King, *One Of The Boys? Changing Views Of Masculinity In New Zealand*; Wellington: Heinemann, 1988, pp.167–8.

8. See, for instance, Lee Davis, "Gore Blimey", in *Metro*, no.219, September 1999, pp.88–94.

9. Brooking, op.cit., p.170.

10. Ritchie, op.cit., p.93.

## Chapter 8

# Horror On The Highway

# ROAD KILL: HORROR ON THE HIGHWAY

## Jim Morton

On September 9th, 1978, 15 year-old Mary Vincent was hitchhiking from Berkeley to Los Angeles. She was picked up by Larry Singleton, a 51 year-old merchant marine with a face like the final stages of Dorian Gray's portrait. He seemed friendly enough at first, but eventually it became apparent that he was not going to take her where she wanted to go. By then it was too late. Singleton tied Mary up, raped and sodomized her, and – for added measure – hacked off both her arms with an axe. She was later found staggering out of California's desolate Del Puerto canyon area, holding up both arm stumps "so the muscles and blood wouldn't fall out".

Singleton got fourteen years for his actions, but got out after eight years with time off for good behaviour. He was later sentenced to death for killing a prostitute in Florida.

This may sound like the plotline from some mooted "Last House On The Left Part IV", but it's a true story. Proof positive that there is little a horror film can throw at you that reality can't match. Mary Vincent's story also vividly demonstrates the primary lesson of all highway horror movies. Once you turn over the course of your life to the chaos of the road, horrible things can happen. M. Scott Peck and Robert Frost may tout the advantages of taking the road less travelled, but deep in the human psyche there is an uncomfortable suspicion that the weed-strewn path remains untrodden for good reasons.

Road films are often metaphors for the "road of life". The classic scenario goes something like this: a troubled man (or woman, or duo) hits the road in search of himself. Along the way he meets interesting people who show him the light. The man grows up, come to terms with what's bothering him, gets over a loss, or whatever else he needs to do to bring the plot to its logical conclusion. This is the model for everything from **Sullivan's Travels** (Preston Sturges, 1943) to **Five Easy Pieces** (Bob Rafelson, 1970).

Horror road films are really no different, but the stakes are much, much higher. You make a wrong decision, you die; usually in some most unpleasant fashion.

In many highway horror films, hitchhiking serves as the catalyst for all the bad things that happen. A young man or woman is either picked up hitchhiking by a psychopath, or picks up a hitchhiker who turns out to be lethal. In road movies, picking up hitchhikers is almost always a bad idea (see for example Tobe Hooper's **Texas Chainsaw Massacre**, 1973), and *being* a hitchhiker is even worse.

In **Devil Thumbs A Ride** (1947), directed by Felix E. Feist, Lawrence Tierney plays Steve Morgan, a homicidal bank robber, on the run from the law. Ted North plays Steve Ferguson, a standard movie nice guy who gives Morgan a ride. Later on down the road, two women join them on their journey. Like other films that Feist wrote and directed (**The Golden Gloves Story** [1950], **Donovan's Brain** [1953]), the pacing is careful and unhurried (which is pretty amazing considering this movie's run time is only 63 minutes), and things are tied up in an exciting conclusion. Much of the credit for the effectiveness of this film must go to Lawrence Tierney (who would go on to appear in **Reservoir Dogs**), who exudes menace from every pore.

Another classic of the form is **Detour** (1946), by Edgar G. Ulmer [see also Chapter 2]. Tom Neal plays Al Roberts, a young musician with a loser's mentality. While hitchhiking across America to meet his girlfriend in California, he is picked up by a man who up and dies on him. Not sure what to do, Roberts takes the man's car and money and hides the body. Down the road, he picks up Vera, played by Ann Savage in her very best role. Vera knows that Roberts is not who he says he is, and uses this to blackmail him. Predictably, nothing but bad things ensue. **Detour** is considered by some to be the greatest B-movie ever made (that's B-movie in the literal sense of the term – a second feature intended as the lower half of a double bill).

In 1953, director Ida Lupino made **The Hitch-Hiker**. As with **Devil Thumbs A Ride**, the danger comes from a homicidal hitchhiker. Two buddies on a fishing trip (played by Edmund O'Brien and Frank Lovejoy) pick up a hitchhiker (William Talman), who turns out to be a psychopath. It's a story that has been filmed dozens of times, but Lupino gives it a nice noir feel. Unfortunately, 1953 was the year that America decided that it didn't want to be noir any more. Films like **The Hitch-Hiker** and Billy Wilder's **Ace In The Hole** (aka **The Big Carnival**, 1951) were rejected by the movie-going public in favour of Technicolor musicals and Cineramic religious spectacles. McCarthy's red-baiting had the country reeling with a paranoid chauvinism that made any attempt at thoughtful filmmaking seem like a subversive act.

To anyone born after 1970, the idea of using hitchhiking as a plot point may seem contrived. To better understand these films it is important to look at hitchhiking in America in the context of the times. During the 1930s and right up until the end of the Second World War, owning an automobile was something of a luxury. All major cities (and most smaller ones) had good mass transit systems to get people around. During Franklin Delano Roosevelt's administration – and again during the Eisenhower administration – millions of dollars were poured into improving America's interstate roadways. Migrant workers and soldiers returning to their bases took advantage of these highways, and it was not unusual for a woman with three kids in the car to give a soldier a lift.

During the sixties the image of hitchhiking was seriously tarnished. Hundreds of hopelessly naive teens headed out on the highways in search of Jack Kerouac's America (although Kerouac himself almost never hitchhiked; he preferred to hop freight trains). A lot of these kids found trouble. Likewise, good Samaritans who picked up hitchhikers occasionally found themselves looking down the wrong end of the barrel of a gun. In truth, these incidents were not that common, but every one of them was reported, giving hitchhiking an aura of death and danger; perfect breeding grounds for exploitation and horror films (The best example of this – although it is not a road movie – is still **Last House On The Left** [Wes Craven, 1972]).

By the nineties, hitchhiking was too contrived to use realistically. Director Dominic Sena, and writer Stephen Levy solved this problem in **Kalifornia** (1993) [see Chapter 10]. Here, the psycho is not hitchhiking; he and his girlfriend are partners in a shared drive-away. Hipsters, Carrie Laughlin and Brian Kessler (Michelle Forbes and David Duchovny) need two other people to help them drive a car from New York to California. They end up sharing the ride with white trash horror, Early Grayce (Brad Pitt in his best role), and his equally lowbrow girlfriend (Juliette Lewis). Duchovny's character is writing a book on serial killers and Brad Pitt is – guess what? On its release, **Kalifornia** pissed a lot of hipsters off. While it has become too cool to gush over the lives of famous killers, **Kalifornia** reminds us that reading about psychopaths and sharing a car with them is not the same thing. You'd like to have known Jeffrey Dahmer? Yeah, right.

Horror works best on the open road in the form of a pursuit. In **Road Games** (1981) [see also Chapter 7], Stacy Keach plays a trucker who, while transporting frozen

Road Games

meat across Australia, becomes involved in a game of cat-and-mouse with a psychopath. **Road Games** was directed by Richard Franklin, who went on to make **Psycho II** right after this. It was written by Everett De Roche, who also wrote **Long Weekend** (Colin Eggleston, 1979), a great example of subtle Aussie horror that few people have seen. Like **Road Games**, much of the action takes place on the quiet highways of the Australian outback, but in this film the bad guys are less obvious.

The purest use of pursuit as a horror film tactic is **The Hitcher** (1986), directed by Robert Harmon, and written by Eric Red. Young Jim Halsey (C. Thomas Howell) picks up an enigmatic stranger named John Ryder (Rutger Hauer) who turns out to be a psychopath of preternatural proportions. **The Hitcher** starts you running with the opening scene and never lets up after that. Wisely, Eric Red's screenplay doesn't bother with explanations or rationalizations. At one point during the film, the young man asks: "Why are you doing this?" To which the killer replies "You're a bright boy. You figure it out."

**The Hitcher** seemed ripe for a sequel, but there has not been one, really. Umberto Lenzi's **Paura Nel Buio (Fear In The Dark aka Hitcher In The Dark)**, received some distribution as **The Hitcher 2**, but any relationship to the original was purely coincidental. In this film, a young pervert kidnaps women to rape and torture. Director Umberto Lenzi is best known for **Cannibal Ferox** (aka **Make Them Die Slowly**), one of the most infamous Italian cannibal films of the early eighties. Likewise, C. Thomas Howell's **Hourglass** – a film he starred in, wrote, and directed – was retitled **The Hitcher '95** to take advantage of his success in the Robert Harmon/Eric Red film, but any similarity was... well, non-existent.

It is left unspoken as to whether John Ryder in **The Hitcher** is genuinely not of this world, but there's no such ambiguity in Jack Starrett's **Race With The Devil** (1975). Peter Fonda, Warren Oates, Loretta Swit, and Lara Parker play two Winnebago-

The Hitcher

riding middle-class couples who inadvertently witness a satanic ritual execution and spend the rest of the movie trying to escape from Satan's minions. Most notable are the early scenes of a night-time Black Mass and human sacrifice (seen through binoculars), and the final (frozen) image of a trailer consumed by a ring of infernal fire as the Satanists close in for the kill. Director Starrett, who got his start as a biker film actor/director, has a flair for chase scenes, but not for human relationships. It's no wonder that he later showed up as a regular director for the enjoyably idiotic *Dukes Of Hazzard* TV series.

The Devil showed up again in the form of a customized Lincoln in **The Car** (Elliot Silverstein, 1977). This is not really a road movie, since all the action takes place in one town, but it bears mentioning in connection with the film that spawned it – **Duel** (Steven Spielberg, 1971). In this famous movie, made by Spielberg for TV, Dennis Weaver plays David Mann, a man on his way to visit relatives one weekend when a truck driver, seemingly angry at being passed, starts playing chicken with Weaver. As the movie progresses, the identity of the trucker (whose face is never shown) becomes less important, as the big rig takes on supernatural qualities. The battle is between the man and the big rig, not its driver.

If one wants to split hairs, **Race With The Devil** and **Duel** aren't really road movies. They are car chase films. At the end of **Duel**, Mr. Mann is none the wiser for what has happened to him. He has learned nothing from his battle. If there are deeper reasons for the events that occur, the audience is left in the dark as to what they might be. In both of these films, the chase is the thing. Any introspection is incidental.

The Devil is not the only creature cruising the American highways. In **Near Dark** (Kathryn Bigelow, 1987) [see Chapter 9], the evil comes in the form of vampires. Although they are often nomadic, vampires rarely end up in road films. They tend to

Duel

find a town or city to feed on and stay there until they are staked, or sun-baked. This all changed with **Near Dark**, the story of a travelling tribe of vampires. **Near Dark** was written by Eric Red, the author of **The Hitcher**. Like **The Hitcher**, **Near Dark** is a true road movie. The geography keeps changing and the protagonist grows wiser by the end of the film.

In 1998, John Carpenter's **Vampires** (aka **John Carpenter's Vampires**) [see Chapter 9] took bloodsuckers out on the road again. Like many of his films, **Vampires** is equal parts cool as hell and stupid as shit. James Woods plays the leader of a band of vampire hunters hired by the Catholic church to roam the American southwest in search of vampires. After a particularly nasty encounter with a fanged, Trent Reznor look-alike, Wood loses most of his team and takes out after this bloodsucking goth-rocker. In spite of some great ideas and striking images, John Carpenter's **Vampires** falls flat. As with many of Carpenter's films, the misogyny and obsessive homophobia displayed here suggest that J.C. could use a couple weeks of wild abandon in San Francisco's Castro district.

Some mention is deserved here of **Psycho** (Alfred Hitchcock, 1960). Not because it is a road movie, but because it leads us to think that it is going to be. We start watching the movie and quickly decide that what we are watching is the story of Marion Crane, a secretary who has just embezzled thousands of dollars from her boss. Suddenly, what started as a fairly compelling thief-on-the-lam kind of road movie, stops moving and becomes a different film entirely. Because of its age and familiarity, it is hard for modern audiences to gauge the effect this sudden shift of style had on the average moviegoer at the time. **Psycho** fooled audiences into thinking they were going to see the story of a woman travelling across country alone and on the run from the police. The sudden shift in focus and in genre was simply against the rules. People left the theatres trembling. Gus Van Sant's misguided scene-for-scene remake didn't even try to surprise us. He also missed the heart of the Hitchcock film, which is about the effects of sexual repression (a favourite topic of Hitch's), not the dangers of pornography, as Van Sant would have us believe.

Years later, Robert and Steven-Charles Jaffe, and Kevin Connor took the **Psycho** model and added equal parts **Texas Chain Saw Massacre** and *Green Acres* (the TV show than ran from 1965–1971). The result was a silly film called **Motel Hell** (Connor, 1980). Rory Calhoun, in his finest performance (really!), plays Farmer Vincent, the owner of a roadside motel that also sells the best homemade sausages around. Farmer Vincent is proud of his secret recipe, which includes humans plucked from the side of the road. Every few nights, Vincent goes out and causes an accident then takes the victims and plants them in his secret garden before pulling them up and butchering them. No logical reason is given for planting people. Logic – or even common sense – was obviously of no importance to the Jaffes when they wrote the script.

It sounds like fun, but it is this lack of logic that eventually scuttles the movie. The comedic elements work slightly better than the horror, making the movie mildly amusing, but not inspired. I'm sure that this jokey approach to horror seemed like a good idea at the time, but audiences weren't buying it. **Motel Hell** did so-so at the box office. Jaffe and Conner needed to do more market research. Horror movie fans don't need jokes to laugh at gore and ghoulishness; they'll laugh at things that appal most people (I've been to screenings where the audiences have laughed at brutal rape scenes). Meanwhile, the rest of the movie-going public found the humour/horror combination unsavoury.

A better use of the concept of the roadside murder factory was in Peter Weir's 1975 film **The Cars That Ate Paris** [see also Chapter 7]. As with **Motel Hell**, the locals intentionally cause accidents, but that's where the similarities end. This time it's an entire town that is responsible for the mayhem. They sell the car parts and human organs, eventually establishing an economy based solely on automotive catastrophes.

In George Sluizer's **The Vanishing** (**Spoorloos**, 1988), all the protagonist needed to do was pull into a service station. While Rex goes inside for a soda, his girlfriend, Saskia seemingly vanishes into thin air. For Rex, finding out what happened to her becomes an obsession. Eventually he meets a man named Raymond Lemorne, who, he is sure, is responsible for Saskia's disappearance. In the character of Lemorne, George Sluizer has created one of the creepiest human monsters this side of Hannibal Lecter. Five years later, Sluizer remade **The Vanishing** (1993) in Hollywood. You might think that because the same director made it that it might actually turn out okay, but this isn't the case. The Hollywood version is about as bad as it could be. To add insult to injury, the story is changed to give it a happy ending.

**Motel Hell**, **The Cars That Ate Paris**, and **The Vanishing** all represent a variation on the road movie concept that is its own sub-genre; pit-stop horror, perhaps. Films like **Mother's Day** (Charles Kaufman, 1981), **Texas Chain Saw Massacre**, and **From Dusk To Dawn** (Robert Rodriguez, 1996) [see Chapter 9] start as potential road movies, but once the protagonists stop for the night at that Old Dark House, all bets are off. One reason for this is the inevitable fact that horror movies (good horror movies, at least) are more about what's going on inside a person's head, than what's going on outside.

The road proves to be an ideal stomping ground for the most extreme of killers, both in movies and real life. Mass murderers such as Charles Starkweather and Ted Bundy probably would not have gotten as far as they did if not for their peripatetic ways. This idea has been explored extensively in recent years with films such

In Cold Blood

as **Henry, Portrait Of A Serial Killer** (John McNaughton, 1990) and **The Doom Generation** (Gregg Araki, 1995).

Perhaps the two best examples of the killers on the road are **In Cold Blood** (1967) and **Badlands** (1974) [see Chapter 10]. Directed by Richard Brooks, **In Cold Blood** is based on Truman Capote's novelized account of two drifters named Dick Hitchcock and Perry Smith, who murdered a family in Kansas. This film is very much a road movie, as we follow the duo from Las Vegas to Kansas, and then to the gallows. We get to know the two, and eventually start to empathize with Perry Smith. In **Badlands,** no explanation for Charlie's killing spree is ever given. The story suggests that he doesn't understand it any more than we do. Terrence Malick seems to be telling us that the killings just happen. Don't look for a reason because there isn't one.

The most exaggerated expression of the killer-on-the-road came in 1995, with Oliver Stone's **Natural Born Killers** [see Chapter 10]. As in **Badlands,** we follow a young couple in love as they cut a swath of death across the countryside. Unlike **Badlands** (or **In Cold Blood,** for that matter) we never care what happens to these people. **Natural Born Killers** could have been an interesting exploration of the way modern culture, by its very nature, feeds into the glorification of the most heinous criminals, but Oliver Stone is too heavy-handed to deliver anything more than the most obvious observations. Like too many critics and senators, Stone seems to think that the fault for this lies entirely within the realm of media control, although Stone seems proud of it. He coats the story with a layer of camera tricks that are intended to dazzle us, but merely end up irritating our retinas. **Natural Born Killers** is so excessively flashy and hammily acted that I can't help but wonder if Stone was going for a cinematic pun by submitting the story of homicidal maniacs to stylistic overkill.

Stone went back on the road with **U-Turn** (1997), but this time the story dead

Bring Me The Head Of Alfredo Garcia

ends in Superior, Arizona, a dusty desert town filled with knuckleheaded eccentrics. Again, Stone keeps things over the top, although considerably less absurd than **Natural Born Killers**.

It took Matthew Bright to realize that one of the first killer-on-the-road stories ever written was *Little Red Riding Hood*. Bright took the story, updated it and called it **Freeway** (1996). In its original form, **Freeway** was a shockingly graphic and deadpan funny. Unfortunately in its final release, much of the nastiness was taken out of the violence, making it more palatable and less bold, but more commercially viable. Once again, hitchhiking is used as a catalyst for all the bad things that happen, but – unlike the films of the sixties – hitchhiking is not a frivolous act here. Young Vanessa Lutz (played to perfection by Reese Witherspoon) uses it to escape her abusive family environment and the threat of foster care.

Occasionally, filmmakers explore the dangers of the road as a place that lets our own madness spring forth. Sam Peckinpah's **Bring Me The Head Of Alfredo Garcia** (1974) is an ultimate example of this. Warren Oates plays Bennie, a down-and-out piano player in Mexico who stumbles into a rich landowner's bounty plan for vengeance against the man who deflowered and impregnated his daughter. When Bennie finds out where the body of Alfredo Garcia lies, he decides to take the corpse's head and claim the bounty for himself.

As he travels across Mexico, the reality of his mission begins to erode his sanity. Bennie's mental deterioration is made manifest in the decaying, fly-covered head he carries across the Mexican countryside. Ingrained with the blackest graveyard imagery, the film ends, inevitably, in a welter of escalating violence as Bennie blows away the landowner and is then himself annihilated in a firestorm of machine-gun bullets as he attempts to reverse his tracks along the infernal highway. Drubbed by the critics at the time of its release, **Bring Me The Head Of Alfredo Garcia** is only just starting to gain critical acceptance for its unique look into the effects of moral compromises on the human psyche.

Despite our increasing recourse to internet "travel" [see Chapter 19], the roads will always remain, facilitating the spread of mobile killers and nurturing highway psychosis. And for as long as cinema continues to mirror life, the screen will brim with human road kill.

## Chapter 9

# Vampire
# Road Movies

# ASPHALT VEINS:
# ON AND OFF THE ROAD
# WITH THE VAMPIRE

## Omayra Cruz & Ray Guins

*"People can drive infinitely and 'freely' without being*
*at all confined yet while still being perfectly controlled"*
—Gilles Deleuze, "Having An Idea In Cinema"[1]

What the vampire film brings to the road is an old story. Ancient Greece, Assyria and Babylon had their vampires, as did Imperial Rome and Druidic Ireland. Asia, Africa and Europe furnished vampires of their own, often of striking resemblance – for as Silver and Ursini note in *The Vampire Film*, "vampires and vampire-like phenomena are prevalent in almost every recorded culture with only minor variations in their subsidiary characteristics."[2] In the Christian West, however, this diversity of narratives came to reside in the figure of the Eastern European vampire, or an "undead" human corpse that feeds on human blood.[3] One of the most basic elements, and for our purposes the most important, of this stringently coded creature is that although it lacks a soul, it is immortal. The question, then, is how does the road film, a genre commonly associated with an imagined America and which Michael Atkinson's "Crossing The Frontiers" calls a "deathless movie species", fare when matched with the undead.[4]

This piece focuses on a rather minor assemblage of genres, what we call the "vampire road film", to explore the alternative denotations that the vampire's presence both makes possible and in some cases demands of the road film. Yet even more specialized than the vampire and the road, is the vampire's relationship to the road in the late-twentieth century Southwestern United States. We work from the basic premise that vampires in the Southwest are something of an oddity, and that this oddity merits attention. Why the attention? Because the driving pronouncement of this article is that the amalgamation of the vampire and the road film complicates the function and formation of identities appropriate to histories of the Southwestern filmic landscape within which the following films are set.

Kathryn Bigelow's **Near Dark** (1987), pioneered the vampire western combination. The film's tension derives from the combating affinities that main characters, Mae (Jenny Wright) and love interest Caleb (Adrian Pasdar), experience for his mortal yet wholesome family, as opposed to her somewhat nightmarish extraordinary family of immortal mobile-home vampires. Robert Rodriguez's **From Dusk Till Dawn** 1996), is a collaboration with writer/actor Quentin Tarantino. An even larger amalgam of sources than **Near Dark** – most notably criminals-on-the-lam and intimacy-through-adversity slants as well as a flood of over-the-top fast-talking action-adventure exploitation – **From Dusk Till Dawn**'s truck stop cum blood-sucking strip show also tells the tale of two families. Bank robber brothers Seth (George Clooney) and Richard Gecko (Quentin Tarantino) commandeer the aid of Jacob (Harvey Keitel) and his two children Kate (Juliette Lewis) and Scott (Ernest Liu) to escape the authorities by crossing the border into (an unexpectedly undead) Mexico. John Carpenter's **Vampires** (1998), differs significantly from both **Near Dark** and **From Dusk Till Dawn** in that professional

Vampires

rather than upstart, makeshift protagonists face the vampires. Master slayer Jack Crow (James Woods) pursues master vampire Valek (Thomas Ian Griffith) who is in turn searching for something. Valek aspires to the apex of immortality, which for a vampire is to conquer sunlight. Their chase takes place in the Southwestern desert amidst the loyalties and treacheries of their companions.

To return to Atkinson, "in the road movie we have an ideogram of human desire and the last-ditch search for self."[5] His point echoes much commentary on the road film, for the massive expanse of road imagery burgeons with possibility; and as Steven Cohan and Ina Rae Hark so rightly point out in their introduction to *The Road Movie Book*, the genre accordingly possesses an "obvious potential for romanticizing alienation". The result of this tendency is a brand of film criticism that invokes what they call "sentimental existentialism",[6] narratives of soul-searching, "watch-the-sunrise" freedom. But we are hardly interested in freedom.

According to Sartrian existentialism, the subject's fate is non-identity. To posit *an* identity would be a form of essentialization that displaces the condition of radical freedom which Sartre uses to characterize Being. However, the torrent of cultural studies which began to be produced in the late 1960s tells a very different story.[7] Subjectivity is closed in and fixed from all sides.

The vampire road film expresses this overdetermination of identity as fixed rather than fluid. In other words, through the existential logic that informs so much commentary on the road film,[8] identity is perpetually in flux; we aim to demonstrate that the ways in which the vampire road film depicts socially and culturally recognized constraints – in this case conceptions of mortality, race and masculinity – work to fix identity. Thus the first section of "Asphalt Veins" entitled *Choose Death Or Die* takes into consideration the ways in which a cultural construct – specifically, the human soul – influences the treatment of mortality in the road film. It will be argued that although figuring the vampire into the schema of Southwestern filmic representations of the road as space of mobility and possibility would suggest support for immortality, repeated negations of this postulate dominate the films in question. Yet mortality is but one of many factors that work to fix identity within the road film genre. In the final section, *The Vampire Road Film: Or A "Half-dead Little Whore" In "Another New Mexican Shithole,"* we will turn to others. Consideration of the categories race and masculinity links textual histories of the vampire to the ways in which the road film as seen through its ancestor, the western, manages to fix rather than liberate identity.

## CHOOSE DEATH OR DIE

Of the three films, **From Dusk Till Dawn** and John Carpenter's **Vampires** seem to conform most readily to traditional existential tropes found in narrative conventions of the road film.[9] After all, as the films open: Seth and Richard are on the run from the law; Jack Crow and his band of slayers size up an enemy's hideout, arm themselves in an extremely ritualistic manner, then advance posse-style to meet their opponents. Here the complexity of the films deepens sharply, for theirs are not typical adversaries. One cannot go after them and they do not attack with knives, guns or fists. They bite and claw. To be injured by one of them is to in time become, like them, undead. How does such an adversary affect the genre expectations of the road film?

One such significant expectation is well encapsulated by Shari Roberts. She writes that, "road narratives are constituted by a search for life, the characters running from death which always threatens at either end of the road". A romantic notion, death may here work to give meaning to life, much as "darkness gives definition to light".[10] Her analysis could not be more appropriate – except that the road film, a genre that previously offered only two options, alive or dead, now contends with several. The category of "alive" appears to be divided into three opportunities that hinge on the status of a religious construct: the human soul. As Ornella Volta proposes in *Le Vampire*,

*"By decreeing that only the soul has a right to immortality, a position has been created by which the body has also demanded its rights. By refusing to accept the limitations posed by physical death (and by not having the patience to wait for the Day of Judgment for a resurrection of the body), might not the vampire simply be seeking to demonstrate the possibility of survival for a body without a soul?"*

For the travellers of **Near Dark**, **From Dusk Till Dawn**, and Carpenter's **Vampires**, the *fully human* await physical death in return for the promise of the everlasting life of the soul. The *fully vampire* forfeit the previous in return for immediate, physical immortality. Finally, those in the peculiar *condition of transformation* that exists between the human and the vampire attest to the unease associated with the journey between them. This condition of transformation produces what we will call "mobilized identities", and they are the true battleground upon which the stakes of these options are exploded.

From Dusk Till Dawn allows for the shortest period of transformation. Mobilization from one condition (human) to another (vampire) occurs within a matter of minutes. Once a vampire absolutely no semblance of personality remains and each creature is quickly killed. Even actors who would normally merit some form of character development such as Selma Hayek and Cheech Marin are immediately destroyed because they play vampires. In this film all vampires are entirely

From Dusk Till Dawn

interchangeable. Unlike identifiable – and thus more sympathetic – vampires such as Dracula, these characters are rarely named, much less awarded an identity. In **From Dusk Till Dawn**, the vampires are nothing more than a misshapen mass.

Despite the exceedingly short period of transition allotted for transformation, most main characters who become infected face a choice. For example, Scott begs his sister, Kate, to kill him rather than allow him to transform. Jacob holds up the film's climactic final battle to require an oath from his children, Scott and Kate. They must swear to God that they will not let him live once he transforms into a "lapdog of Satan". What is most significant about this aspect of the film is Jacob's choice. It furnishes a provocative commonality between **From Dusk Till Dawn** and Carpenter's **Vampires**: the existential determination of religious faith. In **From Dusk Till Dawn**, Jacob loses his faith and quits his ministry due to the capriciousness of the road. His wife's death in an auto wreck is a test which his faith does not pass and a past from which he runs. In Jacob's case, the twisted immortality of the vampires enables him to place the accidental death of his wife into a schema of devotion consistent with faith in God. The end of his journey is a choice. To be a "mean mother-fucking Servant of God" is to turn his back on vampirism and the immortality of the body it bequeaths.

One who does not fare so well in a test of faith is Jack Crow's liaison to the Vatican, Cardinal Alba (Maximilian Schell). In *Death: Interpretations*, Harry Slochower reminds us that "the knowledge of death is the most continuous, most persistent and inevitable, perhaps the most fateful trauma for man",[11] and when faced with the impending certainty of physical death, Cardinal Alba chooses the promise of transformation over the certainty of human mortality. The vampires' travel/attack patterns, revealed to Father Adam Guitto (Tim Guinee) by Jack Crow, illuminate the desire for complete immortality that drives both the Cardinal and Valek:

*"See this map? This map shows all the* [vampire] *encounters in the United States as far back as the 1800's Look at the Southwest. See the spiral pattern? If you time sequence*

*all the encounters, you get a logarithmic pattern ever-widening. It's a search pattern, Padre. They're looking for something."*

That which eludes the vampires, that for which they have been searching is the complete cessation of vulnerability. Valek pursues absolute immortality. The very first vampire to exist, born of a botched Medieval Catholic exorcism, Valek has travelled to the Southwestern United States to locate an ancient relic that has for centuries been hidden in Spanish monasteries, the Cross of Berziers. The Cross is a vital element of a special ceremony. This ceremony, a repetition of the primary exorcism which went wrong must be completed to relieve Valek of the final cumber on immortality that he experiences – vulnerability to daylight.

Valek vows to extend to the Cardinal the full immortality that participation in the ceremony, which requires the presence of a priest as well as the blood and burning crucifixion of a Crusader, will make possible. Cardinal Alba explains his decision to betray the Church in favour of vampirism as follows: "As one grows old, as death approaches, we begin to question our faith. And I found mine lacking." His justifications for, so to speak, striking a bargain with the Devil are that he has had no visions and witnessed no miracles. The Cardinal's decision is, of course, obstructed. Righteous young Father Guitto puts an end to the ceremony which would complete Valek's transformation with a bullet through the chest of Cardinal Alba. More central characters who experience the condition of transformation, or journey, peculiar to vampirism are Katrina (Sheryl Lee) and Montoya (Daniel Baldwin). However, given that for them vampirism involves conspicuously gender-coded phenomena, their situations will be treated in the final section of this article.

This brings us to Caleb and Mae, for whom both vampirism and the journey which leads to it are reversible procedures. Since this reversibility is fairly exceptional in the vampire genre, and of the three films it comes closest to giving a day-in-the-life of vampires, **Near Dark** poses the greatest possibility of ascertaining how its travelling protagonists are affected by and change the existential treatment of mortality associated with the road film genre. It may be posited that the road film makes existential discovery possible because it is a celebrated instrument for bringing about change in the life and outlook of its characters. In short, one learns something about oneself because through the experience of living one becomes different, or perhaps such knowledge itself *makes* one different. Well, that is, of course, if you are alive and if change is possible for you. Change is not possible for these vampires. They may be in a different place, but they are still vampires. Their basic pattern of experience – constant travel to maintain a steady supply of human nourishment – remains unchanged. To begin to think or behave differently, is to cease being a vampire.

A striking aspect of the film is that at no time is the word "vampire" spoken despite numerous codes signalling their presence such as the drinking of blood, aversion to sunlight, superhuman strength and senses. As Needeya Islam writes, the "namelessness of the group, and the absence of iconic and Gothic elements usually required of vampire narratives (castles, bats, silver bullets, crosses, garlic) indicate that it is only specific actions and movements which define them as a group of vampires".[12] She traces this "distillation" of vampirism to its most basic level to the opening image of the film. An extreme close-up of a mosquito feeding on human flesh insinuates what is to come. The vampire can no more stray from its consuming lust for the blood that sustains it than the mosquito. Feed or die, survival is identity.

After initiating Caleb into her vampiric family, Mae counsels him in the final step toward membership. He must make his first kill. However, Caleb falters. He expresses reservations about himself as a viable killer. Mae strongly reassures him that to do so is nothing more than to rely on instinct. Instinct does not change. Yet Caleb never makes that first kill. He resists that practice of vampirism and in so doing is able,

Near Dark

with the help of some patriarchal blood, to extricate himself and later Mae from its influence.

Part of Mae's instinct argument stems from the particularity of her experience. She is immortal. When Caleb half-stupidly asks the standard "You aren't from around here, are you?", followed by "I've never met a girl like you before", the stargazing Mae responds with the details of just how different she is. "Wanna know why you've never met a girl like me before? because I'll still be here when the light from that star gets down here to Earth, in a billion years." Mae considers *her most defining quality* the span of her existence: she survives. What are the results of such an unusual existence? Borrowing from Søren Kierkegaard, the first existentialist, eternity is true repetition.[13] However, the profoundly religious Kierkegaard accounts only for an immortal soul. For the immortal bodies of **Near Dark**, his claim translates differently.

Rely on instinct. Survive. To do so, the vampire cannot stray from the recurrent features of its existence: to travel, feed, and hide.[14] In this way the vampire constantly moves, while staying the same. This defiance to inertia is, however, an impossible position. Bigelow's film indicates that the only option other than the repetition of eternity is death. In some cases, death is immediate. Witness the final station wagon ride into the sun of the film's "vampire parents" Jesse (Lance Henriksen) and Diamondback (Jenette Goldstein). Other deaths are protracted, a reality on the horizon which by choosing to be mortal allow Caleb and Mae to wake quite sweetly into a transfusion chamber turned sunlit garage.

In this respect, the spectre of death so familiar to the road film is upset. The vampire and the road film, two historically violent genres, merge to provide an alternative within which the immortality of vampirism represents an embodiment of the endless American road. But the vampires and those to whom they extend the possibility of transformation in **Near Dark, From Dusk Till Dawn,** and Carpenter's **Vampires** invariably meet opposition. Roads end.

Though it seemed that the vampire road film opened up three options where once there were but two, a different actuality is expressed. The relationship of the vampire to the road indicates that the road may be understood as a lesson in the imminence of mortality rather than the space of transformation of mobilized identities or the eternal movement of immortality. Contrary to expectations, the road requires the cessation of mobility. Identity, even in the simple form of mortality, cannot run fluid. The road so requires the mortality of the "human" that it makes a violently exploitative show of crushing the vampire's immortality and even the tendency/desire for it embodied by those characters who exist in a condition of transformation. Nothing is permanently mobile. The vampire road film bespeaks travel as a condition of transformation that must without exception end. One must always stop. Next stop, the Southwest.

## THE VAMPIRE ROAD FILM: OR A "HALF-DEAD LITTLE WHORE" IN "ANOTHER NEW MEXICAN SHITHOLE"

In "Roads To Freedom", Dargis writes that with **Thelma And Louise**, "the American landscape has ceased to be the exclusive province of white masculinity".[15] Perhaps so, but the battle for the Southwest has long been on its way and is raging if you're a vampire! Why the Southwest? Let us refrain from jumping to a ready answer such as, a good western – even a vampire western – would seem outlandish in an eerie European castle, or lovely Northwestern forest, to pose a few pragmatic questions. Don't deserts promise more rather than less daylight? More rather than less risk of disclosure? Far easier is it to be inconspicuous in a large city than in a small town where everyone is sure to know everyone else, and more importantly, realize when someone mysteriously disappears. This is not to imply that any of the vampires in **Vampires, From Dusk Till Dawn,** or **Near Dark** are actually displaced city-dwellers, but that the association of such creatures with the road system of the Southwest is neither accidental nor insignificant.

Roads officiate this semiotic diaspora. The term semiotic diaspora is required since what is under examination is not a demographic shift (these are after all films), but a variation of imagery. The figure of the vampire is displaced to different positions for a number of reasons and with distinct effects. Certainly worth a mention is that the characters in **Near Dark, From Dusk Till Dawn,** and John Carpenter's **Vampires** do not travel the major freeways and interstates. Instead they rely on less-travelled roads, the web of state and service roads which were the country's primary means of transportation prior to the construction of interstate superhighways in the late 1950s. As Schaber writes, "the minor road links more than it leads, connects, assembles and exposes more than it issues, unifies, and reveals".[16]

Via these minor roads, the vampires in question are connected to the urban face of United States culture. That these roads are minor does not detract from their impact for the many incarnations of the road figure enormously in the national as well as international image of the United States. As Shari Roberts writes, "The mere mention or image of the road has commonly come to symbolize a conceptualization of America".[17] This fabricated America is woven of a belief in freedom, search for identity, desperation and danger, all conveniently expressed by handguns, Levi's, Harley-Davidsons, and banged-up muscle cars. Paradoxically, these roads, the domain of human motorists, are now beset by vampires. The vampirism along America's major arteries is an aspect of its composition from which it cannot disassociate itself.

Yet to return to Dargis' claim, vampires are far from alone on the road. Men were there first. This section addresses the ways in which complementary forms of fixing identity, namely the codes of race and masculinity, interact in the vampire road film to buttress the shutting down of mobilized identities which began as a discussion of mortality. Granted the treatment of both race and masculinity in the vampire road film could easily furnish sufficient material for articles unto themselves. However, close inspection of the films as well as the genres from which they draw indicates that the strictures of race and masculinity experienced on and off the road work most powerfully together.

Moreover, the vigour of the road film genre derives from the many transfusions it has received. One might even consider it an exceptionally promiscuous genre. Fluid pairings with the buddy film, as well as the action-adventure, western and horror genres abound. This is certainly the case with **Near Dark, From Dusk Till Dawn,** and Carpenter's **Vampires**. Most significant of these pairings to a discussion of race and masculinity through the figure of the vampire, is that of the road to the western, for as Roberts contends,

*"The road movie's linear structure and the metaphorical road's connotations of individualism, aggression, independence, and control, combine the Western's ideal conceptions of the American and the masculine. Masculine superiority links itself with racial hierarchies, manifest destiny, and closure through heterosexual romance and marriage."*[18]

This statement is not far from sentiments expressed by the directors themselves. For example, it is common knowledge that John Carpenter, a renowned horror director, is quick to admit that all of his films are Westerns; and during an interview with Ana Maria Bahiana in *Cinema Papers*, Kathryn Bigelow, whose tendency to create violently masculine action films has received considerable attention, states that the vampires in **Near Dark** were a mechanism for acquiring funding in an industry that would not back Westerns.[19] Robert Rodriguez and Quentin Tarantino set out to make a Mexican vampire movie – and they did, but not without an avalanche of support from the Western and road film. The film's first scene marks this union as Seth and Richard's muscle car flees the scene of a hold up at "Benny's World of Liquor" after brutally murdering another Texas Ranger – the epitome of law and order in the Old West.

But vampires? How have they made their way onto the road, much less the Western? To some extent, vampires have always been associated with some form of travel. Bram Stoker's *Dracula*, the most influential of all vampire narratives, begins with a train journey into Eastern Europe. To underscore this point, simply recall the strangeness of Bela Lugosi's "Good Evening" from Universal's 1931 version of **Dracula**. In short, vampires are one of the quintessential foreigners to be vilified and/or romanticized by Western European culture. In its capacity to broach the subject of the foreign, the body of the vampire is the surface upon which discourses of encounter are enacted. Yet Old World Eastern Europe is not the villain that Hollywood has sent its champions out to conquer.

In this article, we are not discussing the particulars of individuals in the films so much as we are extrapolating upon the dynamics cultivated between vampires and slayers – both amateur and professional. Historically, the vampire has been couched in fears of decadence and degeneration, usually in the form of racial infiltration and emasculation.[20] Vampires have provided a means of narrating these fears – at times quite alluringly – without blatant discussions of race or masculinity. This is not to say that such discussions are not possible. They are, and what is more, that the vampire now inhabits the Southwest – the space of real, white "John Wayne" men – commands attention. To reiterate, it is the very presence of images that the vampire road film imparts to the Southwest, a cultural construct itself based on identifiable styles of treating race and masculinity, that comments on the road film's capability to fix identity by relying on it. We will now examine some of the more suggestive images that, although appearing in diverse forms, are pertinent to all three films.

Near Dark

Because all of the major characters in **Near Dark** are white, it may appear an anomaly in a discussion of the junction between race, the road and vampires. Yet as Richard Dyer contends in *White*: "As long as race is something only applied to non-white peoples, as long as white people are not racially seen and named, they/we function as a human norm. Other people are raced, we are just people."[21] Thus the very whiteness of the two families in **Near Dark** provides a position from which to discuss the infusion of race into middle America through the roaming figure of vampirism. Further, according to Dyer, whiteness is at the heart of the vampire myth. Pallor has come to be such a distinctive marker of vampirism that initiates of all skin tones have at some time or another undergone whitening. Recall for instance Udo Kier's ironic *maquillage* in Morrissey/Warhol's **Blood For Dracula** (1973), or the slightly bleached bone structure of Prince Mumuwalde in **Blacula** (1972). Victims of vampires also whiten. As the blood which gives them life and colour is drained, they take on the cadaverous paleness of their undead attackers. Though for Dyer the "horror of vampirism" is expressed in colour, namely "ghastly white", the prospect of such an experience of whiteness is so unsettling, "so menacing that it is often ascribed to those who are not mainstream whites – Jews, South East Europeans (Transylvania in *Dracula* and its derivatives), the denizens of New Orleans (Annè Rice's *Vampire Chronicles*)."[22] I would add "poor" to Dyer's list of, as he terms them, the "liminally white".

Transient and uncouth, the vampires of Bigelow's **Near Dark** are liminally white. They are the mobile home poverty of whiteness. In her article on the films of Kathryn Bigelow, Needeya Islam writes that in **Near Dark**, "the aristocratic figure of the vampire in classic texts has given way to an image of the disenfranchised and homeless; a stark contrast to Nosferatu in his castle".[23] We would, however, contest this statement on several counts. The vampires of **Near Dark** are neither disenfranchised nor homeless. Their numerous stolen vehicles furnish motorized abodes. The automobile's exterior is a temporary protective shell against the inevitable: daylight.

The rough life that they lead is one that the film takes great pains to show they enjoy. Recall the game of slaughter which takes place in the bar-room or the poignancy of references to "good times" shared on the road. The claim for homelessness seems difficult to support given that with the exception of newcomer Caleb, none of the vampires seem to miss "normal" lives. Thus more so than aristocracy, the vampires of Mae's family reject premier middle-class, middle America whiteness. Mae herself only chooses Caleb's life after she is unable to assimilate him to the pleasures of her immortality. Mae and her crew favour gambling, roughhousing, and living day to day over the stability of such as Caleb's glass-of-milk-with-dinner, hard-working farm life. After all, is it not the excitement of the vampire's lifestyle that really lures Caleb to try on another, more dangerous white?

This very white which Caleb obviously finds so appealing also acts as the occasion by which he is able to reassert the masculinity that vampirism has stolen from him. Recall that Mae explains that infecting Caleb was *"sort of* an accident" (italics added). The phrase could just as easily be used to describe a broken condom or premature ejaculation. Perhaps even more appropriately, the phrase could refer to what amounts to a reverse rape scene. Despite Mae's fervent pleas to be driven home – sunrise is approaching – Caleb forcibly insists on a kiss. Mae has little choice but to capitulate since a protracted argument would leave her vulnerable to daylight. It is Caleb, however, who gives more than he intended. He stumbles home weak and bleeding. A more protracted effect of Mae's bite is the dependency it creates in Caleb. He must have blood to survive. Yet as he insists, he is no killer. Mae feeds him with her own blood. Aptly enough, the background to this feeding is a gas pump. Perhaps the most important thing Mae does for Caleb is protect him from the rest of the vampires who view his inability to kill as an intolerable weakness.

Granted Caleb lacks the shrewdness of a gratuitous killer, but when the white that has adopted him threatens to defile the integrity of the whiteness he has left behind, he emerges as a viable protector in his own right. The abduction of Sarah, Caleb's younger sister, by "child" vampire Homer is the catalyst of this transformation. As Roberts' "Western Meets Eastwood: Genre And Gender On The Road" shows, "in the transference from the Western to the road film, the frontier becomes the road".[24] In this instance, the frontier to be protected is still white womanhood. It is the whiteness of the invaders that is in question. Vampirism is this dangerous feminizing white, an unspoken white which is dangerous because its efficacy as lure to victims points to the adroitness with which it simulates the "original". Consider the image of Homer pretending to be a hit-and-run victim by a twisted bicycle or the attraction Mae exudes as she innocently licks a vanilla ice cream cone.

Despite the play on a cross-country family outing that the vampires' recreational vehicle-cum-motorized coffin represents, the mobilization of identities that the vampires engender fails to fool "nature". The first place Caleb takes Mae is to visit his horse, marker of the rugged man's tie to the land. Predictably, the horse rejects her as unnatural, foreign and frightening. This introduces a dichotomy between natural and technological means of transportation resurrected during the film's climax. During his very nearly Western stand-off with older brother vampire, Severen (Bill Paxton), Caleb's glistening blacktop ride into town takes place atop horseback. The horse extends a challenge to the vampire's authority over road-frontier and presents a means by which Caleb may remarry the sturdy farm-life of his handsome ruggedness to the masculinity regained in battle against the vampires.

In **From Dusk Till Dawn**, contemporary pop culture in the form of exploitation pastiche as well as Hollywood and fan culture icons – such as Quentin Tarantino, Juliette Lewis, Harvey Keitel, Fred Williamson, Tom Savini, Cheech Marin, and so on – battles an "ancient enemy"[25] just the other side of the U.S. border-crossing. But what stands out about the film is, of course, the location for this battle: the strip club at the

From Dusk Till Dawn

end of the road, the Titty Twister. The last scene of the film draws back from the Titty Twister to reveal the ziggurat upon which it rests and the carcasses of eighteen-wheelers whose drivers the vampires have devoured. In its incessant extension, the road – pulsing vein of America's mercantile empire – meets an uncanny alien, or perhaps jarringly familiar form of consumption – and there it ends.

The archaic vampires of **From Dusk Till Dawn** are linked to the pre-Colombian cultures of what are now Central and South America. A necessary realization is that these vampires are as natural to the environment as Caleb's horse. The temple upon which the Titty Twister stands existed prior to the road's presence. Its vampiric inhabitants lay a claim to the area which supersedes the U.S. imperialism associated with the area surrounding its borders. The open stretch of road associated with the West falls into relief to reveal itself as an imaginary construct used to camouflage what the (ideological) highways allow America to literally drive over. Contrary to the dictates of manifest destiny which tinges the supposed freedom of the road-frontier, the West has never been an *entirely* empty expanse to be consumed by the strong and daring.

Who shares the road with vampires? A ready flow of expendables. Some are permanent features of the road such as truckers, bikers, prostitutes. Others are, like Jacob and his family, temporary. The relationship between temporary and permanent denizens of the road collapses at the end of the road: the Titty Twister. "This bar is for bikers and truckers only" insists the bartender, yet Jacob's family recreational vehicle is ironically what promotes the group to the space of general undesirables at the end of the road: outlaw culture and the undead make room for the family. Does this hint at a form of revenge? Do the repressed return in, as Jean Baudrillard contends, a more lethal form of hospitality? "Welcome to the Titty Twister".

Significant in this respect is the occasion of Jacob's meeting with Seth and Richard. Despite the chiding admonishment of his children that their mobile home makes them "self-contained" – a claim they've doubtless heard from him numerous times – Jacob pulls over into the "Dewdrop Motel". "One night's sleep in an honest to goodness bed" before going into Mexico resonates with the memory of stability that draws Jacob to the motel. No matter how fervent their desire, however, no one is self-contained. The Gecko brothers use Jacob's mobile haven to an inauspicious end. They escape the law to find themselves accosted by a more invasive enemy. The permeability of the borders (geographical, economic, political and cultural) that expansion erects is played out in the bodies of the characters. All are to some extent in a strange state of suspension peculiar to the road. Travel opens a window of opportunity for the vampires of the Titty Twister in that no one may ever learn of a victim's fate. Unlike in **Near Dark**, the vampires of **From Dusk Till Dawn** do not have to travel for survival. Nourishment eagerly drives itself in. The suspension of knowledge associated with travel and Jacob's myth of "self-contained" escape from the demands of both external and internal affairs predicts the diaphanous relationship of **From Dusk Till Dawn**'s protagonists to the vampires.

For example, during a rather lengthy tirade, the character Sex Machine – played by Tom Savini – points out that the vampires of the Titty Twister are not like "normal" vampires. As Sex Machine puts it, "These vamps, these vamps, they have soft bodies. The texture of their skin is soft. You can push right through them. If you hit one hard enough, you take their head right off." Yet the bar patrons, who all appear to be travellers from the States taking advantage of the cheap times, liquor, and – as barker Cheech Marin extols – the diversity of pussy to be had south of the border, are physically invaded by the claws and fangs of the vampires. The borders marking their "first world" masculine bodies are just as permeable as the shoddy "Made in Mexico" vampires. To illustrate the poor quality of the Mexican vampire, sharpened pencils take the place of wooden stakes. What else makes it to the end of the road? Products left from murdered truckers, a constant supply of plastic junk with which the vampires are themselves later defeated.

Although not necessarily on the road themselves – Carpenter's **Vampires** travel by foot, by flight, or as stowaways – they too must contend with the road. After all, slayers track them by road, and perhaps more significantly, defeat them using specialized road vehicles. An armoured truck and jeep are the motorized mechanisms of destruction used to transport the slayers to the vampires, and drag them into the sunlight where they invariably burst into flames. In **Vampires**, slayers require mechanical prostheses to overcome what appear to be poor rural vampires populating the Southwestern wasteland.

Inhabitants of just "another New Mexican shithole", they are the throng of drab creatures with which the slayers, a covert band of vampire bounty hunters funded by the Catholic Church, make sport directly after the posse-style opening sequence. These are, however, somewhat underhanded and silly heroes. Rather than call out a challenge, the slayers nervously break in. While searching the seemingly abandoned farm house, a member of the team is rattled when he comes upon a dried-up corpse. Jack Crow's response is a disgusted "suck it up". Though himself soon trying to quietly advance, Jack stumbles over a bottle that clatters loudly. Regardless, the slayers proceed to, so to speak, clean up. It is a vicious scene punctuated by maniacal thrusts of Jack's stake into the heart of a vampire, and the acquisition of yet another "goon" skull to decorate the hood of Montoya's all-terrain vehicle.

As compared to **Near Dark** and **From Dusk Till Dawn**, these vampires are subject to the most dramatic whitening during transformation into vampires. Even their eyes take on a pale blue. Yet their relationship to whiteness is complicated by the presence of master vampire, Valek, for he is European white. As earlier indicated, Valek designates Jack as the Crusader to be sacrificed during the ceremony. That Jack should be called a Crusader ushers in a weighty set of historical associations. First and

Vampires

foremost, the Crusades were a tangled web of interests. Revenge, hatred, self-righteousness, personal gain and many other motives drove Europeans to the Holy Land. From these conflicts was born the ideological conglomerate called the East. Returning to the task at hand, if as Silver and Ursini profess, the Christian West once displaced its vampires to Eastern Europe, it would seem right then that Valek, Eastern European master vampire, should travel to the Southwest – America's "East".

However, the image of Valek and his seven well-dressed master vampires emerging from the earth of the serene Southwest wilderness at dusk is strikingly unnatural. It flies in the face of Jack's description of vampires to the novice Father Guitto: "Have you ever seen a vampire? Well first of all, they're not romantic, alright. It's not like they're a bunch of fags hopping around in rented formal wear and seducing everybody in sight with cheesy Euro-trash accents, alright." But these vampires *are* in formal wear and exude sexuality. Why?

Of the three films, Carpenter's **Vampires** is the most hostile environment for women. None exist except as prostitutes, vampires, or a combination thereof. In keeping with popular connotations of the genres, the road film-western cements male bonds. The vampire tears them apart. For example, the slayers' first encounter with Valek takes place at the "Sun-God Motel" during a rowdy victory celebration, saloon style: bravado, straight whiskey and whores. Before savagely decimating the revellers, Valek feeds on Katrina who is on route to Jack's hotel room. The scene, nothing short of orgasmic, leaves her stunned and stumbling around the parking lot with blood dripping from the bite wounds in the tender flesh of her inner thigh.

The only slayers to survive Valek's attack are core members Jack and Montoya. As they flee, they come upon Katrina. The vehement misogyny with which they treat her is startling. Forced to walk after driving their truck off the road, the slayers push

Vampires

and prod the weak and bewildered Katrina on the road back to the Sun-God where Jack and Montoya argue over how to proceed. Montoya, who wants to "kill the girl, and bury the team together", is overpowered by Jack's will. Montoya reconciles himself to caring for the girl while Jack cleans up, and settles for an admonishment: "Don't take too long. I get nervous when you're not around."

Much like Scott and Jacob of **From Dusk Till Dawn**, Katrina chooses death over the transformation into, and eternity of, vampirism. Her decision is not respected. Jack has directed Montoya to keep her, and Montoya does. However, by interfering in her attempted suicide, Montoya himself becomes infected. At this point his relationship to both Katrina and Jack changes. **Vampires** features a much-extended condition of transformation. Over the span of days, Katrina and Montoya undergo gradual and painful changes.

Identifying with the changes in Katrina, the very same that he will soon endure, Montoya's once firmly established masculine attitudes and behaviour are superseded by more subtle, protective tendencies. The brutal and invasive treatment that Jack repeatedly administers to Katrina becomes the occasion for a rift separating him from Montoya. For example, when Jack probes Katrina's mouth looking for fangs, much as one would inspect the teeth of an animal, then pushes her away by the face, Montoya rears in anger. Jack's callous "you're not starting to fall for this half-dead little whore" brings on the first blow. Both during and prior to this encounter, Jack grills Montoya as would a slighted lover. Drawing from Laura Kipnis' "Adultery",[26] the cheated insists on knowing the details of the cheater's adulterous activity. "Are you sure there's nothing you want to tell me?" asks Jack.

The special hatred Jack carries for vampires is a childhood legacy. Father Adam Guitto, who bubbles over with excitement upon meeting Jack, condenses it as follows: "I know all about you, Mr. Crow. I know that your parents were bitten by vampires, and you were raised by the Church to be their master slayer." Adam, a timid scholar, joins the team of slayers to replace his murdered predecessor; and in so doing, quickly sheds his reticence to emerge a fervent killer. He is the perfect partner for Jack in that his celibate devotion to God complements Jack's single-minded rapacity for the destruction of vampires. This is hinted at early in the film. Jack prods the much-flustered young priest as follows: "When I was kicking your ass back there, did that give you wood?". This new male closeness comes at a price, for it not without some regret that Jack parts company with Montoya. He goes so far as to put himself in the path of Father Adam's attack on the transforming Montoya. However, Jack's subsequent, "Vaya con Dios" is not spoken until he stresses the unyielding ferocity of his hyper-masculine identity as slayer: "Wherever you go, I will find you. I will hunt you down and I will kill you – the girl too."

To conclude, we return to a point made earlier. The "old story" that vampirism brings to the road is death – forgive us for saying so, but one might call them dead ends. The figure of the vampire, vampirism itself, proves to be a trivial threat to the fluctuation of identity which their immortality and anomalous presence on the Southwest road system would indirectly suggest. After all, makeshift slayers outfitted with holy tapwater-filled condoms and squirt guns as found in **From Dusk Till Dawn** can defeat a swarm of vampires. The two surviving down-trodden professional slayers of Carpenter's **Vampires**, one of whom is himself en route to vampirism, can defeat eight masters. Finally, even provincial Caleb makes out well against his vampire adversaries in **Near Dark**. Significantly, he gets the girl too. Mortality is assured in **Vampires**, **Near Dark** and **From Dusk Till Dawn**. Furthermore, the freedom that one might have imagined to exist on the road, freedom from the oppressive and invasive codes of race and masculinity, is revealed to be nothing but a stylistic pretence. The corpse of the vampire cements the productive strictures of human intimacies born in battle on and off the road.

# NOTES

1. Gilles Deleuze, "Having An Idea In Cinema" in *Deleuze And Guattari: New Mappings In Politics, Philosophy, And Culture*, ed. by Eleanor Kaufman and Kevin Jon Heller; Minnesota: University of Minnesota Press, 1998, pp.14–19 (p.18).

2. Alain Silver and James Ursini, *The Vampire Film: From Nosferatu To Bram Stoker's Dracula*; New York: Limelight Editions, 1993, p.18.

3. There are a great deal more characteristics. For more on these, see Silver and Ursini (1993).

4. Michael Atkinson, "Crossing The Frontiers", *Sight And Sound*, January 1994, p.16.

5. Atkinson, "Crossing The Frontiers", p.14.

6. Steven Cohan and Ina Rae Hark (eds.), *The Road Movie Book*; London: Routledge, 1997, p.1.

7. It may be argued that this shift owes a great deal to the work of such writers as Franz Fanon and Simone DeBeauvoir.

8. For a full discussion of this theme, see Julian Stringer, "Exposing Intimacy In Russ Meyer's **Motorpsycho! And Faster Pussycat! Kill! Kill!**" in Steven Cohan and Ina Rae Hark (eds.), *The Road Movie Book*; London: Routledge, 1997, pp.165–179.

9. For example, Stringer (1997) writes: "The road movie habitually promotes two narrative situations. In the first, one or more goal-oriented protagonists take off as a means to escape either from pursuers (**A Perfect World**, 1993; **True Romance**, 1993) or from a hitherto boring lifestyle (**Five Easy Pieces**, 1970; **Lost In America**, 1985). In the second, one or more protagonists seek to 'find themselves' existentially, either through sex (**Something Wild**, 1986), violence (**Natural Born Killers**, 1994), or by messing with nature (**Easy Rider**, 1969)" (p.165).

10. Shari Roberts, "Western Meets Eastwood: Genre And Gender On The Road" in Steven Cohan and Ina Rae Hark (eds.), *The Road Movie Book*; London: Routledge, 1997, pp.45–69 (p.55).

11. Cited in Silver and Ursini, *The Vampire Film*: Harry Slochower, "Eros And The Trauma Of Death" in *Death: Interpretations*; New York, 1969.

12. Needeya Islam, "'I Wanted To Shoot People' – Genre, Gender And Action In The Films Of Kathryn Bigelow" in Laleen Jayamanne (ed.), *Kiss Me Deadly: Feminism And Cinema For The Moment*; Sydney: Power Publications, 1995, pp.91–125 (pp.104–105).

13. Søren Kierkegaard, *Fear And Trembling/Repetition*, ed. and trans. by Howard V. Hong and Edna H. Hong; Princeton: Princeton University Press, 1983, p.221.

14. The basic repetitiveness of what it means to these creatures to live forever is well illustrated by the extremely violent bar-room brawl/banquet. Upon entering the bar-room, naturally in the style of Old Western outlaws out for trouble, the group embark on what has obviously achieved the status of ritual: Severen and Jesse make the act of feeding a farcical drama to energize the recurrent features of their existence. For example, rather than merely biting into the neck of his victims, Severen dances along the bar until close enough to gash the bartender's throat with his spurs. He later complains, "I hate it when they ain't been shaved". Jesse spices up what he doubtless knows will be more of the same meal by puzzling the waitress with the following request: "Bring me an empty glass." Of course, he fills it with her blood. Could this be a commentary on road travel in general? Is it always more of the same? More highways. More forgettable towns. More – often detestable – road food? Is this why we've developed a whole repertoire of stupid games to play while on the road?

15. Manhola Dargis, "Roads To Freedom", *Sight And Sound*, July 1991, p.17.

16. Bennet Schaber, "'Hitler Can't Keep 'Em That Long': The Road, The People" in Steven Cohan and Ina Rae Hark (eds.), *The Road Movie Book*; London: Routledge, 1997, pp.17–44 (p.38).

17. Roberts, "Western Meets Eastwood", p.52.

18. Roberts, "Western Meets Eastwood", p.61.

19. Ana Maria Bahiana, "Interview With Kathryn Bigelow", *Cinema Papers*, January 1992, p.33.

20. A rich source in this regard are the numerous appendices which appear in the Broadview edition of Bram Stoker's *Dracula*.

21. Richard Dyer, *White*; London: Routledge, 1997, p.1.

22. Dyer, *White*, p.210.

23. Islam, "'I Wanted To Shoot People'", p.104.

24. Roberts, "Western Meets Eastwood", p.66.

25. This is the phrase used to promote the film in the studio's movie trailer.

26. Laura Kipnis, "Adultery", *Critical Inquiry* #24 (1998), pp.547–566.

# Chapter 10
# Killer Couples

# KILLER COUPLES: FROM NEBRASKA TO ROUTE 666

## Jack Sargeant

### GUN CRAZY

In 1958 America was rocked by a true-life murder case that mirrored – even magnified – the text of Joseph H Lewis' classic film noir **Gun Crazy**, shot some nine years earlier [see Chapter 2]. Delinquent garbageman Charles Starkweather shot and killed the parents of Caril Ann Fugate, his 14-year-old girlfriend, and the young couple then eloped in Starkweather's car on a cross-State murder spree.[1] The Starkweather and Fugate story has formed the basis for a series of films, spanning three decades of both mainstream and marginal cinema. This chapter seeks to examine the most clearly analogous films to the Starkweather slaughterhouse road-trip.

Perhaps the first film to be strongly influenced by the Starkweather case was the 1963 B-movie classic **The Sadist** (*aka* **The Profile Of Terror**). Directed by James Landis the film, starring Arch Hall Jr (whose father Arch Hall Sr produced and distributed the movie), focuses on a delinquent couple who "terrorize three smalltown high school teachers whose car has broken down near a deserted garage."[2] Little of the road element survives, however, in this cult B-movie.

Arthur Penn's **Bonnie And Clyde** (1967) was the first notable manifestation of the "Starkweather trope" in mainstream Hollywood cinema, although the eponymous killer couple were in this case much older. Also based on a true crime story, **Bonnie And Clyde** was remarkable for the graphic violence of its climactic shoot-out, setting a trend which Sam Peckinpah soon capitalised on in **The Wild Bunch** two years later. Killers/lovers-on-the-run Bonnie Parker and Clyde Barrow are mercilessly machine-gunned to death in their car, terminating an adventure in migrant crime in which the female partner is often seen to be stronger than the male, who we infer may be impotent – in contrast to the Starkweather case, where Charles ostensibly dominated his jailbait paramour.

Also worth of interest here is Richard Brooks' **In Cold Blood** (1967), in which a pair of drifters murder a rural family and then take to the road in flight, prefiguring the same-sex fugitives of **Thelma And Louise** [see Chapter 11]. Based on Truman Capote's story, **In Cold Blood** offers a homoerotic spin on the traditional killer couple.

In 1986 underground film director Richard Kern produced the sleaziest of all Starkweather-type movies. Entitled **Fingered**, the film, something of a *noir* 8mm epic, follows a violent greaseball and his girlfriend, who works as a phone sex employee, as they hit the road. The couple talk dirty, fuck, and drive around California, until they come across a young panic-stricken hitch-hiker, who has been raped. They soon attack her themselves in an act of remorseless violence.[3] This nihilistic punk attitude was developed further by Gregg Araki in **The Doom Generation** (1995). Araki's movie is a lurid high-velocity killer couple gut-punch, revelling in sex, violence and black humour.

**Murder In The Heartland**, 1993, directed by Robert Markowitz, is a true crime TV movie which traces the Charles Starkweather and Caril Ann Fugate story, although hardly classifiable as a part of this potential sub-genre with its emphasis on fact and news-reel style reportage the film is noteworthy for its – general – accuracy (despite

Bonnie And Clyde

a brief foray into sexual violence). The film suggests the hypothesis put forward by Caril's defence that she was an unwilling accomplice, and tried to leave signs describing her predicament and asking for help (including a note which asked for help, originally designed to be left in a diner bathroom, but instead found on Caril's person by the arresting officer). **Murder In The Heartland** also devotes considerable time to the trials, especially Fugate's, and raises many questions regarding Starkweather's contradictory statements concerning her involvement with the crimes. **Murder In The Heartland** fails, however, with the casting of ageing Tim Roth as the eighteen-year-old Charles Starkweather (this is all the more surprising given that Fairuza Balk, who plays Caril, is exceptionally well cast).

The Sadist

## BADLANDS

The films this chapter examines are constructed across more than twenty years of film production, and comprise, primarily, a sub-genre of the road movie, but also bear the important distinction of being influenced by Starkweather and Fugate's nihilistic and murderous distortion of the on-the-road teenage romance.

The inaugural gesture, or at least the most clearly apparent articulation, of this sub-genre is in Terrence Malick's **Badlands**[4]. The film – despite its textual protestations to being a work of fiction – is an almost exact recreation of Starkweather and Fugate's relationship, although it is not without its differences. Nevertheless it is to this film that other works within the sub-genre refer; it is **Badlands** – rather than Starkweather's actual story – which serves as the general point of intertextuality throughout this sub-genre (although each film has many other points of intertextuality which are culturally and temporally specific to that text and its particular audience). As **Badlands** maintains such a central position in this sub-genre it is worth examining in some depth before moving on to other texts within the cannon.

**Badlands** depicts the relationship between the twenty-five-year-old Kit Crothers (Martin Sheen) and the fifteen-year-old androgen Holly (Sissy Spacek); the film is narrated by Holly who describes her family background and her move from Texas to the small town of Fort Dupret, South Dakota, with her father, following the death of her mother. The film opens with Holly's narration and simultaneously we see the garbage truck and garbage men, Kit and Cato; Kit is sorting through the trash when he comes across a dead dog, meanwhile Holly's flat – almost naively lifeless – narration intones: "Little did I realize that what began in the alleys and backstreets of this small town would end in the Badlands of Montana". Kit and Holly meet one afternoon while she plays in the street and he walks home from his garbage route, and the two begin talking. While the two become friends Holly immediately articulates her father's displeasure at the idea of her dating a garbage man, but confesses her own desire: "He was handsomer than anyone I'd ever met, he looked just like James Dean". Shortly after this Kit loses his job as a garbage man and becomes a cowboy, all the while Holly's narration describes the growth of their friendship.

Unfortunately Holly's father finds out about their relationship, and forbids the two from seeing each other. Kit goes to speak to Holly's father. Holly, says Kit, "means an awful lot to me". Holly's father is unimpressed by Kit's declarations of love for his daughter, and Kit leaves. Kit later enters Holly's house and packs her bags for her, as he completes the task Holly's father walks in, and demands to know what is happening; Kit produces a gun, Holly's father threatens to tell the authorities and Kit shoots him in the stomach. Holly is obviously upset and thinks they should tell the authorities, to which the coolly nihilistic Kit replies "if you wanna tell the police that's fine, but it wouldn't be so hot for me". Holly, who until the end of the narrative lets others make her decisions (her narration states at one stage that she has no personality), decides against telling the authorities, and Kit goes into town to make a record stating that he and Holly are going to kill themselves. He then dowses the house in petrol and sets it on fire, while a record player positioned in the garden plays the suicide note/record. Holly picks up her school books and her narration states "My destiny now lay with Kit".

Kit and Holly (who are now, according to the narration, suitably renamed – presumably after their chosen idols – James [Dean] and Priscilla [Presley]) initially hide out in the woods, building a Tarzan-style tree house above a small clearing, which Kit fills with suitably Vietnam-style booby traps. They are soon discovered and Kit – hiding in a branch-covered pit – ambushes the three law men presumably sent to investigate, killing them all. The two lovers then hit the road, first stopping off at Cato's lonely house. Here they eat a meal before walking out into the surrounding fields, while Kit and Holly walk ahead Cato turns and flees, heading towards his small house. Kit raises his gun and shoots Cato in the back. They take Cato back to his house, where he slowly bleeds to death. Soon afterwards two teenagers drive up to visit Cato, and when they refuse to offer a lift to Kit and Holly, Kit takes them out to an abandoned cellar, locks them in the cramped space and fires a volley of shots through the trap door, presumably killing the young couple. Holly's voice over: "Kit was the most trigger-happy person I'd ever met".

Kit and Holly drive to a wealthy area of town, where they knock on the door of a large house, which is opened by a deaf maid. Kit and Holly hold the maid and her male employer hostage. While at the house a friend-cum-business associate calls (a brief cameo by Malick), but Kit sends him away warning that everybody has flu. Kit and Holly then lock up the maid and the rich man; as they do this Kit hands the rich man a list of everything that they have "borrowed" from the house. The two lovers then leave and hit the road, driving out across the great plains, following the telephone lines heading towards the distant quasi-mythological mountains of Montana. Eventually – low on fuel – they stop by an oil derrick, but before they can re-fuel a helicopter spots them. To Kit's dismay Holly elects to stay behind, essentially surrendering to the forces of law and order. Kit is pursued across the badlands by a passing police car; Kit engages in a high speed chase before eventually stopping his car, building a small stack of stones as a memorial to where he was caught, and – as the pursuing police car screeches to a halt – surrendering. Finally – awaiting to be returned home to face his trial – Kit stands chained, amiably talking to the police and National Guardsmen and obviously enjoying playing the role of the murderous celebrity. Through the narration we learn that Kit dies in the electric chair, while Holly

Badlands

gets off on parole and eventually marries her lawyer's son.

**Badlands** presents Kit and Holly fleeing the "real" world and immersing themselves in the fantasy of their own world. Everything in their life has a bland boredom to it, as if they are children who are perpetually dissatisfied but lack even the energy to articulate this frustration. Their one attempt at sex presented in the film ends in a blank orgasmless non-climax, followed by a brief conversation (no verbal communication they have in the film appears to go beyond the most superficial exchange of rudimentary information). The murders themselves (other than Holly's very brief show of emotion at her father's death) are greeted with a similar lack of emotion, Kit "just" shoots people and Holly watches, appearing as an emotionless child-waif in contrast to Kit's almost silent nihilism. Kit's nihilism, is however, a lifeless deadening nihilism which marks Kit as its victim rather than its avatar, and ultimately Kit is seduced by the mimesis of nihilistic cool rather than the vertiginous thrill of actual nihilism.

The world which Kit and Holly invent for themselves is a simulation of domestic bliss, this becomes most apparent in the sequence set in the woods, during which the film presents them living as an almost archetypal married couple; the only thing which separates them from the real world being Kit's crimes and the intensity of the emotional void in which they live. What is seen of the relationship between the protagonists – primarily Holly – and the real world is underlined with a spectacular violence. Kit is obviously an outcast, even among his work mates at the garbage department and, later, the ranch, and he is often presented as distanced from other people. More importantly, however, is the depiction of Holly's relationship with her father, a familial relationship which is characterized by an extremity of violence and abuse; thus for example, when Holly begins dating Kit and her father finds out he

Badlands

takes her puppy into a field and shoots it as a punishment.

    **Badlands** is hauntingly scored – to great effect – with music by Carl Orff, which creates an almost hypnagogic effect. The repetition of the piano refrain also emphasizes the naive, child-like quality of the protagonists (the tune is one commonly used for teaching piano to infants). This effect is further emphasized via the deadpan, listless, narration which, for the most part, describes the day to day mundanity of the relationship, rather than Holly's actual emotions or relationship with Kit. During one key sequence, while the lovers are staying at the mansion, Holly goes out for a short walk around its grounds and, in a rarely incisive moment, describes her feeling of exclusion from the world, and as being like an outsider looking in at the "normal world". The journey she has taken with Kit is thus marked as more than purely physical but also as psychic, a journey which has taken them from the realm of the social into their own special world. The dream-like quality evoked by the soundtrack adds to this feeling of exclusion, an effect which is most emphasized by the film's *mise-en-scène*.

    **Badlands'** cinematography similarly serves to emphasize the couple's outsider status. This status is characterised by the disappearance of traditionally ascribed borders. While the narrative focuses on the transgression of the rule of law and entry into a zone of wilful exclusion, of outsiderness, the *mise-en-scène* reiterates this narrative trajectory of the borderless state. This is most apparent in the scenes set in the badlands, here the great plains are shot as an almost hellish infinity of flat, empty miles, mirrored by the flatness of the sky above them. Only Kit and Holly's car breaks the endless monotony of the landscape. The geography is filmed to emphasise its collapse, until the horizon seems to vanish into pure flatness; world and sky as one massive blank canvas. Such a landscape can only ever be identified as borderless; as infinite; the end of distinction between sky and earth merely reiterating the collapse

Badlands

of all other borders and boundaries within the narrative. As the French postmodern theorist Jean Baudrillard writes, when describing the interminable flatness of the American deserts:

*"You are delivered from all depth there – a brilliant, mobile, superficial neutrality, a challenge to meaning and profundity, a challenge to nature and culture, an outer hyperspace, with no origin, no reference-points"*[5].

Except for the teleological ramifications of eschatological thinking, which render it as mere metaphysical construction, it would almost be possible to describe the appearance of this flat, endless landscape as apocalyptic (such an end-time geographic eschatology becoming far more apparent in the other filmic texts mentioned below).

**Badlands** also introduces, and plays with, a series of signifiers which serve to emphasize, and to punctuate, the nature of Kit and Holly's relationship. The most apparent of these is the image of the fire which burns down Holly's family home. This consuming fire is filmed so as to emphasize the flames as they annihilate the very heart of traditionally ascribed values and of order – the family home. The fire serves to delineate the transgression between normal/perverse, between family values/amorality, and between innocence/guilt. Not only does the fire mark a narrative point of no return, it also marks a psychic point of no return, a zenith from which the characters emerge as changed, or – rather – changing, like the distant mountains the characters never reach, so a state of "being" never emerges in their journey; instead the two lovers exist in a state of continually negated being.

Another element introduced by **Badlands** is that of the personalized ritual of affirmation. In **Badlands** there are two major ritualised moments (excluding the burning of the house, which may also be interpreted as a version of a ritual of abandoning childhood). Both are personalized versions of the marriage ceremony. The first ritual is the making of a balloon which Kit and Holly fill with various tokens of their love for each other before sending it to float above the fields on the outskirts of town. The second ritual in the film – performed by Kit and Holly shortly before their separation and Kit's final chase and capture – repeats this, but reverses the gesture, instead of sending the effects spiralling skyward the two lovers bury a bucket of tokens in the desert, marking the different state of their relationship, which has become a thing to be buried and hidden. There are other rituals in the film, although they are less about the couple's relationship than about Kit, for example after their first soulless copulation Kit wants to mark the spot with a stone, and at the film's climax – shortly before Kit is apprehended – he marks the spot with a small stack of stones.

The most obvious – yet perhaps the most crucial – signifier **Badlands** plays with is that of the couple's relationship to the car. The car represents far more than their mode of transport; it represents both the (relative) stability of Kit and Holly's home (primarily when they have to flee into the Badlands) and the very key to achieving their fantasies and desires. At night they can dance in the glare of its headlights, while listening to the music coming from its radio, while on a more general level the car itself is a central element in the mythology of American culture, and specifically youth culture. The car must be seen as a part of teenage culture which, at least in the '50s, was equal to rock'n'roll in its ability to demarcate a territory of difference from previous generations. The car enables them to commit their crimes and escape, it offers them transport and shelter while they drive towards the distant Montana mountains which provide them with their hope, their "Emerald City".

## WHITE LINE FEVER

David Lynch's **Wild At Heart** (1990) [see Chapter 17] and Tony Scott's **True Romance** (1993) are two films which play with the thematic of pursued love, and contain cinematic references to **Badlands** without actually being direct teen killers-on-the-run movies.

As in **Wild At Heart**, **True Romance** plays with the iconography of Elvis Presley, who appears twice in the film to advise Clarence, acting as a symbol of rebellion but also as a paternal figure; a fantasy father. Elvis acts as a signifier for an archetypical American youthful rebellion, and simultaneously offers a camp humour in the film, as well as offering a point of intertextuality with films such as **Wild At Heart** and Jim Jarmusch's **Mystery Train** (1989). **True Romance** also makes repeated references to **Badlands** via its main theme, which is a virtual re-working of the **Badlands** soundtrack. Further **True Romance** utilises an opening and closing narration from Alabama (who, like Holly, has a southern accent, a theme addressed below). This narration describes the nature of true romance, and the fleeting possibilities it offers and the particular violent insanity that this romance inspired. The narration's only difference from Holly's is that it acts as a pure affirmation to the relationship at both the opening and close of the text.

What is remarkable about **True Romance** is that, despite being about love on the run, the central protagonists actually spend very little time on the road, at least as it is generally viewed in road movies. Instead the journey across the country is reduced to the bare minimum, but Los Angeles, rather than representing the utopia at the journey's end (as it would come to mean in the later **Kalifornia**) becomes a zone identified with the journey. Thus, rather than being constructed as a city by the text, Los Angeles becomes identified with the road, as Clarence and Alabama cruise in their pink Cadillac from location to location in order to set up the coke deal. Jean

True Romance

Baudrillard suggests that Los Angeles itself is a zone of freeways which render the city "an inhabited fragment of the desert"[6] The only place of relative stasis, the only geographically fixed home, is the motel room at which the couple stay, and this space can only operate as a temporary haven. Even the "native" residents of the city are always presented as in transit; thus Elliot is busted by the police while driving. For Elliot the car is a bachelor pad on wheels; not just the place where he gets high, but also the place where he makes his phone calls from, and receives blow jobs from dumb starlets, all while driving along the Pacific Coast Highway at high speed. Similarly Dick's apartment is a place characters always either arrive at or leave but never stay at. The only person to remain at the apartment is Floyd, who never appears to leave it, but just sits watching television while continually smoking copious quantities of marijuana and – blissfully unaware – telling collective gangsters about Clarence's dealings; to be still is thus identified with a psychic stasis as much as a physical stasis. By emphasising the city itself as a place of perpetual motion **True Romance** emphasizes the continued velocity of Clarence and Alabama's journey without ever actually emphasizing a "going to" (save for the coda at the film's end). Instead their destination becomes the achievement of their desire to make money with the coke deal. Desire is thus transformed from the physical locale of an actual utopia to a zone of psychic satisfaction.

Dominic Sena's 1993 film **Kalifornia** also engages with a re-working of **Badlands** and the killer couple narrative, although – unlike **Wild At Heart** – the film does not engage with a generic bricolage, but rather returns to the original format, but extends it via the introduction of a second couple of young lovers. **Kalifornia** (the replacement of the "C" with the "K" acting as a signifier of the films thanatopic thematic; Kali – at least in one of her forms, and certainly that most favoured by the generally ethnocentric metanarrative of Hollywood cinema – is the goddess of chaos and destruction) depicts two couples as they drive from the East coast to the West coast of America. One couple, Brian and Carrie, are identified as being middle-class, educated and northern. Brian – who offers both an extra-diegetic and internal narration throughout the film – is a writer who, armed with his dictaphone, is travelling to sites of famous murders and recording his observations and the particular criminal and personal histories which have led to these crimes. Offered the chance of writing his first book, Brian decides to drive across America to California via these grim locales. In order to fully document this journey Brian asks his partner, Carrie, to accompany him. Carrie is an art photographer (this is made apparent by the film's depiction of her repeated rejection at galleries for being too "obscure"; in fact her pictures appear as stark chiaroscuro erotica, most of which appear to depict carefully posed pictures of black men and white women) who agrees to travel across the country taking photographs of the murder sites. The ultimate aim is to produce the book, but – more importantly – it is to reach California, "a place of hopes and dreams" Brian's narration states. In California he will be a writer and Carrie a photographer, for the couple it represents the land of limitless opportunity (as in such earlier films as John Ford's **The Grapes Of Wrath** (1940).

In order to finance the trip Brian and Carrie decide to place an advertisement in the nearby university in order to split the cost of gasoline (noticeably the sign placed on the notice board by Brian reads "Kalifornia"). The sign is immediately picked up by the school janitor (of one day), Early Grayce (Brad Pitt). Early has been sent to the university by his parole officer, a disgusting figure who makes it clear that he feels the derogatory position is more than suitable for the recently paroled Early.

Early lives in a trailer, which is parked in a run down garbage heap, with his girlfriend Adele (Juliette Lewis)[7]. As the film progresses, the audience learn that Adele has been the victim of an exceptionally violent rape at some point in her past. Early decides to jump parole and head with Adele for California, a land he believes has fruit on every tree just waiting to be picked, and where – he tells Adele – "the first month rent is free". Early kills his scumbag landlord, sets fire to the trailer and, with Adele, joins Brian and Carrie on the journey west, the pair unaware that one of their passengers is a homicidal maniac (like **Badlands'** Kit, Early's murderous intensities are linked to "insanity"; while Kit has visions in the early morning hypnogogia between sleep and wakefulness, Early believes in doors which are geo-temporal gateways between dimensions, each offering a new potentiality. It should also be noted that Brian's narration fixes the serial killer as inhabiting a psychic state which is "between dreams and reality").

The two couples are antithetical, while Carrie and Brian are *bourgeois* liberal artists, Early and Adele are described as "Okies" and "white trash". Against the designer black denim of the artists Early and Adele dress in ultra-downbeat thrift store trash; he in faded Hawaiian shirt, she in boob tubes and halter top. More importantly the difference is marked by Early's baseball cap which bares the Confederate cross, and the accents of the "white trash" which are unmistakably Southern. It is thus not merely psychology, profession or class which divide the two couples so much as the Mason Dixie Line. Since the American Civil War the south has been identified with exceptional poverty, and the profound loss of cultural identity. This is, in part, due to both the loss of its separate identity (which was supported by a romantic myth of social harmony), via the ending of slavery and hence its wealth, but also as a result of the North's cultural imperialism.

As the journey progresses so Early funds his petrol contributions by murdering and stealing. Meanwhile Carrie becomes increasingly concerned; first becoming aware that Early has been in prison, then that he beats Adele and finally that he has a gun. While Carrie becomes worried, Brian is seduced by the potential violence inaugurated by Early; firstly when – on a drunken night out – he witnesses Early's prowess in a bar-room brawl, and later when Early lets him fire his gun. Eventually, at a deserted garage in the middle of the desert, Carrie sees a television news program which shows footage of Early before stating that he is wanted for questioning on various murder

Kalifornia

charges after having jumped bail. Early then shows his true colours and takes over, holding Brian and Carrie hostage as he drives them all to California, killing everybody who gets in the way.

In a noticeable reference to **Badlands**, Early pulls the car into the drive of a large house owned by an evidently wealthy elderly couple. In the house Early ties up Brian and Carrie, and kills the elderly male resident, while the elderly female flees into the desert night. Like the house in **Badlands**, the house in **Kalifornia** is a signifier of the wealthy world from which Early and Adele are permanently excluded. Similarly Early and Adele are seduced by the house, exploring it and relishing its opulence (this is primarily true of Adele who marvels at the collection of cacti which sit throughout – and in pots outside – the house). Like Holly in **Badlands**, Adele is marked by her own apparent lack of personality and is frequently ignored by the protagonists (during one early sequence Adele comments on the need of communication and friends in the development of a personality, while she speaks everybody ignores her). While at the house Adele realises – finally – that Early is a scumbag, and she articulates this before clubbing him with a cactus. His response is to kill her.

Having killed Adele, Early beats Brian senseless and kidnaps Carrie. He continues on the planned route, taking Carrie to California, but decides to spend the night in Nevada, hiding out in a simulated town, which is actually an old nuclear test site. Here he rapes Carrie, although not before she stabs him. At dawn the following day Brian arrives; as the sun rises over the nuclear landscape he fights and kills Early. The film cuts, and the audience witnesses Brian and Carrie living in California, his book is nearly finished, and Carrie has had interest from a gallery in showing her work.

**Kalifornia** utilises recognizable iconography, although traditional killer couple movie iconographic elements are re-worked by being either updated or used with a different emphasis. The image of fire does not directly occur in **Kalifornia**, instead Early's initial killing (at the film's opening) takes place in torrential rain; thus the chaos and destruction of fire is mirrored by the chaos and destruction of water, the elemental status of the signifier is still relevant to the narrative. When Early "reveals" his murderous nature it is at a deserted garage during the middle of a massive electrical storm, and the scene is repeatedly marked with images of lightning and wind. The storm threatens and marks change in much a similar way as fire in **Badlands** and **Wild At Heart**.

The film also depicts contrary rituals of affirmation between the two couples; while Carrie and Brian engage in mutual discussions of art or career, Early and Adele repeatedly slide into the zone of their own language, singing childlike sexual (yet simultaneously naive) songs to each other. In a reversal of the affirmation offered by music and dancing, **Kalifornia** depicts music and dancing as an escape from the killer couple's relationship; when Adele is told by Carrie that Early is a murderer, Adele turns the car radio onto full volume and begins to dance. Music thus acts as an anaesthetic for Adele rather than a signifier of her closeness to Early.

**Kalifornia** offers an update of the apocalyptic geography which signifies the boundary transgressions of the genre's murderous protagonists (and which resonates throughout the later **Natural Born Killers**). The landscape goes "beyond" the desert to the post-nuclear apocalyptic test site town. While the family background of Early and Adele remains under suspension[8] throughout the text (during one hilarious sequence Brian tries to stop Early killing a wounded policeman: "Look, he's not your father," Brian states. "I know that," says Early, as if Brian is stating the obvious, then casually blasts the cop to death). The abandoned desert town reiterates the violence which could be said to be characteristic of normal daily life. Standing in the living room of the test site house is the archetypal nuclear family made from mannequins. **Kalifornia** thus expressly makes the connection between the (plastic) post-war family and the mindless rampage of the serial killer, all of whom are linked with the terror of the family home, a place which mirrors the hellish violence of the apocalyptic world beyond the four walls of the house. A world which is clearly signified by the radioactive desert, but is also present throughout the whole film in the abandoned and decrepit industrial wastelands through which the group drives. This apocalyptic theme is further iterated via the rant of a wino seen in the diner where Adele works. Various other supporting characters also have a quasi-apocalyptic appearance, looking as if they have been visited by some grotesque plague: Early's parole officer has a violent hacking cough and is missing a hand, Early and Adele's landlord is obesely overweight and is surrounded by a small pack of ugly copulating dogs, finally a victim who is slaughtered in the toilet of a gas station is seen releasing the contents of a catheter bag into the urinal due – presumably – to some medical dysfunction.

By the introduction of the second couple (Brian and Carrie) **Kalifornia** both explores, and problematizes, the narrative structure. Firstly via the second couple the film allows the audience to engage with a series of complex multiple identifications, which reflect back and forth across couples and genders, this is far more clearly apparent than in **Badlands**, where the audience is never able to fully identify, nor disavow an identification, with the killer couple. **Badlands'** flatness – and the repeated re-emphasis of this flatness – serves to distance the audience from any identification. **Kalifornia**, with its traditional shot/reverse-shot style and pre-established narrative trajectory, allows for what could be considered (at least traditionally) to be a more ready mode of identification, but by switching the audience's possible identifications across four characters throughout the text serves to create a potentially liberating schizophrenia.

Brian and Carrie also serve to emphasize the audience's own ambiguous relationship to the text: the cinematic audience's voyeurism and scopophilia is mirrored by that of Brian and Carrie who are repeatedly depicted acting out their/the audience's thanatopic fascination. Thus the audience witness violence in parallel to the violence which Brian and Carrie's project fetishizes, this reaches its zenith when, in an abandoned slaughterhouse, Brian plays a cassette of a girl begging for her life while being tortured, meanwhile dictating his analysis of her demise into his tape player while Carrie's flash bursts starkly across the ruined building. Meanwhile the audience is aware that the very violence being described by Brian, and implicitly by Carrie, is being barely contained by Early who is savagely fucking Adele in the back of the car (this violence becomes increasingly apparent when Carrie finishes her photography and walks outside and begins to watch Early and Adele fuck; as she watches so Early looks up and leers at her).

This emphasis on the violence of Brian and Carrie's voyeurism is increasingly emphasized by the contrasts and similarities between the two couples. Thus Brian vicariously enjoys Early's violence during the bar room brawl and the general atmosphere of bravado. Simultaneously Carrie – who finds Early repulsively aggressive in his dominance of Adele – enjoys watching Early fuck Adele (the active/passive dichotomy appears to apply to the sex in which the couple engage). But Carrie can distance herself from the reality of her voyeuristic pleasure by watching the copulation via the camera, similarly when – to her dismay – Brian shoots Early's gun, she shoots with her camera. Carrie's camera, and her relationship to it, thus mirrors the relationship of the male protagonists to the gun (Carrie's voyeurism is specifically linked to her gaze via the camera, through which she can unflinchingly watch and photograph, however when she is held hostage by Early and watches the murder of a policeman she turns her head away). Both devices shoot, but while the gun kills, the camera only captures the moment of death and the final images of life. Finally, Carrie does not become a killer (although Brian does), however it is Carrie who has most in common with Early.

## ROUTE 666

The killer-on-the-road sub-genre reached its cinematic zenith in Oliver Stone's **Natural Born Killers** (which, like **True Romance** was based on a script originally by Tarantino[9], although Tarantino would distance himself from Stone's film upon its release). Even before its theatrical release in Britain the film had something of a cult notoriety in the collective discourses which focused on the text and its relationship to contemporary youth culture. The BBFC delayed classifying the film for some time, before demanding several (brief) cuts be made in the (already cut for the MPAA) film before it could be released.

**Natural Born Killers** follows the consummate murder spree (fifty-two victims) of "white trash" husband and wife tag-team-killers, Mickey and Mallory Knox. The film opens with the couple having already embarked on their killing spree, and via flashback the audience gradually becomes aware of the couple's past. Mallory comes from an exceptionally violent family, and has been raped by her fat, disgusting and abusive father since she was a young child. She may even be the mother of her younger brother, a monstrous looking brat with Kiss-style make up adorning his face. One evening, after being groped and threatened by her father, Mallory meets Mickey, who has come to deliver beef to the family home. It is love at first sight, and the two steal Mallory's father's car, for which Mickey is imprisoned on charges of Grand Theft Auto. A freak tornado allows Mickey to escape from the prison ranch and head for Mallory's house (the tornado, of course, being the agent by which Dorothy is removed from home, and consequently must embark on her journey through Oz). Here the couple beat and drown Dad, and burn Mom alive, along – presumably – with the entire house. Mickey and Mallory flee together, while Mallory's brother makes his own escape. Mickey's background is never made completely clear, other than the fact that he witnessed his father's suicide as a child.

Natural Born Killers

On the road Mickey and Mallory create their own marriage, reciting their own vows and mixing their blood. Meanwhile a TV show, *American Maniacs*, recounts their rampage down the apocalyptically named Route 666 (a "road to Hell in front of us" states Mickey). Interviews with teenagers around the world reveal that Mickey and Mallory are becoming a cult ("If I was a mass murderer I'd be Mickey and Mallory" says one teen). Cut to a windswept desert town and Mickey and Mallory going to a motel. In the motel the two watch a rapid edit of violent television and film, alongside a natural history program which depicts various animals copulating. As Mickey and Mallory begin to fuck the view from the motel window changes to a rapid edit of stock footage depicting various historical acts of violence, primarily images of Nazis. Mickey is not looking at Mallory while they make love, and the two begin to argue, the problem being that Mickey wants to rape the girl tied up in the corner of the room. Angry, Mallory storms out and finds a teenager, who she persuades to go down on her, before she kills him. Cut from the film was a violent rape and murder committed by Mickey on his youthful hostage (a cut demanded by the MPAA).

The following day the couple run out of gasoline and become lost in the

Natural Born Killers

desert. Leaving the car they walk and argue through the sand until they come to a small homestead. Here they meet a Native American who lets them into his small hut, a fire burns in its centre and a rattle snake sits coiled on the floor. To his grandson the old man states (in his native tongue) that the murderers are "lost in a world of ghosts" and have "sad sickness", both have watched "too much TV". As the old man articulates this so the words are projected across Mickey's and Mallory's chests. The two gun happy lovers fall asleep, but in the middle of the night Mickey wakes from a dream of his youth, and "accidentally" shoots the elderly man. As Mallory berates him ("Bad. Bad. Bad. Bad. Bad. Bad," she repeats, poking Mickey in the chest with her forefinger), the dying man reveals that he had seen his own death at the hands of the murderous, demonic Mickey in a dream. Mickey and Mallory flee the hut, stealing some petrol on the way. As they walk back to their car dozens of rattle snakes appear and snap at their ankles. Both are bitten and have to drive into town for the antidote. At the pharmacy the killers are recognized and the alarm is raised. Mallory is grabbed by sick-boy detective Jack Scagnetti, who wants to rape her, and who uses the threat of "cutting her tits off" to force Mickey to surrender. As Mickey puts his guns down he is savagely beaten by the cops in an oblique reference to the infamous Rodney King video.

The film cuts to a prison, one year later. Here the violent and stupid Governor McClusky has invited Scagnetti to supervise the transfer of the two killers to an asylum for the criminally insane, with the proviso that the two will "escape" and consequently will have to be shot. The day before this can take place Wayne Gale, the "auteur" behind American Maniacs, will interview Mickey live on air, immediately following the Superbowl. During the interview Mickey – now with a shaven head – refers to Charles Manson as "the king" (Stone stated that much of the interview was inspired by the infamous Geraldo/Manson television interview), as the interview progresses the prison population (portrayed by real convicts) watch in hushed awe, until Mickey states that he is a "Natural Born Killer" and the entire prison explodes in a fury of violence. Mickey grabs a guard's gun and begins to kill guards and TV crew alike, then – while being pursued by Wayne Gale and the few surviving members of his crew – he begins to hunt for Mallory. Meanwhile Mallory is being "seduced" by Scagnetti in her cell, before he can fuck her she turns and begins to beat and kick Scagnetti. The two fight, suddenly the door is blown open by the rifle-toting Mickey who kills Scagnetti. Aided by a suddenly enthusiastic and murderous Gale the killers escape, although not before watching the prisoners take over the prison.

Finally free the two killers shoot Gale, despite his begging and whingeing, "You always leave a witness," he blubs. Mickey and Mallory point to the camera, which is still broadcasting; "We are," they state, and shoot the journalist. The camera dropped by the journalist films his own demise as the audience watch. The film cuts to the future. Mickey is driving a large truck, in the back Mallory is playing with several children. End.

**Natural Born Killers** is shot in a variety styles: 35mm, 16mm black and white, super-8, video, stock footage (the second world war, Texas sniper Charles Whitman[10] and even animation). While each style could be used to suggest a different perspective within the text they do not, instead the film is cut – almost at random – to bring the audience into a visually seductive quasi-narcotic rush of images, which create the effect in the audience of a media orgy, as if the entire film is based on the singular pleasure of channel hopping. The free-play of cinematic styles also denies the viewer the chance to maintain a fixed gaze and static mode of identification, instead the viewer is forced into acting as Jean Baudrillard's "pure screen, a switching centre for all the networks of influence"[11]; rather than attempting to become the "master"[12] of a single gaze, the viewers of **Natural Born Killers** are forced into the position of a viewing schizophrenia (at one point during the confrontation-cum-interview between Mickey and Wayne Gale the film breaks into an advert for Coke; not only does this appear to be a cynical and audacious example of product placing, the advert also acts as a radical break to any vicarious collective pleasure the audience may experience during this key sequence; like the imaginary audience to Wayne's *American Maniacs*, we too must wait to see what will happen).

The multiplicity of styles was made possible by director Oliver Stone's utilization of the technological advances of editing, advances which can be used to circumnavigate the traditional linear style in favour of a high speed computer-based digital edit. The use of such technology enabled an experimentation of editing and styles, and the finished film was "based on editing gut-instinct"[13], and there is – at least according to Stone – no clear narrative perspective delineated by a certain style, so, for example "reality" is not necessarily perceived in harsh black and white and "fantasy" is not necessarily depicted via colour. Instead the text deconstructs such traditional markers of "reality"/"fantasy" by rendering all such cinematic conventions and divisions as ambiguous, removing their traditionally ascribed significations.

**Natural Born Killers**, like the other films in this sub-genre, is set against an apocalyptic desert landscape – the appropriately named Route 666 – yet the desert, with all its eschatological overtones, is neither the only – or indeed the primary – zone of apocalypse within the film. For much of the film's driving sequences Mickey and Mallory are seen driving against a montage of images, which includes fire, fireworks, television shows and films. The apocalypse is thus played out across the flickering screens of the media, and at the film's opening, immediately following the titles, Mickey articulates this; while they sit in the car, television images of fireworks exploding around them he states "the whole world's comin' to an end, Mal". The signifier of fire which has marked the sub-genre becomes no longer necessary (despite

Natural Born Killers

the burning of Mallory's mother) instead merely its representation on television is enough, it does not need to refer to a real fire but to the simulacrum of fire. In the postmodern society of **Natural Born Killers** television has replaced the car, no longer do people have to travel in order to see the world, but via television they can experience the world instantaneously without having to leave home. If the modern landscape of the first half of the twentieth century was designed for the car then the postmodern landscape of the late twentieth century has replaced the car with the experience of television, the experience of distance and time (the time needed to travel) becomes burned out in favour of distance and speed (the speed of images across the globe). Mickey and Mallory do not have to travel into the chaos of the space between cities, it is already there on television; existential nausea has been replaced by the giddying effects of multiple images edited in quick succession across the television.

The narrative of **Natural Born Killers** utilises these television and film images in order to contextualise the crimes of Mickey and Mallory. They are television kids: "TOO MUCH TV" projected across their chests in the desert cabin; Mallory's background is shot on video as a television sit-com *à la Father Knows Best*, complete with laugh track and knowing asides to the audience. The Knox's media-saturated environment defines their "reality", more importantly **Natural Born Killers** suggests that, at least in part, the killer's activities are due to the media, or a result of a media-saturated world which bombards its audience with indiscriminate images of violence. In the prison, during a montage of images, we see Frankenstein's monster, a creature created by, but ultimately beyond the control of, humanity. Cutting the monster in among the other television and film footage which bombards the audience draws a direct link between images and the creation of a society. This is again emphasized by the entire television show within the text, *American Maniacs*.

The media glut which defines **Natural Born Killers'** aesthetic acts as an aporia: it allows the audience a multiplicity of perspectives, and radically destabilises the notion of a homogenous textuality in favour of a heterogeneous intertextuality, created via its channel-surfing aesthetic. However the media is also presented in simplistic, and occasionally even naive, terms as "glorifying" violence and being partly responsible for the breakdown of the social realm which has allowed serial killers to emerge.

This presentation of the media is contrary to the rest of the films in the sub-genre. The earlier films depict the media as having an influence on the killers, from Kit's adolescent identification with James Dean, to Sailor and Clarence's Elvis fixations, but these media figures are rebellious archetypes and are viewed by the protagonists – and the texts – as symbols of rebellion and existential individualism rather than as the reason for the killing spree.

What all these films share is the articulation of the fantasy of being able to escape the repressed violence of the city, of the home and nuclear family, and travel into the chaos and potentiality of the "beyond", aiming for the utopia of their own Emerald City. The zone outside the cities which becomes repeatedly marked as a place beyond all law (symbolic and legislative), a place where boundaries collapse, and order vanishes to a pin prick in the rearview mirror. In **Badlands** this collapse iterated the psychic state of the protagonists, especially Kit, whose journey was doomed from the start. However post-**Badlands** the text's central protagonists always return to the symbolic order, thus in **Wild At Heart**, **True Romance** and **Natural Born Killers** the couple, by the end of the film, have "matured", married and become parents, adopting the traditional values of a monogamous, heterosexual nuclear family. The killers of these films emerge as exceptionally conservative figures, who may annihilate or flee their backgrounds, killing those who dominate them, but who ultimately seek to reproduce these very values within their own lives. **Badlands** is also the only film to expressly articulate the murderer's conservatism, as Malick stated at the time of the film's release:

*"(Kit) thinks of himself as a successor to James Dean – a rebel without a cause – when in reality he's more like an Eisenhower conservative. 'Consider the minority opinion', he says into the rich man's tape recorder, 'but try to get along with the majority opinion once it's accepted'. He doesn't really believe any of this, but he envies the people who do, who can. He wants to be like them, like the rich man he locks in the closet, the only man he dosen't kill, the only man he sympathises with, and the one least in need of sympathy. It's not infrequently the people at the bottom who most vigorously defend the very rules that put and keep them there."*[14]

Much of this conservatism in the texts post-**Badlands** is reflected in the symbolism of chaos outside the cities; in the urban landscape the characters identity is fixed (thus, for example, Mickey is a delivery man, Early is a janitor, Clarence is a sales assistant) but when the characters leave the safety of the metropolis their identity is thrown into question, consequently much of the journey is about searching for an identity (hence the fixation with rebellious archetypes, whose identity could be easily adopted as one's own in the desert). This search for an identity, which can finally only emerge through the embracing of the Oedipal family, and by arriving at a destination, becomes the central focus of these films. Narrative closure can only be achieved when the serial killer/s are able to fix their identity, until this point they are forced to continue to travel, or – like Early – must die. In **Badlands** this textual closure becomes manifested in the irony of Holly's final deadpan narration; Kit is executed and she marries her lawyer's son, thus her identity – or lack of – is gained through a direct return to the

Badlands

urban and also to a – literal – bonding with the law. However, there is little apparent irony in the closure of the other texts.

The most abrupt narrative closure comes in **Kalifornia** via Carrie, who has been identified as sexual – via shots of her in her bra and panties – and simultaneously identified as artistic, independent and strong. Carrie initially appears as an erotic androgen with her skin-tight black clothes and short black hair and she thus must be read as a post-feminist heroine. Like the serial killer she offers a threat to order and raises questions concerning the nature of identity, further Carrie needs to cross the country in order to ascertain her identity, like the murderous boyfriends of **Badlands** and **Natural Born Killers** she inaugurates the journey. However – unlike the killers of the other texts who can fix their identity by the simple repetition of their murderous act – by the film's closure, and her return to the order of the city, Carrie has been forced into her place in the symbolic order. At the film's close she appears in baggy clothes, with long hair. More importantly her photography, which originally was rejected because of its explicit eroticism, has now been accepted. Although the film does not depict her new work its title is articulated by Carrie: "Icons". Such a title infers that her new work – rather than challenging the norms of society as her previous work did, via its images of faceless (and hence lacking an identity[15]) blacks and whites engaged in sexual acts – actually embraces the culturally traditional concept of the icon, the most representative icon being – of course – the Virgin Mary, thus the photographic work shifts Carrie from "whore" to "virgin". Carrie thus returns from the journey across country, having been "punished" for her individualism via her rape at the hands of Early, who expressly articulates his disgust at her erotic photos. Carrie now "knows" and is "accepting" her place in the symbolic order.

These few films, then, use the road as a quest for an identity, and the journey's end – and film's close – become the point at which the characters can re-enter the symbolic order. Crucially the films – bar **Badlands** – use an East/West journey across America (the drive undertaken in **Badlands** is also an East/West journey, but it is far more a journey to nowhere). This is a journey which has a culturally specific resonance, because it is a journey historically identified by American society as pioneering, as travelling to a promised land, a new world of opportunity away from the Eurocentrism of the East Coast. The frontier of the American west represents the birth place of the American national identity; thus by journeying west the characters of these films are enacting a culturally specific voyage which seeks to articulate an identity.

Charles Starkweather and Caril Ann Fugate, the couple who "inspired" these films, remain absent from them, their shadows remain cast across the text but they are blurred, barely recognisable shapes. It is only **Badlands**, with its narrative that echoes the story of Starkweather, which makes any direct reference to his life and crimes. Those other films described here engage with a repetition of cinematic texts, with **Badlands** as paternal nexus via its depiction of murderous youth on the run. Even **Natural Born Killers**, with its name-checks to Manson and Whitman amongst others (not to mention its sly nods to such classic road movies as **Vanishing Point** and **Easy Rider**), fails to allude to the Starkweather case directly, despite its conscious engagement with the very concept of rebellious youth on the lam. Similarly of all the crimes alluded to in the subplot of **Kalifornia** concerning Brian's book, none even transpire on the road, they are instead oblique iconic references to "pit-stop" films such as **The Texas Chainsaw Massacre**. Furthermore **Wild At Heart** and **True Romance** both embrace a postmodern pastiche of previous texts, genres and – more importantly – culture, a large number of which come from '50s popular culture; Nicholas Ray's classic film **Johnny Guitar** (1953), Elvis Presley, and '50s retro-style fashion. The '50s represent, at least in these films, a golden age:

*"The real high spot for the US ('when things were going on') and you can still feel the nostalgia for those years, for the ecstasy of power, when power held power."*[16]

Finally, then, these films play with images of alienation and angst, but always resolve the protagonists' dilemmas with a return to the conservatism of "being" (be it via the mechanisms of an arrival at the destination, or the destruction of the killer). The potentialities of chaos remain ungrasped. Rebellion is rendered merely as a pastiche of previous rebellious icons. Only **Badlands** fully recognises the killer as victim and, simultaneously, as fundamentally conservative: as a nihilist unable to grasp either the velocity or necessity of his own nihilism. While the other films in this sub-genre offer a spectacle of rebellion that becomes merely another image, without meaning and yet offering the illusion (and believing in the mystique) of depth and authenticity.

# NOTES

1. For the full story of Starkweather and Fugate, see Jack Sargeant, *Born Bad*; Creation Books, 1996.

2. Charles Beesley, in Michael Weldon, *The Psychotronic Encyclopedia Of Film*, Plexus: London, 1989, p.601.

3. See Jack Sargeant, *Deathtripping: The Cinema Of Transgression*; Creation Books, 1995, for further details.

4. An independent production, written, produced and directed by Malick, and made for $300,000, *Badlands* was brought by Warners for a million dollars.

5. Baudrillard, *America*; London: Verso, 1988, p.24.

6. Baudrillard, *America*, p.53.

7. Lewis and Pitt later played a homicidal young trailer-trash couple on the run in **Too Young To Die** (Robert Markowitz, 1994), and Lewis of course went on to star as Mallory Knox in **Natural Born Killers**.

8. Race also remains an issue at the margins of the text. Carrie's photos depict black/white sex scenarios, and when Early, who is identified with the South and thus with the "negative", finds them he mocks and degrades Carrie for her work but – perhaps surprisingly – ignores the racial element of the pictures.

9. **Natural Born Killers** was Tarantino's second script.

10. Whitman was an architectural engineering student who, on August 1st, 1966, climbed to the top of the bell tower at the University of Texas and, armed with a variety of rifles, began to shoot at passers by. He killed three people – including his wife and mother – before going to the university, here he killed a further eighteen people, before three policemen gunned him down. An autopsy revealed a massive brain tumour pushing onto the aggression centre of his brain. The Whitman case inspired Peter Bogdanovitch's debut feature **Targets** (1967).

11. Baudrillard, "The Ecstasy Of Communication", in Hal Foster, editor, *Postmodern Culture*; Pluto Press: London & Concord, MA, 1990, p.133.

12. Master because, as feminist film theorist Laura Mulvey articulated in her essay "Visual Pleasure And Narrative Fiction", the Hollywood film text creates a male scopophilic or voyeuristic pleasure. Where Mulvey's work fails is that it assumes cinematic gaze and modes of identification are constructed on a psychoanalytic and gendered basis, Mulvey thus privileges the phallo-centric constructed psychoanalytic discourse as a "truth" discourse.

13. Stone quoted in Smith, "Oliver Stone: Why Do I Have To Provoke?" in *Sight And Sound*, December, 1994, p.12.

14. Walker, "Malick On Badlands" in *Sight And Sound*, Spring 1975, Volume 44, No.2, p.82.

15. Crucially, Early recognises the woman in the photographs as Carrie – hence linking the two figures via their lack of a fixed identity.

16. Baudrillard, *America*, p.107.

# Chapter 11

# 'Thelma And Louise'

# OUR IDEA OF FUN: 'THELMA AND LOUISE' ON TRIAL

## Alistair Daniel

> LOUISE: "You think you've found your callin'"?
> THELMA: "Yep. The call of the wild!"

If **Thelma And Louise** (1991) was only a modest commercial success on its release in 1991, its enduring cultural impact has far outstripped its initial profits. As Ridley Scott's most notable film since **Blade Runner** (1982), it made a star of Geena Davis, introduced audiences to Brad Pitt, and set Susan Sarandon on a career path which culminated in an Oscar for **Dead Man Walking** (Tim Robbins, 1995), while even the unassuming supporting role of Detective Hal Slocum helped to resurrect the career of Harvey Keitel. Furthermore it revitalized the road movie genre, reworking its masculine image and inspiring a fresh wave of films such as **My Own Private Idaho** (Gus Van Sant, 1992) and **Leaving Normal** (Edward Zwick, 1992). At the time of its release some critics argued that the film generated more debate that its content justified, that it was a film coated with a thin veneer of feminism, a road movie whose female protagonists behaved like men for the titillation of a mainstream audience. But **Thelma And Louise** is more complex than that. If it is hardly your average buddy movie, it seems even less akin to contemporaneous "women's pictures" such as **Mystic Pizza** (Donald Petrie, 1988) or **Fried Green Tomatoes** (Jon Avnet, 1991).[1] Its blend of hitherto unrelated genres coupled with its exploration of female agency in a hostile southern landscape, produces a powerful mixture of strident didacticism and ambivalence which still resonates ten years on.

## MY IDEA OF FUN

**Thelma And Louise** does not set out as a road movie, it becomes one. The intended car journey is brief, its destination the fishing hut owned by Louise's colleague. What turns the film into a road movie, a flight across several States which transforms its protagonists inside and out, is the attempted rape of Thelma by Harlan, a local womanizer who picks Thelma up in the bar where they stop *en route* to the fishing lodge. Harlan is shot in the chest by Louise, not to prevent Thelma's rape, but in a moment of rage at Harlan's unrepentant insults as the two women back away. With no witnesses and sufficient physical evidence of injury, Louise, we might suppose, would be able to claim that Harlan was shot in defence of Thelma. Discussing the events much later, Thelma, whose original impulse was to go to the police, makes this very suggestion. But Louise doesn't see it that way. From the start she believes, or recognizes, that a jury would call in question the rape itself: "A hundred people saw you dancing cheek to cheek with him all night... who's gonna believe that?... we don't live in that kind of world Thelma". The world they *do* live in, she implies, is one which still invests in the virgin/whore myth. A jury, Louise believes, would assume that a woman who decides to flirt, or to dance, is a woman who will consent to sex. The flight from the scene of the crime, then, and all that follows, is precipitated by the question of Thelma's actions, not Louise's.

It seems astonishing that women's right to sexual autonomy might still need to be asserted, but the controversy generated three years earlier by Jonathan Kaplan's **The Accused,** suggests otherwise. Jodie Foster's character, Sarah Tobias, is brutally gang raped in a bar. The ensuing courtroom drama centres on the attempted discrediting of the victim's status *as victim* by focusing on her supposedly unbridled sexuality. The "accused" of the title becomes the woman bringing the charges. Though the film ends on a triumphant note for Sarah, the victory registered is a hollow one, a minor charge brought not against the rapists themselves but the crowd who cheered them on, while the perpetrators escape unpunished. In terms of film history at least Louise is right. Rather than vindicating the women, a jury, we can assume, would dismiss the claims of rape out of hand.

We, on the other hand, know the truth. Thelma, spun around on the dancefloor, and full of drink, begins to feel dizzy and sick. She agrees to leave the crowded bar and go into the car park with Harlan for fresh air. Once there she fends off his attempts to kiss her and tries first to "keep walking", and then to go back inside. When Harlan becomes violent she argues, pleads, struggles and resists, slapping his face, an action which turns Harlan's coercion into psychotic aggression. For the viewer, the gap between Thelma's willing participation in a line dance and her rape is made abundantly clear. The recurrent use of "fun" - a keyword throughout the film - reinforces the point. When Thelma accepts Harlan's invitation to dance with "Sure, that'd be fun", her conception of fun involves drinking, dancing, some mild flirtation, and an escape into the mountains for one weekend only for a holiday with her best friend. Thelma is not looking for sex. Her infidelity only comes much later, motivated by the realization that Darryl is an "asshole", and himself entirely faithless.

Harlan himself has a very different idea of fun. "Calm down," he says - apparently without irony - to Louise, who has just caught him in a frenzy of violence, "we were just having a little fun, that's all". "Looks like you've got a pretty fucked up idea of fun," retorts Louise, backing away. The gap between Harlan and Thelma's idea of fun is self-evident, but the film is anxious to remind us at every opportunity of Thelma's opposition to Harlan's personal conception of fun. After the shooting and their initial getaway, the women stop at a café while Louise tries to calm herself and "figure out what to do". Still visibly shaking, trying to take in what she has done, she allows herself to lash out at Thelma: "If you weren't concerned with having so much fun we wouldn't be here right now," she hisses across the table. Louise momentarily sides with the hypothetical jury whose prejudices she is trying to escape, suggesting that Thelma's behaviour had somehow, paradoxically, encouraged her rape. Thelma understands the implication: "So this is all my fault?" she asks, knocking cups over as she leaves the table. Significantly, Louise doesn't answer her, registering the unfairness of her accusation. In this way the film constantly raises the question of Thelma's responsibility, only to refute the idea. Louise, like us, is a witness of Thelma's resistance to Harlan. Only in the depths of emotional despair could she suggest Thelma is anything other than innocent and later, when Thelma herself expresses doubt, it is Louise who dismisses it:

THELMA: "I know this whole thing is my fault."
LOUISE: "If there's one thing you should know by now it wasn't your fault."

If there's one thing the audience, too, should have grasped by now, it is this central idea. Like **The Accused, Thelma And Louise** seeks to undermine the virgin/whore dialectic and reclaim women's active sexuality from its traditional associations with promiscuity, hysteria and madness. Asserting that women have the right to express their sexuality without moral censure, it delivers an implicit critique of conventional

Hollywood cinema, in which female sexuality unregulated by traditional social structures and spaces such as marriage and the home, from the duplicitous and sexually predatory *femmes fatales* of *film noir* to the contemporary heroines of **Fatal Attraction** (Adrian Lye, 1987), **Black Widow** (Bob Rafelson, 1986) or **Basic Instinct** (Paul Verhoeven, 1992), leads inevitably to violence and punishment. However Thelma and Louise are ultimately apprehended, it is not for having fun in a bar. "Fun" becomes the measure of the psychological transformation that Thelma undergoes on the road. "At least now I'm having some fun," she says after locking a police officer in the trunk of his car. By this stage Thelma's idea of fun has come to include (among other things): fleeing to Mexico with a murderer, casual sex, blowing up trucks, and armed robbery. But this does not undermine or question her original resistance to Harlan. In fact Thelma's night with JD (Brad Pitt), a charismatic convict on parole, while part of her emancipation, is specifically designed to contrast with the attempted rape scene. Here we are presented with a model of the circumstances under which Thelma would choose sex. After a succession of scenes in which she is shown watching and actively pursuing JD, she invites him into her motel room. In the first instance Thelma is dancing, drunk, in a public space which she only leaves when unwell, and into another supposedly public space for "fresh air" where the attack takes place. In the second, after a sustained period of mutual flirtation, she invites JD into the private space of her motel room. If she becomes a sexually confident woman, Thelma never becomes the kind of person who would consent to sex with Harlan.

## WHAT DID YOU SAY?

If the film is a defence of Thelma, of a woman's right to sexual freedom, it must equally defend Louise, who is, after all, the one who kills Harlan. Of the two, this is certainly the harder project. At the time of the shooting Louise is not, strictly speaking, in physical danger, nor is she protecting Thelma, as the threat of the gun pressed against Harlan's neck has already enabled her to escape. Louise's defence, then, cannot rest on behaviour alone, we need insight into who she is, and what motivates her.

In many ways the entire narrative of **Thelma And Louise** is constructed as a defence of Louise's point of view, with the viewer positioned as an ideal juror in a trial that never ultimately takes place. Ideal in the sense that we are given privileged access to information, access which would be impossible in real life. We are witnesses where there are none. The camera takes us into the private space of motel rooms, it soars above Louise's car to show the fugitives pursued by legions of squad cars. Most importantly, we see the attempted rape, the beating delivered to Thelma, and the murder, note Louise's wild swing of the arm as she brings the gun round horizontally to fire - a swing which seems unlikely to result in an accurate aim - her slightly crazed stare, her hand shaking as she lowers the gun, her nonsensical whispered demand that Harlan, now dead, "watch [his] mouth". What this enables us to do is assemble evidence that a police investigation could never unearth. Louise's behaviour at the moment of the shooting, from the viewer's perspective, suggests she is not entirely in control of herself. And when the women flee the scene of the crime we know this is not, entirely, an expression of guilt, but a recognition of the impossibility of a fair trial.

That our privileged perspective is not possible for the characters is confirmed by Hal (Harvey Keitel), the sympathetic detective who pursues the women. "Would you believe me if I told you it was an accident?" Louise asks him during one of their phone conversations. "I do believe you," replies Hal. "That's what I want everyone to believe. Trouble is, it doesn't look like an accident." Hal's "belief" is more a faith, unjustified, unsupported by evidence. The evidence accumulated by the investigators is hopelessly partial and fragmentary in comparison with our own knowledge of events, but it is the only evidence admissible. As Thelma says, "the law is some tricky shit".

## NATURAL BORN KILLERS

If Hal comes to believe that the shooting was "an accident", he is certain from the beginning that either woman was capable of killing Harlan. Interviewed by Hal in the car park while Harlan's body is carried away, Lena, the waitress, opines repeatedly that: "neither of those two was the murderin' type", her prime candidates being "some old gal, some old gal's husband". But Lena is completely wrong, and in fact the film mocks the idea that there is such a thing as a "murderin' type". Given the means, as Hal knows, anyone is capable of murder.

Lena is not the only one with such assumptions about who "killers" are and how they behave. Thelma's fantasies about criminality are also derived directly from pop culture representations. She insists on bringing a gas lamp on the journey "in case there's some escaped psycho killer on the loose who cuts the electricity off and tries to come in and kill us", while the gun she passes to Louise has multi-purpose utility against "psycho killers, bears, snakes". Louise is familiar with Thelma's ideas. She knows, for instance that her imaginary killer is male: "Maybe we should tow your car behind in case *he* steals the spark plugs," she retorts. Ironically the only killer Thelma does encounter is the one sitting next to her, a fact which makes a mockery of her conception of the kind of people who are capable of violence. Thelma herself demonstrates that there is no such kind. In the packing sequence she picks up her gun like a dead rat, by the end of the film she feels she has been holding up stores all her life.

Some critics even described the film on its release as an advert for the NRA. While there is certainly an uncomfortable element to the visual pleasure derived from seeing them destroy an oil truck, and an extremely troubling satisfaction to be had from watching Louise blow Harlan away, **Thelma And Louise** is far more responsible than the average Hollywood action film or police thriller, with its unthinking endorsement of gun law. In fact it ridicules the right-wing argument that weapons may be safely licenced to responsible people. Who could be a more responsible gun owner than Thelma, who refuses to touch hers for years? And yet, eventually, because it is there it is used, and because it is used, one person (and indirectly, two more) dies.

## THAT KIND OF WORLD

But the specific circumstances of the killing and Louise's possession of a gun are not defence enough on its own. Harlan is not shot simply for insulting Louise. Harlan is a representation of the "kind of world" Louise is obliged to live in. In fact, the film is populated by patriarchal archetypes, salacious violent cartoons of masculinity, rather than realist characters. The drooling, gesturing truck driver they encounter three times on the road is another cartoon, his unsubtle invitations betraying a mentality unpleasantly similar to Harlan's:

LOUISE: "Pointing to your lap - what is that supposed to mean exactly?..."
THELMA: "Does that mean 'suck my dick?'"

Though here the protagonists content themselves with shooting his truck. But Harlan and the truck driver are only the worst of the bunch. Thelma's husband Darryl (Christopher McDonald) is an egotistical buffoon who would rather watch a football game than listen to his wife. Though Thelma is clearly afraid of him in the early scenes, too nervous even to ask his permission to go away for the weekend, Darryl is too comic a figure to be threatening. He thinks the phone tap the FBI installs in his house is going to cost him. When Slocum tells him his wife is wanted for armed robbery, he steps backwards into his pizza, able only to utter "Wha–?" repeatedly, a grunt of incomprehension which is also the trucker's favourite phrase. Though Thelma has to wait to get her own back, Darryl is being punished for his idiocy from the first scene, in which he falls over trying to get to his beloved (and predictably red) sportscar. His car's licence plate is "THE 1", which is both "the one" and, ironically, nearly "Thelma". Ironic because Thelma, though his wife, is not "the one" for Darryl. Darryl's real marriage is to the vehicle which takes him away from the house and into the world he truly inhabits, the world outside his house, the world of his office and his (implied) girlfriend(s).

Louise constantly taunts Thelma for her passivity in the face of Darryl's overbearing arrogance: "Is he your husband or your father?" she asks in the first scene. Louise implies that Thelma is allowing Darryl to retain the authority of a father over her, an accusation she makes explicit in her next sentence: "Don't be a child". The power relation between husband and wife, in this kind of world, is the same as that between father and child. Thelma, in marrying Darryl, has simply been passed from one male to another. While there are no real parents in **Thelma And Louise** (neither women seeming to have any family), characters constantly reproduce parent-child roles between themselves. Darryl's assumption of the authority of a father is particularly ironic because he, as Thelma acknowledges, "prides himself on being infantile". In some ways the film is like a custody battle between Darryl and Louise (who, especially in the early scenes, behaves like a fussy, slightly overbearing mother) for Thelma.

Louise's boyfriend Jimmy (Michael Madsen) is little better. If he flies across two States to deliver her savings to her in Oklahoma City, he is still "no different from any other guy, he just loves the chase is all". When Louise refuses to explain the situation to him he vents his frustration on the hotel furniture, throwing stuff off work surfaces and kicking over a table. Even Hal Slocum, though well-meaning, is on the other side of a seemingly unbridgeable divide. His belief in his ability to "do them some good" is unshakeable, but the indifference of his peers and superiors attests otherwise, and his persistence ultimately worsens the situation. As Cathy Griggers notes, Hal, as a representative of:

"the sympathetic but paternalistic authority, turns out to be the most dangerous because he believes in his won ability to 'do the right thing' in regard to the women. Enticing Louise to stay too long on the phone... Slocum is the one who puts the two women in the hands of the feds..."[2]

These figures not only people Thelma and Louise's world, they order and control it. When Thelma goes into a store, apparently to buy groceries, the camera stays on Louise who notices an old woman watching her from a window, her face framed as if behind bars and her expression pained as she blinks into the light. It is, Louise knows, a vision of domestic entrapment summarizing the only future that this "kind of world" has to offer her. Thelma, meanwhile, has made the same realisation. Her response is to hold up the store.

The relentlessly negative stereotypes of men in the film are too grotesque to be real characters. Rather they are projections of Louise's jaded experience of the world. We see men through Louise's eyes, acknowledging their constant inclination to treat women as slaves and objects, and we begin, retrospectively, to understand Louise's irrational reaction to Harlan's "suck my cock". What seems a banal insult in the aftermath of attempted rape now appears as the straw that breaks Louise's back, the final verbal attempt at subjugation which, coming from another would-be rapist, seems to threaten a second rape. The violent retribution exacted by Louise against Harlan is then, not to be taken literally, as an appalling endorsement of vigilantism and gun culture (after all, the narrative does not permit them to profit from Louise's action but rather locks them into an escalating cycle of desperation), but as a symbolic attempt to destroy patriarchal society's control over her.

## TEXAS

If the supporting characters are archetypes rather than individuals, the landscapes of Thelma and Louise cannot quite be taken literally either. "Something crossed over in me and I can't go back," says Thelma, drawing an explicit parallel between the State borders they traverse and her own internal transformation, as if the landscape is an expressionist projection of her character's emotional and psychological journey. Geographical spaces, come, in both women's minds, to function as emblems of society, and they polarize into two opposing possibilities, "Texas" and "Mexico".

From their arrival in Oklahoma City, Thelma and Louise's behaviour is determined, both literally and metaphorically, by the desire to reach Mexico by avoiding Texas. The word "Texas" signifies both the State itself and the experiences Louise suffered here, it becomes the shorthand euphemism by which Louise raises the issue of her past trauma without directly talking about it, and it is the means by which the viewer pieces together an idea of Louise's past. As they pull into the car park of the bar where the rape and murder take place, Louise comments: "I haven't seen a place like this since I left Texas". After blowing up the oil truck Thelma asks her where she learned to shoot like that. "Texas," says Louise. By the time Thelma confronts Louise with a direct question "It happened to you didn't it... you was raped?", the repeated associations of "Texas" with chauvinism and violence, coupled with Louise's shooting of Harlan, make her answer (which she never makes) unnecessary to our understanding of her motivation.

On a literal level, then, Louise's insistence on reaching Mexico from Oklahoma City without going through Texas is absurd, suicidal. As Thelma reasonably notes, "we're running for our lives, can't you make an exception?" In their progression from Oklahoma City to the Grand Canyon the Thunderbird covers a mileage which, had the car been pointed in the right direction, would have taken them well across the border. But on a symbolic level it is a desperately poignant decision. Louise is attempting the impossible. Texas is a kind of society, a kind of reality; it cannot simply be avoided - neither by her decision to leave the State of Texas in her youth nor by their circuitous itinerary now - because they are already in it, it surrounds them, it is patriarchy. Louise is obsessed with Texas even as she resists it, her resistance is determined by her obsession. As Sharon Willis says, Louise's route is "the detour that circumscribes 'the heart of the matter', the personal history that is at once obscure, empty and structuring".[3] As a word, as a geographical place, as a symbol, Texas is the multi-functional sign of their undoing, their nemesis. The final seal on their entrapment comes when Hal reveals during their second phone conversation that "I know what happened to you in Texas". Louise pauses with the receiver in her hand, stunned, just long enough for the police to trace the call.

## MEXICO

Even more so than Texas, Mexico is less a real than an imaginative space, and it is everything Texas is not. In Louise's mind it represents not just freedom from arrest, but freedom from patriarchy. In fact Thelma and Louise make little attempt to reach the real Mexico, perhaps suspecting that the country itself will not match their utopian projections. While their trunk is already overstuffed with a weekend's worth of provisions, they make copious stops for food and in motels. Thelma has time for a passionate romance with JD. Louise and Jimmy spend a final night together discussing their relationship. Louise makes dangerous phone calls to Detective Slocum, her own motives for doing so apparently unclear. Even after circumventing Texas they do not turn sharply through New Mexico and head for the border but at the time of their capture are still moving due west. Their decision to blow up the truck, sending a smoke signal of their position hundreds of feet into the desert air, betrays a fatalism about their eventual capture. This is not the behaviour of people desperate for survival.

Realising they will never reach their "Mexico", Thelma and Louise try to create their own private "Mexico" *en route*, in opposition to the Texas which oppresses them. And their first step in this direction is a simple reversal of traditional gender roles. Thelma leaves home and takes to the road with Louise. This act both highlights the traditional status of the road (and implicitly, the road movie) as a masculine realm, and destroys it. In the first domestic scene of the film, Darryl, dressed for work, is shown leaving the house while Thelma, wearing a dressing gown, stays behind. The instant Thelma and Louise climb into Louise's car, everything changes. "I just got fed up with the passive role of women," wrote screenwriter Callie Khouri. "They were never driving the story, because they were never driving the car."[4] From this point, they are, and Darryl, except when he is obliged to assist the police, is never seen out of doors again. He, and all the police officers who fill the house, is tied to the home, reduced to impotent rage and astonishment, waiting for the phone to ring. So too Jimmy, who is no more than a voice on an answering machine in the early scenes, is soon obliged to sit by the phone, waiting for Louise's call. The women, meanwhile, are seated in the Thunderbird, heading for the expansive western desert where they can give full vent to their untested autonomy.

Once there, and now wanted by the police, this "autonomy" takes ever more extreme forms. Both Darryl and eventually Jimmy, dwindle to irrelevance. Louise rejects Jimmy's poignantly ill-timed offer of marriage and keeping the ring as a memento, gently refusing to let him come with her. It is, she says, "probably not a good idea": the very words with which she initially refused to give JD a lift. Jimmy is relegated to the incidental status of JD, a hitchhiking stranger. Meanwhile, the south-west becomes a kind of incredible space in which they enact a succession of "feminine revenge fantas(ies)"[5]. Feminist resistance to "Texas" becomes blurred with the women's status as criminals. As Louise notes, "We're fugitives now, let's start behaving like that".

## I'M LOUISE

Thelma and Louise's embracing of a gender-political version of traditional outlaw behaviour, coupled with their intense relationship which sees off all competition from men, has made the film hugely popular within queer theory. Certainly there is plenty of space for lesbian readings. A persistent thread of suggestion runs through the dialogue from the first scenes (a colleague of Louise's in the cafe asks Thelma "When are you going to run away with me?"; "Not this weekend sweetie," says Louise, grabbing the phone; "She's running away with me") to the closing kiss as they drive, hands clasped together, over the edge. Louise, for much of the film, adopts a butch protective attitude towards Louise. Her demand that Harlan "let her go" places her firmly in the traditional male rescuer position, and her driving is at time outrageously macho. After refusing to allow Thelma to offer JD a lift, she drives backwards at high speed to a gas station and tells the attendant to "fill her up". Louise, on the other hand, assumes all the tropes of feminine passivity; being rescued, crying, being seduced. She is even unable to manage money properly, losing $20 in the wind while trying to count their savings, and allowing JD to make off with Louise's entire savings. In this respect, Thelma and Louise appropriate all the stereotyped behavioural patterns of a straight couple in a particularly clichéd romance.

But the film continually resists and undercuts such coherent readings. Louise's protective behaviour towards Thelma is more maternal than erotic, while the overtly heterosexual behaviour of both women contradicts the lesbian undertones. Besides, a pivotal moment in the two women's relationship occurs when Thelma loses all Louise's savings. While Louise crumples to the motel room floor in resignation and despair, Thelma suddenly takes charge: "Don't you worry about it Louise. Stand up... come on dammit! Move! Jesus Christ!". Thereafter it is Thelma, rather than Louise, who adopts the more active role. While Louise fiddles with make-up and waits in the car, Thelma is holding up a store. And her turn duly comes to save Louise when she is nearly arrested for speeding, forcing the policeman at gunpoint into the trunk of his own car. During this scene, Louise takes on the "feminine" role of comic befuddlement, shooting the wrong radio in the police car.

But this gender role reversal is not consistent either.[6] In fact the text tantalizes us with its openness, the constant alternations in identity and role within the movie. At other moments, the two women achieve the balance not of opposites but of (Platonic) twins. "I'm Louise," says Thelma on their first drive, pretending to smoke a cigarette and watching herself in the wing mirror, as if a little girl copying her mother. By the end of the film, the emulation has been perfected, both women are so synchronized that their dress, behaviour, dialogue is all in tandem. Their clothes become increasingly androgynous, and their hair colour, Thelma's especially, changes perceptibly with the desert light, sometimes it is blonde, and sometimes, in the evening sun, it takes on an auburn luminosity almost identical to Louise's.

In this sense neither Thelma nor Louise can be said to progress or develop as characters in the way in which you would expect in a road or buddy movie. Thelma's inner journey is not an easy linear one from housewife to harpy. The store security video which records her robbery shows her acting out the gentlemanly method JD described for her, throwing in ad-libs (eg. her request for a bottle of Wild Turkey) to make the performance her own. Thelma's hold-up emphasizes the performative element of their behaviour, the way in which they adopt and inhabit a succession of (supposedly gendered) roles as the need arises, drawing on different potentialities within themselves. Louise, too, does not so much become a new person as rediscover long-suppressed elements of her identity. In the opening sequences she is a model of mature responsibility. The final shot in the packing sequence lingers on the kitchen sink which she has left spotless. Our first sight of her is in the diner where she tells two female customers they are "kinda young to be smoking, don'tya think?". But her demeanour of weary asexual self-restraint protests too much: another Louise is never far from the surface. Louise is equally complex and contradictory, and only in the utopian space of the desert can she really explore herself. Both women, then, improvise their "Mexico" en route, making of the road a space for a kind of desperate, utopian play with identity.[7] In so doing they expose femininity and masculinity as learned patterns of behaviour, removing the chains which tie both sexes to their traditional roles.

## YOU WOMEN ARE CRAZY!

Of course, the male characters do not interpret Thelma and Louise's emancipated behaviour in this way. They try persistently to dismiss, categorize and contain female behaviour by characterizing anything they don't like as insanity and hysteria. The truck driver calls the women "crazy" when they suggest his obscenities might be disgusting. Learning of Thelma's flight with Louise, Darryl describes her as a "nutcase". Neither of these actions could seriously be considered "crazy", they are merely *inconvenient* for the men on the receiving end. The label of insanity is a way of aggrandizing and legitimizing their complaints. When Thelma is not waiting patiently at home on his eventual return, Darryl protests: "I *leave* for work, and you take complete *leave* of your senses". Women's sanity and normality is tied to the specific domestic space of the family home. While Darryl can "leave" the home at will with his identity intact, Thelma's departure involves leaving her "senses" behind. Louise suggests she should "tell (Darryl) I'm having a nervous breakdown". "That won't carry much weight with Darryl," retorts Thelma, "he already thinks you're out of your mind". We are left to guess exactly why Darryl would think this, but it is likely to be connected to the fact that Louise is an independent woman. Certainly Darryl regards her as a threat. When Thelma repeats Louise's assertion that he is "my husband not my father", Darryl instantly realizes the idea is Louise's not Thelma's: "That Louise is nothin' but a bad influence".

And yet the women sometimes characterize themselves in the same way: "I guess I went a little crazy," says Thelma after their shooting fest has destroyed the oil truck. "You've always been crazy," replies Louise, "this is just the first chance you've had to express yourself". But they are joking. Louise herself highlights the traditional link between female sexuality and madness when Thelma appears at breakfast after her night with JD with her hair "messed up". "You look like you're crazy or you're on drugs," comments Louise. If their behaviour is, or becomes, extreme, it is the product of extreme provocation. If Harlan is unhinged, Louise too appears genuinely unstable in the shooting, and there is a hysterical tone to the escalating gun play of the closing scenes.

THELMA: "It feels like I've been doing it all my life."
LOUISE: "Think you've found your callin'?"
THELMA: "Yep, the call of the wild."
LOUISE: "You are disturbed."
THELMA: "I believe I am".

"Disturbed" is a better word. By the final sequence, both women are, in different ways, traumatized by their experiences, by the stress of their opposition to "Texas".

## LET'S KEEP GOING

The association of western outlaw mythology with a feminist parable makes **Thelma And Louise** a problematic film for feminism. By linking feminism with anarchic violence, it makes women's self-determination seem both more romantic, and more threatening, than it is. It also resorts to ever cruder male stereotypes to justify its protagonists' behaviour to audiences. In some respects the grotesque nature of the male characters betrays the filmmakers' anxieties over the audience's response. Part of the function of the scene between Hal and Lena is to remind us what kind of a man Harlan was, to block any encroaching audience sympathy for his lifeless body. And he was, Lena tells us, a faithless husband hated by men and women alike. It seems curious that we might need to be told that Harlan is an unfaithful husband when we already know him to be a rapist, as if he is not already hateful enough. Even if such characters are symbols rather than "real" figures within the logic of the film, at its darkest moments, **Thelma And Louise** strays dangerously towards endorsing a violent vigilantism.

The heavy-handedness of the confrontation scene with the trucker who has been annoying them betrays a kind of exhaustion, encouraging us to indulge impulses of disgust and revenge. Certainly both women show signs towards the end of succumbing to the same inclinations, to stop resisting patriarchal violence and to simply return it like avenging furies. Their position hardens as the police close in. Thelma claims to be "not sorry that sonofabitch is dead. I'm just sorry it was you did it and not me". She starts to sound like Lena, who is positively cheerful about Harlan's murder. And Louise, in the final showdown at the Grand Canyon, does not drop her weapon when called on to do so, she loads it. By the end the female fugitives and their male pursuers are encamped on opposite sides in a literal battle of the sexes. A series of close-ups show guns being loaded and huge numbers of marksmen arrayed in ranks, kneeling in a firing squad style line, as if ready to execute them. Small wonder Louise comments "it looks like the army".

This is followed by the officer's absurd command to "turn off your engine". They are surrounded by police cars on one side, and the Grand Canyon on the other, but the engine still somehow threatens escape. The demand is an attempt to control the terms of the end, to leave them only the choice between surrender and execution. For a moment, as Louise loads her gun, the film seems set to play out a final gun battle in the Butch Cassidy style. But Thelma has a different idea: "Let's keep going," she urges, her face bright with elation. Louise doesn't follow her at first, but once she understands, she shares Thelma's euphoria. As the car starts, Hal makes a despairing, futile run into no man's land, confirming what Louise always suspected, his inability to "do them some good". It is hard to regard suicide as a positive resolution, but in the desperation of the moment, it comes to seem so. Thelma's idea to "keep going", they realise, is what saves them from the bloody shoot-out which the police seem to want, a final flurry of violence which would leave them, in death, with only more blood on their hands. Instead Thelma reconfigures the end as a final act of resistance, registering their disgust at the terms (surrender or fight) offered to them. If the outlaw pursuit narrative which has gathered pace throughout the film demands such a climax, Scott finds an ending which both acknowledges the outlaw genre and evades it, reworking the protagonists' inevitable deaths as a euphoric final act of resistance. The original cut followed the car to its destruction in the canyon below, but in the final cut, Scott leaves us with the point of triumphant escape, freezing the car just as its arc begins to fall.

# NOTES

1. As Yvonne Tasker puts it: "The situation of a female friendship scenario within the context of violence, the mobilisation of the iconography of the Western and the evocation of the rape-revenge narrative, all suggest the movie's peculiar status as a text that is both unconventional and generic." (Yvonne Tasker, *Working Girls*; London: Routledge, 1998, p.199).

2. Cathy Griggers, "Thelma And Louise And The Cultural Generation Of The New Butch-Femme" in Jim Collins, Hilary Radner and Ava Preacher Collins (eds), *Film Theory Goes To The Movies*; New York: Routledge, 1993, p.137.

3. Sharon Willis, "Hardware And Hardbodies, What Do Women Want?: A Reading Of **Thelma And Louise**" in *Film Theory Goes To The Movies*, p.123.

4. Cited in Willis, p.125.

5. Cathy Griggers, "Thelma And Louise And The Cultural Generation Of The New Butch-Femme', p.137.

6. In fact there is a constant alternation of masculine/feminine roles between Thelma and Louise: "The degree to which Louise can maintain her femininity in a given situation depends on the degree to which Thelma can give up some of hers. The femme-butch line of flight requires a constant adaption and variation." (Griggers, p.139).

7. Cathy Griggers summarises the complexity of Thelma and Louise's self-exploration: "Empowered with their machines (pistols and cars), wearing blue jeans, boots, T-shirts, and a just-so touch of lipstick, they can signify the multiple and contradictory regimes of signs from which they construct, day to day, a sense of identity." (Griggers, p.139).

# Chapter 12
# Queens Of The Road

# QUEENS OF THE ROAD: DRAG AND THE '90s ROAD MOVIE

## Estella Tincknell

### INTRODUCTION

The road movie is a curious genre. Its various permutations have been more complex and radical than the popular image often allows for, and its own journey from the picaresque romance to the post-modern anti-quest narrative has been more tortuous and much longer than might be imagined. While it is true that "the road has always been a persistent theme of American culture. Its significance, embedded in both popular mythology and social history, goes back to the nation's frontier ethos", as Steve Cohan and Ina Rae Hark argue in the introduction to their *Road Movie Book*[1]. The best road movies have not always been American and nor have the roads being travelled. Even if the road movie is the definitively American genre (which it possibly is), it is one that has excluded, marginalised or dealt only partially with much of American life. And because the road movie has largely been a genre that privileged the figure of the young white man in search of himself, it has often excluded or has been silent about others. This essay is about two road movies which are both very alike and radically different: **The Adventures Of Priscilla, Queen Of The Desert** (Stephan Elliot, 1994) and **To Wong Foo, Thanks For Everything, Julie Newmar** (Beeban Kidron, 1995). The first film, **Priscilla**, deploys the conventions of an American genre in order to interrogate *Australian* society and identities, while the second uses them for sentimental comedy. Both films share a basic premise, that of the journey of three drag queens across country leading to a series of transformatory encounters. In **Priscilla**, Felicia/Adam, Mitzy/Tick and transsexual Bernadette attempt to deal with their tragedies and failures by journeying to a gig in Alice Springs; while in **To Wong Foo**, "Miss Vida Boheme" and "Miss Noxeema Jackson" are two fully-fledged drag queens who take pity on the young Latino, Chi Chi, taking "her" with them to the grand final of a national drag "beauty contest" in Hollywood. **To Wong Foo** has been read as a poor imitation of the more innovative and acidic **Priscilla** and as a text which substitutes saccharine sentimentality for subversive wit, but this is too reductive as a critical analysis, as we will see. Both films loosely situate themselves in relation to the emergence of a new "queer" cinema in the 1990s through the central characters and through a textual preoccupation with performance, visual display and ironic self-reflexivity, although **Priscilla**'s take on such themes is undoubtedly sharper-edged. Most noticeably, both films, while offering homosexual desire as a key narrative theme, evade a fully meaningful critical engagement with the topic by refusing to represent that desire pictorially and by displacing it onto heterosexual characters. This displacement is the factor that, arguably, makes both films "commercial" – that is, acceptable to a mainstream (heterosexual) audience – but it is also problematic to their narrative success.

### SETTING OUT...

As Steve Cohan points out, road movies are not simply about individual transformation and fulfilment, they offer a commentary on the state of America as a nation and

America as a nation state. The development of the road narrative as a specifically American film genre from the 1930s is therefore significant. It articulated the restlessness of a new and relatively nomadic society, and charted social changes linked to the use of new and more individualised modes of transport, as the train gave way to the car and motorcycle, and the model of the mass society was replaced by that of fragmentation and diversity. Like the western, the road movie offers a space in which to explore the ways in which ideas about Americanness, culture and identity are expressed and defended (a thematic trope taken up by **To Wong Foo** in its western-style small town, complete with main street on which the final symbolic "shoot-out" takes place); but unlike that genre, the road movie articulates the search for sensory experience which has been central to post-war popular culture. It is, therefore, a genre that stages some of the key tropes of modernity in its dramatisation of the individual's search for self-determination and its charting of social change. Unlike the pre-industrial form of the picaresque tale, the road movie offers not an account of the sentimental and moral education of a hero whose "self" remains bounded by Cartesian duality, but an exploration of the *relationship* between the personal and the social. To be "on the road" is not only to be ever in search of an authentic self, but also to experience modernity.

Early road movies of the '30s and '40s tended to trace a journey in which the flight from home was also a journey back there, emphasising the importance of the individual's relationship to a broader community. Just as Dorothy in **The Wizard Of Oz** (Victor Fleming, 1939) found that the yellow brick road led back to Kansas, other travellers discovered that home was finally the best place to be and that their journey worked to make them recognise this. Indeed, from **It Happened One Night** (Frank Capra, 1934) through the Hope/Crosby/Lamour series of **Road** films in the forties, the road (however exotic its ostensible location or destination) led firmly back to an America which was pluralistic yet homogenous – a thoroughly United States. And showbusiness itself was often the discourse through which this was figured, as Cohan argues, "Made right before the United States' entrance into the war, **Sullivan's Travels** (1941) glosses the road through a mythology of national coherence that draws on popular entertainment for its rationale. A film director seeking first-hand knowledge of 'real' American life that will allow his new film to overcome the escapism connoted by Hollywood entertainment, John L. Sullivan (Joel McCrea) tours the road in disguise as a hobo only to discover right away that he cannot escape Hollywood, his home town."[2]

As Cohan points out, Preston Sturges' **Sullivan's Travels** offers popular entertainment as the glue which sticks America together, so that when the hero is thrown into jail he witnesses the shared pleasure of his fellow convicts in a Disney cartoon despite their ethnic differences. Thus, "[the] road is the utopian path linking popular culture and the nation through Hollywood, which provides the comfort of home"[3] and the values of Hollywood are the values of America. Paradoxically, the queer, postmodern version of the genre exemplified by **The Adventures Of Priscilla, Queen of the Desert** and by **To Wong Foo, Thanks for Everything, Julie Newmar**, returns to this discourse of showbiz style, glamour and energy, even though it does so ironically. The latter, in particular, posits Hollywood as the "home" to which the drag queens are travelling (Sharon Willis argues that the characters never really leave it![4]), while in both films the journey is also a quest. The trip to Hollywood and the beauty contest in **To Wong Foo**, and to Alice Springs in **Priscilla** is figured in both films as a search for a better self, while both places are represented as an "essence" of the nation being traversed, even though **Priscilla** attempts to undercut this with ironic knowingness. If Hollywood is the bloated but still vigorous heart of America and Alice Springs represents the austere, spiritual centre of Australia, both can be recovered and remade anywhere. As Noxie says in **To Wong Foo**, if she can't get to Hollywood "I gonna make Hollywood wherever I am at".

Yet despite this apparent continuity between early and more recent films, it is important to note that the genre has not simply "returned" to an earlier version of itself or even recovered the values of the '30s and '40s. The road movie of the '60s and '70s offered a journey through an America that was increasingly fragmented and heterogenous, divided not only by differing values but also by competing and contradictory definitions of what America itself was supposed to be. If **Easy Rider** redefined the road movie in 1969 [see Chapter 4], it did so in the context of America's own identity crisis in the late '60s, which the film staged through its clash between conforming and alternative cultural values. The road was increasingly identified as the space for the marginalised and the alienated, the journey taken one which led away from rather than back towards mainstream society.

Even before **Easy Rider** in 1969, the road movie had become increasingly identified as a genre that articulated highly masculine fantasies of escape and personal freedom, in which emotional commitment was conflated with a bourgeois femininity that stifled both the authentic (male) self and sexual liberation.[5] The road was primarily a masculine space in which the power and mobility of the male body was aestheticised and fetishised and the intense emotional relationship between men – "buddies" – celebrated. While early road movies such as **It Happened One Night** and **Sullivan's Travels** featured heterosexual couples in a relationship of idealised companionship, the "buddy" movie of the 1970s replaced this with homosocial bonding. In the 1990s, however, the "queer" road movie has entered another paradigm shift in which aggressively heterosexual forms of masculinity have been critically represented. The seminal **Thelma And Louise** (Ridley Scott, 1991) [see Chapter 11], **My Own Private Idaho** (Gus Van Sant, 1991) and **The Living End** (Gregg Araki, 1992) offer narratives in which patriarchal and normative masculinity is a threat rather than a solution, and in which the quest for masculine authenticity is replaced by an increasing interrogation of the very basis of gendered identity, desire and sexuality. **To Wong Foo** and **Priscilla** clearly belong to this moment. Yet while both films offer a critical refusal of dominant masculinity their appropriation of "feminine" cultural modes is itself highly problematic.

In both **Priscilla** and **To Wong Foo** the male body's association with power, strength and mobility is repeatedly problematised by the replacement of the streamlined car or motorbike with, respectively, an old bus and a beaten-up open-top cadillac. Neither vehicle is able to make the journey without breaking down. The unreliability of the transport thus seems to mirror the problematic masculinity of those it carries, so that to be in drag is to be mechanically inept. Indeed, in **To Wong Foo**, the drag queens choose the cadillac entirely on the basis of its appearance not its reliability, setting up the film's message that style is more important than anything else. This uncoupling of the marriage between male power and the internal combustion engine is less radical than it looks, however, for by linking a feminised masculinity with a preference for style over power it tends to reify the relationship between heterosexual patriarchy and a command of the road. Indeed, **To Wong Foo** resolutely sets out to offer a narrative of integration, *reincorporating* its drag queens into mainstream America at the end of the film and restoring heterosexual coupledom. In this respect, the film seems to belong firmly within the tradition of the romantic comedy.

## MILITARY CAMP – CARY GRANT'S (UN)EASY RIDE

Indeed, the emphasis on drag in the contemporary queer road movie has an interesting precedent in the Howard Hawks comedy, **I Was A Male War Bride** (1949) which, while firmly foregrounding heterosexual romance, also plays with other sexual

I Was A Male War Bride

possibilities. The film's plot revolves around the screwball romance between Cary Grant as the French Captain, Henri Rochard, and Ann Sheridan as the feisty American Lieutenant, Katherine Gates. The film begins with their second meeting (they already have a past) in occupied Germany to be sent on a final secret mission together before leaving the armed forces. The mission involves them in a hair-raising journey across Germany in a motorcycle combination during which they fall in love; and in the second half of the film they take another kind of trip in an attempt to marry and go to the USA together. Grant, of course, can only be approved by the US authorities if he accepts his role as a "war bride", that is if he concedes the power and authority properly belonging to patriarchal masculinity to his wife,[6] and this humiliation is finally effected in the last sequence when he is forced to masquerade as an admiral's bride in order to be allowed on board the ship.

From its opening frame, in which Grant as Henri Rochard is being driven to the US military headquarters, to its final shot, in which the statue of liberty is sighted through a ship's porthole, I Was A Male War Bride draws on many of the elements of the early road movie. Rochard's "real" journey is his Journey to America and to the American values that he embraces by falling in love with Katherine Gates, of course, and this is symbolised through the picaresque adventure he and Gates must take. Characteristically, Rochard proceeds through various forms of increasingly uncomfortable modes of transport during his journey. From the car he transfers to the motorcycle combination driven by Sheridan (she's got the permit), in which he is forced to huddle in the sidecar, to a bus for the "war brides", and finally to the ship which takes them to America. Grant and Sheridan bicker and wisecrack all the way, and throughout the film he is subjected to repeated physical discomfort and humiliation: he is drenched with rain, splattered with paint, falls from a window into a chicken coop and from the sidecar into a haystack.

Significantly, Grant prefigures his final female drag early in the film by disguising himself in the "feminised" (and therefore absurd) costume of a German burgermeister, complete with knee breeches and stockings. Sheridan responds to this sight with laughter and ridicule, as the audience is plainly also expected to do. Thus, while *her* body is repeatedly offered as an object of increasing desire for Grant's character – he tries to kiss her, touch her and constantly surveys and assesses her – *his* is firmly established as unavailable as an erotic spectacle. The sight of his stocking-clad limbs is represented as absurd not alluring, in marked contrast to the scene in which Sheridan rolls up her trousers to scratch her leg and Grant looks on appreciatively and encouragingly. Thus, in the final set-piece in which Grant is forced to disguise himself as a woman in order to be recognised by the US navy as a "war-bride" and be allowed to board the ship leaving for the USA his drag is deliberately set up as both ridiculous and uninviting. Forced to wear a "wig" fashioned from horses' tails by Sheridan, military skirt and thick stockings, Grant's status as a profoundly non-erotic spectacle is emphasised visually and confirmed by the dialogue. Indeed, as Stella Bruzzi argues, "The intention is not to create a credible illusion of femininity, but to reflectively allude back to masculinity via an ill-composed caricature created from a few thrown-together signifiers."[7]

Yet the film also plays with the possibility of sexual ambiguity as well as the spectacle of femininity. Grant stops to hitch up his stocking and is wolf-whistled by a passing sailor. Finally permitted to board by the two sailors checking passes, he is watched as he struggles to maintain a "feminine" progress along the ship – the "conventionalised gestural slip" which reminds the audience of his unease in women's clothing, as Bruzzi points out [8]. "First time I ever felt sorry for an Admiral", comments the first sailor, but "she isn't so bad", says the other – hinting at the possibility of transgressive desire – to be met by the rejoinder, "now I feel sorry for you". The point of all this is to re-establish the impossibility of Grant's femininity at the level of the ideological trajectory of the narrative, even while the possibility of sexual ambiguity is opened up. Grant's unflattering disguise works to demonstrate that he cannot "pass", that his drag serves only to confirm a straight masculinity – even though the film plays with queer desire. Of course, such ambiguous possibilities are cut off by the film's narrative and ideological closure, in a heterosexual embrace that promises to last for weeks – "until we see the statue of liberty" – and which will presumably erase the memory of Grant's foray into drag. And yet, the film has traced the "taming" of Henri Rochard not that of his wife, who remains the dominant partner. As Constanza del Rio has argued, **I Was A Male War Bride** belongs to a transgressive category of romantic comedies in which "masochistic male attachment and humiliation are sustained and envisaged as a valid structure for the couple's future relationship".[9]

## SURFACES, STYLE, SEXUALITIES

If **I Was A Male War Bride** may be read as a kind of ur-text for the drag road movie, the two films discussed below are more properly representative of the sub-genre, not least because both films are openly celebratory of the outrageously camp and of queer identities. In both **The Adventures Of Priscilla Queen Of The Desert** and **To Wong Foo, Thanks For Everything, Julie Newmar** the three male stars (Terence Stamp, Guy Pearce and Hugo Weaving, and Wesley Snipes, Patrick Swayze and John Leguizamo respectively) are on-screen in drag almost continuously. The costume designers for **Priscilla** received an academy award for their work and there can be little doubt that the spectacular, grotesque and fantastical clothing worn by the three queens is crucial to the visual pleasure of the text. Where Cary Grant is supposed to be unambiguously hideous in drag, the male characters in both **Priscilla** and **To Wong Foo** are offered as specular delights. Yet this shift to a celebration of the male body as visual spectacle is also problematic. For while both films create space for male characters to appropriate the pleasures of femininity, they also marginalise female ones. **Priscilla** in particular demonises and renders grotesque its female characters, from Cynthia the screeching Filipina "male-order bride", to Shirl, the homophobic bar owner whose physical unattractiveness is contrasted unfavourably with the glamour and wit of the transsexual, Bernadette. In **To Wong Foo** female characters are more fully present, less one-dimensional, but they are primarily passive. The main secondary character, the oppressed and dowdy Carol Ann (played by Stockard Channing), who runs the lodging house where Vida, Noxie and Chi Chi stay, is markedly offered as a victim in contrast to the life-affirming, empowered drag queens. In both texts, however, the marginalisation of women is more than a matter of the specific concerns of the plot; it is as though the transfer of the spectacular elements of performance to male bodies leaves little else for female bodies to do. Although the women of Snidersville effect a physical transformation of themselves which involves both dressing up and "performing" femininity as a spectacle of desire, this can only take place once the drag queens have made it possible by disrupting the conventions of normal life.

Thus, in both films, the foregrounding of the male body as the site of performance and spectacle effectively problematises this role for the female body. Indeed, this process is actually staged at one point in **Priscilla**, when Cynthia performs an explicitly vulgar striptease in an outback bar immediately after the failure of the queens' own drag show to please the crowd: an audience composed of a mob of homophobic males. Cynthia's performance is offered as lacking in the ironic self-reflexivity of the drag show as well as pathologised and punished: her body is forcibly removed from the stage in the bar just as her character is removed from the narrative.

Both films thus offer a stylised, performative version of "femininity" that is grotesque, exaggerated, parodic. If, in **Priscilla** especially, this is partly about the drag queens *own* problematic relationship with their sense of identity, desire and gender it is compounded by the absence of credible female characters to counterpoint the spectacular grotesquerie of the drag, ensuring that "femininity" itself is reduced to a masquerade. For both films are fascinated by and play with the idea that femininity can be "put on" and "taken off": it is as though the spectacle of parodic femininity being offered means that there is nothing else – that femininity is always already about surface and masquerade.

Thus, the conventional fragmentation and fetishisation of the *female* body as desirable object in classical cinema is both reworked and subverted in the opening sequences of both these queer road movies. **Priscilla** begins with Tick/Mitzy's lipsynched performance of a song which sets up his existential dilemma – "I've been to Paradise, but I've never been to me" – and which is rapidly followed by a sequence in the dressing-room in which he removes his wig and glamorous costume to reveal the male body underneath. **To Wong Foo** begins with its main star, Patrick Swayze, stepping out of the shower and walking towards the camera, the corporeality of his maleness thoroughly established in this opening shot. Swayze then sits down in front of a mirror facing the camera and begins to make up, transforming himself into Miss Vida Boheme, the drag queen. In extreme close-up we see him tuck back his short hair and begin to apply foundation, mascara, and eye-liner. This is followed by a rapid cut to a parallel shot of Wesley Snipes, also in extreme close-up and already glittering as Miss Noxeema Jackson. To the diegetically produced sounds of "Body Beautiful" the film alternates shots of the camera panning up and down the bodies of Swayze and Snipes as they dress themselves in costumes that cross camp with vamp ready for the New York drag beauty contest.

These early montages are important. First, they work to emphasise the artifice, the constructedness of the "femininity" that Vida and Noxie embrace, but do so by

To Wong Foo, Thanks For Everything, Julie Newmar

drawing on an already established set of Hollywood conventions, those of the transformation of the ordinary girl into glamour princess found in countless musicals, "women's films" and romantic comedies from **Now, Voyager** to **Pretty Woman**. Second, they are the only moment in the film when we see Swayze and Snipes out of drag, recognisably "themselves", or rather their star personae. For the rest of the narrative, Vida and Noxie sustain their drag queen characters, even at night when Vida floats around in a silk negligee. And since part of the film's ideological project is to insist that the drag queens' transvestism is part of their authentic selves, not something which is easily put on or taken off, the opening sequence is ambivalent in its assertion of the presence of phallic masculinity beneath the costumes. It is as though it is thoroughly anxious to confirm the established and conventionally masculine star identities of Swayze and Snipes before it can proceed to present them in their drag characters. Later in the film much of the comic play depends upon the drag queens rigorously maintaining their "feminine" status while fending off the sexual overtures of the Snidersville boys, who not only regard any woman as fair game but see them as highly desirable, glamorous "city girls". The dissonance between the appearance of feminine fragility and the "real" strength of masculinity is also foregrounded in a scene in which Swayze's character is able to call on his muscularity to punish Carol Ann's abusing husband, yet he does this as "Vida Boheme", the avenging angel of female victims, not as an angry man. Vida and Noxie, it seems, do not simply imitate "real" women, they exceed them. And they do this most significantly as active agents of change rather than passive victims.

Some of the film's comic tension derives from the exaggerated contrast it offers between the immaculately groomed drag queens and the dowdy and ill-kempt "real" women who inhabit Snidersville. Indeed, Noxie, Chi Chi and Vida all offer a different and highly stereotypical "version" of stylised femininity: the "sassy" African American, the sweet and "hot" Latino and the ladylike Anglo. Significantly, Vida, the

Priscilla, Queen Of The Desert

figure who is closest to the dominant culture and effectively the leader of the group, and also the character who offers the town women an alternative and idealised model of femininity, is also the one whose sexual desire is rendered most opaque.

In **Priscilla**, Bernadette the transsexual also performs femininity in more complex and nuanced ways than Mitzy and Felicia, her drag companions. Bernadette's modulated voice and elegantly simple clothes mark hers as the same kind of styled femininity as Vida's – that of the perfect lady. Indeed, the film offers a "queer fantasy" of a world in which desire and masculine identity are fluid, unfixed and endlessly re-makeable, while femininity is pathologised through parody.

And as John Champagne points out, "In order to produce a 'queer' narrative identification with **Priscilla**'s transsexual Bernadette and her quest for love, the film must posit her in opposition to Cynthia,... Bernadette is poised, Cynthia is out of control; Bernadette is 'classy', Cynthia is 'crude'; Bernadette is a lady, Cynthia is a slut".[10] For, not only does the film set up the transsexual, Bernadette, and the Filipina, Cynthia, as opposites, it makes it clear that Bernadette is the "better" *woman*. That is, Bernadette's performance of femininity is more effective than Cynthia's because it is closer to an idealised version in which the female body is neutralised and made safe. Moreover, in both films, the possibility that a drag queen may be more desirable to a straight man than a biological woman is posited. In **Priscilla**, Bob, the "gentleman" mechanic who rescues them when the bus breaks down in the outback, falls in love with Bernadette. In **To Wong Foo**, Chi Chi becomes an object of romantic interest to Bobby Ray, the similarly "gentlemanly" boy who rescues "her" from rape. But as Sharon Willis points out, while **To Wong Foo** claims to be a film all about "being true to yourself", the drag queens themselves are not permitted to show any sexual longing; "Only Chi Chi exhibits any desire and she quickly sacrifices her longing for Bobby Ray on the altar of an altruism that really translates into a sense of ethical duty to the norm; she's a fairy who brings the heterosexual couple together"[11]. In other words, while the film represents itself as a "queer" text, the very thing which makes the drag queens queer – their desire for men's bodies rather than women's – is repressed. Instead, what is offered is a glossy fantasy in which the surface details of drag style stands in for queer sexuality.

In both films, then, biological femininity is offered as flawed and problematic, while the fantastical glamour of the drag queens works to emphasise their powerful otherness: these queens are too good to be women. Where **Priscilla** asserts this through vicious misogyny, **To Wong Foo** substitutes the camp make-over. In the key set piece sequence noted above, the drag queens effectively remake the downtrodden females of Snidersville by doing their hair and make-up, and dressing them up in the '60s clothes found hidden in the attic of the town store. The women emerge, one by one, to parade and to "vogue" up and down Snidersville's dusty main street in their new finery, and for the first time demand and are accorded the courtesy from the local boys which they have never had. Perversely, by making themselves over they have become "real" women. The film offers this as a moment in which the women recover their self-respect and are therefore empowered to demand it from men; but by emphasising surface appearance as the key to authentic femininity it simply manages to emphasise that styling oneself as a desirable *object* is the only authenticity available to women. The new clothes and make-up are the "magical resolution" to the problem of patriarchal brutality (enacted by Virgil's beating of Carol Ann) yet the women are not the active agents of their transformation or of their own story. In this way, **To Wong Foo's** already limited critique of patriarchal power is further enfeebled: not only are the women offered a lesson in therapeutic self-help rather than politics, they have to wait for a bunch of men dressed as women to tell them what to do.

It is also significant that the clothes themselves invoke the late '60s, the key moment of symbolic modernity, sexual liberation and of feminism in the twentieth century, as well as the first time in over one hundred years when men could safely enjoy dressing up and experimenting with style. The psychedelic patterns and bright primary colours of the clothes thus doubly symbolise the "liberation" of Snidersville's women from their oppression, yet it is unclear to what better future they are being directed, since the film offers an equally problematic model of appropriate femininity.

## "WHITER TRASH" – EXCESSIVE MASCULINITY AND FANTASIES OF COMMUNITY

**To Wong Foo's** limitations as critique of patriarchal masculinity are manifested most clearly in the sequence discussed above, yet the film's failure to address the issue seriously is evident from the moment the three drag queens arrive in Snidersville, a town which seems to be offered by the film as representative of a generalised rural community. There is a curious absence of mature adult males, for the place seems to be inhabited mainly by women and adolescent men, with the exception of Jimmy Joe, the token black male and Virgil, Carol Ann's husband. Indeed, Virgil and Sheriff Dollard, the villain, are the only exemplars of conventional white heterosexual masculinity offered and, as such, they severely limit the film's attempt to celebrate women's empowerment. Both are little more than versions of the familiar stereotype of the Southern redneck and it is significant that the film conflates such a position with a masculinity that is both excessive and absurd.

Virgil is a wholly one-dimensional character – his narrative function is primarily to demonstrate the inadequacy of conventional marriage through his violence to Carol Ann. This is emphasised in a series of scenes which, while presumably intended to be dramatic and menacing, are perversely comic. Carol Ann spends her days in the kitchen as a drudge, drearily stirring an unpleasant looking stew which is regularly condemned and hurled to the floor by Virgil, from which Carol Ann wearily mops it and where she is found by Vida. The latter's culinary advice – "this needs a little spice and a little garlic" – is greeted with horror by Carol Ann, who knows what Virgil's reaction will be. But the scene also works to link Virgil's preference for bland, tasteless food, his lack of "good taste", with his violent and abusive personality. Virgil is vulgar. He is incapable of the kind of sophisticated appreciation of food and indeed of other good things which Vida and Noxie demonstrate. Virgil's class position as a mechanic is also implicitly conflated with this lack of taste. He is "white trash", to deploy an offensive term, and therefore fair game for liberal horror. Just as the young men in the town demonstrate their excesses through a discourse of class as well as gender – they are "rough" working men, ill-educated and therefore suspect – Virgil's physical brutality is too readily conflated with his position as a rural white working class male.

Sheriff Dollard, too, is a figure of both menace and of comic absurdity, and like Virgil he is roundly defeated at the end of the film. In this penultimate sequence, Dollard returns to Snidersville having finally tracked down Vida, whom he mistakenly took for a woman and attempted to rape at the beginning of the story, and enters the main street shouting for her, convinced that the townsfolk will turn a drag queen in once they learn that "she" is really he. Yet, in a scene reminiscent of **Spartacus** (Stanley Kubrick, 1960) – and the only genuinely innovative moment in the film – the women of the town confront Dollard, each dressed in a spectacular red dress, and each claiming that *she* is a drag queen, too. Indeed, in terms of the women's appropriation of a spectacular and stylised femininity this is effectively the case: they are all in drag. But the transgressive potential of this moment is lost. While Dollard is forced to leave, defeated by the new kind of community into which Snidersville has been transformed, the precise terms of that community are left open; and while the scene itself may leave the viewer with a warm glow (or perhaps simply a queasy feeling) the easy utopianism being offered is inadequate. The absence of a recognisable masculine community in Snidersville makes the transformation unconvincing, and seems to underline the film's well-meaning populism. Without adequately representing the real (complex, liberal, contradictory) power of patriarchal masculinity it cannot hope to make such a transformation meaningful beyond a brief "feel good" moment.

Both **Priscilla** and **To Wong Foo** thus contrast the values of urban cosmopolitanism with rural traditionalism, offering versions of "good" and "bad" communities in which rural bigotry and sexual repression are transformed by urban liberalism and sexual liberation. **Priscilla**'s journey across Australia is also a journey through different kinds of communities in which the spatial is linked to the performance of gender. Sydney is represented as a sophisticated, cosmopolitan cultural space in which a gay lifestyle can be pursued and is contrasted with the resistance and aggression encountered in the inhabited parts of the outback where the drag queens are confronted by small-town homophobia and hick barbarity. Yet in both films, resistance to queer culture is largely conflated with an excessive masculinity that is not only heterosexual, it is poor and white. To posit caricatures such as Sheriff Dollard or the sweaty "mates" of Australia's outback as the villains of queer romance is therefore both too easy and too problematic.

Notwithstanding the celebration of "feminine" spectacle and performance in these two films, the queer drag road movie, like other examples of the genre, continues to see the road as masculine space and to be concerned with the kinds of authentic selfhood primarily available to white males. For all their emphases on a liberal pluralist version of queer identity both **To Wong Foo** and **Priscilla** foreground white male characters as the key figures, rendering women as passive, demonised or marginal. Indeed, we have to look back to 1949 and **I Was A Male War Bride** for anything resembling an independent, assertive and witty heterosexual female in such a context. If **Thelma And Louise**, by killing off its heroines, radically asserted the impossibility of the road as a safe space for women, the emergence of the queer drag road movie concerned only with femininity as style reinforces that disturbing claim.

# NOTES

1. *The Road Movie Book*; London: Routledge, 1997, p1.

2. Steven Cohan, "Almost Like Being At Home: Showbiz Culture And Hollywood Road Trips In The 1940s And 1950s" in Steven Cohan & Ina Rae Hark (eds), *The Road Movie Book*; London: Routledge, 1997, p.123.

3. Steven Cohan, Almost Like Being At Home: Showbiz Culture And Hollywood Road Trips In The 1940s and 1950s", p.124.

4. Sharon Willis, "Race On The Road: Crossover Dreams" in Steve Cohan & Ina Rae Hark (eds), *The Road Movie Book*; London: Routledge, 1997, p.295.

5. And even outside the road movie the popular teen culture of the '50s celebrated the figure of a romanticised male rebel – Elvis, James Dean – who rejected the inauthentic and feminine demands of domesticity and sexual fidelity.

6. Somewhat unsubtly, Grant's capitulation to American hegemony closely resembles that of Europe itself. Time and again his "European" expectations and behaviour are contrasted with and transformed by the feisty spirit and moral values of his new American wife, who demands sexual fidelity as well as marital equality in their relationship.

7. Stella Bruzzi, *Undressing Cinema: Clothing And Identity In The Movies*; London: Routledge, 1997, p.151.

8. Stella Bruzzi, p.151.

9. Constanza del Rio, "Something Wild: Take A Walk On The Wild Side (But Be Home Before Midnight)" in Peter William Evans & Celestine Deleyto (eds), *Terms Of Endearment: Hollywood Romantic Comedy Of The 1980s And 1990s*; Edinburgh University Press, 1998, p83.

10. John Champagne, "Dancing Queen? Feminist And Gay Male Spectatorship In Three Recent Films From Australia", *Film Criticism*, 21(3), pp.70–71.

11. Sharon Willis, "Race On The Road: Crossover Dreams" in Steve Cohan & Ina Rae Hark (eds), *The Road Movie Book*; London: Routledge, 1997, p.294.

# Chapter 13
# Travelling Children

# "SUCH TIME WHEN YOUNG'UNS RUN THE ROADS": THE DEPICTION OF TRAVELLING CHILDREN

## Kay Dickinson

Amidst the heavy traffic of Walrus-moustached white men in road movies, the character of the child often slips by the wayside of academic engagements with the genre. This oddly potent manifestation of the child driven from his or her "natural" habitat and caught up in the matrix of adult representation with its concomitant desires, habits, nostalgia and neuroses will be the focus for this chapter. The wealth of film material fascinated by children or involving child-identified characters has an overt pool of source literature (various fairy-tales and quest narratives, Charles Dickens' *David Copperfield*, Rudyard Kipling's *Kim*, Mark Twain's *The Adventures Of Huckleberry Finn*, Kenneth Grahame's *The Wind In The Willows*, J.R Tolkein's *The Hobbit* and so on) providing a diverse array of examples for our perusal. The following films, although perhaps at first glance incongruous, display often startling unity in their ideological treatment of the wandering child.

The first choice is an archetypal film, an ultimate road movie if we peer beyond open-topped cars and bogarted joints: **The Wizard Of Oz** (Victor Fleming, 1939). The second, **Night Of The Hunter** (Charles Laughton, 1955), sandwiches John and Pearl's flight from their wicked step-father down not a road, but a river, between broader narrative sections, and this particular portion will be isolated and scrutinized. Film three, **Walkabout** (Nicholas Roeg, 1971), lacks a designated path as the viewer might know it, but is perhaps thematically the closest of the group to the traditional road movie. The "Walkabout" of the film's title represents an existential quest, a rites of passage for not only the Aborigine, but also the English-speaking girl and boy he saves in the outback.[1] The deeper connotations of the road, of course, vary from film to film, but the theme of self-discovery – familiar also from **The Wizard Of Oz** – is deeply ingrained in the genre.

One common denominator which sets these works apart from traditional road movies is their lack of a car. In fact the luxury of technologically advanced (or magical) transport is often only afforded to their baddies – the Wicked Witch of the West traverses Oz by broomstick, Powell rides along in a jalopy in **Night Of The Hunter** and **Walkabout's** father drives his children into the wilderness, leaving them chauffeur-less when he commits suicide. That the car can only signify individual freedom at a price and with an age limit, that the oblivion of speed or access to technology is not granted everyone, is often overlooked in the genre's literature. By default the road is largely a (masculine) adult preserve and the dubious rewards of eventual disillusionment may at least dawn on the road movie protagonist as he roams rather than – as might be the case with children and obedient house-wives – while stuck indoors. The privilege of freedom, of "boysy" beat-existentialism – however ambiguous it becomes on the road – is virtually denied the child adventurer in such movies. The exclusion of children from both actual road travel and active cultural representation betrays the fact that geographical space might only signify freedom for a minority. In line with generic convention, these narratives interrogate the place of the figure in the landscape and, more broadly, geographical space as the concretization of politics – how location might relate to one's inner state or social position – but they do so from very different vantage points. The power to own space, to feel at home in it, to encode it cartographically and to decipher these inscriptions of territory are all part of a particular white male empire-building historical trend.

Unlike many of their road movie counterparts, these children cannot follow maps, although the greater rule systems of which maps are only a part forever bear down upon them as they travel. Roads, after all, are always built by someone who has come before you and whose purpose is partly encapsulated in the mapped road itself. In **Walkabout**, the father's study of a map and a list of American States only moments before his suicide hardly seems incidental. For his children, the road also stands for civilization, order and safety (although it is yet to seem so stifling to them); the decimation of the car and the running down of their radio battery distance them further and further from "civilization". The road in this sense is what the white children are looking for, the road in the road movie sense is what they are actually travelling along. Being lost and finding oneself, two key elements of the genre, are played out along this semantically weighty concept of the road.

For Kirby, being lost "becomes something like a crisis of differentiation, a dysfunction of the logic ensuring ordered space"[2]. While an ability to survive and thrive in this situation is admirable in the adult, children are shielded from this existence, their defencelessness retained at all costs. These are children on the road out of desperation rather than some self-expressive whim. "Such time when young'uns run the roads," sighs the woman who feeds John and Pearl on their travels, her comment epitomizing despair of social dissolution and its attendant parental inadequacies.

In accordance with such sensibilities, all three of these films chart not so much the process of finding oneself, but of finding someone else – and who this might be is highly social encrypted. Fundamentally they focus on coming back (or "back" to a different though similar familial setting) rather than venturing forth. Hansel And Gretel is an obvious precedent, while, at another end of the spectrum, **Picnic At Hanging Rock** (Peter Weir, 1975) insinuates the horrors of what happens when the return is bungled and William Golding's Lord Of The Flies reminds us what happens when children "find themselves". Maybe this is why, in **The Night Of The Hunter** and **The Wizard Of Oz**, the children follow an adamantly defined path (the course of a river, the yellow brick road) and are thus never really lost. **Walkabout**, on the other hand, is initially spattered with aerial and extreme long shots whose landscapes overwhelm its young protagonists, quietly intimating that they are socially as well as geographically lost. By the end of the film, the appearance of the sought after road prompts near-indifference in the children – or, rather, the sense of difference that has comfortably suspended them in urban plenitude has diminished considerably. Unlike the two earlier films, **Walkabout's** lost children become a profoundly damning symbol of the perils of this enforced vulnerability of the young. Yet whatever the underlying ethos, these movies persuade us that children are "lost" without adults.

Whether this is true, whether indeed any of this touches upon "what children really want or need" is beside the point. It must be stressed that we as adults neither understand, nor have the means to represent the child's perspective – all these ideas are merely grown up discourse. The vast expense and the protracted expertise necessary to filmmaking denies the child anything more than the chance to play out their given role, to bond together these odd and unique fragments of adult perception. Yet, despite all these infractions and unfounded interpretations, each of these films aims to convey the child's viewpoint through very literal scenic and

Walkabout

cinematographic renditions of how a child supposedly sees the world. Before engrossing ourselves in the tacit motives for these artistic endeavours, we must briefly examine how they achieve an aesthetic of juvenility.

Referring to **The Night Of The Hunter**, Sinyard suggests that "By conjuring up stylistic recollections of cinema in its infancy Charles Laughton is seeking to approximate visually the instinctive and innocent point of view of the children."[3] Laughton apparently pored over Griffiths' films before embarking on his own, and the innocent-child-versus-brutal-father-figure scenario is reminiscent of **Broken Blossoms** (1919) whose star, Lillian Gish, also takes on the role of fairy godmother and parental substitute, Rachel in **The Night Of The Hunter**. The film makes conspicuous use of an iris and Robert Mitchum's invocation of villainy is often absurd and pantomimic – a realm of horror appropriated for children just as much as it is a tell-tale sign of pre-talkie acting style.

A similar reference is inferred by Margaret Hamilton's Wicked Witch in **The Wizard Of Oz**, but, on the whole, the film achieves its childlike perspective without recourse to a parallel of early cinema with child development. The captivated encircling shots which depict Dorothy's first moments over the rainbow are replete with a recurrent adult rendition of a child's point of view. Everything glistens – the water in the fountain, the plants' leaves, Glinda's jewelled outfit, the ruby slippers, iridescence wherever possible. Luminosity and colour (in all senses of the word) encourage wonder and childish enlightenment as we confront this "youthful" view of a strange land – the tantalizing implications of which will be tackled later. The **Wizard Of Oz**, while its narrative temporarily suspends childhood spoiling – indeed suggests that this is Dorothy's motive for running away – nevertheless over-indulges us with the saturated

The Wizard Of Oz

nature of its *mise-en-scène* and, in particular, its palette. Both Dorothy and the viewer are lavished sensuously by the adult film world, furnished with treats thought to delight and win favour from the child (in all of us).

However, **The Wizard Of Oz** simultaneously fails, perhaps deliberately, to disguise its adultness. Judy Garland's Dorothy makes for a physically unconvincing child – her breasts swell beyond the vital statistics of Auntie Em and the Wicked Witch and, squashed into gingham and ankle socks, her body rings out plangently against standard child proportions. The fact that such an incongruous physique fleshes out this role and that such an obvious teenager (directed by adults) works so hard to gesticulate and intone childish naiveté underlines the falseness of such a representation making it charmingly, even willingly ersatz.

The Wizard Of Oz's dedication to the "Young at Heart" divulges its adult investment from the very start and I do not wish to claim any false glory for ensnaring the complex hybrid it has bred. That children in art forms might act as ventriloquist dummies for the adult voice is a worn out proposition; the only sport (or political satisfaction) on offer is the hunting out of its underlying motives.

By far the most popular approach for achieving this end is to filter these adult-perspective texts through the Freudian understanding of childhood as the site of sexual trauma. In such a reading one could pinpoint the formulation of identity in terms of sexuality and desire in the child (or better still the filmic fantasy of the child), one could investigate the circular structure of the road movie quest as a replication of Freud's *Fort Da* game. But I do not wish to roam too far into psychoanalysis when it is an over-populated discourse as concerns children, however much these films deal with fantasy and however much fantasy may be the preserve of the Freudians. Instead I shall steer towards the slightly less crowded arena of Marxian investigation to contemplate how the child characters in all these films uphold or question their contemporary divisions of labour.

Tellingly, the child has only occupied a central position in art and literature (with the exception of the infant Jesus) since the first phases of the Industrial Revolution. And yet the child-figure's proximity to the pillars of this phase of capitalism has repeatedly been evaded or hushed up. As Rose points out: "Money is something impure... It is contaminated by association and exchange. Not so childhood... Childhood is always a moment *before* – once it is contaminated, it is lost."[4] However, just as it is impossible to conceive of the child existing outside the sphere of economics (and, increasingly the economics of the film industry and all its profitable off-shoots), so too must it be noted that all these utopian representations of childhood are fetish objects available to us for purchase. Interestingly, none of these films' children use money, nor do they steal, a distinction that sets them apart from the economic desperation that drives the road narrative in such texts as Jack Kerouac's *On the Road* and films from Bonnie And Clyde (Arthur Penn, 1967) [see Chapter 10] to Thelma And Louise (Ridley Scott, 1991) [see Chapter 11].

Nevertheless, the films forge a sturdy bond between childhood security and the structures of capitalism. Children on the road are largely running away from home or are lost and looking for it. Ultimately, they realize that there's no place like it and that all their routes lead to roots. While "home" means all manner of things, these ideas' condensation into *property* is consequential. The home is the largest adult purchase, the dream of ownership (with everything else that noun might stand for) fulfilled – none of these parents appear to be renting. Miss Gulch, The Wizard Of Oz's villain owns "half the county" – her abuse of power and her property are subtly conflated. Dorothy's now-creaky line: "If I ever go looking for my heart's desire again I won't go any further than my own back yard, because if it isn't there I never really lost it to begin with" may have exhausted the limits of critical discourse, but its over-bearing (or risible) presence is still integral to the film. As Schaber suggests in reference to Oz's Kansas counterparts, it is "not so much that there is no place *like* home, but there is no place *but* home."[5]

And yet the home Dorothy pines for seems markedly bleak: her beloved Auntie Em treats the farm hands brusquely and scolds Dorothy about Toto. Most tellingly, Em's exasperation derives from Dorothy's uselessness on the farm, she must "find some place where there isn't any trouble", get out of their way rather than help

The Wizard Of Oz

out. Such indolence (however it is thought of) functions as the fulcrum for prescribed child behaviour both here and in **Walkabout**. Haunted by phantoms such as Victorian child labour, adults toil so that their off-spring need not. Working even twice as hard in order to suspend our children in this idyll provides the adult with one of the strongest arguments for upholding the present capitalist system. All three of these films examine this ideal (without necessarily endorsing it) within the relative historical boundaries of their narratives. Significantly, the overpowering economic depression depicted in **The Wizard Of Oz** and **The Night Of The Hunter** jolts the traditionally firm aspiration of one's children not having to work.

The sympathetic rendition of the murderous and thieving father in the latter is underpinned by his "honourable" motive: "I got tired of seeing children roam in the woodlands without food, children roaming highways in this year of depression, children sleeping in old abandoned car bodies in junk heaps." Ironically the repercussions of his crimes predispose his children to this very same desperation. Early on in the film we are presented with a seemingly superfluous vignette of the father's hangman returning home; a vocational despondence provoked by sympathy for the day's victim precedes an adoring gaze upon his own sleeping children. A companion scene occurs near the film's end – "this time it'll be a privilege" he declares on the advent of Powell's execution for crimes against infants and vulnerable women.

Powell too is a thief, but he steals for wrong reasons, rebelling against the ethics which secure capitalist stability without opting for the immunity granted by child care. The overlap between the violation of capitalism and the violation of children's rights anchors Powell's villainy. When bargaining with the John and Pearl for their money, for example, he withholds their supper. Failure to provide food and material necessities amounts to reprehensible, even criminal fatherhood, here as well as in

Night Of The Hunter

**Walkabout**. Unlike standard road movies, our sympathies lie not with the type of men who run away, take drugs, live illegally by their wits and relinquish responsibilities, but with those they might leave behind.

However, rebellion against the family (through running away) is still central to these plots. The divergent factor which translates such waywardness into conservatism is that the children in **The Wizard Of Oz, The Night Of The Hunter** and **Walkabout** are reluctant renegades who long for the bliss of the family unit. Essentially these films exalt the specific safety and security on offer at home, while admonishing the parent who withholds it. While agonizing over children's well-being, these texts also conveniently soothe the adult viewer, two of them patting us on the head for our faith in property and financial stability because it is what children aspire to as well.

While none of our child protagonists can claim to have two parents[6] for the duration of the diegesis (and indeed they often seem better off without them), they still instinctively seek out a family-type arrangement. The quests which structure **The Wizard Of Oz** and **The Night Of The Hunter** are for mother figures (not the traditional heterosexual princess/partner) and consequently relay the idea that the nuclear family or its unwavering substitutes provide the ultimate in reassurance. Despite the haphazard nature of these initial or eventual groupings, their warmth derives from reactionary embers. **The Night Of The Hunter**'s rebel father, for instance, squanders his remaining freedom speedily summarizing sexual politics for his son: he must now look after his sister and their money keeping his father's secret from his mother because she has "no sense". Without her husband, their mother becomes vulnerable, preyed upon by a new and dangerous suitor the moment she attempts renewed sexual activity. And, lest we forget other stereotypes, what might be implied by the unsympathetic Miss

Gulch/Wicked Witch of the West, who is flagrantly single and overly fond of her cat?

Within this enclosed familial ideal, outlined by the misfits and outcasts that it refuses to contain, the child represents one constant that is, paradoxically, impossible – diminutive stature. While **The Wizard Of Oz** proclaims himself "the great and powerful", the film's heroine calls herself "small and meek". "It's a hard world for little things," Rachel sympathizes in **The Night Of The Hunter**, merging smallness into vulnerability. This fascination with scale will be elaborated upon later, but one of its most conspicuous imprints is the desire to care for these children, to watch over them, which, of course, as the film's audience, we are licensed to do. Among other things, adult superiority flexes its muscles through an obsession with remaining vigilant over the child.

When a human diegetic stand-in cannot be found, more removed replacements volunteer their services. In **The Night Of The Hunter**, the animal community watch over the unprotected children as they drift downstream and swooping aerial shots give us the sense that the heavens, or at least the stars (which feature prominently at various intervals) are looking down kindly. This plea for surveillance – the voyeurism inherent in cinema aside – strikes a blow against the usual road movie's heartfelt flight from such constraints. The freedom to not be watched over so intently which, after all, appeals to children as well as adults, is quashed in this representation. **The Wizard Of Oz** demonstrates a more ambiguous arrangement and response: Professor Marvel's harmlessly fraudulent prophesies that Aunt Em is looking for her niece clash with their menacing counterpart, the witch's crystal ball with which she spies upon the realm of Oz.

This vacillation between freedom and surveillance draws us closer to a central paradox embodied by the child character. While we long to wrap our children in cotton-wool (if only to prove that we can afford it), the figure of the child simultaneously signifies the allure of imagination, escapism and independence, perhaps so that it might avail itself to the adult, so that a Dorothy might remove us from our post or rescue us from rust. Such films present fantasy fulfilment for the adult and child alike in an ideologically sensitive manner. While they deal to a greater or lesser extent with dream worlds, we should speculate upon whose flights of fancy these might actually be? As ever, dreams (conducted awake or asleep) are a mixture of unconscious fantasy and cultural convention.

This association of children with dreaming (most obvious in **The Wizard Of Oz**) runs on into in the opening sequence of **The Night Of The Hunter** with its invitation to "dream little one, dream" set against a starry backdrop where the heads of Rachel and the children are ludicrously superimposed. While John and Pearl's journey often seems a nightmare, the troubled children are eventually hushed into another more pleasant dream by their guardian angel, Rachel. Continuing the themes of safety, the child's dream also proffers an antidote to harsh reality: juvenile imagination evades the quotidian and adventure is possible even when supine. How this might be evoked visually discloses a fair amount about what its adult creators wish to situate within this realm. Most overtly these definitions eschew filmic realism and, by implication, everyday living (to which they are all too obviously also tethered). In **The Night Of The Hunter** lyrical imaginings come in the form of twinkling picture-book stars and the constructed naiveté of the aforementioned superimposition – the charming ignorance of the child becomes a haven from the supposed complexities of troubling adult perception.

Similar stylistic inferences are made in **The Wizard Of Oz**. The long shots of Kansas are fairly conscientious in their muted description of a barren expanse. The depictions of Oz, however, harbour no pretences of realism in their colour or attention to detail – again the look of a child's dream appears more vivid and seductive than adult reality. Curiously, this colourful fantasy realm where the liberating ideals of the road movie can be acted upon, is a particularly cramped space.

The pillowy hills of Munchkinland and the bulbous mushroom-like roofs of its buildings squash everything into the foreground. Although characters in **The Wizard Of Oz** are sometimes shown on the brink of wide open spaces (the poppy field, for example), they rarely blend with them or seem undaunted by their expanses. More often, the narrative unfolds in bounded spaces such as the two forests and the walled Emerald City. This confined *mise-en-scène* constructs the child protagonist as more "at home" in closeted spaces – regardless of their (supposed) outdoor locations – and proposes the child/child-like viewer to be fascinated by what is nearby, by detail. Child freedom, we are told, comes, rather conveniently, from the local rather than the distant. These films deny us the opportunities of the vistas we see in, say, John Ford's **Stagecoach** [see also Chapter 1], Dennis Hopper's **Easy Rider** [see Chapter 4] or Terrence Malick's **Badlands** [see Chapter 10] – a sense of restriction must be seen to prevail happily and regardless of the implications of the adventurous narrative.

Similarly there are no distant vanishing points in John and Pearl's river journey. The earlier aerial shots give way to closer framing as their travels get underway and their preference for night-time boating narrows down our field of vision considerably. As in **The Wizard Of Oz**, this cordoned space is conveyed with the precision of deep focus – we can (indeed should) pay attention to detail. Although both films limit what we see, the tiniest detail of what we *are* given is clarified, from the individual blades of grass on the riverbank to the ornamentation on the jackets of the Wicked Witch's guards. In **The Wizard Of Oz**, moving shots skirt behind the fantastical foliage presenting nature (more of which later) in extreme close up. **The Night Of The Hunter**'s flora and fauna also receive the majority of this treatment, framing each establishing shot of the river. We see the children through an intricately represented spider's web, in the background as a toad looks on, and intercut between rabbits, foxes and owls.

Of course this miniature world is warped, expanded by the size of the cinema screen into somewhat Expressionist wackiness. The flowers in Oz are overly large, blown up to evoke child proportions through a sense of oddity and fun that serious adults must, for some reason, project elsewhere. The most transparent example of this is the dinkiness invested in the (adult midget) Munchkins – in their comical voices, clashing clothes and pantomimic gestures. With similar bias, Toto, **The Wizard Of Oz**'s meagrest protagonist, is also its most resourceful. His size allows him to both escape the Witch and reveal the Wizard to be a sham – cute rules the day.

Evidently, this microcosmic attention to detail, this favouritism of the small bears more macrocosmic referentiality. Bachelard exposes the implications: "the minuscule, a narrow gate, opens up an entire world. The details of a thing can be the sign of a new world which, like all worlds, contains the attributes of greatness. Miniature is one of the refuges of greatness."[7]

The ascription of this quality to the child's eye view has always baffled me: I find small children, although, of course, physically small, in no way particularly attracted to things of those dimensions, or at all entertained by sustained engagement with them.[8] Close regard is largely an adult preoccupation. Children in these films become a repository for the concepts of naive wonderment and delight in more subtly visible objects – highly prized *adult* pursuits.

The time that such scrutiny takes up might offer a clue to the motives for such a heavy investment. Adult involvement in distracting, exhausting and time-guzzling work may mean that we cast these privileges (hobbies too engrossing for us to engage in on a regular basis) into our fantastical perception of freer childhood activity. This preoccupation with time-is-money spills over into the traditional road movie's obsession with the fast vehicle, a device which forbids our attention to detail in favour of shaving hours off journey time. As with the rendition of labour in such films, if

Night Of The Hunter

one's position within capitalism means one cannot "afford" to entertain such a scrutinizing relationship with its objects, then all that hard earned cash must be spent making sure one's off-spring can (whether they like it or not). From here, children are integrated into the nuclear unit as the guardians of some of the ideals that capitalism treasures, encourages us to buy into, yet offers us little time to explore.

While such ideas may seem far from conscious in **The Wizard Of Oz** and **The Night Of The Hunter**, their treatment becomes deliberately political in **Walkabout**. The close-ups of the animals which the white children seem not to notice slot into the film's critique of "civilization" as indicators of their ignorance of life outside their regime of school uniforms and elocution lessons. The children not seeing the outback's monstrous lizards or the wombat that snuffles them in their sleep implies that the adult world is robbing them of their childhood response of awed observation by stuffing their time with the acquisition of its rules. These beasts are more David Attenborough than magic realism – the stylistic debt is to adult-controlled television rather than to anything supposedly more intrinsic to childhood, or anything which might make them realise that such animals are potential meals.

This diatribe upon the capitalist child continues by damning the fragmentation of work our systems of production encourage. Shots of a butcher hacking at meat are cross cut with the white children's starved wanderings hinting that such specialists' roles in their lives mean that they are incapable of fending for themselves. The film's relentless attention to the Aborigine's hunting and preparation of meat underscores not only his superiority in this environment, but also the other two's uselessness, despite their expensive education.

A similar vulnerability is presented in **The Night Of The Hunter** where, on spotting a turtle, John declares that these animals can be made into soup, before

Walkabout

admitting that he would not know how. Here the point is less cynical than a tug for pathos, a plea to keep children within our sights and well looked after – the very idea that **Walkabout** confounds.

Later on in **Walkabout**, the girl brushes the ants from the now dead Aborigine's body. Her sense of decency is at odds with nature here, her understanding of life more mannered, Christian and linear than cyclical or ecological. His tragic demise results from this seemingly illogical culture and the girl's morally motivated reasons for refusing his advances have, essentially, killed him.

The supposed neutrality of this natural backdrop to her learnt etiquette is an ideological shield covering a distinctly anthropomorphized wilderness. Apparently the erasure of culture is not only possible, but such an action would reveal an unsullied other world. This persuasive supposition might run as follows: something natural actually exists and is a stable entity, corruption (read acculturation) may be suspended and this blank canvas of "nature" bears no traces of socio-historical palimpsest. Here we fly headlong into Rousseau territory: the child, the "savage" and nature embody purity[9] with their interaction generating this self-perpetuating rhetoric. All this might be retained regardless of children's almost immediate acculturation, the human circumscription (not to mention harness) of nature and the intricate social systems of "savages"[10].

Despite its flaws, despite its contradiction of the capitalist marketplace and its security procedures, this logic is extremely pervasive and puissant in our arts. **The Night Of The Hunter** strengthens the affinity between the child and nature by positioning the latter as John and Pearl's ally. As they run from Powell, he struggles through a thicket and then sinks in the mud they were light and nimble enough to traverse. The benign animals along the riverbank act as guardian figures, while the house where they hear Powell's singing once more displays a caged bird on its porch – curtailing nature's freedom can only foretell disaster. As Powell stalks the children to Rachel's house, an owl swoops down on a bunny before Rachel proclaims "it's a hard world for little things". The harsh side to nature provokes our pity for all things small and vulnerable while "good nature" can be found in selected adults. Rachel later declares that she is "a strong tree with branches for many birds".

Although distinctly more embittered an understanding of childhood, **Walkabout** also props up Rousseau's philosophy not only in its dubious rendition of the "noble savage" Aborigine adolescent, but in the white girl's nostalgic adult flashback to her Walkabout at the film's end. The Edenic qualities attributed to her reminiscence, the suggestion that childhood represents innocence, freedom and "naturalness" in the face of distorting manners and morals (not to mention sexual initiation), links the film more closely than one might initially assume to the other two. The ultimate glorification of childhood and the desire to clearly distinguish it from the adult world hark back another of Rousseau's fantasies, an ideal which tellingly centres itself more around eventual adult behaviour than youthfulness: "Nature wants children to be children before they are men. If we deliberately pervert this order, we shall get premature fruits which are neither ripe nor well-flavoured, and which soon decay."[11]

Rose loops all these insinuations of innocence and their underlying adult motivations back to a Freudian formation of sexuality: "The child is sexual, but its sexuality (bisexual, polymorphous, perverse) threatens our own at its roots. Setting up the child as innocent is not, therefore, repressing its sexuality – it is above all holding off any possible challenge to our own."[12] Again, whatever our analytical methodology, the child is the empty vessel we fill with our unfulfilled desires and the negation of our anxieties. In considering Freud, we might think back to the importance of sleep to all these films' diegeses. Sleep equates with innocence here: when children go to bed they do not have sex, they dream, and dream very specifically of what we want them to.

The barely equivocal innocence of these children disguises, as Rose suggests, anything that might prove uncategorizable, disturbing or uncontrollable about childhood. The adult notion of the natural child in these films betrays none of the *unheimlich* qualities which haunt the characters we find in **The Innocents** (Jack Clayton, 1961) or Kubrick's **Lolita** (1962, another child-on-the-road movie well worth poring over)[13], children who are, significantly, set up as repellent for the most part. John and Pearl, the children who stray the closest to these themes, are forthrightly pitied for their lack of innocence: an adult secret, "guilty knowledge" has driven them from home and made them of interest to evil forces. Despite corruption, though, they struggle to retain their innate purity and do so through, amongst other things, an affiliation with nature. All our protagonists' specific relationship with the outdoor world and with animals means their goodness, their lack of wilfulness or unpredictability becomes a kind of "second nature", despite being moored to adult cultural systems (or, rather, because of it).

Although these niceties ostensibly represent the child's perspective – a child, after all, would not consider itself unsettling – there is evidently more at stake. Exposing the child to nature fairly comprehensively immunizes it to closer scrutiny. Dismantling this child-product might prove a fruitless, implausible or never-ending task, especially if finding the "true" child is one's aim. However, scrabbling around in the debris might disclose much about how adult identity might be built from ideas about the road, freedom, time, scale, cultural corruption, our environment and the child – all of which, though, as physical entities, are vulnerable to falling rubble from this continual reconstruction process.

# NOTES

1. Obviously the pairing of these children throws up questions about "racial" representation, questions which are so consuming that, were I to let them, they might fill the entire space of this chapter. As I would like to leave room for other ideas, I shall keep this discussion to the minimum because it can be readily found in almost any other writing on this particular film.

2. K. Kirby, *Indifferent Boundaries: Spatial Concepts Of Human Subjectivity*; New York and London: The Guildford Press, 1969, p.53.

3. N. Sinyard, *Children In The Movies*; London: B.T. Batsford Ltd, 1992, p.62.

4. J. Rose, *The Case Of Peter Pan Or The Impossibility Of Children's Fiction*; Basingstoke: The Macmillan Press Ltd, 1984, p.87.

5. Schaber, B. "'Hitler Can't Keep 'Em That Long': The Road, The People" in Steven Cohan and Ira Hark (eds.), *The Road Movie Book*; London: Routledge, 1997, p.25.

6. It is interesting to note how many children's films and books feature orphans and how fascinated children themselves are by these figures.

7. Bachelard, G. (trans. Jolas, M.) (1969), *The Poetics Of Space*; Boston: Beacon Press, 1969, p.155.

8. I am not proposing my idea as the truth, I simply wish to suggest that there are other views on children's perspectives and that this particular one might not be as persuasive as it imagines.

9. Rousseau commences *Émile* with: "God makes all things good: man meddles with them and they become evil" (J.J. Rousseau, trans. Foxley, B., *Émile*; London: Everyman Library, 1966, p.5).

10. Rousseau tells us that the savage is "tied to no one place, he has no prescribed task, no superior to obey, he knows no law but his own will" (J.J Rousseau, *Émile*, p.83), but one wonders who these savages are and whether they dwell any place other than in Rousseau's imperialist mind-set.

11. J.J Rousseau, *Émile*, p.54.

12. J. Rose, *The Case Of Peter Pan Or The Impossibility Of Children's Fiction*; Basingstoke: The Macmillan Press Ltd, 1984, p.4.

13. Even Judy Garland's criss-crossing of the divisions of child and adult, her preposterously strapped down breasts and incongruous plaits, is nowhere near abject.

# Chapter 14

# The Road As River

# INTERRUPTED FLOWS: THE RIVER JOURNEY FILM

## David Sorfa

Before the invention of the internal combustion engine and the almost simultaneous rise of the cinema, stories detailing journeys and the adventures to be had along the way were a mainstay of the narrative experience. In the many centuries preceding the emergence of mechanically powered means of transport, it should come as no surprise that the three modes favoured by fictional travellers have involved either the literally pedestrian (Geoffrey Chaucer's *Canterbury Tales* [1387–1400], John Bunyan's *The Pilgrim's Progress* [1672]); the equestrian (from Miguel de Cervantes' *Don Quixote* [1605–1615] to the saddle-sore heroes of countless Western novels and films); and, of course, the aquatic.

Perhaps the most famous of stories which takes boat travel as its structuring device begins:

*"Tell me, O Muse, of the man of many devices, who wandered full many ways after he had sacked the sacred citadel of Troy. Many were the men whose cities he saw and whose mind he learned, aye, and many the woes he suffered in his heart upon the sea, seeking to win his own life and the return of his comrades."*

The *Odyssey* (and Virgil's much later Romanisation, the *Aeneid*), with its themes of exploration, destiny and change, would seem to herald many of the features now so easily attributed to the genre of the "road movie". It is the strong metaphoric link between physical travel and psychic experience that seems to draw narrative so strongly to the structuring device of the journey; a connection of which Shari Roberts writes:

*"While other elements of the Western remain important to the road film, the transformation of the frontier into an often metaphorical road introduces the crucial, structuring device of the road – the dual journey, the interdependent physical and spiritual journeys. The road as theme may appear in any film, regardless of historical context, whereas, in the road film genre, the metaphor of the road becomes the main structuring device through this interdependence of the physical and spiritual journeys."*[1]

Here I intend to return to a broader notion of the "road" (a word which is often used metaphorically in itself) in the context of travel and consider a few of the significant films that have taken the river as the ground for their stories (and I am mixing my metaphors deliberately). There are many other literary antecedents to the river journey saga and these are often alluded to, more or less explicitly, in some of the films I will be discussing. Joseph Conrad's *Heart Of Darkness* (1902) is perhaps only rivalled in influence by Mark Twain's *The Adventures Of Huckleberry Finn* (1884), while Herman Melville's *Moby Dick* (1851) and, to a lesser extent, Edgar Allan Poe's *The Narrative Of Arthur Gordon Pym Of Nantucket* (1838) seem to loom large on the horizon of many of the films (especially those set in the U.S.A). Although I will not be explicitly investigating the connections between literary source or influence and any particular film, this is an area which would benefit from a more detailed exploration.

One of the differences between the traditional road movie and the river journey film lies in the force of flow in the river itself – unlike the road (and also the sea) which is often depicted as a frictionless field traversed by transient vehicles purely under their own power, and by extension, by their passenger's volition. The river, on the other hand, powerfully and inexorably flows in a certain direction and, depending on whether a protagonist decides to head up or downstream, the surface on which the journey takes place will feature as a significant part of the narrative. In addition to this, any river always has very definite beginnings and endings: head upstream far enough and the river will eventually disappear; while downstream the vast expanse of the sea always waits. The very insubstantiality of the river seems in some way to permeate the narratives which take place on it and, once again, the metaphoric slippage here seems to be one that is echoed in the very language of narrative criticism itself. Wolfgang Iser writes of the necessary incompleteness of every story:

*"No tale can be told in its entirety. Indeed, it is only through inevitable omissions that a story will gain its dynamism. Thus whenever the flow is interrupted and we are led off in unexpected directions, the opportunity is given to us to bring into play our own faculty for establishing connections – for filling in gaps left by the text itself."*[2]

Thus if one is forced to use the metaphors of river travel ("flow", "interrupted", "directions") to describe narrative, it seems that river travel itself will be in some way the model of all narrative. This will remain one of the unfilled gaps of this chapter.

This chapter is divided into four sections. The first will discuss **Aguirre, Wrath Of God** (Werner Herzog, 1972), **Deliverance** (John Boorman, 1972) and **Apocalypse Now** (Francis Ford Coppola, 1979) as films that represent impossible journeys of one sort or another. These films are fundamentally concerned with the silence that is ever present beneath the surface of the river. The second will concern films which end happily with regeneration and the re-establishment of proper order: **River Of No Return** (Otto Preminger, 1954), **Fitzcarraldo** (Werner Herzog, 1982) and The River Wild (Curtis Hanson, 1994). The third section will compare the rape sequences in **Deliverance** and **River Of No Return** as the marker of the absolute limits of civilisation, and I will conclude with a brief consideration of **Piranha** (Joe Dante, 1978) which stretches to breaking point the tenuous credibility of the river journey film as a reputable genre.

It is unavoidable that I have ignored many other films in this selection. For instance, the mass of films dealing more explicitly with sea travel and exploration from the mythic adventures of **Jason And The Argonauts** (Don Chaffey, 1963) and **The Seventh Voyage Of Sinbad** (Nathan Juran, 1958) to the hardly less fantastic celebrations of **1492: The Conquest Of Paradise** (Ridley Scott, 1992) and **Christopher Columbus: The Discovery** (John Glen, 1992). Nor have I considered the many cinematic remakes of *Huckleberry Finn* which seem to begin with Norman Taurog's 1931 version and continue steadily through to Stephen Sommers' recent 1993 **The Adventures Of Huck Finn**.

## IMPOSSIBLE JOURNEYS

At the very beginning of **Apocalypse Now**, Captain Willard (Martin Sheen) is summoned to a briefing at Nha Trang by Com-Sec Intelligence. He is asked about a previous assassination mission and he answers: "Sir, I am unaware of any such activity or operation – nor would I be disposed to discuss such an operation if it did in fact exist, sir." His exemplary rectitude is quietly acknowledged by the assembled soldiers

Apocalypse Now

and the briefing continues to detail the actions of Colonel Walter E. Kurtz (Marlon Brando) in the Nu Mung Ba area, culminating in Colonel Corman's melodramatic speech:

*"Well, you see Willard... In this war, things get confused out there, power, ideals, the old morality, and practical military necessity. Out there with these natives it must be a temptation to be god. Because there's a conflict in every human heart between the rational and the irrational, between good and evil. The good does not always triumph. Sometimes the dark side overcomes what Lincoln called the better angels of our nature. Every man has got a breaking point. You and I have. Walter Kurtz has reached his. And very obviously, he has gone insane."*

The mission is thus already marked with rather heavy-handed metaphysical portents tied in with the image of the end of the serpentine river. Earlier, in a voice-over, Willard reflects from who knows what future time: "I was going to the worst place in the world, and I didn't even know it yet. Weeks away and hundreds of miles up a river that snaked through the war like a main circuit cable and plugged straight into Kurtz." In this electrical metaphor, Kurtz is in fact the very battery which fuels the greater insanity of the war in Vietnam. As Willard begins his journey he begins to identify more and more, not so much with Kurtz as such, but rather with the logic of the Vietnamese conflict which seems to be exemplified in the actions of Kurtz. This is brought home to Willard after their encounter with Bill Kilgore in the hallucinogenic "Charlie don't surf" sequence:

*"If that's how Kilgore fought the war, I began to wonder what they really had against*

Apocalypse Now

*Kurtz. It wasn't just insanity and murder. There was enough of that to go around for everyone."*

The sequence, of course, plays ironically on the Western cliché of the arrival of the cavalry with Willard explaining that the "First of the Ninth was an old cavalry division that had cashed in its horses for choppers, and gone tear-assing around 'Nam, looking for the shit." Kurtz, then, has become the insanity of the American myth itself and it is this dream that Willard is sent out to stop in a symbolic and ultimately useless and self-negating gesture of control. No-one will be able to wake from the nightmare because no-one is asleep. This double-logic of negation is exemplified in Willard's final command at the initial briefing: "You understand, Captain, that this operation does not exist, nor will it ever exist".

This command undermines the possibility of Willard's voice-over: his voice echoes over the film from no-place. It creates the illusion that the film we are seeing is some form of truth but it can only do so by forgetting that it cannot possibly exist. The very narration of the film indulges in the enigma that is Kurtz.

As the crew and Willard travel upstream towards the centre of horror, they move from one bizarre experience to the next; from cold-blooded murder to dancing Bunny Girls dressed up as cowboys and indians. At one point, Chef decides to forage on land and he and Willard are frightened back on board by the sudden appearance of a tiger. Chef hysterically screams: "Never get out of the boat! Never get out of the boat!" as Willard's even voice-over intones:

*"Absolutely goddamn right. Unless you were going all the way. Kurtz got off the boat. He split from the whole fucking program."*

The boat, then, becomes the only point of stability in the maelstrom of the river and of the war. Evil and uncertainty are everywhere except in the dubious safety of the over-exposed boat. It is this absolute visibility that induces Lance to paint his face with camouflage in a drug-induced and paranoid attempt to stop "them" from seeing him. It is true that "they" do exist but it becomes increasingly pointless to hide from their gaze. Thus when they finally arrive at Kurtz' camp, his army of followers merely observe, just as Willard has done throughout, as if waiting for an inevitable death to happen. The fact that this death happens to be Kurtz' seems of little significance and is almost expected in the sacrificial logic surrounding his cult. However, it is unclear what has been learnt, since the lesson that Kurtz appears to be teaching is that relating that lesson is impossible. **Apocalypse Now** ends with Kurtz' silhouetted body echoing John Wayne's exit from **The Searchers** (John Ford, 1956) [see Chapter 1], marking not so much the death of the American dream (and frontier) but its absolute impossibility.

The frontier spirit is very much to the fore in **Deliverance**, with three of the four city men desperately trying to come to terms with the dull inevitability of their suburban existence. Only Lewis, Burt Reynold's survivalist, seems to have no family or background but even he, as Ed points out, cannot come to terms with the wilderness. The group cannot even find the river at first and when they do their entry into unknown territory is marked by the blank stare of the duelling-banjo boy as his banjo swings like a pendulum over the canoeists' heads: marking time (earlier Drew was unable to keep up with the boy's playing – and soon time will overtake them and events will lead to Drew's suicide). Their journey begins well with a successful run at some tricky rapids. Lewis muses: "The first explorers saw this country, saw it just like us, in a canoe".

DREW: I can imagine how they felt.
BOBBY: Yeah, we beat it, didn't we? Did we beat that?
LEWIS: You don't beat it. You don't beat this river.

This early ominous note quickly fulfils itself when Ed and Bobby are accosted by two "mountain men" when they stop for some water: "Boy, you're lost, ain't you?" says one before they tie Ed to a tree and rape Bobby. Lewis comes to their rescue and kills one mountain man with an arrow while the other escapes. The four men then have to decide what to do with the body and Drew pleads with them to obey the rule of law and to turn the body over to the police. The others decide to bury the body instead and to leave the incident behind them. They bury the body in silence with their bare hands (even though their canoes are loaded with equipment) and it is understood that this particular story will never be told. In fact, the story only "surfaces" along with the hand of the corpse in Ed's nightmare at the very end of the film. Thus, again, we are faced with a narrative that cannot possibly have a narrator. The impossible secret of Bobby's rape (more forceful than the rather more prosaic death of the mountain man) is one to which I will return later in this chapter.

Werner Herzog's **Aguirre, Wrath Of God** begins with an inter-title explaining that Pizarro and a "large expedition of Spanish adventurers" left the Peruvian Sierras in late 1560 in search of the fabled El Dorado and that "the only document to survive from the lost expedition is the diary of monk Gaspar de Carvajal". The film is, then, ostensibly reconstructed from Carvajal's diary and is often quoted in voice-over.

Pizarro's expedition finds itself trapped and he decides to send a small group led by Don Pedro de Ursua forward on rafts. While resting one night, the avant-garde's

Aguirre, Wrath Of God

rafts are washed away and Don Lope de Aguirre (Klaus Kinski) orders materials to be gathered to make a new one, against Ursua's wishes who now decides to march back to Pizarro. Aguirre leads a mutiny and declares his apostasy:

*"We rebel to the death. Our hands shall perish and our tongues dry up if this is not so. The House of Hapsburg is overthrown. You, Philip the Second, are dethroned. By the power of this declaration you are obliterated."*

It is the uselessness of this declaration that comments so dramatically on the colonial project of expansion based on greed and hypocrisy. Later, Don Fernando de Guzman, the corpulent and ineffectual nobleman whom Aguirre elects as their Emperor, reads out yet another declaration as their raft drifts further and further downstream into the unknown Amazon interior:

*"All the territory to our left and to our right now belongs to us. I solemnly and formally take possession of all this land. Our country is already six times larger than Spain. Everyday we drift makes it bigger."*

Guzman signs a tattered document with great ceremony while Aguirre sneers: "Have you seen any solid ground that could support your weight?" As they continue their journey down the river more men die of sickness and from attack until Guzman himself is found dead. It is now that Aguirre delivers his quiet speech of megalomania, aligning himself with Lucifer and the fallen angels:

*"I am the great traitor. There can be none greater. When I, Aguirre, want the birds to*

Aguirre, Wrath Of God

*drop dead from the trees then the birds will drop dead from the trees. I am the Wrath of God. The earth I walk upon sees me and quakes. Who follows me and the river will win untold riches."*

Sickness continues to spread on the raft and the priest's voice-over reads (and perhaps the translator's frequent mistakes at this point are indicative of another kind of weariness):

*"Most men have fever and hallucinations. Hardley [sic] anyone can stand upright. Just Gonzales [sic] drank my ink. He thouht [sic] it was medicine. I can write no more. We are going round in circles."*

They then sail past a ship perched in the highest branches of a tree and the monk claims that it is another illusion, although Aguirre sees in it the mad possibility of reaching the Atlantic. The negro sits and stares blankly at the ship: "That is no ship. That is no forest," an arrow appears in his leg and he continues without flinching, "That is no arrow. We just imagine arrows because we fear them." The monk says, "This arrow cannot harm me. That is not rain." It is here that the narration should logically end since the priest can no longer write and has no ink left to do so in any case. As the film enters the impossible imaginary of the unwritten, the voice-over, for the first time, becomes that of Aguirre. It is as if his voice will only truly be heard when it cannot possibly have an audience. This impossible audience materialises on the raft in the form of dozens of squirrel monkeys, to whom Aguirre delivers his final speech:

*"When we reach the sea, we will build a bigger ship and sails [sic] North in it to take Trinidad from the Spanish crown. Then we'll sail and take Mexico away from Cortés. What great treachery that will be! Then we shall control all of New Spain and will produce history as others produce plays. I, the Wrath of God, will marry my own daughter and with her I'll found the purest dynasty the earth has ever seen. Together we shall rull [sic] rule the whole of this continent. [Aguirre picks up one of the monkeys and addresses it directly] We'll endure. I am the Wrath of God. Who else is with me?"*

The answer is, of course, no-one. At the end of these three river journeys the protagonists can only experience blankness instead of closure, not so much tragedy as ennui. Their various rivers finally lead to the negation of all value.

## WATER UNDER THE BRIDGE

It is not, however, inevitable that the river traveller finds him or herself confronting the very depths of the abyss, although there are always a set of unexpected rapids ahead. **River Of No Return** sees Matt Calder (Robert Mitchum), Kay Weston (Marilyn Monroe) and Calder's son, Mark, escaping by raft from a band of marauding Indians (who appear to have been doing nothing but wait for the very moment that Kay's no good, gambler fiancé, Harry, steals Calder's gun and horse in order to stake his claim further down the river in Council City). The three on the raft continue to float down river and Calder vows to kill Harry despite Kay's protests that her desperate fiancé should not be blamed for his actions. Inevitably, the family romance of mother/father/ son is confirmed by three acts of violence: Calder's near-rape of Kay, Mark's shooting of Harry to protect his unarmed father (and thus confirming his father's earlier lesson that, at times, it is necessary to shoot a person in the back), and Calder's final comic abduction of Kay from her job as a saloon singer. In this final sequence (echoed in the *Taming Of The Shrew*-like plot of 1956's **Bus Stop** [Joshua Logan]), Kay reprises the ballad which begins the film (sung then by Ken Darby), perched on a piano, wearing the glittering, ruby shoes (marking her as a grown-up Dorothy) which are her only possessions:

> *"There is a river called the River of No Return*
> *Sometimes it's peaceful and sometimes wild and free*
> *Love is a traveller on the River of No Return*
> *Swept on forever to be lost in the stormy sea.*
> *I can hear the river call.*
> *I can hear my lover call. Come to me.*
> *I lost my love on the river*
> *And forever my heart will yearn.*
> *Gone, gone forever,*
> *Down the River of No Return."*

She ends almost in tears while the crowd applaud the maudlin sentimentality of the song. Calder walks in, hoists Kay over his shoulder to the consternation of the assembled drinkers and deposits her next to his son on the horse-trap outside. "Where are you taking me?" shouts Kay. "Home," is the answer. The film ends with a pan down to the red shoes abandoned in the trap's tracks.

In a slightly less convoluted plot, the mother/father/son triad of **The River Wild** learn to rely on each other through the dual tribulations of kidnapping by two gunmen and the increasingly dangerous rapids. The emasculated father, Tom (David Strathairn), eventually takes an active role and allows Gail (Meryl Streep) to shoot the

Fitzcarraldo

gunman, Wade (Kevin Bacon). Safely ashore, Tom and Gail rediscover their love for each other and are joined in silhouette by their son and their dog as the river rages on. At the end of this river lies the re-establishment of home and normality.

A slightly less trite, but nevertheless deliriously happy, ending awaits **Fitzcarraldo**'s genial opera-obsessed maniac, Brian Sweeney Fitzgerald (Kinski again), "conquistador of the worthless". After persuading a rubber baron to fund a ship, the Molly Aida, to find more rubber plantation land further in the Amazon basin, Fitzcarraldo sets off upstream (much to the consternation of the baron who was under the impression that the boat was going in the opposite direction) with Captain "I don't trust maps" Paul at the helm. It is Fitzcarraldo's dream to build an opera house in the depths of the Amazon; he sees opera as the final weapon of civilisation and often plays the gramophone to silence the rhythms of the jungle's inhabitants. Heading up a tributary of the Amazon, the Pachitea, no-one is quite sure of Fitzcarraldo's strategy until he reveals that he plans to drag the ship over a mountain to join another tributary, the Ucayali, above its rapids where no other ships have been able to travel. The rubber he dreams of finding here will fund his projected opera house. Unbelievably the massive steam ship is successfully pulled over the mountain (a feat documented in Les Blank's **Burden Of Dreams** [1982]), set adrift into the rapids of the Ucayali and miraculously makes it back to port. Fitzcarraldo sells the ship back to the baron and uses the money to transport the entire cast of Bellini's "The Puritans" on board for a final operatic journey down the river. Fitzcarraldo, grinning and posturing on deck with a huge cigar, looks as if he has achieved his life's goal: a triumph of giddying worthlessness.

This particular journey ends in a success of sorts, but one which doesn't

Deliverance

celebrate the comforts of home and civilisation, nor does it allow the deep pessimism of **Aguirre** to infect the pleasure of this mad enterprise. Fitzcarraldo is finally alone, without wife or child, but is also bereft of the comforting angst of nihilistic existentialism. He truly plays and flows with the senseless logic of the river.

## FORGET RAPE

There are two moments of violence in **Deliverance** and **River Of No Return** which deserve slightly fuller discussion. The homosexual rape of Bobby in **Deliverance** is often commented on and it is clear that the moral centre of the film is concerned with this violation rather than with the rather tendentious legal discussion surrounding the death of the mountain man. As Bobby says, "I don't want this getting around". The entire film has to erase the memory of that rape with more and more violence: Drew's suicide, Lewis' broken leg, Ed's self-stabbing and shooting of another hunter. The surviving men are bloodied and broken to an almost comic degree but still the memory of the rape is the one that lives on in any description of the film. It is as if their earlier misgivings about the staidness of suburban life are answered by the revelation of its complete opposite, anal rape, a fate so terrible that it has to be sublimated into the guilt of murder. Even Ed's loving wife cannot stop the dream of the stiff hand piercing the dark pool of his nightmare.

In contrast to this macabre fantasy, **The River Of No Return** moves with a grim inevitability to the near-rape of Kay by Calder. Although Calder has been presented as a staunch adherent to the frontier code, even if he has been to jail for shooting someone in the back, it is obvious that the close quarters of the raft, and the necessity of providing a mother for the boy, will eventually lead to some form of sexual contact.

Piranha

Since Kay already has a fiancé there is no way in which Calder can approach her without breaking the code of honour which he purports to uphold. Quite a long way into their journey, while on the bank one night, Calder snaps and tries to kiss Kay. When she struggles to escape, he drags her to the ground and manages extract his kiss. Although Kay has been struggling throughout, it is the kiss which finally calms her down, fulfilling another sort of masculine fantasy. It is at this point that the frontier myth has to protect itself since the violence of the impending rape cannot be morally borne by the narrative and the sudden fortuitous appearance of a cougar allows Calder to save face by protecting Kay from a fate possibly *worse* than rape. The finale, of course, following the death of her fiancé and the audience's knowledge that Kay will now acquiesce to Calder's kiss, repeats in comic form the very inevitability of the attempted rape. The line, "Love is a traveller on the River of No Return" seems somehow more sinister than it might at first have appeared.

## THE END

The river journey film is not a genre. These films are not connected in any real way. The encounter of boat, river and human is not inevitable or formulaic, but it is possibly beautiful. Perhaps it is necessary to turn our attention to a film that will make the pretensions of the previous discussion obvious. In Joe Dante's **Piranha**, the traveller has no boat but is a genetically mutated school of fish with a rather ludicrous line in electronic biting sounds. As the fish travel down the Lost River, chewing feet and attacking children, they learn nothing and neither do they find true love nor develop feelings of compassion.

The human dramas on shore seem to pale in comparison to the unthinking movement of the piranha. Characters discuss *Huckleberry Finn* and one of the soon-to-be-eaten sunbathers reads *Moby Dick*. Heroic actions and burgeoning romances fail to

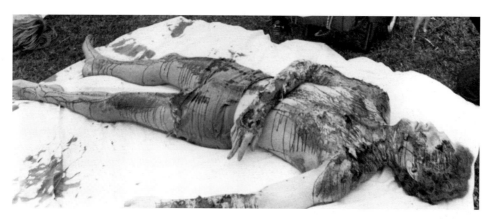

Piranha

stop the piranhas' entry into the sea from where their ridiculous threat will spread to all corners of the globe. The river conceals the silent threat of destruction and it is this fear that seems to haunt the river journey film.

# NOTES

1. Roberts, Shari; "Western Meets Eastwood: Genre And Gender On The Road", *The Road Movie Book*, (eds.) Steven Cohan & Ina Rae Hark; London: Routledge, 1997, p.53.

2. "Indeterminacy And The Reader's Response To Prose Fiction" (*Aspects Of Narrative*, (ed.) J. Hillis Miller. New York, Columbia University Press, 1971); quoted in Shlomith Rimmon-Kenan, *Narrative Fiction: Contemporary Poetics*; New York & London: Routledge, 1991 (1983).

**Chapter 15**

# British Road Movies

# HIGHWAYS, BY-WAYS AND LAY-BYS: THE GREAT BRITISH ROAD MOVIE

## Susan Picken

*"To travel hopefully is a better thing than to arrive,
and the true success is to labour"*
—Robert Louis Stevenson (1850–1894)

As popular wisdom would have it, in Britain you're never more than sixty miles from the sea. Actually, due to the convoluted shape of mainland Britain (which, as Paul Theroux commented, resembles nothing so much as "a witch riding a pig"), one is never more than 77 miles (125km) away from the sea at any point. Inaccurately romantic, the saying does, however, give a pretty good indication of the prominence of the sea in the British psyche. Isolating and insulating, the proximity of the ocean to every point of the British Isles only reinforces the consciousness of Britain as a "sceptred isle", serves as a constant reminder of a sea-faring, empire-building history.

At the margins of the island, constantly shifting, lies the natural interface with the sea, the coastline: all 6,000 plus miles of it. Rough and rugged, wild and windswept or safe and sandy this interzone between land and sea, between the foreign and the familiar exerts its own strange attraction on the national consciousness. From Graham Greene's *Brighton Rock* to **Genevieve** (Henry Cornelius, 1953) and the **Carry On** films[1], to **Quadrophenia** (Franc Roddam, 1979) and **Mona Lisa** (Neil Jordan, 1986), to be beside the sea has provided the inspiration for a significant part of British culture. The border between the elements of earth and water; the threshold between geographical territories; the coastline is a liminal space where known and unknown converge; the seaside the last resort of the *carnivalesque* where everyday reality is turned upside-down.

Enclosed within this coastal barricade, Britain is a small island dominated by an abundance of water. Despite the labyrinthine length of Britain's coastal profile, to go from north to south, Land's End to John O'Groats, one need only travel for 560 miles while the furthest points from east to west are only about 250 miles apart. For all the supposed "green and pleasant" attractions of the interior landscape there's no escaping the limitations of geography: sooner or later one hits the edge of the world, the end of the road, the sea.

Of necessity, the British road is brief. It's not really surprising that the mythology of the road never quite took hold of the British imagination the way it did the American. Lacking the mystique of distance the British road finds glamour conferred on it from a different source: the aura of age, the sheer weight of history incumbent on the land. The Roman invaders may have constructed the first proper highways almost a millennium ago (and indeed fragments of these still remain), but even before this the rolling ridges and troughs of the British terrain formed natural pathways for ancient travellers. Like the seaside, the road too is a liminal space, a place with its own laws and conditions; neither one place or the other but always

Radio On

somewhere in-between. In the British landscape, on the British road-map, the psychic and the physical converge, the spiritual and the secular overlap. Ley-lines are overlaid by miles and miles of motorway, while commuters gaze upon ancient monuments from express coach windows.

Without the charisma of its US counterpart (somehow the M4 to Bristol doesn't have the same allure as, say, Route 66), travelling on the British road offers a curiously enervating experience. Surrounded by sculpted banks and barriers, punctuated by the blandly repetitive architecture of "Happy Eater" and "Little Chef" diners, these ribbons of tarmac and gravel pass through the natural world without ever touching it. Like a vast, open-air movie screen landscape is turned into spectacle, environment is transformed into scenery.

Functional and pragmatic and, of course, limited, the geography of the British road network is at best uninspiring, at worst banal. The American highway has its Nebraskan plains and Arizona desert, the British have Spaghetti Junction, that mass of intersecting roads just outside Birmingham. No inspiration here for an *On The Road* or **Easy Rider**, we prefer **On The Buses** (Harry Booth, 1971). One could almost say that there is no such thing as a British road culture, no such thing, especially, as a British road movie. Almost – but not quite.

Apart from extremely rare excursions fringing onto the genre, such as the early **They Drive By Night** (Arthur Woods, 1938) or '50s realist dramas like **Hell Drivers** (Cy Endfield, 1957), or later efforts like Chris Petit's **Radio On** (1979), the most notable examples of the British road movie have come in the last few years, from film makers who are less concerned with geography *per se* than with the intuitive reading of the landscape: "psychogeography". Interactive rather than empirical, the psychogeographical imperative charts the "precise effects of geographical setting, consciously managed or not, acting directly on the mood and behaviour of the individual", and considers the relation between the human and the environment.

As initially conceived by the Situationist International (SI) in France in the late 1950s, the study of "psychogeography"[2] evolved from the notion of *détournement* (subversion)[3], part of the "revolution of everyday life"[4]. Originating in the artistic avant-gardes of Dada and Surrealism, the process of *détournement* soon expanded to include virtually all aspects of day-to day existence, in particular, especially, the urban environment. Co-opted by the radical theories of the SI, new vistas opened up in hitherto drab city streets, new possibilities of exploration and pleasure emerged:

*"The sudden change of ambience in a street within the space of a few meters; the evident division of a city into zones of distinct psychic atmospheres; the path of least resistance which is automatically followed in aimless strolls (and which has no relation to the physical contour of the ground); the appealing or repelling character of certain places"[5]*

Fundamental to the psychogeographical study of the environment was the concept of the *dérive* or the drift, a strategy of random wandering which relied upon serendipity and chance encounter to garner new information about the seemingly familiar:

*"Psychogeography is about the instinctual exploration of the emotional contours of one's environment. It aims to discover subversive and anti-authoritarian places and journeys that can be used in the development of new, more liberating, kinds of locales. Situationist psychogeographers adopted the practice of the **dérive** (the "drift") as their basic tool. To dérive is to go on an unhindered, unstructured wander through the restrictive landscapes of everyday Space."[6]*

Appearing in the work of film-makers such as Patrick Keiller (**London, Robinson In Space**) and Chris Petit, the translation of psychogeography into the representation of the British landscape has mapped a whole new emotional terrain onto the otherwise flat topography of the British road movie. The two films to be discussed here, Andrew Kotting's **Gallivant** (1996) and Michael Winterbottom's **Butterfly Kiss** (1994) also evince an unspoken fascination with the psychogeographical, with the human exploration of and interaction with the environment. Road movies of a sort (although Kotting in particular is keen to distance his film from the genre), both films, however, rely less on the linear progression of the road for their structure and more on the random encounters and happenstance of the *dérive*.

## HOW LONG *IS* A PIECE OF STRING?: 'GALLIVANT'
*"gal' li'vant': to wander about seeking pleasure or diversion; gad; to go about with members of the opposite sex."*

A runaway home-movie, Andrew Kotting's **Gallivant** is, in the most literal sense, a road movie, a hurtling circular jaunt round the coastline of mainland Britain whose "script" is the *AA Road Map Of Coastal Britain*. A "zig-zagging 6,000 mile trip fairly full to overflowing"[7], **Gallivant** winds its way from cosy south coast to the most northerly points of Scotland and back again, all during the few months when autumn becomes winter.

    This apparent exercise in futility (what could be more pointless than to go round in circles?), is of course anything but. In his desire to create "a journey without it being a road movie"[8], Kotting leaves the conventions of the genre far, far behind. Travelling becomes more than a means to an end, a way of getting from A to B. The road in **Gallivant** becomes the narrative: the act of the journey, its chance encounters and passing moments forming the fabric of the film itself.

    Meticulously avoiding the urban sprawl **Gallivant** trades in the picturesque as much as the picaresque, conjuring up the incredible diversity of the British landscape from the crumbling Cornish coastline to the brooding peaks of the Welsh mountains

Gallivant

and the rainbow-hued expanses of the Scottish highlands. A psychogeographical explorer mapping the very limits of Britain, Kotting insistently positions the human at the heart of all this wild beauty: encountering those who live at the extremities of the island, giving a voice to those who are, quite literally, marginalised.

A voyage of discovery in more ways than one, Kotting does not undertake his journey alone. On an extended, eccentric family holiday, he is accompanied by two of his nearest and dearest (apart, of course, from a minimal crew). Along for the ride are Kotting's octogenarian grandmother Gladys, and his 6-year-old daughter, Eden. Bridging the generations of this one family, "Big Granny" and little Eden have a lot more in common than blood. Positioned at either end of age's spectrum both are in equal proximity to death: Gladys because of her advanced years, Eden because of a rare genetic disorder.

Grandmother and child are pivotal to the film. Initially Kotting wanted this to be a solo journey, a personal account of his reaction to the shifting British landscape and the people who inhabited it. Production politics intervened, however, and the decision was made to introduce other figures: beefing up the storyline, broadening the experience. "Casting" Gladys and Eden seemed a natural choice:

*"I hit on the idea of Gladys and Eden and it just began to make more and more sense that if I could go on this trip with the two of them, be together for three, four, five, six months, we didn't know at the time how long it would take, to travel en famille then something might come of it"[9]*

Fabricating **Gallivant** from the most basic of elements: people, places, the road, Kotting has constructed a film which is not only about human beings communing with the landscape but is about their communication with each other. Suffering from Joubert's Syndrome, which severely impairs her ability to speak, to move, Eden's only form of communication is through a simple form of sign language. Initially almost strangers to one another (Kotting and his family spend a large part of their time in France), a bond is soon forged between Eden and her great-grandmother, the gap in their ages eroded by their shared experience of the world around them.

The "drift" transmuted into celluloid, transplanted into the rural landscape, the film is scripted according to the vagaries of location, structured according to the laws of chance. Kotting again:

*"The film is strangely structured, it's a mess of a structure. One minute you feel there is a structure and the next it's all out the window, and then you think "where are Gladys and Eden?"*[10]

Structurally freeform, an impressionistic exercise in map reading, **Gallivant** is revelatory of Kotting's experimental roots, his interest in dada and performance, the legacy of the British landscape film[11].("What has always interested me was to do something in the landscape, something that was beautiful but also powerful and meaningful. Performance and landscape..."[12]). The vicissitudes of the headlong, 6,000 mile dash also provide the excuse for some rather more formal experimentation. Hurtling through the lexicon of film techniques from A through Z, **Gallivant** is, at the very least, an exhilaratingly colourful patchwork of sped-up, slowed-down, hand-held, jump-cut film.

Kotting wrests a surreal humour from the film's freestyle experimentation. A sort of prologue featuring a manically signing weatherman pokes fun at the British obsession with the weather as well as the plummy tones of BBC English. On the seafront at Cornwall a telescope "focuses" on footage of a naughtily naked lady. He's not averse to getting in on the joke himself: as the journey progresses he, Gladys, and Eden build up their own personal iconography, Gladys and Eden cast as lollipop lady and Virgin Mary respectively, while the anything but monkish Kotting appears as just that, a monk.

An absurdist appropriation of the traditional seaside holiday, Kotting's expedition sets out from (and eventually returns to) the shingle-strewn shore of Bexhill-on-Sea. An appreciation for the kitsch soon becomes apparent, whether it's the cosily familiar seaside iconography of piers and pavilions, kiss-me-quick hats and candy floss, the gorgeously tacky lights of Blackpool Illuminations or the lavishly, lovingly decorated interior of a public toilet on the Isle of Lochalsh, Scotland.

Parallel with all this cheerful tat, however, a darker, stranger, more dangerous Britain emerges during the course of the journey. Passing through, an outsider looking in, the impartial gaze of Kotting's camera reveals the dual nature of the end-of-season seaside resort, the drab reality behind the colourful facade, the hollow spaces left by departing holidaymakers. As the road-trip progresses, the land itself begins to seem inconstant and impermanent; the lost village in Cornwall which slides into the sea, the Norfolk coastline disintegrating under visitor's feet.

The journey, too, is not without its own dangers and discomforts. It is especially punishing for Gladys and Eden who, at times, must interrupt their journey in order to rest. Occasionally, Kotting's desire to document the reactions of the old woman and the child to the landscape around them borders on the cruel. At one point Eden signs, "I'm cold, Daddy ...I'm hungry", at another the sight of an exhausted Gladys climbing towards John O'Groats is only marginally offset by the armchair which Kotting is, surreally, carrying for her. Even Kotting suffers for the film. Entertaining a teary Eden, larking about, he falls and smashes his ankle (an accident which does, however, prompt an interesting excursion to the emergency room).

The regions of this tiny island exist in close physical proximity but in every other way are worlds apart. Behind the passing scenery, beneath the unfurling tarmac, age-old tensions emerge: between North and South, city and country, Welsh and

English, old and young. On Tyneside one angry passer-by proclaims "You can fuck off back down South straightaway", while, deep in the beauty of the Welsh countryside an old man warns Gladys "Keep away from Swansea on a Saturday night... it's like the Wild West".

The only certainty, it seems, in this turbulent landscape is in tradition, in history. The film layers past upon present, finding inspiration in the reminiscences of the elderly – "What is traditional? Traditional is something you should never forget" – in their weather-beaten faces. The pagan roots of Britain, its bloodthirsty past resurfaces again and again. In Cornwall, for instance, the gruesome legend of how the young beautiful St Agnes tricked the giant Bolster into bleeding to death survives to be re-enacted by local schoolchildren and stilt-walkers. Likewise, the bloody invasion of Wessex by the Vikings lingers on in folk memory in the form of a ritualised, sanitised sword-dance. Scratch the surface of this modern Christian Britain and another, pagan past soon appears: at Offa's Dyke, Cootywell, Hastings.

Charting what is, in many respects, an invisible landscape, **Gallivant** sets out to be, to some degree, definitive: a mile for mile voyage round the perimeter of Britain. This is, of course, an impossible mission; not just because of the sheer inaccessibility of some areas but also, more importantly, because of the changing landscape of the island itself, its constant erosion by the ever-encroaching sea. As the film makes explicit the coastline of Britain is akin to a piece of wet string: immeasurable, unknowable. Lacking the empirical "evidence" of his journey Kotting must instead opt for what is ultimately a much more intriguing *modus operandi*: an emotional rather than a physical process of mapping, through the eyes of Gladys, Eden, himself, as well as the many, many folk he meets along the way.

## ROAD RAGE: 'BUTTERFLY KISS'

While on his circular journey, Andrew Kotting undoubtedly passed within a couple of miles of the Midlands, the setting of Michael Winterbottom's **Butterfly Kiss**. Kotting probably never gave these bleak locales a second glance. Why would he? Why would anyone? The film takes place in the most bleakly banal of environments; the protagonists of **Butterfly Kiss** inhabiting a traveller's no-man's-land, lingering in the sort of roadside spaces that the rest of the world passes through, ignores. Anonymous way-stations for those who are permanently on the road to somewhere else: last minute toilet stops for screaming kids; refuelling points for Kleenex and cigarettes; cooked breakfasts and cups of tea for weary motorists.

How different, this, from the vast open prairie and rolling tumble-weeds of the United States, the ineluctable allure of big horizons and even bigger skies. How glamorous, how mythic the road of the American dream. Kerouac and Cassady, Bonnie and Clyde, the US road, unlike its British counterpart, is peopled by those who are larger than life, bigger than death.

A vast circulatory system, movement is the life-blood of the American road, the motor-car its red blood cells. Like our own bodies, however, this circulatory system is not without its pathogens, in fact as well as fiction: carriers of disease, destruction and death.

In the cinematic imagination, murder and movement are inextricably linked, the US road movie in particular has had no shortage of itinerant killers. From Robert Mitchum's god-fearing psychopath in **Night Of The Hunter** (1955) [see Chapter 13], via Rutger Hauer's homicidal **Hitcher** (1986) [see Chapter 8], through to the white trash pairings of Brad Pitt and Juliette Lewis in **Kalifornia** (1993) and Woody Harrelson and Lewis in **Natural Born Killers** (1994) [see Chapter 10], the transience of the road has provided the perfect opportunity for murder, while the scale of the landscape has promised obscurity, invisibility, escape.

Odd, perhaps, then, that Michael Winterbottom chooses to transplant this most American of genres, "roadkill", to British soil. Lacking the backdrop of the trans-continental vastness of the US, the anonymity of the endless road, **Butterfly Kiss** plays out against more intimate, insular vistas, emphasising the claustrophobic repetition of the British road, the inescapable "smallness" of the immediate world. Twisting the road movie almost out of recognition, Winterbottom's film leaves behind the machismo of murder, focusing on a peculiarly feminine psychopathology (and thereby living up to the hoary old cliché that the female is, truly, deadlier than the male).

Eunice, or "Eu" (Amanda Plummer), drifts along the motorways and slip-roads of the Midlands on a bizarre mission. Searching for a mysterious woman, "Judith", and the name of a song she cannot quite remember, Eunice compulsively pursues her ritual quest in service stations and petrol kiosks, questioning the women who work there, killing them when they fail to be the long-sought Judith.

At one stop, however, Eunice encounters the naive, kindly Miriam, or "Mi" (Saskia Reeves) ("Eu" and "Mi", natural born killing partners!). Doing her best to help the charismatic yet obviously unstable Eunice, Miriam invites her to stay at the flat which she shares with her invalid grandmother.

Lonely and inexperienced, Miriam is easily seduced by Eunice, taking for granted her dangerous eccentricity, the chains and tattoos which adorn Eunice's scarred, bruised body. Waking to find Eunice gone, Miriam sets off in pursuit, leaving her grandmother alone and helpless.

Duty, responsibility, morality: Miriam abandons them all for Eunice. Reunited with Eunice, joining her on her mad quest, Miriam soon becomes aware of the true extent of Eunice's violent urges, the trail of corpses she has left behind her. Rationalising the irrational, forgiving the unforgivable, Miriam soon becomes inexorably swept up in Eunice's deranged existence, where murder becomes a commonplace, and sex is a prelude to death.

The geography against which **Butterfly Kiss** situates its tale of transgressive romance and murderous obsession is one which is sinisterly commonplace. Familiar from J.G. Ballard's bleakly auto-erotic novel *Crash* and his follow-up *Concrete Island* (and, to a lesser extent, David Cronenberg's film version of the former), this is a drably functional landscape of slip-roads and hard shoulders. In nature, but not of nature, in this environment the human form, flesh and blood becomes a fragile incongruity. The true inhabitants of the world, it seems, are the speeding metal boxes which endlessly whizz by in a blur of movement. The banality of the everyday extends to the act of murder itself. Selecting her victims from the dreary self-enclosed world of the motorway, Eunice is indiscriminate in her slaughter of workmen and shop assistants, travelling salesmen and long-distance lorry-drivers, the flotsam and jetsam of the road.

Conceived with a modicum of morbid humour, the character of Eunice has constructed a complexly psychotic world for herself which weaves together Old Testament orthodoxy with sexual sadism. Like some latter-day self-flagellating saint she physically wraps herself in chains, while her body has frequently, willingly submitted to the sting of the tattooist's needle. What, historically, might have been seen as a sign of religious devotion now seems, however, in the post-modern, post-Christian cynicism of the late twentieth century, like obsessive masochism.

This perverse take on Christianity extends throughout **Butterfly Kiss**. While it never really becomes certain exactly who the "Judith" is that Eunice is looking for, her biblical antecedent is clearly evoked: the Israelite Judith, beheader of the Assyrian general Holofernes. Quasi-blasphemous, too, is Eunice's oft-repeated wish to be cleansed. Literally reaching the end of the road, the sea, the closing moments of the film culminate in Eunice's simultaneous baptism and execution, drowned in the waves by a loyal, grieving Miriam.

Butterfly Kiss

While sharing the American cinema's fascination with the road, its dual status as both nightmare and dreamscape, Winterbottom sets his film within a radically different geography. A tentative experiment in fusing narrative with psychogeographical enquiry, **Butterfly Kiss** maps the human psyche onto the physical environment. The humble, humdrum "A" and "B" roads of the British transport system become routes to a murderess' redemption, the directionless to-and-fro of Eunice's obsession a homicidal derivation of the drift. A modern pilgrim, Eunice is on a metaphysical quest; beneath the tarmac, at the end of the road, lies her salvation.

Apart from language, there is, perhaps, little else that the British road movie shares with its American antecedent. Maybe even to call films like **Gallivant** and **Butterfly Kiss** road movies does them a disservice. Unimpressed by burning rubber, unconcerned with guzzling gas and eating the miles, these British films focus less on the attractions of the road than on that which the road passes through: the landscape which surrounds it. If the American road movie ultimately originated from the 19th century drive west, the "manifest destiny" of the white settlers to make their mark upon the land, the British road film, by contrast, derives from an entirely different tradition, a painterly tradition which concerns itself with contemplation rather than conquest.

# NOTES

1. The long-running **Carry On** series of comedy films were produced between the fifties and seventies, characterised by scripts rich in innuendo and references to British life. They frequently include days out and trips to the seaside within their narratives; see, for example **Carry On At Your Convenience** (Gerald Thomas, 1971) and **Carry On Girls** (Thomas, 1973) amongst others.

2. A definition of this and other key Situationist terms can be found in Libero Andreotti, Xavier Costa (eds), *Theory Of The Dérive And Other Situationist Writings On The City*; ACTAR, 1996.

3. Alastair Bonnett defines the process of *détournement* thus: "*Détournement* involves taking elements from a social stereotype and, through their mutation and reversal, turning them against it so it becomes disrupted and exposed as a product of alienation". Alastair Bonnett, "The Situationist Legacy" in Stewart Home, (ed), *What Is Situationism? A Reader*; AK Press, 1996.

4. For more see Raoul Vaneigem, *The Revolution Of Everyday Life*; Rebel Press, 1983.

5. Guy Debord, "Introduction To A Critique Of Urban Geography", reprinted in *Theory Of The Dérive And Other Situationist Writings On The City*.

6. Alastair Bonnett, "The Situationist Legacy".

7. Taken from **Gallivant**, Andrew Kotting, 1996.

8. Barbara Pichler, "Interview With Andrew Kotting", (unpublished, July 1998). Transcript held in British Film Institute, London.

9. Barbara Pichler, "Interview With Andrew Kotting", (unpublished, July 1998).

10. Barbara Pichler, "Interview With Andrew Kotting", (unpublished, July 1998).

11. As practised by film makers such as Chris Welsby and William Raban and, now, Patrick Keiller and Andrew Kotting, the landscape film has formed a minor but significant strand in British avant-garde cinema. For more see Michael O'Pray (ed), *The British Avant-Garde Film: 1926–1995*; University of Luton Press/Arts Council of England, 1996.

12. Barbara Pichler, "Interview With Andrew Kotting".

# Chapter 16

# Wim Wenders And The Road

# LAY-BYS & LULLABIES: ROCK'S ROLE IN WIM WENDERS' ROAD MOVIES

## Ian Garwood

If a character is caught smiling in a Wim Wenders movie, it is likely that (s)he is listening to music: troubled travel writer Philip (Rudiger Vogler) enjoys a brief stop-off at a Chuck Berry concert in **Alice In The Cities** (1974); Robert (Hanns Zischler) and Bruno (Vogler) never have more fun than when they provide additional vocals to Heinz' "Just Like Eddie" as they drive along the East German border in **Kings Of The Road** (1976); and the angel Damiel (Bruno Ganz) delights in surveying the scene as he walks into a Nick Cave concert after disowning his celestial roots in **Wings Of Desire** (1987).

Wenders himself has claimed that American rock'n'roll saved his life as a teenager, and it is tempting to view the incidents cited above, and many other musical moments from his films, as examples of the enthusiastic pop fan getting the better of the reflective filmmaker. If his road movies generally follow their alienated protagonists as they search for some sense of identity through travel, the characters' interactions with music can appear as moments where that identity is suddenly, and uncomplicatedly, secured, as they enact a possession of a particular song.

Regarded in this way, music would be cast in a familiarly transcendent role, providing in the immediacy of its "unmediated" language ("pure form" according to Wenders[1]) a safe haven for characters otherwise suspicious of and at odds with alternative systems of social communication, whether that be articulated as an estrangement from images (Philip in **Alice In The Cities**), the institution of the family (especially Travis in **Paris, Texas** [1984]) or verbal language itself (Josef in **The Goalkeeper's Fear Of The Penalty** [1972]).

Indeed, there is evidence in Wenders' movies to suggest his use of music ought to be characterised in such a manner. The most notorious line of dialogue from a Wenders' film – Robert's cheerful observation in **Kings Of The Road** that "the Americans have colonized our subconscious" – comes in response to Bruno's admission that he has a song lyric going around in his head which he had hummed throughout an argument with an ex-girlfriend and which had stayed with him ever since ("I've got a woman, mean as she can be"). It is certainly easier to imagine Bruno seeking emotional protection in the comforting repetition of a song than it is to envisage him engaging in anything as messily intimate as a lovers' quarrel.

Yet, **Kings Of The Road**, which does feature its two heroes bonding over the records Bruno feeds his in-truck diskette player, is exceptional rather than exemplary in the space it provides for its music. It is not generally the case that pop provides his otherwise self-doubting protagonists a ready-made means of survival. Examples from other Wenders films such as **Alice In The Cities** and **Wings Of Desire** feature characters whose relationship with the music they listen to represents their frustration in searching for a useable identity, or who ultimately reject music as a site of identity at all.

Kings Of The Road

The very act of "singing along", a male bonding exercise in **Kings Of The Road,** becomes an index of Philip's failed attempts to create self-made idylls in **Alice In The Cities.** Philip has been sent to America to write a travel piece for a magazine, but is suffering from writer's block. In the opening sequence, he is viewed sitting beneath a pier on a deserted beach, taking a Polaroid of a wooden structure in front of him. Looking at the photo and lining it up against others in front of him, he starts singing the chorus of The Drifters' "Under The Boardwalk": "Under the boardwalk/ Down by the sea/On a blanket with my baby/that's where I wanna be".

Smiling wryly whilst singing, the moment encapsulates both Philip's desire to capture experiences and his awareness of the shortfall between the "authentic" originary point of an experience and his attempts at its preservation. If the row of photos picturing the same object bear out his frustration that "they never really show what you saw", his low-key, half-spoken delivery of a classic piece of Atlantic soul demonstrates a similar inability to combat his self-isolation by drawing upon the emotional plenitude of the song. Rather than ameliorating his visible loneliness by conjuring up a romantic scenario through his singing, Philip's self-deprecating performance succeeds only in highlighting for the viewer the gap between his present situation and the utopian reach of the song, both in the lyrics cited and in the awareness of the original's musical richness.

Philip's tacit admission of his inability to sing along convincingly turns to frustration soon after, when his harmonizing to a piece of string-laden, gospel inflected funk on his car radio is interrupted by a DJ's voiceover. Stroppily kicking at the off-button, he complains that he's never been allowed to hear the end of the song. Soon after, Philip rages against America's packaging of images by trashing his hotel room TV, the two sequences combined exhibiting his alienation from the mainstream delivery routes of both vision and sound. However, rather than acting as

Alice In The Cities

a simple critique of a culture that turns all its art into commerce, Philip's sudden bursts of anger stem from a desperate need, and evident inability, to participate with the world. His failure to do so is as much in evidence in his own delivery of "Under The Boardwalk" as it is in his efforts to exploit the more obviously mediated opportunities provided by radio and TV.

The jukebox, a prominent symbol of Americana in Wenders' films, features twice in **Alice In The Cities**, and both occasions depict a continuing estrangement between pop song and protagonist, rather than the bestowing of a comforting identity upon him. Soon after leaving the beach, Philip stops off at a roadside café. The camera remains looking in on Philip from outside the building as he lays his photos, as in the boardwalk sequence, in a row along the window sill, the cafe's jukebox visible behind him. Another male on his own (actually Wenders himself) walks into the back of the frame, selects a song from the jukebox and, like Philip, stares out a window blankly, this time facing out to the right: two solitary figures, both attempting to fill the voids in their existence with recordings, one visual, the other musical.

In terms of Wenders' character and the music he selects ("Psychotic Reaction", a '60s hit for Yardbirds imitators The Count Five), the attempt is shown to fail for a number of reasons: firstly his status as an autonomous subject is compromised by his deployment as a mere double for Philip, the figure who holds centre stage (as much as is possible for such a diffident personality) both in terms of the composition of the individual shot (he is front of frame) and in his centrality to the events that have already taken place; secondly attention is further diverted to Philip as the film cuts to a close up of him drinking from a paper cup and then a shot of the anonymous road he looks out onto. The song's opening lyrics ("I feel depressed, I feel so bad"), as well as its title for viewers who recognise the intro, has clear relevance to Philip's state of mind at the time.

However, a further diversion takes place throughout the scene that prevents the song becoming a commentary on Philip's character. The spindly riff that opens the track quickly gives way to a shuffling railroad rhythm, complete with wailing harmonica. Apart from Philip's observable lack of attention to the song's building dynamics, the song is cut off jarringly just as it appears it may indeed become attached to Philip's point of view. The song is only a reflection of Philip's state of mind in its extremely tenuous and brief connection to a distracted consciousness drifting listlessly without direction.

Tenuous connections also pervade the second jukebox scene, with Philip now in the German town of Wuppertal, trying to deliver Alice, the small girl he has been asked to escort back from America, to her grandmother. Popping into a cafe for a bite to eat, Canned Heat's "On The Road Again" emanates from the jukebox, the sequence choreographed to last for the entire duration of the song. A small boy leans against the jukebox, acting as a double for Alice, both of similar age and both eating ice-cream. Alice's ravenous appetite acts as a counterpoint to her surrogate father's unfulfilled craving for emotional sustenance, and the boy also stands as a taunting figure for Philip, successfully gaining such sustenance through the music from which Philip has proved himself to be estranged. The scene ends with Philip looking on at the boy, who has rested his head against the jukebox and hummed along throughout the scene, as if the machine were his mother coaxing him to sleep with a lullaby.

However, whilst the boy displays an unbroken connection to the song (and in his simple humming escapes the complications of adult language), the relationship with Alice which seems to offer Philip the possibility of connection reaches a crisis point. Alice admits that her grandparents do not live in Wuppertal at all, a revelation that prompts Philip to give up their search and hand her over to the police. "Psychotic Reaction" is allowed to build up its own head of steam only to be cut short by the film. "On The Road Again", in contrast, with its droning pulse threading itself throughout the sequence, retains a rhythmic certainty to its own journey which plays against the uncertain hesitations of Alice and Philip's.

That Philip has made tentative steps towards a less estranged participation with the world is represented through a combination of music and image towards the end of the film. However, this reconnection does not involve him achieving the child-like, unmediated, relationship with music suggested by the boy's association with "On The Road Again". Philip stops taking photos after he is entrusted the care of Alice, but picks up the camera one last time as they cross the Rhine on the ferry, just before the police come to take Alice from him (she had run away from them). Through his viewfinder, we see Alice framed in a family grouping, standing in front of a woman with her child in her arms. On the soundtrack, the woman continues singing a folk song with the repeated refrain "my dad and my son". This moment signals Philip's acceptance of the potential for photography to conjure satisfying illusions (Alice reintegrated with a family), as compensation for its inability to preserve reality. No less important to this fantasy is the woman's musical inscription of Philip into the scene with her naming of male family figures. When Philip smiles during the Chuck Berry concert (which he visits straight after taking Alice to the police station), it is in recognition both of the musician's visible virtuosity (referenced in close ups of Berry on-stage), and in relief at seeing music emanating from a particular body rather than floating ephemerally. Philip does not achieve a surer sense of self by merging with music, by successfully realizing his early attempts to sing along, but rather by recognising a separateness from the music that allows him to use it as a vehicle for fulfilling fantasy.

If **Kings Of The Road**, at least superficially, seems determined to disavow this sense of separateness between music and its on-screen listeners, **Wings Of Desire** reopens the gap and, in its final moments, enacts a separation between character and music that sets limits on the ability of a particular song to secure a satisfying sense of identity.

Of all Wenders' road movies, **Wings Of Desire** is the most homely, tipping the genre onto a vertical axis, bringing the world (and the heavens) into one city, Berlin, rather than setting its characters out into the world, and featuring a protagonist whose quest is predicated on the desire for human interaction rather than a wary shying away from it. Damiel (Bruno Ganz) is an angel who longs to escape his celestial duties and feel the weight of the world – a weight which is evidenced in the music that plays diegetically within the film and which is lacking in the non-diegetic choral strains that soundtrack his heavenly observation.

The diegetic music, the music of the earth, is characterised by its "earthy" tones, provided by the tangled lines of heavy brass and clumsy fairground rhythms that accompany the performance of the trapeze artist heroine Marion (Solveig Dommartin), the woman Damiel loves, and the dark industrial beats that float around the city streets throughout the film. Changing its textures according to the distance of the camera from its diegetic source, the music is demonstrative of the weight of the world that Damiel craves to be able to experience, rather than merely to observe.

In one sequence, Damiel, invisible to Marion as he stands in her circus trailer, enacts a fantasy of earthly presence to Nick Cave's song "The Carny", which Marion has put on her record player. Responding to the song's menacing piano and twisted Wurlitzer rhythm, he choreographs his movement towards Marion in time with the music, demonstrating his desire to feel his own presence (the *mise-en-scène* encouraging the fantasy that his movement holds a physical threat), as well as the effectiveness of Nick Cave's song in suggesting weightiness.

The song reappears in a live form at the end of the film together with another Cave track, "From Her To Eternity", and, given both's sense of weightiness, should provide an appropriate setting for the moment where the now earthbound Damiel achieves the physical contact with Marion about which he could earlier only fantasize. Indeed, there is within the sequence evidence of the music's weight and of Damiel's new found ability to appreciate that weight. Cave's music is particularly marked by his visceral treatment of folk music forms, in the case of the two songs on show here those of the fairground ("The Carny") and the blues ("From Her To Eternity"). Each song adds texture to its musically simple rhythmic base with baroque instrumentation (the deeply resonant piano and menacing organ in "The Carny"; the squall of distorted electric guitar attacking the remorselessly chugging guitar and insistent bass line beneath it in "From Her To Eternity"). In addition, Cave's voice moves from the mock-stately in "The Carny" to a scream in "From Her To Eternity". Both music and voice contain the variety of texture and uncertain dynamics of delivery that differentiate the diegetic music from the non-diegetic score throughout the film.

The sequence also indicates how Damiel is able to appreciate this music as a human being now that he has lost his wings, hearing the performance from an undisturbed auditory perspective, rather than being assailed by the thoughts of those he passes as was his lot as an angel. Damiel takes joy from having his point of view, like that of the rest of the audience, limited to focusing upon Cave's music as the chief sensory experience available to them in this location. Great play is made of approximating the level of sound as Damiel would hear it as he traverses the length of the club in one long tracking shot, as if to emphasise Damiel's wonder at having an earthly point of view to articulate at all.

However, Wim Wenders has claimed that there is a certain irony in the choice of Nick Cave's song "From Her To Eternity" to soundtrack the film's climactic sequence: "the film is really the opposite," he has said, "It's 'From Eternity To Her'".[2] There is indeed textual evidence that the song acts as a counterpoint, rather than complement,

Wings Of Desire

to the action that once and for all vouchsafes Damiel's place in the real world.

The title track from Cave's first album as part of the Bad Seeds, "From Her To Eternity" details a man's obsession with the woman living in the apartment above. Lying awake through the night, he listens to her crying, and imagines catching her tears in his mouth. As the song progresses, his fantasies become ever more feverish until he comes to the conclusion that in order to retain this level of desire for her, he will have to kill her, because he knows "to possess her is, therefore, not to desire". As Simon Reynolds and Joy Press note, "he fastens on murder as a means to make her permanently his, yet eternally out of reach".[3]

The repeated refrain of "from her to eternity" indicates the singer's wish to escape the bonds of transient, earthly desires, a clear reversal of Damiel's longing for mortality. As the first word of the chorus is sung, the film begins to enact a distancing from its sentiments. Damiel turns away and walks out of the concert hall into the bar, leaving the escalating impreachments of Nick Cave behind him. Similarly, Marion makes her exit during the first line of the second chorus. As the song becomes ever more fervently in thrall to its own psychotic fantasy, the absenting of the film's chief representatives of the two elements to which the song refers (of womanhood and the eternal) is completed. The paths of Damiel and Marion are shown literally to follow the opposite trajectory to that yearned for in the song.

The fantasy of the song to escape the limits of earthly desire is expressed ironically in the final shot of the performance, as the film makes the shift to black and white that has always indicated the viewpoint of the eternal. Initially, however, there is no angel to be seen, the camera holding on the two guitarists as they crowd a

Kings Of The Road

microphone, chanting the refrain yet again (with Nick Cave audible off-screen). Thereafter, there is a pan to the left, fixing on the angel Cassiel, but the trick of his exclusion from the frame provides the song with an image that suggests its fantasy has come true (and Cassiel's re-inclusion denotes that the song is precisely that, a fantasy). The focus on the song is undermined for a final time, as the camera cuts away from a black and white shot of the stage to Marion entering the bar, thereby muffling the sound and returning to colour (the "real world") at just the second Nick Cave reaches his climactic decision that "that girl must go". The singer's cries for the death of a woman are replaced by a vision of woman as life-giving, a characterisation confirmed when Marion equates her and Damiel's love to that of Adam and Eve.

The sequence reverses the moment of Damiel's earlier fantasy of feeling present to the world to the rhythm of "The Carny" in Marion's trailer. There, his benign desire to achieve human weight was briefly articulated as something menacing. In the final sequence, Cave's own menacing fantasy is undercut to become the soundtrack for Damiel's benign attainment of worldly weight.

Thomas Elsaesser has argued that Wenders' "partisanship for images" is spurred by a neo-romantic revulsion against words.[4] In its emphasis on the textural qualities of Cave's song, **Wings Of Desire** demonstrates Wenders' equal interest in the expressive possibilities of music. However, this does not result in a mystification of the relationship between music and listener. Even in **Kings Of The Road**, there is an element of self-awareness in the representation of characters who seem happy to allow the songs they listen to represent them (to colonize their subconscious). Bruno and Robert have hardly exchanged a word before they are gazing tenderly over the steering wheel at each other, to the chintzy shuffle of Chris Montez' "The More I See You" (a '60s cover of an old show-tune by Harry Warren). However, the film moves away from the intimate close-ups of the couple to a sustained shot of their van from outside, with the music continuing, but engine noise to the fore. In this shift of perspective, the collusion of music and machine to stand in for more direct forms of human interaction becomes apparent: pop, even in **Kings Of The Road**, is as much an alibi as a lullaby for its listeners.

In this light, the emphasis in Wenders' films on the means (jukeboxes, diskette players, live performance) by which his beloved rock'n'roll is delivered to the world can be seen as more than a glamorization of pop's paraphernalia. Rather, the careful establishment of a particular source for the music within the diegesis points to the song's separateness from its listener: and thus its potential for providing fantasies that can be temporarily inhabited or even rejected, rather than ready made identities in which characters can become safely cocooned.

## NOTES

1. Jan Dawson, *Wim Wenders*; New York, Zoetrope, 1976, p12.

2. **Wings Of Desire**, Connoisseur Video, sleevenotes.

3. Simon Reynolds and Joy Press, *The Sex Revolts*; London: Serpent's Tail, 1995, p29.

4. Thomas Elsaesser, *New German Cinema: A History*; New Brunswick, Rutgers University Press, 1989, p57.

## Chapter 17

# David Lynch
# And The Road

# HOW SECRETS TRAVEL: DAVID LYNCH AND THE ROAD

## Stuart Mitchell

David Lynch loves to travel. An American film-maker weaving in and out of the mainstream, unafraid of the ill-lit, poorly maintained path. Wide-eyed David has discovered gateways deep into his and our subconscious, linking his films from one to the next and to those of the other "coolest" directors in the memory banks of this "boy scout from Montana". The ear, the garden hose, the phone cord and the intercom can all offer uneasy passage beyond our ostensible reality and into the realm of fantasy and nightmare.

Whether he likes the description or not, David Lynch is an avant-garde artist producing films for the Hollywood studios. He may still worry the hell out of "the money", but his name can play above a movie and command bums on seats. And once we are there he can play with our minds.

In his search for ideas Lynch has bemoaned the opportunities in modern life to find the necessary time and peace in which to drift off into waking nightmares. To sit still with the only disturbance being your own errant mind. Going for a long drive, down an empty road, proves hard to beat.

### LYNCH & HIS WAY TO THE EMERALD CITY

Lynch has been dabbling with the road movie genre for quite some time. People can take on new identities on the road. They can fantasise, lie and get confused. The journey can provide the time and distance to overcome class, age and conformity. The passenger can be taken on a rites-of-passage experience. David Lynch has explored the road movie's concepts and preoccupations most noticeably in **Blue Velvet** (1985), **Wild At Heart** (1990) and **Lost Highway** (1997).

His major influences and inspirations come from other film-makers who have themselves featured the road in various guises, such as the work of an undoubted favourite, Stanley Kubrick; Alfred Hitchcock; Jean-Luc Godard; avant-garde film-makers Luis Bunuel/Salvador Dali, Maya Deren and Man Ray; and most specifically the much plundered children's road classic, watched every Christmas by homes across America, **The Wizard Of Oz** [see Chapter 13].

It was in **Blue Velvet** that Lynch first made reference to the mother of modern road movies, **The Wizard Of Oz**: Dorothy coming home in her ruby slippers to sexually negotiate with the monstrous Frank Booth in a bid to regain her kidnapped husband and child. The original plan had been to use even more explicit references to Oz, not as well absorbed into the story, but these were cut from the script and saved for the more burlesque creation of **Wild At Heart**. **Lost Highway**, is an even darker tormentor of the Oz themes, doubling back over familiar ground and turning a paranoid mind upon itself.

These three Lynch films occupy consecutive life-stage journeys: through adolescence, to the early 20's and into mid-life crises; revealing the sexually troubled, the parentally liberated and the anxiously paranoid. **Wild At Heart** is the only film explicitly framed as a "road movie", but the others are just as concerned with the fear

Wild At Heart

associated with being in or out of the driver's seat and draw heavily on the symbolism and metaphor, as well as the film history, of the road.

America is a nation founded on the journey West, a venture through barren desert toward the promised land of the mythic Californian paradise. However, the road as the traditional emblem of pioneering America drops over the horizon in a Lynch film, into identity loss, a sense of foreboding, and unreliable memory, disabusing an audience of its reliance upon underpinning genre. By alluding to other road movies the audience may only be lulled into a false sense of security, doubling Lynch's impact.

David Lynch, like any good avant-garde artist, uses and abuses conventional narrative and aesthetic strategies. By genre deconstruction, pastiche and intertextuality he produces highly original work, strongly identifiable as a David Lynch film, yet dangling its film-consciousness for all to see from the rear-view mirror.

His lead characters in **Wild At Heart** – Sailor and Lula – adopt pop fantasy to escape the terrifying fictional narrative they find themselves in. They are fleeing from bitterly jealous parents and seeking sanctuary on the road. They are "Elvis and Marilyn burning to Oz in a convertible". Icons of arrested development, glowing with innocence while simultaneously terrorising the adults.

Sailor croons Elvis songs to display the purity of his love for Lula and brandishes his snake-skin jacket "as a sign of my individuality and my belief in personal freedom". But, like this jacket, **Wild At Heart** is far from individual; it has been produced for the masses and is brazenly synthetic.

The films **The Fugitive Kind** (Sidney Lumet, 1960) and **Pierrot Le Fou** (Jean-Luc Godard, 1968) [see also Chapter 18] are two clear influences for **Wild At Heart**: Lumet's beatnik Adam & Eve, played by Marlon Brando and Anna Magnani, inspire the Lynch character traits and Godard's road movie provides precedence for the assault on genre and narrative.

Sailor's rebel mantra echoes Brando's "wild things leave skins behind... tokens

Wild At Heart

passed from one to another so that the fugitive kind can follow their kind". While Belmondo and Karina in **Pierrot Le Fou** also start out complicit to murder at a party and flee South; to the Cote D'Azur rather than New Orleans.

Lynch's plundering of **The Wizard Of Oz** is equally unabashed. Characters constantly refer to the Yellow Brick Road, The Emerald City and getting over that Rainbow. Lula clicks the heels of her ruby slippers in the forlorn hope of cleansing herself from the sexual intrusion of Bobby Peru. And both lovers see imaginary witches circling the action, dropping candy-coated pearls of wisdom: "Don't turn away from love, Sailor". Lula and Sailor behave as though more a part of this fantasy world than the one full of assorted crazies hot on their trail. Their ludicrous destination of Big Tuna, promotes the imaginary status of a map just as fantastic as the signposts to Oz.

The crudeness of **Wild At Heart**'s references and the post-modern, arm- waving antics of the characters annoyed most critics – all the more it seemed after winning the Cannes Film Festival Palme D'Or. They were offended at the apparent loss of the assured director who supplied such dark and deft comedy with **Blue Velvet**. They preferred fucked-up sexual anxiety to confident, highly sexed lovers. There are those who also blame him for ushering in a glut of US indies with a visceral and brutal sensibility not seen since the reign of the '70s slasher movie. Its narcissistic heroes leading a wave of neo-conservative pleasure seekers: most famously the couples-on-the-run of the two Tarantino scripts, hurled at the screen by Tony Scott and Oliver Stone, **True Romance** (1993) and **Natural Born Killers** (1994) [see Chapter 10].

## NEXT EXIT: LOST HIGHWAY

David Lynch achieves a much finer film when he avoids playing mainstream Hollywood at its own game and wanders off into his favourite woods, back into his unique cinema of unease. He pitched **Lost Highway** as:

*A 21st century noir horror film.*
*A graphic investigation into parallel identity crises.*
*A world where time is dangerously out of control.*
*A terrifying ride down the lost highway.*

And described his lead character, Fred Madison, as a man "lost in confusion and darkness, where fear is in the driver's seat... A lot of **Lost Highway** is internal. It's Fred's story. It's not a dream. It's realistic, though according to Fred's logic". This enigmatic journey, beyond the limits of reason, is an internal road movie; a dissection of a human brain – happy Lynch territory. A man in crisis, hiding from the consequences of his own thoughts and actions, hoping to change his destiny.

In **Wild At Heart**, when Sailor confesses to Lula, during a long night drive, that he witnessed – again from a car – the death of her good daddy, Lula's anguished response could be a prophesy for Fred Madison's future predicament: "It's shocking when things aren't the way you thought they were. We're out in the middle of it now" – the camera surging forward, into the dark road ahead.

**Lost Highway** opens and closes with an image of the road rushing under us, a yellow-dotted line flickering and weaving into a double-register, through a land shrouded in inky darkness. At first we can only hear the slithering hiss of the tyres over asphalt (or could it be the amplified noise of the film itself spooling through the projector) before the warbling strains of David Bowie's track "I'm Deranged", drifts in with "Funny, how secrets travel, I start to believe, as if I was a dream..." and the drumbeat kicks in and the titles surge forward, each actor's name slapping the screen to be whisked away.

This spinning road image recurs throughout and becomes synonymous with a mind reeling out of control, so that whenever someone gets in a car you fear this could be the moment they meet their destiny. It is a familiar Lynch image. Being plunged onto an ominous road by a driver ignorant of speed restrictions has appeared so memorably in all three of his mentioned films that you might be forgiven for thinking it has become stock footage for editor and partner, Mary Sweeney.

**Lost Highway** takes the road film, twists it and turns it back on itself. The narrative is cyclical as opposed to linear or circular. It bears a marked resemblance to one of the most influential films of the American avant-garde, Maya Deren and Alexander Hammid's **Meshes Of The Afternoon** (1942), and the inexorable mind-bending of Stanley Kubrick's **The Shining** (1980), both of which bear later discussion. After two hours of events increasing in their uncomfortable familiarity – as dialogue and gestures echo and reflect – the lead character arrives back where he began, not at a final destination or a return to home, but at another point of departure. If the exhibitors would allow it, **Lost Highway** would work wonderfully as an endless loop, with the audience able to enter at any given moment and, like cinema-goers of the

Lost Highway

early 1960s, leave when they reached the point where they came in.

The first part of **Lost Highway** occupies the home of Fred and Renee Madison. They live in an indefinite present that already feels like the past. An apartment adrift in a cloud of suspicion, directionless clues, impossible acts and pregnant pauses. Fred is shaken from a brooding reverie by the chilling buzz of his front door intercom. The message informs him that "Dick Laurent is dead". He tries to get a look at the messenger, but his windows only offer a view of his empty drive. Just like the discovery of the ear at the opening to **Blue Velvet**, Lynch provides an aural enticement into one man's mind. In typical picaresque fashion, David Lynch has claimed in interviews that just such a message was left on his home intercom, letting him know of the demise of a Dick Laurent and thus his imagination was sparked (this from the same man who claimed the robin at the end of **Blue Velvet** was a real bird playing a role).

Fred and Renee keep close to the walls of their apartment, as if in hiding, perhaps only from each other. Fred plays sax at the Luna Lounge while Renee stays in "to read". But at the end of his frantic set Fred calls home and gets no answer. He returns to find his wife in bed, sleeping innocently.

An unmarked envelope containing a videotape appears on their front steps. They glance at each other as if this could be the moment when Renee's guilty secret is exposed. When its images leap out from the static they only provide a view of the outside of the house. Just a single bluey surveillance shot dumped onto tape. Renee seems relieved, "Must be from a real estate agent". The comic naivete of such a banal explanation in a David Lynch film immediately sets the hip tone for the audience.

A second tape arrives and the dread thickens. A second shot has entered their home, moving hand-held into the bedroom to peer down at our couple in their sleep. Suitably spooked they inform the police and the first of Lynch's comic double-acts pitch up to investigate and further Fred's sense of paranoia.

They get out of the house and go to a party. Renee is getting tipsy and flirty with the host, Andy. The wonderfully sinister Mystery Man arrives and makes a beeline for Fred. The party music dips and we're in for a legendary Lynch head-to-head. (This technique of receding music making way for a private audience with our main protagonist – invisible to other guests – is familiar from *Twin Peaks*, when the very tall man appeared, to inform Agent Cooper of another murder).

The Mystery Man claims to have met Fred before, at his house. When Fred fails to remember he tops it with the absurd claim that he's there right now and invites Fred to call him there on his cellular phone. The unmistakable Mystery voice answers. "Who are you?", ventures Fred. "Mmmm, good question". The laughter echoes between the Mystery Man and his double. Fred drags Renee from the party. He is cracking up. His previous, unanswered call home had been bugging him... and now this.

Fred wanders the dark corridors of their home and seems to disappear into the shadows. Renee calls his name; fulfilling a dream Fred recounted to her earlier. The third videotape arrives and only Fred sits down to watch. In a frenzied rush of images, time and space, Fred witnesses the electric images of Renee's dismembered corpse, his despairing screams cut short by a heavy punch from a police officer and it's an open and shut case: Fred Madison is found guilty and condemned to death row.

Between huge bouts of head-splitting pain Fred has only his unwanted memories for company: the same snatched views of a video surveillance camera. An unacceptable documentary "truth".

As Fred's mind reaches fever state and we prepare for a Cronenberg-type head explosion, relief comes in the form of the original image of the onrushing highway and an equally disconcerted young stranger appears roadside.

Next morning the guards need good excuses; Fred is gone, his cell now occupied by the swollen-headed younger man. "What's the situation?" "I'm not

Blue Velvet

entirely certain, Captain. You'll have to see for yourself". A direct appeal to the audience to not expect any cute *X-Files* explanations, this would rob Lynch of his beautiful space to dream.

The new prisoner is identified as Pete Dayton, with no more than a traffic violation on his crime sheet; not exactly the wild man of the road. He is released to his blue-collar parents, his job as a car mechanic and his small-town girlfriend. As the cops keep tabs on him, Pete looks unsure as to who or what he should be.

The film has shifted gears in performance and visual style. We have jumped the central reservation and started down the opposite side of the highway. Out of the dark and the crawling terror, into the painful light of day and an eager sense of the over-familiar. From Fred staring at the buzzing fluorescent lamp above his prison bunk, we have arrived at Pete squinting at the midday sun.

Pete tries to relax on a garden sun-lounger, until his tranquil surroundings begin to unsettle him. We can recognise him as Jeffrey Beaumont at the end of **Blue Velvet**, laying back, his torment over. The same lawns and white picket fence. And as he takes a look into next door's garden he finds the same dog, last seen biting playfully at the fountain of water from a hose still held by Jeffrey's collapsed father, here looking pitifully dazed and confused to be in another Lynch movie, sniffing at the ground for clues.

A regular to the garage, Mr Eddy brings in his Cadillac for a Pete tune-up – "the best ears in town". He has also brought upon Pete one incredible head-fuck: out of his car, in delicious slo-mo, lifted into myth by Lou Reed's "This Perfect Moment", steps Alice. A blond temptress, femme fatale, uncannily familiar to Pete, and to us as Renee in a wig, plunging the viewer into dream-time, movie-time, the dizzy sensation of Kim Novak emerging from the bathroom in Hitchcock's **Vertigo** (1958). This is love for David Lynch, our "Jimmy Stewart from Mars".

As in **Wild At Heart** – only this time pursued by the police and Mr Eddy, rather than hired killers and a jealous mother – our new couple go at it in a series of clammy hotel rooms. No matter how hard they fuck they're still left wanting more.

Alice hatches an escape plan to rob her pimp and party friend, Andy. She met this guy at a place called "Mokes"; the same place Renee told Fred she had met their party host and been offered a job.

Pete obediently arrives at Andy's to discover a porno film featuring Alice roaring out from a giant video screen. It is disorientating when Alice appears slinking down the stairs as the porno scene continues. You may have had the distinct feeling that those images were a live feed from an upstairs bedroom. Or maybe this viewer was just getting too caught up in the Renee/Alice spell, becoming as jealously confused as Fred/Pete.

In a grotesquely hilarious accident Andy is speared headfirst onto a glass-cornered coffee table and our lovers are well and truly on the road. But Pete's brain is in just as much pain; he has glimpsed a photograph featuring Andy and Mr Eddy either side of Alice and Renee. Out in the swirling desert, waiting for Alice's fence, who will return and buy their stolen goods, Pete once more tries to "have" her. They make love in the blinding car headlights, only for Alice to viciously whisper "You will never have me". She walks away, toward the desert shack seen before in Fred's fevered mind: a house that de-exploded in gasping rewind.

Out of the headlights emerges the naked Fred – "How did I get here? Where does that highway lead to? This is not my beautiful house. This is not my beautiful wife". Waiting for him in the familiar shack is not Renee, or even Alice, but the Mystery Man, who chases him back to his car, recording his getaway on a surveillance camera clamped to one eye.

Fred stops at the Lost Highway Hotel. Behind the same room number that Pete discovered at Andy's place, Renee is fucking Mr Eddy. The police investigation is under way at Andy's house. They discover the photograph: Renee is now the only woman standing between Andy and Mr Eddy. The fantasy is coming to an end.

Renee leaves the hotel and Fred attacks Mr Eddy, stuffing him into the boot of his car. In the desert Fred is rescued by the Mystery Man while wrestling with Mr Eddy. No longer his menace but his ally, he hands Fred a knife to slit Mr Eddy's throat.

In a spooky rerun of the Mystery Man's mobile phone trick, he hands Mr Eddy a mini-TV playing blue-tinged images of his pornographic transgressions as Dick Laurent, before the picture zaps to a view of Fred and the Mystery Man, reaching for his TV back.

Fred arrives back home, ascends to his front door and delivers the opening message, "Dick Laurent is dead". Only this time there is someone outside (should another Fred be peering down from the window): the police have arrived to see Fred rush to his car and head for the highway. As darkness falls and a stream of police cars give chase, Fred's mind whirls out of control. At the wheel of his car his head thrashes to and fro in a Baconesque blur. The soundtrack roars, then gives way to the hiss of the unravelling road and the sensation of the film itself flapping loose from the projector.

This film has left many viewers thrilled but baffled. They imagine the director must know what all of it means, but has wilfully locked the answers away. Lynch favours generating just enough confusion to allow dreaming. Has Pete Dayton temporarily usurped or occupied Fred Madison, in the way of Bob and Agent Cooper at the close of *Twin Peaks*? Or has Fred adopted the likeness of Pete; his memories still spooling away behind the mask? There are tantalising shared characteristics: Pete has an intuitive ear for fixing car engines, but finds it all too much when he hears Fred's squealing sax solo on the radio, shutting it off as if it threatens to explode the fantasy.

Lynch doesn't clearly distinguish between any possible fantasies and reality. He doesn't make sure that the Pete episodes will be read as Fred's fantasy in the way the film has come to be accepted. It is quite possible, though highly frustrating, to take events at face value. The director's disregard for ontological differences is a determined strategy; the viewer's experience spiralling into empathetic confusion and madness.

David Lynch has a great fear of the rational explanation. "The intellect can hold back so many wonderful things. One of the reasons I like painting in black & white is that your mind can travel in there and dream. Colour is a little too real. It doesn't make you dream much". This is no doubt why he prefers to create his visual effects "in-camera" – paintings that move by themselves rather than by digital stop-frame effects. These days we expect the transformation of Fred into Pete to be served up in morphing science fiction-style. This would flatten all the glorious mystery for Lynch.

This preference for mystery extends to exposition and character motivation. Scenes were written in which the doctors, family and police tried to rationalise the weird transformation, but they must have appeared appallingly dull in the edit and were cut. Lynch always shrugs off as much responsibility to such realistic, procedural detail as he can get away with. He likes to keep his police investigations and the associations between his criminal-types as unclear as possible: what Mr Eddy, Andy and the Mystery Man are really up to remains just as uninteresting to Lynch as clearing up the activities of Frank, "suave" Bob and police detective "The Yellow Man" in **Blue Velvet**.

Alice's betrayal of Mr Eddy to run away with Pete is equally senseless, perfunctory, for its own sake. But it fits when considered as servicing Fred's impatient, masochistic fantasy; like the porn film we discover Renee appearing in, Fred skips believable set-ups to get to the sex. Fred has a road movie spinning in his head and in road movies the lovers must flee the crime boss and the law, so let them get on with it.

A psychogenic fugue: a temporarily delusional, yet fully aware, state of mind, of which the subject retains no subsequent memory; the adoption of a new identity and personality, creating its own history and associations.

David Lynch has long struggled to bring his own version of Franz Kafka's "Metamorphosis" to the screen. A man who wakes up to discover he has become someone (or something) else. A psychogenic fugue sounds like a fine substitute. Lynch and the co-writer, Barry Gifford, claim never to have heard of this mental condition until it was pointed out to them during the shoot, but its definition so neatly encapsulates Fred Madison's journey that this may be the director once again retaining his right to dream.

The structural model they have admitted to, however, is that of the Mobius Strip: a long strip of paper given a 180 twist before connecting the opposing ends to form a loop. The strip (or story) turns inside-out half-way along, folding back underneath itself and continuing. Fred turns into Pete and back to Fred again. Lynch movies have always generated unease by twisting genres together, in **Lost Highway** the change is made distinct as the tormented Fred interior world opens out into a desperate fantasy rerun. His mind scrabbling for equilibrium, Fred copes with the horror of his wife's murder, and his part in it, by creating a fantasy in which he is a virile, young dude, sought after by the voracious blonde, rather than shut out by the hiply disaffected brunette. Sticking a wig on the wife and attempting to have it both ways.

The film shifts perspective with the spooky transformation, from a psycho-sexual thriller into a semi-parodic noir. The anguished hero is inextricably tangled within a narrative of his own making, and his predicament is reborn with the classic motifs of a femme fatale, crime-boss threats and multiple double-crosses. A man obsessed with the wrong woman.

## HOME, HORROR & THE WIZARD OF OZ

"There's no place like home": the line that permeates every scene of **The Wizard Of Oz**, beckoning Dorothy to return, wiser, more experienced but able to appreciate the value of family and structure. It would be easy to imagine the Mystery Man's sick laugh reverberating after Dorothy's sweet incantation; a way for Lynch to posit his movie as the post-modern antidote to naive faith in home as centre and store of identity. Home is the point of origin and the destination of the road. Traditional narrative involves flight and return, even if the destination is a different and separate place, it still embodies the notion of home: a new home.

Estrangement and disorientation are so acute in Lynch it is inconceivable to feel "at home". Dorothy's motto is held dear, for it already contains a dual meaning. In **Blue Velvet** Jeffrey was able to return home more experienced in the ways of sex and still be able to cherish the security of a well-kept lawn, meal-times and safer sex with a steady girl. Sailor Ripley at the end of **Wild At Heart** is about to walk away from his son and lover, because too much has happened to allow for a fresh start, but having some sense knocked into him by a gang of wayward hoods and a visit from the Good Witch convinces him there is always a place where you belong, no matter how fragmented its history.

"There's no place like home" can imply that home is a fantasy, a fiction, a non-place, or that home is supreme, fundamental. It's only a matter of tone or emphasis. To runaway from "home" is to acknowledge and accept its very notion; an artist learning the rules before they break them. **Lost Highway** shuts out its protagonist from the comfort of simply returning home. Fred is condemned to an eternal cycle, but always orbiting the fantasy of home and permanence.

Home in the world of David Lynch is not a sanctuary; there will always be intrusion. Jeffrey sneaks in to Dorothy's apartment, to observe and gain knowledge; Lula's Daddy is set on fire in his own living room, witnessed by her future beau from his car; Fred and Renee are videotaped while sleeping and the Mystery Man can answer their phone. In both **Wild At Heart** and **Lost Highway** the protagonists seek refuge in roadside motels; usually an illusional hiding place.

David Lynch's evident relationship with **The Wizard Of Oz** also extends to their visual indexes. In Victor Fleming's 1939 film "reality" was signified by the then familiar image index of black and white, and the realm of fantasy by the extraordinary spectacle of the new Technicolour. For the same reasons, now that colour is the norm, Lynch used the opposite scheme for his early films; employing black and white to create an unreal world in **Eraserhead** (1977). For **Blue Velvet**, no doubt under marketing pressure to use colour, Lynch derived a hyper-real design to work emotionally rather than realistically – like a painter. He defamiliarised our standard perceptions of the real with deeply saturated colours.

Lynch had expressed an interest in returning to black and white for **Lost Highway**, but instead kept the colours in Fred's apartment to muted shades with the blackest shadows known to cinema. By the time Fred is transformed into Pete and released from jail the weakest outdoor colours feel fresh and deceptively welcoming. Monochrome is confined to the video surveillance footage that provides the damning evidence to convict Fred of murdering his wife. The latest signifier of documentary "truth", able to make the most innocent action appear illicit and criminal, is desperately questioned by Lynch as his empathetic hero cannot entertain their scenes as possible, "No!!!!!!". Fred earlier admitted to the cops that he doesn't like video cameras, that he likes to remember things his own way, not necessarily the way they happened. These tapes must haunt Fred like postcards from his own sick mind.

## MIRRORS, FILMS & DAVID LYNCH

**Lost Highway** is a film conscious of film. It tantalises with doubles and parallel worlds – within its own world, those of past Lynch sojourns and those of film history. The Mystery Man (and film-maker within the film) ignites the journey with his unique home-movie service, delivering images blandly familiar, scarily hypnotic, alluringly incriminating and yet ultimately unfathomable.

David Lynch is a descendent of Edgar Allan Poe. Homely, benign interiors become disrupted by the invasion of the alien. Often appearing in the form of the double, the threat bearing uncanny similarities to the self, all the more terrifying for its strange familiarity.

The use of doubles and mirror images has been so useful to cinema it can these days lumpenly stare back as cliché. It has signalled the divided self and the boundary between dream and reality, between one world and the next. In past work Lynch has relished the creepiness of mirrors providing false reflections (Bob staring back at Leland Palmer in *Twin Peaks*) and extended it to other faithful recording devices, returning shifty results (Agent Cooper able to rush from a security observed corridor to catch himself on the monitor in a different room in his 1992 **Fire Walk With Me**). For **Lost Highway** Lynch is not quite so literal in his scheme of doubling up as to overload his scenes with actual mirrors, but he alludes to their properties constantly.

The Mystery Man can be in two places at once with the questionable help of his mobile phone; one man can be transposed into another in a high-security cell and Renee and Alice can appear side by side in a photograph for Pete to see, but have receded to only Renee for the cops to discover.

The naming of Fred's nemesis as Renee is tempting to read as an allusion to that great master of impossible reflections and optical views, René Magritte; and her double on the other side of Fred's mind, as Alice, Through The Looking Glass.

The double is both divided and one. And the passage between the two a zone where it's possible to be neither. The road is such a passageway in **Lost Highway**. Its yellow broken dotted line flashing beneath the windscreen – by some sleight of double exposure – wavering and undulating as two potential paths.

As a highly film-conscious director intertextuality is an important aesthetic strategy to Lynch. There are obvious homages to **Vertigo** (Jimmy Stewart, haunted by the death of Kim Novak, remodelling another woman in her image – when she is in fact the same woman) and Hitchcock's later **Psycho** (for its structural twist of brutally murdering the heroine part way into the film, severely unbalancing the audience's expectations) [see also Chapter 8]. But the two films I would most like to look at again for their intertextual value to **Lost Highway** are Stanley Kubrick's **The Shining** and Maya Deren and Alexander Hammid's **Meshes Of The Afternoon**. Both of these films draw upon "the road" as metaphor and can be read as unorthodox "road movies": internal, psychological road movies. And both are films which David Lynch is undoubtedly very familiar with (whether consciously or unconsciously during the creation of **Lost Highway**): Maya Deren being a hugely important figure in the post-war American avant-garde, whose work Lynch would have undoubtedly been exposed to while at art school, and Kubrick the director who Lynch has declared on numerous occasions to be simply "the coolest".

It should be no surprise that Lynch finds such inspiration in the work of Kubrick. He is a director who also firmly believes that film communicates not with the intellect, but the emotions and subconscious. For many **The Shining** is still regarded as the last great psychological horror film. It can also be read as a *noir* conducted in glaring brightness. Like **Lost Highway** it is the story of an unacknowledged artist,

Lost Highway

beleaguered by a nagging sense of déjà-vu, unable to stop himself harming his wife (and child, in the case of **The Shining**'s Jack Torrance). Menaced and aided by demonic forces and mental aberrations, his confused mind is caught in its own maze of corridors and paths, scuttling for the truth about himself. An infernal cycle of self-annihilation. A journey of death and transfiguration, which terminates in the past with the realisation of the protagonist's place in a perpetual cycle: Jack Torrance trapped and frozen in a maze, his image appearing in the old ballroom photograph; Fred Madison thrashing in a frenzied tableau, entombed within his car, after inconceivably delivering the message he received at the outset.

The road/labyrinth motif is linked in both films to the concept of infinity. And the idea of personality splitting is constantly alluded to by double images: (The Shining) Jack/the previous caretaker; Danny/his imaginary friend, Tony; the twin sisters; the garden maze/its model and its reflection in the corridors of the hotel; (Lost Highway) Fred/Pete; Mr Eddy/Dick Laurent; Renee/Alice; and the comedy double acts of detectives, prison guards and bodyguards.

Lynch adopts a structural technique also favoured by Kubrick of splitting the narrative into distinct acts so that the menacing action of one part continues to haunt every gesture and utterance of the next, without the reassurance of any direct correlation. Key scenes bear distinct parallels. Jack Torrance and Fred Madison are both troubled by nightmares in which they murder their wife. They desperately recount the details in the morning in a bid to dispel them, but in doing so only succeed in creating prophecy.

And just like Fred Madison's nefarious Mystery Man, Jack Torrance is visited by a deadly commanding spirit – Grady, the previous Overlook caretaker. After gulping down a bourbon Jack and Fred are both treated to an evil encounter at a party, to be given chilling lessons in the possibilities of time and space:

*Jack:* Haven't I seen you before?
*Grady:* I don't believe so.

The Shining

*Jack:*  Aren't you the caretaker?
*Grady:*  No, Mr Torrance. You are the caretaker. You... have always been the caretaker.

*Mystery Man:*  We've met before, haven't we?
*Fred:*  I don't think so. Where was it you think we've met?
*Mystery Man:*  At your house. Don't you remember?
*Fred:*  No, no I don't. Are you sure?
*Mystery Man:*  Of course. In fact, I'm there right now.

Grady and the Mystery Man both keep a look out for their charges, ensuring they stick to their destined path. The Mystery Man comes to Fred's aid when he is succumbing to the attack of Mr Eddy, handing him a knife out of nowhere. Grady arrives to defy the scientific laws of space and release Jack from the premature death-by-freezing of the hotel's cold-storage room.

**The Shining** and **Lost Highway** leave their audiences with the feeling of having witnessed a looping of time, fate and identity; the knowledge that the Overlook and Lost Highway Hotel have added another victim to their grisly cycle, to be eternally reborn.

**Meshes Of The Afternoon** is an outstanding work of the avant-garde, a dream narrative inspired by Expressionism. It has an intricate spiral structure, based on the sensation of repetition with its opening sequence. And, as with the central theme of many psycho-dramas of the American avant-garde, it endures the quest for sexual identity, in the form of dream or fantasy, unfolded within shifting perspectives.

Maya Deren declared herself concerned "with the interior experiences of an individual. It reproduces the way in which the subconscious will develop, interpret and elaborate an apparently simple and casual incident into a critical emotional

Meshes Of The Afternoon

experience... The film is culminated by a double-ending in which it would seem that the imagined achieved such force that it became reality".

**Meshes** simulates the dream/fantasy experience of a heroine, played by Deren herself. Previous events and objects become potently transfigured in dream, and the dreamer may be aware that it's a dream and may dream that they wake.

The heroine travelling along a road glimpses a mysterious figure turning the bend ahead of her. She reaches a house and enters. She stalks around before falling asleep in a chair. The camera then moves subjectively, imitating her vision and movements. A black figure, with a mirror for a face, appears at the side of the road and follows the woman's path. The objects in the house (an unhooked phone and a knife) are again present but moved. She sees herself asleep in the chair. These events are repeated with accelerated variations. She goes to the window to see herself chasing the black figure around the bend of the road. As she is about to stab her sleeping self, the sleeper's eyes open to see a man waking her. Upstairs he caresses her. A flower next to her turns into a knife, she grabs it and stabs him in the face – which turns out to be a mirror and smashes. The man is walking along the original road. He enters the house and finds the woman slumped in the chair with her throat slit. End.

The devil is in the details and the similarities to **Lost Highway** are unmistakable. Unanswered phones generating suspicion; strangers appearing at roadside; protagonists looking out of windows to see themselves running away; mirror faces breaking to reveal Magritte-style voids; and suddenly appearing knives used to slash throats. Apart from the evocation of the dream state, **Meshes** is also a psycho-drama-as-quest for sexual identity clouded by anxiety; a representation of a mind in a state of terrible ambivalence between verifiable reality and subconscious violence.

The structure of **Meshes** is a far more open spiral than **Lost Highway's** hermetically sealed universe. But even for Lynch the road-as-cycle is not simply an endless loop set to replay itself precisely. He has loaded it with fresh elements to spin it towards another orbit: the police officers arrive to witness the recurrence of the intercom message. An open chase commences as Lynch refuses to bring the car and the film to rest.

Road movies have traditionally carried the responsibility of communicating an attitude towards human progress and particularly a reaction to the advance of America. David Lynch's vision of America has never sought to be condemning or embracing. His primary interest has been the dissection of the family and the experience of seeing too much; exposing his own psyche and displaying fantasies that convention may have categorised as obscene. A David Lynch film has become known for its own brand of black humour and pastiche. Never idly playful or coldly nihilistic, as his mentor Stanley Kubrick has so often been accused. The growing problem for Lynch is that his humour can no longer be used for its unsettling value – we can never again be as uncomfortable as we were watching **Blue Velvet's** raw journey. We are more knowing passengers, not as vulnerable, the view through the windscreen no longer completely unfamiliar.

# Chapter 18

# 'Weekend'

# FROM THE FRENCH REVOLUTION TO GAULLIST WEEKENDS: JEAN-LUC GODARD'S 'WEEKEND' ROAD TRIP

## Peter Rojas

Made in 1967 on the brink of the abortive revolution of May 1968, Jean-Luc Godard's **Weekend** is the end of weekends, of banal leisure, of programmed consumption and mass media spectacles. Godard puts the bourgeois road trip on the big screen, and in so doing exhibits a sensationalistic spectacle of an ironic apocalypse. At once enthraled with post-industrial society and deeply disturbed by it, Godard depicts a middle class couple's weekend journey through the rapidly eroding landscape of (what was thought at the time) to be capitalism's waning days. The two main characters, Roland and Corinne, are a married couple filled with mutual enmity who set off on a road trip only to have the collapse of society hot on their heels. While each is secretly plotting to kill the other, they leave Paris for Oinville, the home of Corinne's aging parents, where they hope to collect a huge inheritance from the imminent death of her father. Their planned weekend in the French countryside stretches into days and then weeks as Roland and Corinne drift further and further away from the safe space of capitalism and into the absurd and the barbaric until they land straight into the heart of revolution. This is the road trip no bourgeois hopes to make.

Weekend is the road trip that heads off the map and into the miserable and unmapped terrain of revolution. This road movie is set in the geography of capitalism, but instead of telling the story of star-crossed lovers on the run, attempting to escape society, it is the inverse, of a hate-consumed couple that never intends to stray from the safe path of petit bourgeois society. With its role reversals, **Weekend** is the negative image of a road movie. Unlike the archetype of the road movie, which typically depicts a marginal or criminal couple on the run from the law or a disapproving society (like in Arthur Penn's **Bonnie And Clyde** [see Chapter 10], Terence Malick's **Badlands** [see Chapter 10], Joseph Lewis' **Gun Crazy** [see Chapter 2], or Godard's own **Pierrot Le Fou**[1]), Roland and Corinne are a privileged couple who never intend to escape the comfortable bounds of French middle class society. In fact, their entire purpose in undertaking this road trip is to improve their standing in this social order, not to abandon it. They leave Paris and hit the road in order to get richer. Because of this, the road does not automatically equal rebellion in **Weekend** like it does in **Easy Rider** [see Chapter 4] or **Thelma And Louise** [see Chapter 11]. The French countryside is already recuperated by a capitalism that has seized upon it as a zone of weekend leisure. Instead the revolutionary potentiality of the countryside must be forcibly carved out, and it is this possibility of altering the geography of capitalism that Godard sets out to investigate in **Weekend**.

Though it ends in disaster, as many road movies must, many of the themes and motifs of those films are missing from **Weekend**. The romanticized road of this cinema is nowhere to be found in the film; the freedom from social constraints that the open

Pierrot Le Fou

highway represents in movies like **Easy Rider,** for instance, simply does not exist here. Roland and Corinne do not take to the road to become "free". Rather the selfish individualism of the car culture is repeatedly condemned. Roland and the other drivers in this film are reckless and extremely dangerous. Consumed with road rage and an irrationally impatient desire to get wherever they are going with absolutely no delay, the result is endless death and destruction. In single, long tracking shot of an enormous traffic back-up in the French countryside which happens to be one of the most striking set pieces in the history of the cinema, Godard exhibits the sheer ludicrousness to which modern existence has come. For several minutes we see Roland and Corinne in their car, weaving in and out of a line of cars that appears to stretch for miles and miles. Despite the expected frustrations and shortness of tempers, people seem oddly accepting of their fate. People honk their horns, but also children play games by an overturned car, people toss balls back and forth, a couple plays chess next to their immobilized vehicle. People's lives go on as if it had never been any other way. Godard seems to be saying that a civilization that would allow people to live this way simply cannot continue. And at the head of the line we see what is causing all the traffic: a deadly accident with multiple bodies lying about. Roland and Corinne appear to pay little attention as they zoom by, only concerned with how this will delay them on their way to collecting their millions. The blind complacency of those stuck in the traffic jam speak of a society which is so enamoured of cars and the consumer lifestyle that the can see no alternative to just waiting in traffic. The sheer callousness of Roland and Corinne point to a middle class mentality that will ensure that we will all be in our cars when the end comes. Godard depicts our obsession with the automobile as literally driving us to our deaths and as pushing civilization towards extinction all throughout this movie: mangled bodies and the burning hulks of cars lie strewn about nearly every place that Roland and Corinne go. They cease to even take note of it after a certain point, and for that matter, neither do we.

All road movies, being journeys through space, are fundamentally depictions of a space and its social and political underpinnings. The road becomes a nomadic space in these archetypal road movies; it is a fluid, endangered, yet liberating space from which the outlaw couple can sporadically attack society. Not surprisingly, the traditional road movie uses the geography of the open road in a metaphorical way; rebels and social malcontents take to the road in order to escape from society and "be themselves". Their road trip comes to symbolize unspoken desires to break free of the system. These road movies are a contestation of the geography of capitalism and of the way that this social system organizes space. The unconstrained movement across the map implicit in these road trips is a disruption of the restrictive spatial mapping of a capitalism which seeks to construct life around work, leisure, and consumption. It is the ultimate futility of these attempts that reminds us that it is capital which draws the road map; that is, as Henri Lefebvre asserts, social space is a social product. Thus, one cannot fundamentally challenge society without challenging its organization of space and vice-versa. Thus just as the genre of film noir is intimately tied to the geography of the city, road movies are always connected to the relationship between the city and the countryside, of the dichotomy of zones of control and zones of freedom. The boundaries of capital and its power come into play whenever an attempt is made to escape them. In a movie like **Gun Crazy**, one of the classics which combines the road movie and film noir genres, John Dall and Peggy Cummins play two sharpshooting lovers who take to robbing banks rather than face poverty. On the run from the law, they eventually die together in a spectacular shoot-out. For a few brief moments they escape the system, but they soon discover that there is no place to hide. The only space of freedom is unmapped. It is in the open road that Godard finds a similar space of rebellion. **Weekend** is the depiction of a world in which the fixed geography of capitalism is coming undone, where hiding places and even places from which to launch an assault might be discovered in the ensuing anarchy.

Accordingly, Godard eschews traditional narrative structure and casts Roland and Corinne adrift in unfamiliar terrain. Their safe French countryside of comfortable weekends is swept away and they find themselves hopelessly lost on the way to Oinville. They wander from situation to situation, further and further into the surreal, having encounters with, among others, a hitchhiker with a god complex, a pianist named Gegauff, and an African and Arab who discuss colonialism. Godard rejects the conventions of film in an attempt to develop a cinema in which social criticism can be elucidated. With little necessary connection between scenes, Godard's road movie takes place on a road map he has cut up and entirely rearranged. This experimental use of narrative and structure is reminiscent of the work of the Situationists (who incidentally despised Godard). Hoping to break through the very mundanity of life under capitalism by disrupting its organization of space, the Situationists used psychogeography (the study of the ambience of certain locales) and the *dèrive* (the practice of drifting through a place) to recontextualize the city. It was thought that through these recontextualizations, and by challenging an urban landscape so given over to cars and consumerism, they could create a space or situation in which life was not totally organized around the needs of capitalism and a transcendent art could be created. Guy Debord, the primary Situationist theorist, writes in "Introduction To A Critique Of Urban Geography" that, "The production of psychogeographic maps, or even the introduction of alterations such as more or less arbitrarily transposing maps of two different regions, can contribute to clarifying certain wanderings that express not subordination to randomness, but complete *insubordination* to habitual influences (influences generally categorized as tourism, that popular drug as repugnant as sports, or buying on credit)." Roland and Corinne's jaunt leads them to meet fictional and historical characters, revolutionaries and farmers. Their trip is through a French countryside rearranged as social critique. Godard's stringing together of seemingly unconnected scenes is his way of jolting viewers out of their accustomed cinematic habits; by depicting a road trip in such a way, he attempts to fracture the smooth

Weekend

ordered space of capitalism and discover a revolutionary potentiality laying in the cracks within. Godard forcibly recontextualizes the road in **Weekend**, laying bare its origins as a social space and its position within capitalism.

Godard's disruption of the geography of capitalism serves as his method of critiquing the very ways in which capitalism constructs space-time. This is a world in which citizens are replaced with consumers and communities with demographic groups. Space in both the city and the countryside are designed more along the needs of automobiles than people, and time is organized around work and leisure. Roland and Corinne can understand no world outside of this. When a hitchhiker offers them anything they could imagine in exchange for taking him to London, all they can think to ask for, for instance, are a Mercedes-Benz, an Yves Saint-Laurent evening dress, a hotel on Miami beach, and for Corinne to be a real blonde. Their very dreams are dismally consumerist. Godard is utterly fascinated with this world, but while he is mesmerized by the vibrancy of pop culture, this child of Mao and Coca-Cola is at the same virulently disgusted by its emptiness and its disempowering nature. The fundamental duality of his stance makes it difficult to discern his position on the potential for a revolutionary movement. In a perfectly dialectical manner, he portrays a society hurtling towards destruction, and in the ruptures we see spaces of revolutionary promise develop. But Godard depicts the social disintegration in very negative terms, as a breakdown in civility and sociality, and gives few hints of any positive steps towards a new and better world, which indicates that the collapse of Western civilization is less at the hands of any Marxist revolutionary organization, and more due to the very overextension of a logic of hypermodernization such that it brings about a systemic collapse. It is through Godard's remixing of the road movie that he is able to represent this. He reworks the space and geography of the road, taking us away from familiar contexts and motifs, and at the same time generating an immensely negationist critique of both the left and the right.

Godard represents the turpitude of the middle classes, but also shows a revolutionary movement that only knows how to usurp this depravity through a descent into barbarism. However because of his negationist and highly ambivalent stance, Godard is unable to depict the violence and destruction on screen in anything except an ironic, distant manner. The events in **Weekend** are sickly hilarious, and Godard runs the risk of having the audience either recoil in disgust or laugh off what they're seeing. Either way, they are able to distance themselves from what is going on. Knowing that his audience consisted primarily of educated and middle class cinemagoers, Godard goes to great lengths to offend and disturb their sensibilities (by scenes of theft, murder, and cannibalism). Not only does he do this, but he goes further and attempts to fully implicate these viewers in the destruction transpiring on-screen with his use of meta-commentary. There are several points where characters in the film reflect on their status as fictional characters in a film. Shortly after coming upon Saint-Just, Roland and Corinne stumble across two more historical characters, Tom Thumb and Emily Brontë. Frustrated with the absurdity they are encountering, Roland exclaims, "What a rotten film. All we meet are crazy people." When Emily Brontë fails to provide them with directions to Oinville, Corinne pleads with her, asking her to, "Cut it out. This isn't a novel. It's life. A film is life." Roland and Corinne then proceed to set her on fire. Afterwards, Corinne laments to Roland that, "We are beastly, you know, we've no right to burn anyone, not even a philosopher." Roland sees no problem with their actions, replying that, "Can't you see they're only imaginary characters." To which Corinne responds, "We're little more than that ourselves." This glimmer of conscience is quickly washed away in the next scene, in which Roland and Corinne steal the clothes off of the dead victims of an auto accident. Yet the point remains. Godard forces viewers to confront what it is they are doing sitting there in the dark witnessing the collapse of civilization. Roland and Corinne are fiction, but what is the viewer's own role in this breakdown?

But if the viewer has trouble taking the events on screen seriously, it can be claimed that **Weekend** is a film which has trouble taking *itself* seriously. Godard can be accused of a certain callousness in depicting violence and destruction in a comical manner, but like Oliver Stone's **Natural Born Killers** [see Chapter 10] it is easy to confuse the emptiness and violence on screen with the message of the filmmaker, when in fact these represent a certain ambivalence on the part of Godard. The revolutionaries that Roland and Corinne encounter at the end of the film illustrate this perfectly. Finally reaching Oinville, Roland and Corinne kill Corinne's mother when she refuses to cut them in on the inheritance left by Corinne's father. After disposing of the corpse by making appear as if she had perished in an auto accident, Roland and Corinne take once again to the road. It isn't long before they are kidnapped by members of the Seine et Oise Liberation Front. These hippie guerrillas respect no social conventions: they gun down picnickers with impunity and are cannibalistic. It is a vision of the anarchic end of civilization; there is scarcely a glimmer of hope for a better future society in this revolution. When Roland is shot to death by the revolutionaries while trying to escape, Kalfon, the group's leader, dismisses Corinne's shock at what has just transpired stating that, "We can only overcome the horror of the bourgeoisie by even more horror." Here we see Godard's scepticism of the left (we see a similar scepticism in **La Chinoise**, another movie he made that same year), of a revolution which sees a descent into inhumanity as humanity's only hope.

After the death of her husband, Corinne becomes fully integrated into the guerrilla group, and we see that her appearance has changed to become similar to that of the others in the group. In the final scene we see her eating with the other guerrillas, and when she is informed that the meat she is eating comes from her husband she does not react except to ask for some more. Her transformation from despicable bourgeois to deplorable revolutionary is complete. In the heart of the *bourgeoisie* lie the seeds of revolution, but it is also the end of the road for civilization. Within the gaps in the map that capitalism has drawn, Roland and Corinne's unintended wanderings lead them into the space of rebellion. Through their violence Roland and Corinne leave Paris only to find themselves in a wilderness where all the road maps are being violently redrawn to lead towards revolution.

**Weekend** breaks violently with road movie convention. Instead of the establishment coming to get the rebellious couple, we see the establishment couple get caught by the rebels. We are never sympathetic to Roland and Corinne's plight. Seeing them at their worst, we root against them. This contradicts traditional road movies like **Thelma And Louise** or **Gun Crazy** where we have an unrealizable desire to see the couple escape. Yes, Corinne survives and joins the hippie guerrillas, but she survives only by committing acts of savagery even more repulsive than those which she committed with her husband Roland earlier in the film. All of the rules, conventions, and customs which constitute civilization are abandoned at this point in favour of a perilous space of revolution. But is this revolution the stepping stone to a new society or a descent into pure anarchy? Godard's contrasting of guerrilla leader Kalfon's thoughtful musings on society and the group's cannibalism connote an unresolved ambiguity in his position. Godard is at once fascinated and disgusted with this crumbling world he has depicted, and disappointed by what has come along to take its place.

Godard's **Weekend** road trip exists purely in the imaginary terrain of revolutionary possibility, in the interstitial space of what he saw in 1967 as a rapidly fragmenting capitalist society. This apocalyptic vision is frightening and captivating. Godard is convinced of the necessity of destroying this world but unsure of whether he trusts anyone, including himself, to create something better in its place. Remapping the space of capitalism is a risky matter, and in the events of May 1968 many thought that a completely new world was at hand. This abortive revolution made **Weekend** and its ambivalent geographics obsolete when revolutionary space appeared and then disappeared so quickly. **Weekend** is oddly prescient in this respect. Roland and Corinne's falling off of the map is significant in its very possibility, but it also underscores the extent to which today the road trip has become the domain of middle class banality and leisure. There is no danger, only more McDonald's. The subsequent retrenchment of capitalism and its ever more restrictive redrawing of the political and social terrain means that the space of contestation imagined in **Weekend** seems practically unimaginable today. This is reflected in the sheer futility of the road movies following this era (**Thieves Like Us** [1974, Robert Altman's remake of Nicholas Ray's **They Live By Night**], or **Badlands** for example). The current domination of our landscape by suburbs and shopping malls leaves no space on the map for the revolutionary. Godard's fragmentary space of **Weekend** disappears as the mythic status of the road-as-rebellion is demolished in a suburbanized world designed solely to facilitate the circulation of automobiles and capital. The only road maps for revolutionaries are the ones they must draw for themselves.

# NOTES

1. **Pierrot Le Fou** (1965) is Godard's play on the pulp thriler, in which a married man (Jean-Paul Belmondo) runs off with a former girlfriend (Anna Karina), who involves him in her world of violence and crime. Belmondo, of course, had previously figured in Godard's archetypal French lovers-on-the-run movie **A Bout De Souffle** (1960).

**Chapter 19**

# The Road In SF Film

# WE'RE VIRTUALLY THERE: SF FILM ON THE ROAD TO RUIN

## Karl Phillips

Five souped-up hot rods transverse a near-future fascist America in the ultimate race, aptly described as "a cross country road wreck" on the billboards. Each of the cars' drivers gains points for hitting and killing pedestrians. This is the future world imagined in the Roger Corman produced **Death Race 2000** (Paul Bartel, 1975), a cult classic that starred David Carradine as king racer Frankenstein and also featured Sylvester Stallone and Mary Woronov. In **Death Race 2000** the road becomes the terrain in which the Social Darwinists of the future exercise their strengths (the film includes scenes in which hospital patients are left in front of speeding cars); more importantly, it is also where they are defeated. **Death Race 2000** suggests that battles of the future will be fought on the road. The film announced the road as an apocalyptic-race-track, as a space for future confrontations, as an arena for terminal road rage.

In 1977 the future prognosis was equally as grim in **Damnation Alley** (aka **Survival Run**, directed by Jack Smight from Roger Zelazny's cult novel). In this post-World War 3 road movie George Peppard and Jan-Michael Vincent lead a group of survivors in a glorified RV across America in the search for further survivors. The nuclear apocalypse that has befallen the Earth has resulted in freak weather conditions and tectonic movement, all of which must be endured by the survivors in addition to the numerous mutant insects they battle along the way. Lacking both the necessary understanding of the cultural significance of the road trip and the camp velocity of **Death Race 2000, Damnation Alley** flopped at the box office.

It wasn't until 1979 that Mel Gibson made a name for himself, and for director George Miller, with the release of **Mad Max** [see also Chapter 7]. **Mad Max**, the tale of an avenging policeman whose wife and child are killed by a motorcycle gang in a post-World War Three future close to apocalypse and where fuel is the only commodity worth fighting (literally) for, is arguably the most revered of that hybrid genre – the post-apocalyptic road movie. Indeed "Mad Max-style" has become a catch-all phrase for anything that features a hint of bastardised automobiles driven by maniac scavengers in desolate landscapes. Similarly the film's plot has been equally influential; "Only a few oil producing nations build their economic systems around the concept of 'black gold' as a store of value. And yet it is easy to comprehend the post-apocalyptic world of **Mad Max**, in which gasoline is the currency upon which all life and death hangs"[1].

Successful in numerous territories (with the exception of America), **Mad Max** spawned two sequels: **Mad Max 2** (aka **Road Warrior**, 1981) and **Mad Max Beyond Thunderdome** (1985).[2]

However, what is noticeable across the three films, aside from the enlarged budget's ambitions, is an increasing tendency to go "off-road". The roads, or rather aptly titled Anarchie Road, of **Mad Max** give way to the dirt tracks of **Mad Max 2**. The third part of the trilogy provides little in the way of a "marked" road, instead offering "a trackless landscape of desert dunes, fertile gorges, and post-nuclear dust." (Falconer).

Death Race 2000

      Delia Falconer finds significance in this move away from the road, suggesting that it offers:

*"a complex (re)negotiation of Australia's spatial history. In the first film, the road appears as a specific and violently contested site. By the last film it has disappeared into a landscape of mythic 'sights'. This disappearance* [she argues] *represents both the road's liberation from colonial narratives of empire and its absorption into a* **deregulated** *postcolonial spatiality"*[3]

However, it is not Falconer's post-colonial theory with which I wish to engage. Rather, it is the fact that many of the chapters in this book are concerned with "concrete" journeys, journeys that are made, literally, along roads that are made up physically of, to use an old-fashioned term, tarmacadam or asphalt. This chapter, like Mad Max, also wants to go "off-road". To chart journeys that travel along alternative routes, and not merely the dirt tracks of **Mad Max 2**.

      The road I wish to travel weaves its way through the post-apocalyptic landscape. Landscapes that have been damaged, obliterated, made useless as a result of apocalyptic destruction – lands marked by a visit from at least one of the Four Horsemen of the Apocalypse (war, famine, pestilence and death). However, I want to go further off-road, and examine what I shall term the "virtual road", or rather, "a Baudrillian hyperreal road" as travelled by the protagonists of **Until The End Of The World** (Wim Wenders, 1991), **La Jetée** (Chris Marker, 1962), **Twelve Monkeys** (Terry Gilliam, 1995), and **The Matrix** (Wachowski Bros., 1999).

Mad Max

Mad Max 2

The question that I would ask is: "is there some intrinsic value in being on the road?". Or is it, simply, perhaps by default rather than intention? Post-apocalyptic movies are often defined by a sense of wandering (the nomadic tribe searching for a home, often juxtaposed with the lone wanderer eking out a living); the breakdown in communications and goods supply necessitating the need for continual movement. Not unlike the Western perhaps – indeed the road movie often operates along the same lines as the Western, only perhaps more brutally so – except the *mise-en-scène* is more brutal in its landscape, and the people are more brutal. I don't just mean the villains either; Mad Max, like the Dirty Harry of the pre-Apocalypse, is separated only by a thin line from the villains that he polices (a point Gibson's character acknowledges in the film). Likewise, the plot is not too far removed from that of the classic revenge Western.

But if Mel Gibson is the lone wanderer of the Australian wasteland, then his American counterpart is surely Kevin Costner. Whilst **Dances With Wolves** (Costner, 1990) is not post-apocalyptic, it is a road movie of sorts and the "journey" contained therein further establishes the close relationship that the road movie has with the Western, revisionist or not. I'm actually thinking here, though, more of Costner's roles in **Waterworld** (Reynolds, 1995) and **The Postman** (Costner, 1997).

**Waterworld**, as was noted by many of the critics reviewing the film, is essentially **Mad Max** set on water whereas **The Postman** is set in 2013, in a somewhat feudalistic America recovering from World War Three. A lone, travelling actor, with debatable acting merits and something of a chancer, plies his trade offering performances for food, shelter and whatever else is on offer. Coming across the wreck of an old mail van he dons the postman's clothes and proceeds to the next town armed with a sackful of mail. The bluff works, albeit rather too effectively as the townspeople are desperate for news of their kinfolk. His claim to be a representative of the newly formed government is welcomed by a people seemingly waiting for some sort of authority to guide their lives.

Thus **The Postman** is more interesting in that its main agenda seems to suggest that in the post-apocalyptic world it is communication that binds society together and gives the public a sense of belonging. It is not the road travelled that is important, nor the traveller, but the information that has been transmitted.

Costner's lone crusade to save the world aside, it is to Mel Gibson's territory that I wish to return for it is also the desert that signifies the end of the road in **Until The End Of The World**. Wenders' film, set in 1999, travels from Paris to Australia via Siberia, Beijing, Tokyo and San Francisco, not an inconsiderable distance, and yet seems somehow wholly unconcerned by the journey (a journey which is made under the threatening cloud of an out of control nuclear satellite). Wenders, no stranger to road movies with **Alice In The Cities** (1974), **Wrong Movement** (1975), **Kings Of The Road** (1976) and **Paris, Texas** (1984), is never at pains to fetishize the viewpoint of his protagonists as so many traditional road movies do (his own **Paris, Texas**, being one the guiltiest parties).

I'd argue that the road in the post-apocalyptic road movie is less significant than it used to be, simply because we now live in a media age where "to travel" no longer means quite the same thing that it used to. We no longer travel along roads, we travel along information highways – it is information that travels. McLuhan's "global village" is now a reality. I'm writing this on the bridge between 1999 and 2000 and within the space of 24 hours I've visited the new Millennium celebrations of most countries between New Zealand and America, including a couple of remote islands that I've never heard of, let alone will ever visit. If television broadened the space we travel within our minds, then the computer, or rather computer networks, have increased the travel speed, and continue to do so at ever-faster rates.

Manohla Dargis claims that, "The road defines the space between town and country. It is an empty expanse, a *tabula rasa*, the last true frontier"[4]. Of course the problem here is twofold. For many the space between town and country is not so noticeable any more, certainly not when every town starts to look like every *other* town. The ubiquity of the same chainstores and the same shopping malls, the same people buying the same clothes in the same stores, and then eating in either McDonalds or the "Choices from Around the World" food court means that we have lost any sense of difference. In a year that saw the Seattle Trade Conference disturbed by protestors challenging the global power of corporations (note the words global and corporate), we have every reason to be concerned about the tranquillising effects of the "anytown" syndrome. The problem for me is that we no longer travel from A to B, we now travel from A to A(nother?), the second A merely being a copy of the first. As a result the sense of journey between the two becomes less important because we are travelling all that distance and arriving nowhere new. Secondly, and as a result of this, what new frontiers are there left to conquer? And were road movies ever about conquest in the first place?

Thus in Wenders' film it is less about the road travelled and more about what happens when the traveller arrives. Maybe this is why the overall arc of Wenders' film travels not from town to town, or city to city, but from town *to* country or, in this instance, the Australian outback.

What appears at first to be something of a suspense thriller (and one not that dissimilar to Wenders' 1977 film **The American Friend**), **Until The End of The World** in fact turns out to be a mix of traditional romance and futuristic science fiction. Henry Farber (Max von Sydow) is resident in a bunker bedded in the Australian outback, his laboratory home to his recent invention: a device that will enable his blind wife (Jeanne Moreau) to see, through electronic impulses to the brain. These images have been recorded on a camcorder-like device by the travellers, his son Sam Farber[5] (William Hurt) and, later, Claire Tourneur (Solveig Dommartin).

In essence then Hurt and Martin are not so much the travellers, but the carriers of the images. But unlike Costner's postman, they are not merely empty vessels as it transpires that they also have to recreate the emotional charge of seeing the image, as it is this that enables the image to be recorded in the first instance.

**Until The End Of The World** is also interesting in the way that we do not really witness its post-apocalyptic vision. Other than the freak force that cripples computers which have been exposed to the unseen radioactive blast, we are not even aware of the disaster (the film never appears to make its mind up on this point). Thus ultimately, **Until The End Of The World**, despite being considered an apocalyptic road movie[6], is concerned neither with the road nor the apocalypse. Rather beyond its love story element, and a sub-plot involving familial strife between father and son, the film is concerned only with images. In this sense the film picks up on that Baudrillardian notion of simulated images that are more real than the real. The images Hurt's mother sees, processed and simulated, are more real than the real could ever be because she is blind and could never know the real image and because of the technical proviso that the images must be (re)processed through the mind of the original recorder. Given that the exercise proves mentally and physically exhausting for both carrier and receiver, Wenders is clearly attempting to deliver a critical sub-text on the danger of simulated images over the real, but this is only ever hinted at, rather than fully developed.

It is this notion of the image being more important than the actual journey, which for me, is the central concern of films such as **Twelve Monkeys** and **The Matrix**. Here the physical road has drifted away into oblivion, it is no longer the physical road that is travelled, but time itself. Of course road movies have always travelled through time, but it has always been a linear time, as linear as the A to B along which the road protagonist travels. Cinema itself, even more than the automobile, is a time machine.

"You ever been in a time machine?" arch felon Kevin Costner asks his young,

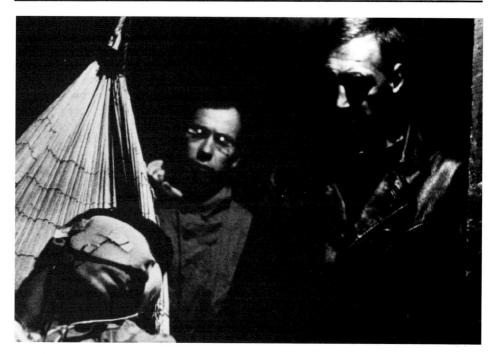

La Jetée

kidnapped passenger in Clint Eastwood's **A Perfect World** (Eastwood, 1993). "There's the future", he says, pointing forward through the windscreen, "and there, well, there's the past", pointing back to the ass-end of the highway they're on. "This here's the present, Philip – enjoy it while you can."[7]

In this respect the road movie has always been about travelling through time – the Baudrillardian combination of "space, speed, cinema, technology" that symbolises America.

In the future the roads that must be travelled are found in the time and space of a new dimension, but still bound up with this is the inescapable notion of the image.

Chris Marker's **La Jetée**, a remarkable film that achieves more in its short 29-minute running time than many Hollywood full-length features, is told entirely through still images (bar one brief but nonetheless haunting, dreamlike moment).

The story concerns an unnamed man held prisoner in a post-apocalyptic prison situated in the tunnels below a bombed-out Paris. As a child the man witnesses the murder of a stranger at Orly airport, and the image of a girl also present at the scene stays with him his entire life. It is because of this that the man is selected by his captors to undergo an experiment. They believe that such a man might be able to travel back in time to the point of the image that he remembers so well. The experiments are exhaustive but eventually the man makes contact with the past, if only for a short while. As the experiments continue the man is able to stay in the past for longer periods of time. His captors, now satisfied that he can travel in time, send him towards the future where he meets those that have survived the crippling aftermath of the Third World War. As with most time travel movies there is a paradox; here it is that the future cannot deny the traveller the information to guarantee its own existence, and thus the man travels back to the present with the necessary information to safeguard the future. Aware that he will now be executed, the man is offered the chance to return to the future by those he has visited but he declines, instead asking to return to the past, and to the point, or rather the *image*, that he so vividly remembers. His wish granted, it emerges that the murder he witnessed at Orly airport was in fact his own assassination at the hands of his captors. **La Jetée**, then, picks up on a frequent theme of the road movie that goes back to **They Live By Night** (Ray, 1949), namely that the characters rarely escape their past. **La Jetée**'s protagonist, may, in a perverse twist, be running towards rather than away from his past, but nonetheless it is a combination of the past and the present that catches up with him.

In **La Jetée** the man's life is disposable, and we learn little about his character. Rather, what is more important is his ability to hold onto a strong image and the possibility that he can carry information, information which will save the human race, through time.

**Twelve Monkeys**, then, is credited as being based upon Marker's film. But director Terry Gilliam, or rather the scriptwriting duo of David and Janet Peoples, play with the story in interesting ways. Not simply in the fact that they have fleshed out Marker's story to feature length, but in their treatment of time, space and image. The process of simulation runs rife throughout the film. The opening scenes of James Cole in his future world of 2036 where a virus has wiped out all but a small percentage of the population – the wire cages, the board of inquisitors, the scrubbing down – are repeated almost immediately as soon as he lands, accidentally, in 1990.

In **La Jetée**, the protagonist, along with the woman he has met and fallen in love with, visits a tree whose concentric rings show the passing of time. The woman makes reference to an English name the protagonist "did not understand". It is in fact Alfred Hitchcock, who had visited the very same tree-trunk in **Vertigo** (Hitchcock, 1958), a film itself concerned with issues of simulation and reality.

However, the Peoples' do not have their protagonists James Cole (Bruce Willis) and Kathryn Railly (Madeline Stowe) visit the same scene, rather in a moment of post-modern self-reflexivity, they hide out in a cinema which is screening **Vertigo**. The real is lost, the simulation is made present, a point extended by Railly's wearing of a blonde wig as a disguise.

This Baudrillardian world of the real and the simulated is met head-on in another post-apocalypse movie, **The Matrix**. If the protagonists in the traditional road movie are often on the run (usually *from* something rather than *to* something) then so are the protagonists of **The Matrix**. Although it is less clear where they have to run to, they are nonetheless nearly always on the run and the film has a restless quality that suggests that they would die if they were ever to stand still (*cf* **Speed**, another Keanu Reeves vehicle, in which the very finiteness of the road – and the passage of time – threatens almost inevitable death).

On the surface this film appears to be a triumph of style over substance, but closer examination reveals an interesting working out of the relationship between the real and the simulated. There is much talk of travel, the dialogue consisting of lines such as "our way or the highway", "you've been down that road before", and "Kansas is going bye-bye"[8]. The latter a prophetic statement, given that **The Matrix** will ultimately concern itself with a fantasy world. There are also copious references to *Alice In Wonderland* – "follow the white rabbit" (also an LSD pattern) Thomas Anderson (Reeves) is told early on in the film before his transformation into Neo. Just as Alice is enticed to journey into Wonderland, so too is Thomas, and as with Caroll's Wonderful, so too does the "Matrix" of the film become "curiouser and curiouser".

The world of 1999 is the ultimate simulation, an illusion created by a world-controlling artificial intelligence to house the planet's inhabitants who provide the energy and sustenance for the Matrix. The rebels, a small band who appear to be living outside of the Matrix, can only do battle with the system by entering the computer programme that makes up the Matrix. As a result the time travellers leave their bodies behind, and enter the system as mental projections in a computer-simulated world. The need for physical travel is completely abolished, in favour of journeys made in and by the mind.

Furthermore, **The Matrix** plays with time in ways that other films referred to do not. It is not merely time which is travelled through, but it is time which is distorted not only as a plot element (*déjà vu* is actually a glitch in the system), but also for its stylistic qualities when the action is either slowed down, speeded up or just simply frozen. These devices are particularly noticeable in the fight scenes that take on the absurdly quick-fire and repetitious form of computer games. Thus given the suggestion that the Matrix is just one huge computer programme, these fight scenes are just another computer game.

Parental concerns have always been focused on the addictive nature of computer games; **The Matrix** turns this on its head and asks what if the world we know is itself one being computer game – a simulated world where not only as Baudrillard would have it, the Gulf War never happened, but in fact the world as we know it does not exist.

In "Crossing The Frontiers", Michael Atkinson says, "Today there's little frontier to speak of and little hope of national rediscovery, and the movies confirm the general sense of Generation X defeatism by transforming the travelled landscape into a bricolage of cinematic tropes", and he goes on to posit that "Instead we may be nearing the age of the anti-road movie, or the revisionist road movie."[9] But can the road movie be revised? As the information highway gathers speed (even if it sometimes feels like one is on the hard shoulder at times) and becomes a superhighway, images and information that once had to travel by road, by air and by sea, will circulate in nano-seconds. The world will be remapped, not by countries but by global corporations, and the road will no longer exist – instead it will be replaced by networks. We will still travel, but it will be to virtual worlds and by looking through the computer screen not the car windscreen.

What then the future of the road movie, post-apocalyptic or otherwise? If, as the introduction to the book *The Road Movie* suggests, a "road movie provides a ready space for the exploration of the tensions and crises of the historical moment during which it is produced"[10], what then will be the next "upheaval and dislocation"? Which "dominant ideologies" will fuel "fantasies of escape and opposition"? Is it the fear of where our computers will take us? Or even, that they will take us *over*? *HAL 2000* has become a real threat, even if the Millennium Bug proved to be almost non-existent. Certainly, the journey men of the post-apocalypse are not living out fantasies of escape and opposition, but one of survival, all the more often in the wake of machines that have spun out of our control – if Godard's **Weekend** [see Chapter 18] and J.G Ballard's *Crash* [see Chapter 20] hinted at an autogeddon, then the post-apocalyptic road movie is now more concerned with a new form of transportation and the dangers contained therein.

For me the period of dislocation, as I hope I have argued, is this new age of information: internet, intranets, world wide webs, and virtual realities, all serving to shrink the world and yet simultaneously cutting us off from one another. Whereas I might have once been cocooned in my car, I am now cocooned in my own private space, linked to the outside world by a couple of wires[11].

Will our old social skills became defunct as we become, at worst, passive receivers of images and information, at best, chatty on-line alter-egos where we do not even have to be ourselves – but a simulation of something that we would like to be visiting simulations of places that we would like to go, living out our vicarious thrills online in virtual worlds that are only limited by the technology that creates them?

# NOTES

1. *The Guardian*, 10 July 1999.

2. And the first two **Mad Max** movies themselves inspired a host of sub-standard imitators. These include New Zealand's **Battletruck** (1982) [see Chapter 7], France's **The Last Battle** (Luc Besson, 1983), and American efforts such as **Megaforce** (1982), **Survival Zone** (1983), and **Deathsport** (1978, a sequel of sorts to **Death Race 2000**). Italy, ever quick to exploit a trend, produced a whole body of "post-apocalyptic" films, most notably: **1990: The Bronx Warriors** (1982), **The New Barbarians** (1983), and **She** (1983). And from Japan came Sogo Ishii's **Crazy Thunder Road** (1980), a mean, rough-house road movie in which a man takes revenge on a group of vicious bikers who molest and kill his girlfriend.

3. Delia Falconer, "'We Don't Need To Know The Way Home': The Disappearance Of The Road In The Mad Max Trilogy", in Steven Cohan and Ina Rae Hark (eds.), *The Road Movie Book*; London: Routledge, p.246.

4. Manohla Dargis, "The Road To Freedom", *Sight And Sound*, July 1991, Vol. 1, issue 3.

5. Sam Farber has earlier been masquerading under the assumed identity of Trevor McPhee.

6. Derek Winnert's 1994 *Radio Times Film And Video Guide* describes it as such.

7. Michael Atkinson, "Crossing The Frontiers", *Sight And Sound*, January 1994, Vol 4, issue 1.

8. David Lynch's road movie **Wild At Heart** (1990) also makes references to **The Wizard Of Oz** (Fleming, 1939) [see Chapters 17 and 13, respectively].

9. Michael Atkinson, "Crossing The Frontiers", *Sight And Sound*, January 1994, Vol 4, issue 1.

10. Steven Cohan and Ina Rae Hark (eds.), *The Road Movie Book*, p.2.

11. In **eXistenZ** (1998), David Cronenberg takes the idea of the road movie as an internal journey to its logical conclusion. At the start of the film, a brilliant young computer game designer (Jennifer Jason Leigh) is shown beta-testing her new virtual reality game for a team of people. After a homicidal Luddite tries to kill Leigh for contributing to the state of modern software, Leigh and her bodyguard take it on the lam, chased by various anti-VR zealots. The protagonists spend most of the film travelling around the Canadian countryside, trying to find a way to hook into the game. Yet it soon becomes apparent that much of the trip (if not all of it) is taking place within their own minds. The act of travel loses all value in the face of virtual reality; all that is left is the perceptual content of the journey. In the final analysis, this journey leads to a conclusion of no value, merely more confusion. Perhaps Cronenberg is telling us that these journeys through virtual space offer no growth – and that virtual living can indeed only lead to the reduction of our status from "real" people, to simulacra. [Jim Morton]

# Chapter 20

# 'Crash'

# END OF THE ROAD: CRONENBERG'S 'CRASH' AND THE FADING OF THE WEST

## Mikita Brottman & Christopher Sharrett

*"A point is that which hath no parts, or which hath no magnitude"*
—Euclid

*"...Shall he drive*
*His horses upward, bring again the day?*
*It will but rise to die"*
—Seneca, *Thyestes*

In **Crash** (1997), David Cronenberg negotiates our ambivalent attitudes towards death and destruction on the roads, as well as the attractions of car crashes, using the car and the architecture of contemporary road systems as symbols of the convergence between humanity's unconscious desires and its technological artifacts. Cronenberg's film, like Ballard's novel, is an exploration of the ambiguous fascination and excitement of the car crash and the latent identity of the machine. This exploration, in the film and the novel, re-examines the contentions of some basic genres. It is a "road film" in the sense that it's an eccentric examination of the cult of adventure, journey and discovery that has animated that form. Ballard is British and Cronenberg Canadian, but **Crash** seems peculiarly American since its narrative deals with the exhaustion of the civilizing process, and of the final expenditures of the horizontal, forward-moving momentum that drove this enterprise. It is energy incipient within the Western, the biker film, and all manner of male-oriented identity that affirms the potency of a burgeoning society. In **Crash**, the traditional journey of discovery becomes a downward spiral, a frustrated, ever-circling implosion of the defeated bourgeois self at the end of the millennium.

Although the film was condemned in England as "a movie beyond the bounds of depravity"[1], Cronenberg's film does not fit well within the traditions of pornography. Clearly, sexual arousal in its audience is not the primary motive of the film, and, more significantly, none of the characters seem able to relate to one another in an emotional way. For this reason, in part, Cronenberg himself has described the film as "anti-pornographic"[2]. Arousal can hardly be on the agenda since Ballard, faithfully adapted here, has long been concerned with the "death of affect", a concept now basic to postmodernity that has been applied by Ballard in various locations to describe, rather moralistically, the depletion of bourgeois life. Cronenberg's evocation of sex seems iconic; Deborah Kara Unger leans on a balcony, pulling aside her gown to expose her bare buttocks as if to quote fashion photography, or Dali's "Young Virgin Auto-Sodomized By Her Own Chastity". Pornography is employed here as the end product of the culture of representation that has dissolved all lived experience through filters of mediation.

Other critics, picking up on the film's sense of surgical precision and its fascination with technology, attempted to locate Cronenberg's **Crash** in the tradition of science fiction. Many of Ballard's novels, including *Crash*, certainly adopt a number of sci-fi formations, including the metaphysics and biophysics of time and space-time paradigms and the ontologies of psychic realities. Unlike Ballard's novel, however, Cronenberg's **Crash** deals with the technology of the present rather than that of the future, and, in fact, is interested in the future only as a perspective from which to understand the current moment. It has been observed that the movie "looks and feels as if it were made long, long ago in a parallel universe"[3], a reference to its *mise en scène* of pillars and pylons, crash barriers, disused hangars and gas stations, dumped cars and derelict parking lots. This is no sci-fi dystopia, but a coruscating vision of the horror that is to be found in the bleak everyday of contemporary life.

Indeed, if Cronenberg's **Crash** fits into a tradition at all, it is that of the road movie – albeit in the form of a hardcore, apocalyptic, endtime variant. As Cronenberg makes explicit, the car crash is to the traditional road movie what the sex scene is to the classical romantic comedy – the unspoken culmination, the hidden act towards which all others tend, the secret, implicit, concealed finale. In effect, Cronenberg's **Crash** is the terminal form of the genre. Its obsession with the aftermath of car accidents vivifies the pathological truth of all previous road movie cycles – that our obsession with the automobile is, in fact, an obsession with atrocity and disaster.

As in all road movies, the road in **Crash** functions on many different levels. Among other things, it serves as a metaphor for the cultural condition of western civilization – in this case, a bleak, gaping expanse of vacancy. This is explicit in scenes where James Spader – the actor who represents blank yuppiedom *par excellence* – surveys traffic-clogged highway webworks from his terrace. A representative of "spectator culture", Spader muses anxiously about the increased number of vehicles on the roads, which would serve to disturb him after a disabling car crash, yet he and his wife yearn for "the next time", as their dream of perfect orgasm is conflated with death in the final fusion of eros/thanotos in the technoscape. The character is still able to enjoy orgasm even as his emotional life is arid, evidenced best by the chill grey-blue and amber twilight that saturates the film. Sex is arousing chiefly because it becomes associated with self-annihilation, and with urban-primitive cultism, replete with tattoos and talismans, of the crash re-enactors organized by renegade researcher Vaughan (Elias Koteas). The cult recapitulates a humanist theme that Cronenberg asserts, albeit half-heartedly, in all of his major works, as characters' panicked pursuit of meaning and coherence tends to recoup dead belief systems that ultimately hasten dystopia and provoke the holocaust. As in Freud's *Beyond The Pleasure Principle*, the pursuit of the death wish has reduced the self to the base material of the repetition compulsion. In **Crash**, as in Scorsese's **Taxi Driver** (1976), the repetition compulsion takes the form of an inability to be still, a kind of circling insomnia reminiscent of Spengler's "organicist" view of a "denatured" culture gradually winding itself down. Of course, as Freud reminds us, the repetition compulsion is essentially a means of both repeating and avoiding the initial trauma – which, in the case of **Crash**, is bourgeois life itself. In this way, perhaps, Cronenberg's film can be regarded as a mournful, anti-illusionist, anti-Brechtian version of Godard's bourgeois road fantasy, **Weekend** [see Chapter 18].

Those who choose to defend Cronenberg against the charge of nihilism do so by drawing attention to the way in which he often attempts to uncover new unifying principles, new myths in the modern technological landscape. It has been argued that the fetishization of the car accident in **Crash** triggers the emergence of both a new sexuality, and a new form of creativity and imagination. In other words – for all its dangers – the techno-sex of **Crash** bestows a certain radical potential on humanity by allowing us to jettison bourgeois notions of "appropriate" sexual encounters[4]. In Cronenberg's script, for example, the renegade scientist Vaughan – in a line straight out of Ballard – claims that the car crash should be seen as a "fertilizing event", not a destructive one. By describing the car crash as "the marriage between sex, the human organism and technology"[5], Ballard seems to be suggesting that such "fertilizing events" can provide people with some kind of collective liberation from their repressed existences. Yet the notion of the car crash – and sexual pathologies in general – as liberatory seems undercut by the gloom of the film, especially in the primal moment when the Spader and Unger characters couple on a piece of roadside wasteland after a near-deadly car crash.

Cronenberg's new unifying myths seem peculiarly appropriate to the postmodern scene. His earlier films have often been analyzed in terms of their presentation of a series of irresistible transformations, wherein the boundaries between Self and Other dissolve, annexing identity. Sometimes this transformation takes the form of the abandonment of self to a collective urge or *gestalt* (**Shivers, Rabid**); sometimes it takes the form of a merging between two beings (**Dead Ringers, The Fly, M. Butterfly**), sometimes in the surrender of independence to enlistment in conspiracies almost beyond human comprehension (**Scanners, Videodrome, Naked Lunch**)[6]. Like **Scanners** and **Videodrome**, **Crash** contains a cult-like group that attempts to reinvigorate society (or, at least, a marginal sector of society, since in Cronenberg larger social transformation seems impossible) through the creation of a new mythology appropriate to a secular, post-industrial environment. As noted, it becomes clear that the group's plan is bankrupt, and speaks merely to the panic of a postmodern setting that has exhausted all belief systems. Yet Cronenberg's narratives involve a traditional sacrificial ritual with propitiatory victims (Vale and Revok in **Scanners**, Max Renn in **Videodrome**, Vaughan and possibly the main character in **Crash**). This radical, futuristic construction of Self and Other in these films has been read in relation to Richard Slotkin's concept of "regeneration through violence"[7], the magic potential of destruction and the will-to-myth (the will to read experience mythically through the apparatus of victimisation), reviving old mythologies, or creating new ones more befitting to the contemporary wasteland.

In Cronenberg's **Crash**, however, none of these previous models or paradigms have any real application. Something of a departure for Cronenberg, **Crash** is a film whose apocalypticism is conservative, rather than regenerative. This is a film in which the symbiosis and dispersal of self produce a terminal, degenerate state of isolation and estrangement. In effect, the destruction in **Crash** is neither magical, nor sacrificial, nor regenerative, but pure suicidal immolation in the failure of collective philosophies. The protagonists of **Crash** lack any sustaining faith in mythical or spiritual belief systems previously supplying consensus to society. The film's apocalyptic spirit is profoundly secular and pessimistic, reflecting the postmodern refusal of both sacred and ideological conceptions of reality, depicting a culture totally cut off from its mythic past. **Crash** is a film about the impulses of western consciousness towards the worship of catastrophe and self-annihilation. It is a disaster story, though with none of the frantic, panicky overtones of the usual disaster story, since the catastrophe needed to provoke revelation never comes.

Instead, the attention of the audience is focused on a small group of rather calm, detached, sexually promiscuous though emotionally barren people; James Ballard (Spader), his wife Catherine (Unger), and the defiant, compulsive Vaughan (Koteas). As in much self-consciously decadent art, the sexuality of the protagonists is closely bound up with the notion of surplus violence – the need to prove one is alive by lacerating the flesh. And, as René Girard explains, "violence, if left unappeased, will accumulate until it overflows and contaminates the surrounding area"[8]. Moreover, in relation to the sexual violence and promiscuity of this distant triad, Cronenberg himself has pointed out that the film's showcasing of rear-entry and anal sex is meant to express its practitioners' disconnectedness from and defiance of the world[9], evoking

Puritan notions of anality as death, waste, the cul de sac of experience. As an act of paraphilia, anal sex is a metaphor for a profoundly degenerate attitude towards human life. The pursuit of satisfactions in **Crash** is the pursuit of a Sadean void; as in Pasolini's **Salo** (1975), anality becomes an emblem of the transmogrification of transgressive sexuality. Although **Crash**, unlike **Salo**, doesn't associate anal sex with tyranny and sadism, it does liken this taboo – almost as a pun – to the dead end of human experience. Anal sex also suggests the peculiar paucity of accumulation and violation of taboos, a succinct summation of bourgeois life.

In the traditional road movie, the road movie functions as a metaphor for the path of history, the impetus and trajectory of human civilization. In his 1895 work *The Law Of Civilization And Decay,* historian Brooks Adams analyzed the relationship between intellectual tendencies and the economic laws governing the movements of the material universe, concluding that human society must pass through a number of distinct intellectual phases in its oscillations between barbarism and civilization. According to Adams, when any human race reaches the limit of its material energy, that energy becomes surplus, and needs to be dissipated through economic competition. When surplus energy accumulates in such bulk as to preponderate over productive energy, it becomes the controlling social force, "and energy vents itself through those organisms best fitted to give expression to the power of capital"[10]. In such highly civilized and centralized societies, according to Adams, the imagination slowly fades and eventually falls into contempt, whereas "the economic intellect" grows gradually "less tolerant of any departure from those representations of nature which have appealed to the highly gifted of the monied type among successive generations"[11]. In the end, this loss of energy is manifested by a gradual dissipation of capital, which, at last, leads to disintegration: the pressure of economic capitalism has exhausted the energy of the race. "Consequently," writes Adams "the survivors of such a race lack the power necessary for renewed concentration, and must probably remain inert, until supplied with fresh energetic material by the infusion of barbarian blood."[12]

Adams's doleful, apocalyptic interpretation of history is an interesting way of making sense of the entropy and mythic dysfunction of Cronenberg's **Crash** – an elliptical, interiorized film with no final narrative release, only dissolution and disintegration. Here, the recognizably postmodern (yet actually rather puritan) theme of the downfall of civilization lacks any restorative mythic dimension. James, Catherine and Vaughan are the survivors of a declining civilization in the decadent stages of late capitalism, whose excess economic energy has been sublimated into a universalizing death-drive. Their descent into barbarism is willed, either consciously or unconsciously, by each of them, suggesting an acknowledgment of the failure of myth to revitalize society, to generate consensus, and to give energy to the construction of a new order. These are characters who do not hesitate to embrace the revelations about themselves and their sexuality that technology has made possible. Cronenberg argues that the Darwinian version of evolution having to do with survival is anachronistic within a capitalist society:

*"What I think has happened is that we have seized control of evolution without being aware of it. Survival of the fittest as a principle – one now has to say, what does "fittest" mean? ...It might be the guy who makes money the best in a capitalist society. There are cultures which embody the notion of suicide within them... [I]f you can get enough people to will it along with you, it is the reality..."*[13]

The logic of the film unfolds in accordance with the economic system that makes such a narrative possible, vivified most clearly by the alienating effect of its depicted technology (the camera gazes fetishistically over bent fenders, crutches, stretchers, the brushes and levers of the car wash), the lifeless intensity of its *mise en scène* (street lights are reflected hazily in windscreens, wet roads, and the hoods of cars). The dolorous, liturgical tone of the film and the distant, laconic interactions of its characters are Cronenberg's attempt to depict the dehumanized eroticism of late capitalism, the failure of the imagination characterized by Adams. A movie about the end of the historical road, Cronenberg's **Crash** is set on the downward edge of the historical cycle. The film explores the contradictions of a decadent capitalist system out of control, as well as the psychological consequences of this superproductive consumer society. These consequences include not only the failure of the imagination and the descent into barbarism, obsession, pathology and collective rage suggested by Adams, but also the forceful desire to tear society apart, to "throw stones at the Crystal Palace", as Dostoevsky puts it. As a consequence, the destroyed commodity becomes part of a nostalgic reliquary for lost ritual and consensus built around shared myth and language systems. In **Crash**, the particular commodity facing ritualized destruction is that most symbolic artifact of American consumer culture – that wasteful, aggressive, violent totem of western civilization, the car.

The obsession with technology in **Crash** is not – as it is elsewhere in Cronenberg – an attempt to create new meanings from the minglings of flesh and machine, but to reflect an increasing preoccupation amongst commercial designers and architects with the relationship between the technological environment and the design, gestures and contours of the human body. This commercial relationship between human and machine reaches a perverse fruition in the car crash, with its "blood-soaked instrument panels, seat-belts smeared with excrement, sun-visors lined with brain tissue... The intimate time and space of a human being... fossilized forever in this web of chromium knives and frosted glass"[14]. Ballard's perception that "the precise make and model-year of my car could have been reconstructed by an automobile engineer from the pattern of my wounds"[15] has nothing to do with what **Videodrome** describes as the "new flesh", but is rather a symptom of immanent apocalypse. It is a symbolic representation of a society obsessed with violence, brand names, destruction, machines, time, boredom, and repetitive sex, a society on the cusp of collapse into nihilistic dereliction and disaster.

One of the most symbolic constructions of capitalism is the notion of celebrity. Celebrity is only possible within the framework of a consumer culture, which provides the economic forces necessary for the formation of the public relations and the motion picture industries. Writer Jay McInerney claims that it's an indication of a collapsed value system, when the "great chain of being" seems to be defined by our distance from these empty luminaries, or our connection to them, however vague. Only in a particular kind of consumer culture could the highest rung on the social ladder be occupied by people who are "essentially not anything". This is because the celebrity is, essentially, an ego ideal. Our fascination with celebrity death is a vicarious extension of our own death drive, and its endless cycle of repetition compulsion. The dead celebrity stands for the surrogate propitiatory victim, the "mirror image" whose failed sacrifice serves only to highlight the miserable charade of commodity culture. Consequently, the public death of a celebrity has become one of the most horrifying and fascinating taboos that can be transgressed in our time.

Part of the horror of such a death is the fetishized body's sudden loss of revelatory power. The celebrity body, once so expressive and so intensely scrutinized, is abruptly transformed into a limp marionette, the strings suddenly cut that once attached it to the complex and hidden mechanisms of media relations and industrial investment. If death itself has become fetishized within capitalism, the celebrity death has become so much more symbolic, the object of so much violent eroticism, voyeurism, and obsessive curiosity. This notion of the celebrity death is always present in the background of Cronenberg's **Crash**, whose clinical atmosphere evokes the tone of news reports and other accounts of disasters. In the film's cold landscape, private terrors merge with public possibilities, personal nightmares with the nightmare of history, and the inner spaces of psychoses with imaginable large-scale disasters.

In Ballard's novel, Vaughan becomes obsessed with the death of Elizabeth Taylor and takes to following her home from the film studios, hoping to engage her in a violent, frenzied, sexual collision. In his attempts to induce the actress's death by automobile, Vaughan himself is finally killed – "his only true accident" – while Elizabeth Taylor escapes unharmed. Taylor is not mentioned in Cronenberg's film – perhaps for legal reasons – but other celebrities are equally fetishized. Vaughan, who in the novel "dreamed endlessly of the deaths of the famous, inventing imaginary crashes for them"[16], in Cronenberg's film becomes a crazed impresario, restaging his own performances of such celebrity accidents as James Dean's "death by Porsche". In the small, floodlit stadium, Vaughan relates all the details of the crash to his audience of midnight connoisseurs, including the date (September 9th, 1955) and the "performance cast". Dean, played by the psychotic stuntman Seagrave, will slam his new Porsche Spyder into the side of the Ford driven by college student Donald Turnupseed, who, according to Vaughan, was very important. "The two would meet for a moment", Vaughan shouts gleefully to his fans on the bleachers, "a moment that created a Hollywood legend. I myself will play engineer Rolf Wutherich from Zuffenhausen, Germany..."

In Cronenberg's film, Seagrave meets his end by re-enacting in drag Jayne Mansfield's fatal crash of 1967, around which he has built "an abattoir of sexual mutilation"[17]. Seagrave's highly detailed and authentic re-enactment dispels the myth that the truck under which Mansfield steered her car decapitated her. Seagrave gets it right. After the crash, his wig is stuck on the same door as had been Mansfield's, which led the first eyewitnesses to the crash to conclude that the actress had been decapitated[18]. This connection between death, celebrity and the automobile embodies the totemic iconography of all crash vehicles and other dysfunctional commodities in

Cronenberg's *mise-en-scène*, and is reinforced by the fact that Vaughan himself roams the freeways in a car which itself has mythic dimensions – a black 1963 Lincoln Continental convertible, the model in which Kennedy was assassinated. Indeed, in a piece of dialogue taken directly from the novel, Vaughan proposes the Kennedy assassination as "a special kind of car crash"[19]. In the novel, James Ballard, confined to his apartment, fantasizes about the injuries of film actresses and television personalities, "whose bodies would flower into dozens of auxiliary artifices, points of sexual conjunction with their audiences formed by the swerving technology of the automobile"[20]. If the obsession with celebrity is a by-product of capitalism, then the obsession with the celebrity car crash is a fantasy of literalization: the final and much longed-for union between the celebrity and members of their audience.

The traditional road movie is often regarded in psychoanalytic terms as a story of birth and regeneration. The car can easily be read as a symbol of a claustral (womb-like) environment, within which its driver feels safe and secure, and from which, at the same time, experiences an ambivalent urge to escape. If the classical road movie deals with birth and regeneration, however, then **Crash** is a narrative of abortion.

In psychoanalytic terms, the car accidents depicted by Cronenberg (both "live" and televised in the Swedish crash-test films screened by Vaughan) – especially those in which a figure is projected through the windscreen – suggest a number of parallels with the forcible expulsion from the womb and the anxiety associated with birth trauma, or stillbirth. The obsession with car accidents shared by the characters in **Crash** suggests the death wish underneath much apocalyptic thought, and resonates closely with a number of psychodynamic constructs that psychoanalyst Henry Murray describes as "anti-claustral complexes"[21]. These include "cathection of claustra" – strong emotional investment in claustral enclosures such as the car, feelings of chaos and lack of control, and a violent terror of suffocation and confinement.

Sexuality in **Crash** does not lead to birth and renewal, but instead represents an emblem of chaos and alienation. Vaughan and Seagrave's compulsive sexual desire to both observe and re-enact crashes in which a figure is forcibly ejected from the car seem to suggest, among other things, an "egression complex" – an anti-claustral tendency associated with active attempts to separate from the mother's body. In most cases, this yearning to escape from the womb is associated with strong desires for autonomy and the establishment of an independent identity. Birth traumas are usually re-enacted in order to master the anxieties associated with the birth process. In the case of **Crash**, however, the magic of birth no longer has any regenerative function, because what is at stake here is stillbirth. No creation comes out of this chaos. In the crashes enacted by Vaughan and Seagrave, the forced ejection of a body from the car results not in the establishment of an independent identity, but in sudden, violent, and premature death.

"In *Crash*," writes Fritz Leiber in his review of Ballard's novel, "geometry is king." Leiber argues that in this novel, "Ballard is seeking to satisfy a compulsion or an imperative"[22] which manifests itself in the form of "a delirium of Euclidian eroticism". In his film of Ballard's novel, Cronenberg realizes this imperative by configuring the traditional horizon of the classical road movie as circular, leading endlessly back on itself, as empty and as meaningless as a Euclidian dot. The horizon in **Crash** is like Vaughan's ill-lit, clandestine racetrack where cars pile into one another pointlessly, chaotically – as Ballard puts it, "cars meeting head-on in complex collisions endlessly repeated in slow-motion films"[23].

Consequently, unlike most road movies, there is no real sense of narrative form in **Crash**; the plot is merely a gateway to a certain cultural, historical and psychological locale in which the power of myth has given way to a barbarism whose violence lacks any restorative or regenerative function. Repetitive and insistent, Cronenberg's film is like a piece of newsreel footage being played over and over again, a circular re-run of obsessions, a pointless, elliptical quest to find interconnections between apparently inexplicable phenomena. Where the traditional road movie follows a linear horizon, Cronenberg's regressive fantasy is vertiginous and entropic, giving its audience a sense of queasy dislocation and foreboding.

**Crash** is a compulsive nightmare, a film about the end of culture and of history, the road movie of the apocalypse. It is full of those "premonitions of disaster" that James Ballard senses as he sits at home on his veranda, watching through his binoculars the traffic move along the motorway, "determined to spot the first signs of the end of the world by automobile"[24].

# NOTES

1. Alexander Walker, *The London Evening Standard*, 3rd June 1996. Walker went on to describe the film as containing "some of the most perverted acts and theories of sexual deviance I have ever seen propagated in mainstream cinema". In the 9th November issue of the 1996 *Daily Mail*, "critic" Christopher Tookey added his voice to the outrage, declaring that Cronenberg's film promulgates "the morality of the satyr, the nymphomaniac, the rapist, the paedophile, the danger to society", and marks "the point at which even a liberal society should draw the line". As evidence of the director's allegedly perverted morality, the reader's attention is drawn to the fact that "the initially heterosexual characters lose their inhibitions [and] they experiment pleasurably with gay sex, lesbian sex, and sex with cripples".

2. Xavier Mendik, "Logic, Creativity And (Critical) Misinterpretations: An Interview With David Cronenberg", unpublished, p.17.

3. Chris Rodley, "**Crash**: An Interview With David Cronenberg", *Sight And Sound*, June 1996, p.6. Rodley goes on to comment that "one is forcibly struck by the overwhelming impression that this is early Cronenberg".

4. See, for example, Roy Grundmann, "Plight Of The Crash Fest Mummies: David Cronenberg's **Crash**", *Cineaste* XXII/4, March 1997: 24–27. Grundmann points out that the sexual encounters featured in **Crash** challenge notions of "who has sex with whom, in what kind of environment, in what manner, and for what purpose".

5. J.G. Ballard, interview with David Pringle, cit. in Introduction to *J.G. Ballard: A Primary And Secondary Bibliography*; G.K. Hall & Co., Boston, 1994: xxix.

6. See, for example, Gavin Smith, "Mind Over Matter: Canada's Radical Director Interviewed", *Film Comment* XXXIII/2, March/April 1997: 14.

7. See Richard Slotkin, *Regeneration Through Violence: The Mythology Of The American Frontier 1600–1860*; Middletown, Conn: Wesleyan University Press, 1973.

8. René Girard, *Violence And The Sacred*, trans. by Patrick Gregory; Baltimore: Johns Hopkins University Press, 1977: 10.

9. See Grundmann, 27. Grundmann goes on to point out that "[t]hey don't seem to fuck each other so much as they fuck the world from which they're alienated. As rear-entry sex involves a refusal to face the sex partner and to confront his or her humanity, the film uses it as a close analogy to the cult members' practice of crashing one another's cars. This practice, too, involves a calculated refusal to see the crash partner as a human being".

10. Brooks Adams, *The Law Of Civilization And Decay*; Sonnenschein & Co., London & Macmillan, NY, 1895: viii.

11. Ibid., 294.

12. Ibid., viii.

13. Cronenberg, cit. in Smith, 18.

14. Ballard, 12.

15. Ballard, 28.

16. Ibid., 15.

17. Ibid., 135.

18. See Grundmann, 25. Grundmann points out that "[t]he lowly Seagrave is to Vaughan what Renfield is to Dracula. Seagrave is Vaughan's assistant in all important affairs". He also discusses "the Dean intertext of Fifties drag strip races, teen rebellion and car sex", which "suggests the close link between the sexual revolution and the car culture", giving "the fetishistic techno-play" of the film's characters some historical grounding.

19. In the novel, Vaughan also refers to "[t]he special involvement of at least two of the Kennedys with the automobile" – see Ballard, 183.

20. Ibid., 180.

21. See Henry Murray et al, *Explorations In Personality*; OUP: NY 1947.

22. Fritz Leiber, "Fantasy Books", *Fantastic Stories* 26. 1 (February): 129–30.

23. Ballard, 8.

24. Ibid, 50.

# INDEX OF FILMS

*Page number in bold indicates an illustration*